D0891845

Everett Dirksen and His Presidents

Everett Dirksen and His Presidents

How a Senate Giant Shaped American Politics

Byron C. Hulsey

University Press of Kansas

Published by the University Press of Kansas (Lawrence, Kansas 66049), which
was organized by the Kansas Board of Regents and is operated and funded by
Emporia State University, Fort Hays State University, Kansas State University,
Pittsburg State University, the University of Kansas, and Wichita State
University

Library of Congress Cataloging-in-Publication Data

Hulsey, Byron C., 1967–

    Everett Dirksen and his presidents : how a Senate giant shaped American
politics / Byron C. Hulsey.

      p. cm.

    Includes bibliographical references and index.

    ISBN 0-7006-1036-7 (alk. paper)

    1. Dirksen, Everett McKinley. 2. United States—Politics and
government—1945–1989. 3. Legislators—United States—Biography.
4. United States. Congress. Senate—Biography. I. Title.

E748.D557 H85 2000
328.73′092—dc21
[B]

00-027279

British Library Cataloguing in Publication Data is available.

Printed in the United States of America

10 9 8 7 6 5 4 3 2 1

The paper used in this publication meets the minimum requirements of the
American National Standard for Permanence of Paper for Printed Library
Materials Z39.48-1984.

For my mother and father,
Linda and Sam Hulsey

Contents

Acknowledgments

This book has been a labor of love. Nonetheless, I have profited in countless ways from the unflinching support and guidance of my mentor, Lewis L. Gould. Lew's standard of excellence and his commitment to professionalism inspired me at every turn. All scholars endure periods of doubt and confusion. With his quick wit and gentle prodding, Lew spurred me on and gave me the affirmation I needed to get over the top. Mike Briggs at the University Press of Kansas guided my book through the publication process, and to everyone who helped at the press I will always be grateful. Robert Divine and Randall Woods read the entire manuscript and offered prescient suggestions for its improvement. I owe a special debt of gratitude to Frank H. Mackaman, Executive Director of the Dirksen Congressional Center in Pekin, Illinois. No one knows the world of Everett Dirksen better than Frank. He kindly read an early draft of the manuscript, and his sharp eye and pointed criticism greatly enhanced the final product. He and his expert staff went beyond the call to make my trips to Pekin as productive as possible.

Dirksen's reluctance to commit himself to paper forced me to travel near and far to fill in the gaps. From Maine to California and from Georgia to Minnesota, I tracked Dirksen's record and the politics of the 1950s and 1960s. My efforts would have come to little were it not for the eager attention of archivists at almost every stop. Deserving special praise are Dwight Miller at the Hoover Library, Maura Porter and June Payne at the Kennedy Library, Thomas W. Branigar at the Eisenhower Library, and Linda Seelke and Mike Parrish at the Johnson Library. Mike's careful reading of an early draft and his interest in my ideas have greatly enriched my work. On multiple occasions he has sent me books, articles, and clippings that relate to our mutual interests. To him I will always be grateful. Richard Baker, the Historian of the United States Senate, was invaluable. He read a draft of the manuscript, and his suggestions made for a more tightly focused product. Dick helped me to the very end, patiently listening to my ideas about the change and continuity in the Capitol Hill milieu. Don Ritchie and the rest of the staff at the Senate Historical Office gave me unbroken assistance throughout the project.

Timely financial support enhanced the research for this book. The Kennedy and Hoover libraries provided me with welcome travel grants, and the Dirksen Center gave me critical financial support to finish the project. A David Bruton Jr. stipend from the University of Texas and a Patterson-Bannister Fellowship from the history department at the University of Texas were enough to give me an academic year to pull the narrative of my work together. Portions of this book appeared in the *Journal of Illinois History* and *Congress and the Presidency.*

Historical scholarship is a lonely and solitary endeavor. Friends in and out of the academy lured me out of the library and helped me immeasurably along the way. One of the great pleasures of working at Woodberry Forest is spending professional and personal time with men and women dedicated to the world of teaching. It is a special privilege to work closely with Nat Jobe, who sparked my love for history in high school and endured my meager efforts on the baseball diamond those many years ago. Jennifer Thornburrow spent countless hours helping me clean up the manuscript, but it is her love of life and affection for me that mean the most. My mother, Linda, is the most loyal woman I know. Her unconditional love has taught me more than the books I have read, the collections I have researched, or the schools I have attended. I will never forget her grace and courage through the most difficult times. My father, Sam, is the most giving person I know. From him I have learned that service to others is the true measure of life.

Introduction

After weeks of relentless heat and humidity, September 9, 1969, dawned bright and brisk in the nation's capital. Everett Dirksen, minority leader of the Republican Senate, had died two days before, and his body lay in state in the Capitol rotunda. A Washington icon who had served his native Illinois for almost twenty years, Dirksen was the fourth person in American history to be so honored for his Senate service. At noon senators, members of the House of Representatives, justices from the Supreme Court, and representatives from the diplomatic corps filed into their positions to pay their last respects in a thirty-minute service. President Richard Nixon delivered the eulogy, and he praised the senator as a "politician in the finest sense of that much-abused word." In a moving tribute, Nixon described Dirksen as a master legislator, a democratic craftsman who brought opposing sides together and found honor and dignity in compromise and conciliation. The president pointed to Dirksen's spellbinding oratory, his "self-deprecating sense of humor," and his ever-ruffled appearance. "He was at once," Nixon declared, "a tough-minded man and a complete gentleman. He could take issue without taking offense." Most important, "He could be persuaded. . . . He was not afraid to change his position if he were persuaded that he had been wrong. That tolerance and sympathy were elements of his character; and that character gained him the affection and esteem of millions of his fellow Americans." Two weeks later in the *National Review,* conservative intellectual William F. Buckley acknowledged Dirksen's importance to the nation's political culture but complained that the GOP's minority leader was "so much the pragmatist that you couldn't really count on him in a pinch."[1] The gist of Buckley's critique was that Dirksen was a wily political operator who bumbled and stumbled his way through life without a core set of beliefs to guide his leadership.

Dirksen was not particularly close to Nixon, and he was completely unfazed by Buckley's increasing prominence in America's political life. Nevertheless, Nixon and Buckley captured the essence of the historical debate about the life and career of Everett Dirksen. Most Americans who were politically conscious in the 1950s and 1960s remember Dirksen's melodious voice, his tousled hair, and his unkempt appearance. Comedian Bob Hope, for instance, once likened the disheveled Dirksen to a man who had been electrocuted and lived. Other Americans point to Dirksen's background as a fiscal conservative from the small midwestern town of Pekin, Illinois, and recall a pithy quote that he may never have uttered but certainly would have approved: "A billion here, a billion there, sooner or later you're talking about real money."[2]

Dirksen's honeylike baritone, his rumpled look, and his supposed aphorisms are wrapped up in his historical identity, but the nation's memory of the Illinois giant is both simplistic and superficial. Though the divide between Nixon's celebration of Dirksen's importance and Buckley's lamentations over his lack of ideological rigor yields itself to no simple reconstruction, in this book I uncover the multilayered reasons for Dirksen's centrality in relation to the most defining issues and events of post–World War II American politics and examine Dirksen's place in the conflict-ridden history of the modern Republican party.

I first encountered the world of Everett Dirksen in fall 1992 as a first-year graduate student at the University of Texas, Austin. I had returned to my native state primarily to study Lyndon Johnson's presidency, and my first research project investigated Johnson's belief that communists and left-wing radicals were orchestrating the antiwar protest at the height of the Vietnam conflict. Dirksen shared the president's conviction that domestic radicals were whipping up dissent in order to blunt the military's ability to do its job in Vietnam. Most familiar with the slash-and-burn political culture of contemporary America, I was moved by the depth and intimacy of Johnson's relationship with Dirksen. Even though President Johnson was a Democrat and Dirksen was a Republican, the two Washington giants risked precious political capital in order to protect one another from critics who were fed up with the war and with the prevailing political style that had shaped Washington culture since Dwight Eisenhower's presidency.

That first research paper provided the seed that grew into this project.

I wrote my master's thesis on Dirksen's relationship with Johnson and knew even then that the whole of Dirksen's career had captured my intellectual imagination. Unlike Johnson, Dirksen was an understudied political figure who nonetheless played a critical yet sometimes contradictory role in the defining issues and events that shaped modern American history. Fascinated as I was by the twists and turns of Everett Dirksen, however, I was reluctant to abandon my preference for examining the minority leader in the context of the presidents under whom he served. Too much political biography assumes that the principal character acts in a vacuum; I wanted to write a book that transcended Dirksen's importance.

Piecing together Dirksen's relationships with the modern presidents was fascinating work that took me to archival collections in nineteen states and to five presidential libraries. Because of the peculiar structures of the American system, good politics requires a healthy respect for the interdependence of Congress and the White House from both ends of Pennsylvania Avenue. Dirksen's interaction with Harry Truman, Dwight Eisenhower, John Kennedy, and Lyndon Johnson enabled me to assess the political skills of the primary characters and the prevailing circumstances that shaped their administrations. What follows is a unique look at how four of the modern presidents handled the critical tasks of coalition-building and interparty relationships as each administration worked to accomplish its most important goals. Even more important, I come face to face with the change, continuity, and conflict that shaped the Republican party from 1950 to 1970.

Intraparty conflict was one continuous strand that characterized the GOP during Dirksen's Senate career. Blocs of eastern and midwestern Republicans debated the most important issues of the day and fought to win control of the party. In short, Republicans in the 1950s struggled to establish the party's identity with regard to Franklin Roosevelt's New Deal and the Democratic policy of global containment that emerged after World War II. In the 1960s the focus of intraparty factionalism shifted to the federal government's appropriate responsibility in the area of civil rights and the soundness of the nation's open-ended commitment to anticommunism in Southeast Asia.

Divided as the GOP was, there were also important elements of continuity. Dirksen reflected the party's instinctive preference for a smaller federal government that returned power to its state and local counterparts.

All things being equal, the GOP believed in an unfettered economy but-tressed by private enterprise. Party chieftains and foot soldiers alike held that an antistatist free economy was the surest means to roll back the liberal reforms of the New and Fair Deals. The GOP during Dirksen's career was also known for its militant anticommunism and its reflexive distaste for social radicalism. Characteristic of the mainstream Republi-can party, Everett Dirksen was a patriotic and sentimental institutional-ist who blanched at any and every threat to his conventional conception of American society.

But there were also important elements of change that marked the GOP during Dirksen's Senate career. Much of this book revolves around an examination of the reasons for and meaning behind Dirksen's dra-matic policy reversals. At bottom, Dirksen's (and the mainstream GOP's) eventual affirmation of the responsibilities and powers of the modern presidency was the defining change that marked the Republican party's active contribution to the liberal consensus. By the end of his career, Dirksen had embraced the notion that the White House was at the center of the nation's political life. While his early years were marked by a jeal-ous protection of congressional power consistent with his Republican lineage, Dirksen came to accept and then champion the executive branch's assumption of increased authority to provide for the social welfare, con-tain the spread of communism, and guarantee the civil rights of all citizens.

Elected to the Senate as an Asia-firster and a midwestern isolationist in 1950, Dirksen was one of many Republicans who spoke openly about the dangers of a leviathan executive and the importance of rolling back the New and Fair Deals. Eventually serving as one of Dwight Eisen-hower's most faithful Republican legislators, Dirksen abandoned the conservative wing of the party and became an important actor in the GOP's decision to legitimate an activist presidency while absorbing the New Deal reforms and pursuing a bipartisan foreign policy based on global containment. He had been a relentless critic of Harry Truman's prosecution of the Korean War, but in the 1960s Minority Leader Dirk-sen developed into a strong supporter of unchecked presidential power and became one of Lyndon Johnson's staunchest allies. Once bitterly op-posed to a strong civil rights law that required federal enforcement by the executive branch, Dirksen proved to be the essential catalyst that en-abled the passage of landmark legislation.

Dirksen's centrality to the history of the modern Republican party obscures his importance as an actor in a Washington culture unique to the times. The more secondary literature I read and the more primary sources I unearthed, the more convinced I became that the manner and style of doing national politics in the Eisenhower, Kennedy, and Johnson presidencies were markedly different from what went before or came after. After his colleagues elected him minority leader in January 1959, Dirksen emerged as a central player in the Washington political establishment. These were also the years in which Minority Leader Dirksen created and perfected a leadership style that emphasized inclusiveness and teamwork in the GOP caucus. Even more important, Dirksen was initiated into the suprapartisan workings of the Washington political establishment. He saw firsthand how Eisenhower, during times of cold war crisis, discarded all pretenses of partisan gain and sought the favor of Democratic leaders Sam Rayburn and Lyndon Johnson.

The emergence of suprapartisanship as a political style was closely tethered to the interparty consolidation of the modern presidency that occurred during the Eisenhower administration. Suprapartisan politics differs from its nonpartisan, bipartisan, and consensus varieties in important ways. Nonpartisan politics fails to acknowledge that partisan interests bubbled below the surface even when Republicans and Democrats came together as one to address the problems of the day. Establishment leaders expected their fellow members from the other side of the aisle to fight ferociously for partisan advantage on a number of issues that were perceived to be uncritical. Yet during times of national emergency, the unwritten but unchallenged code of conduct mandated that the leaders come together behind closed doors and abandon any and all partisan calculations in order to pursue their notion of the national interest. Bipartisan politics falls short because the prevailing culture was much more resonant than a short-term deal or legislative compromise. Consensus politics ignores the important issues on which there was little to no agreement between Republicans and Democrats.

Cold war politics and Eisenhower's personal preference for the politics of suprapartisanship drove him to seek foreign policy support from Democratic congressional leaders. The political need to win control of the GOP motivated Ike to embark on an uphill struggle to secure Dirksen's unbroken allegiance. From the earliest days of his administration, the president wooed and courted Dirksen in an effort to push his program

through Congress. Eisenhower's enduring popularity, his awesome powers of persuasion, and the accepted norms of national leadership combined to convince Dirksen to join the president's team and fight for the
administration at every opportunity. By 1959 Dirksen was the president's
most trusted confidant on Capitol Hill. Even more important, Dirksen
had been baptized into the politics of suprapartisanship and, not coinci-
dentally, embraced the modern presidency in ways that he would have
found repugnant just years before.

Perhaps the most striking characteristic of suprapartisanship was its
endurance through and across three presidential administrations. Although Eisenhower was not the first president to include the congressional opposition in the innermost activities of his administration, his
unyielding commitment to a style of politics that transcended partisanship at defining times distinguished him from both Franklin Roosevelt
and Harry Truman. Even when the GOP enjoyed a nominal majority
early in the first two years of the Eisenhower administration, the president cooperated more closely with internationalist Democrats than he
did with isolationist Republicans. Both Roosevelt and Truman singled
out their conservative critics and profited from their attacks; Eisenhower
emphasized national consensus, unity, and harmony. Unlike his predecessors, Ike rarely lashed out at his foes publicly; more often than not he
relegated his most savage assaults on his opponents to his private diary
and his personal correspondence. More similar to Eisenhower than many
historians allow, John Kennedy continued his predecessor's promotion
of a suprapartisan national political establishment. Kennedy's intuitive
aversion to doctrinaire liberalism and Dirksen's principled affirmation of
the modern presidency, regardless of which party occupied the White
House, redoubled the minority leader's importance in the 1960s and cemented suprapartisanship as Washington's dominant political style.

For most of Dirksen's Senate career, his instinct for the center bolstered his national prominence. His leadership style revolved around a
belief that government was an organic process and that the "Senate is a
public institution; it must work; it's a two-way street; and that requires
efforts of both parties."[3] But Dirksen's predilection for the suprapartisan
establishment was by no means a full-time endeavor. His greatest asset
as a politician was the ease with which he moved within and between
his ritualistic roles as a member of the establishment and as a partisan
fighter for his GOP colleagues. His place in the establishment depended

on the trust and faith he earned from his party colleagues. Moreover, the pre-Watergate, uncritical Washington press corps kept Dirksen at the center of the nation's news and treated him as if he were an honorary member of their fraternity. Essentially, Dirksen was a protean politician who used a kaleidoscopic sixth sense to juggle his own agenda, the interests of influential Republicans, and his evolving understanding of the national good.

Until the Cuban missile crisis in October 1962, the Washington political establishment had been primarily a function of the cold war and the perceived need to present the world with a united front. Domestic politics, by and large, remained a partisan affair, with Democrats and Republicans engaged in ruthless competition for the support of a national majority. But after 1962 the African-American push for long-deprived civil rights altered the pattern of the Washington establishment. With Southern Democrats inexorably opposed to any meaningful bill and with black Americans fed up with Washington's apparent disregard for the basic rights of all citizens, Democratic presidents John Kennedy and Lyndon Johnson were forced to seek support from mainstream Republicans as the nation confronted its most acute domestic crisis since the Great Depression. Wooed by Johnson, pushed from below by the essential morality of the civil rights cause, and inspired by the historical record of Illinois's Abraham Lincoln, Everett Dirksen responded to the call. After months of intense infighting and negotiation, Dirksen shed his conservative mantle and pursued his conception of the national interest, regardless of its partisan implications.

The Civil Rights Act of 1964 and the Voting Rights Act of 1965 were the two signal achievements of the suprapartisan Washington political establishment. In the realm of foreign policy, the results were decidedly mixed. The establishment's exercise of the powers of the modern presidency enabled the White House to respond expeditiously to cold war emergencies. Just as important, the bipartisan commitment to global containment produced a consistent and continuous policy that served the nation well through the early 1960s. But the establishment was weaker than it appeared. Paradoxically, the source of its greatest successes (a transcendent pursuit of an unsullied national interest at the expense of cheap partisan gain) was also the principal cause of the establishment's decline by the end of Dirksen's Senate career.

As the fighting in the jungles of Vietnam resulted in escalating American casualties and costs the nation was unable to pay, Johnson and Dirksen doggedly resorted to the suprapartisan politics of the Washington establishment and refused to promote an open and honest debate on the implications of global containment. Johnson's unwillingness to engage the nation in this debate eroded his credibility and ultimately forced him into submission. For Dirksen, the results were less dramatic, but real enough. By the time of Johnson's retirement, Dirksen's prestige in the GOP was at an all-time low. Though his failing health contributed to his political decline, Dirksen's unflinching contribution to the palace politics of the Washington establishment was the primary cause of his diminished authority and his inability to have his way in a changed political atmosphere.

Dirksen's eventual decline masks his overall importance to a unique era in this nation's political history. His career mirrored the tortured journey that the GOP took in the party's eventual affirmation of presidential power as the surest means to pursue the national interest and compete for a national majority. Dirksen, however, was far more than a weathervane who pegged his every move on the prevailing political winds. His ultimate achievement was to have made himself into a central actor in the national establishment while still maintaining and cultivating those distinctive and individual traits (the hair, the voice, the manner, and the demeanor) that account for his esteemed place in the historical memories of middle-aged and older Americans and that will ensure his historical significance for generations to come.

1. "He Should Be in Politics"

Situated halfway between Chicago and St. Louis, and just south of Peoria, Illinois, lies the midwestern and middle American town of Pekin. It was here that Antje Conrady, who arrived with little more than "a ticket around her neck," settled after emigrating from Germany in the early 1870s. After her first husband died, in 1892 she married Johann Frederick Dirksen, a semiprosperous decorator for Smith's Wagon Works and a fellow first-generation German immigrant. Less than four years after marrying, the couple had three sons. Consistent with the reflexive Republicanism of downstate Illinois, Dirksen named his sons after the GOP's most prominent figures. The oldest of the three was called Benjamin Harrison Dirksen; the twins born on January 4, 1896, were given the names of contemporary Republican leaders. Thomas Reed Dirksen was named for the Republican Speaker of the House of Representatives; Everett Dirksen was given the middle name of McKinley, then the governor of Ohio but soon to become the nation's next president.[1]

Except for naming his sons after the nation's most notable Republicans, Johann Dirksen had little impact on the personal development of his children. Before the twins were old enough to enter Pekin's public schools, their father suffered a severe stroke that left him bedridden and helpless until his death in 1905. Antje Dirksen was a frugal woman with the ability to "stretch a dollar and make two," and she took upon herself the responsibility of raising her family. Everett Dirksen's many chores began before school. His duties included milking the family cows and selling pails of milk "suspended from a notched broomstick over his shoulder" to his neighbors on the way to the schoolhouse. Sundays were given over entirely to worship, which began with a service at a Dutch Reformed church that Antje Dirksen helped "build with her own hands." The Dirksens studied the Bible on Sunday afternoon, so much so that

Everett claimed later in life that he had "read it from cover to cover three times."[2]

Antje Dirksen and her sons lived in a predominantly German neighborhood called "Bohnchefiddle," otherwise known as "Beantown." The Dirksen home was big enough for the boys, but Dirksen later remembered that the "rooms were almost as porous as a pair of fishnet hose." He recalled how "snow could and did filter in beside the window casings so that the first barefooted step out of bed would land on a neat pile of snow and elicit an exclamation both long and horrendous." Without the convenience of an indoor toilet, the Dirksens made use of a slopjar during cold winter nights. Rustic as his existence in Beantown was, Dirksen remembered fondly the stretch of land adjacent to his family home: "I had an innate desire to grow things. That acre, therefore, became the most intriguing of all the resources of my childhood and youth. To me it was 'one acre and liberty.'"[3]

Life for young Everett was rugged and dour, but the Dirksen boys had their share of fun as well. On Saturdays Antje Dirksen gave her sons a nickel for a "divvy" of candy and the local matinee. But more so than his friends, Everett was a loner. Driven by a relentless faith in the power of language to fulfill his personal potential, Everett showed more interest in books and ideas than in friends and boyhood games. From an early age he was a voracious reader, the son who, his mother noted, often "had his nose in a book." Morning after morning young Everett rose before dawn to build his vocabulary and read the likes of Horatio Alger's *Ragged Dick*. His brother Henry remembered Everett's ceaseless determination to educate himself: "There was Ev at five o'clock on a cold morning, in his nightshirt, just out of bed, in his bare feet, standing by the table reading his damn book. First he would hoist one foot up to warm it against the other leg. Then he'd put that foot down, and hoist the other one up. Just like a rooster in the snow."[4]

Dirksen's passion for learning extended into high school, where he also served as vice president of his class, business manager of the yearbook, member of the debating team, 150-pound center on the football team, and miler on the track and field team. Only Everett's ninth grade report card survives. That year he was rarely absent from class and never tardy. Besides excelling in the area of deportment, young Dirksen mastered German and history. He was slightly less proficient in English, but the only course in which he went the entire year without an A of any sort was algebra. In the yearbook his peers cited Everett's playful pretentiousness, describing their classmate as afflicted with "bigworditis." Another claimed that Dirksen "must have swallowed a dictionary."[5]

Everett's peers may have deemed him detached and aloof, but he later insisted that his "slightly antisocial complex" was a function of the dour conventionality that defined life in Pekin. "Anything smacking of art or culture or self-expression," he remembered, "had no particular place in their lives." Everett knew from an early age that he was saddled with an "irrepressible urge for expression," and in his high school years he began a lifelong interest in theater. He also excelled in debate, where he enjoyed the give and take of forensic combat. In 1913 he participated in the National Oratorical Finals in Lexington, Kentucky, where he also met Democratic standard-bearer William Jennings Bryan. Dirksen asked Bryan how he kept the attention of indifferent audiences, and Bryan advised, "Always speak to the folks in the back rows and the rest will be sure to hear you." Not long thereafter family members and friends remembered Everett retiring to the family barn to practice his speechmaking and to exercise his urge to be a showman. Tom Dirksen recalled that on Saturday mornings Everett "would preach and preach and we could just hear him from the barn to the kitchen, and my mother says [sic], 'Now sometimes just listen to him talk.'"[6]

After graduating as salutatorian of his Pekin High School class in 1913, wearing his first tailored suit to the ceremonies, Dirksen left home and attended the University of Minnesota. He pursued undergraduate studies in law, but was forced to work his way through college and found a job at the classified advertising desk at the *Minneapolis Tribune*. Dirksen worked twenty-nine nights a month from 6:00 to 11:00. His crowded schedule left him little time for socializing or extracurricular activities and contributed to some understandable academic difficulties. In his general studies courses, he hovered around a high C, low B average. He achieved only two As in college, one in a rhetoric class and the other in a political science course on American government. Interestingly, he dropped to a C when in the second semester of his sophomore year he took the companion political science course on state and local government. Dirksen found his law courses even more challenging. Out of nine completed courses, he failed to merit an A, earning instead two

Bs, three Cs, and four Ds.[7] Though he had to struggle mightily to balance his grueling work schedule with his academic responsibilities, he never failed a college course.

World War I interrupted his studies and embroiled Pekin in a wave of ethnic conflict. Pekin's German-American bank was coerced into dropping the "German" from its name, and the local Methodist church was implored to hold "English-only services." Pekin "patriots" threatened to burn a terrified Antje Dirksen's home to the ground because she refused to remove a picture of Kaiser Wilhelm from the living room wall. Young Everett pled with his mother to remove the photograph until the end of the war, but Antje insisted that America "was a free country." With one brother married and another medically exempt, it was up to Everett to "prove the family's allegiance" by volunteering for the army. Dirksen hoped that the service star in the front window of his home would give comfort to his mother and "would be a loud and clear announcement to the neighborhood and to the world" that he and his family were loyal Americans.[8]

Dirksen served in France with the Nineteenth Balloon Company of the 328th Artillery, eventually achieving the rank of second lieutenant. He saw sporadic combat and later recalled the hazards he endured as a military balloonist spying behind enemy lines without allied air protection. The war's end afforded him the opportunity to travel widely through Europe, but he longed for his familiar surroundings and in 1919 returned home to Pekin. For the next several years he worked at a variety of local jobs, all of which he found unsatisfying. First he joined his brothers in the grocery business. Unfulfilled, he formed a short-lived partnership for the manufacturing and selling of washing machines. From 1923 to 1925 Dirksen managed the C. L. Cook Dredge Company.[9]

Though postwar life left Dirksen "floundering," "unhappy and bewildered," he found some personal satisfaction outside the workplace. He rekindled his passion for theater and began writing, producing, and acting in plays for local production. At the urging of his church's deacons, Dirksen also preached every Sunday evening for two months while the church searched for a permanent pastor. Nothing could have prepared him for his beloved mother's sudden death in December 1923. Before she died, Antje Dirksen discouraged her son's budding interest in theater as a lifelong vocation. Dirksen later remembered that "she had a typical old-country, small-town, puritanistic view of the stage as a wicked domain. She demanded that I assure her . . . that I would not essay it as a career. . . . But that, of course, did not destroy the urge. I *had* to appear before people."[10]

It was two months after his mother's death that Dirksen, through the production of a local play that he had cowritten, met Louella Carver. She was not favorably impressed on first meeting her future husband, describing him later as "tall and gawky with a lot of tousled hair that hung down like a mop over his forehead. He was smoking a smelly pipe and he looked rumpled in his ill-fitting clothes." But Dirksen would not be deterred. He at once embarked on an unceasing mission to win her affection. An inveterate romantic, Dirksen wrote amateur, unpunctuated love poems to Louella. Once, when Louella was out of town, Dirksen pined, "Received your card yesterday / And your letter today / And so I'm quite happy / Altho terribly lonesome / And beginning to realize more and more / How much you mean to me / And how important you are in the scheme of life / And how much of my happiness is bound up in you / And centered in you."[11]

Dirksen's letters to Louella in the early stages of their relationship reveal more than his romantic interests. In 1924 he traveled by train through the South looking for business prospects for the dredging company. To Dirksen, the region was backward and undeveloped. He admitted that he enjoyed the southern drawl and the "un-anxious" appreciation of happiness as an end in itself rather than an "incident of life." But his critique of the South was searing and unbecoming. He wrote of a "terrible country" where "one would think that the Creator had either run out of fair material for this part of the south or had purposely created it as it is for punishment." Dirksen's racial and class prejudices were wrapped up into his assessment of the southern topography: "Nothing but yellow and red soil from which the energy and fertility has been sapped years ago and at the same time, the energy and ambition of those who till the land must have flowed away and left a residue of indolent white trash and niggers." In Vicksburg he wrote Louella that "this country was never intended for white men." Southern Jews, he believed, dominated Vicksburg's business district: "Take away the Jews and the niggers and Mr. O'Mara [his traveling companion] and I would have to fry our own eggs for breakfast."[12]

Dirksen's prejudices reflected the provincialism of the small-town Midwest. The Ku Klux Klan operated the *Pekin Daily Times* for the majority of the 1920s, and three or four times a week the paper ran an editorial entitled either "Klan's Korner" or "Klan Komments." Promoting "One Hundred Percent Americanism," "White Supremacy Now and Forever," and "Absolute Independence," the Pekin KKK lashed out at urban immigrants, Catholics, Jews, and blacks. Throughout his early life, Dirksen was saturated with the Midwest's parochial glorification of the "native-born, white, Gentile Protestant" as the "flower of America." Dirksen struggled for years to overcome the narrow intolerance of his upbringing.[13]

In 1927 Dirksen quit the dredging venture and entered into a thriving bakery business with his brothers. Incorporated as "Dirksen Brothers—Bakers," their motto ran, "If it's made of dough we make it." Dirksen helped with the baking, but his primary responsibility was to sell and deliver the finished products to grocers, delicatessens, and hotels. Though he remained consumed by unfulfilled ambition, his life was settling down. On Christmas Eve 1927, after nearly four years of constant courtship, he married Louella. The couple honeymooned in Chicago, where they spent their time sightseeing and window-shopping, in addition to enjoying their "first real steak dinner" at their "first real night club." On February 10, 1929, Louella gave birth to the couple's first and only child, a daughter, Danice Joy, whom they called Joy.[14]

Through the 1920s Dirksen's participation in politics was haphazard and informal. His life experience was unabashedly Republican, but, as his biographer Neil MacNeil has persuasively argued, "His commitment to Republicanism was emotional, sentimental, irrational, like his sense of the meaningfulness of Lincoln; it was not predicated on intellectual postures or reasoned logic." In 1922 his friend and fellow veteran Scott Lucas from Havana, Illinois, persuaded Dirksen to join the American Legion. By 1926 Dirksen was elected district commander, the boundaries of which matched Illinois's Sixteenth Congressional District. In his capacities with the nonpartisan American Legion, he expanded his political net by traveling widely and speaking frequently to Illinois veterans.[15]

Dirksen's first encounter with formal politics came with his election to Pekin's nonpartisan city council in 1927. From the beginning he operated under the assumption that a responsible government could enact laws and promote necessary projects in the interests of the people. While he advocated the creation of a Board of Local Improvements and championed the importance of a bridge across the Illinois River, he also displayed a penchant for balanced budgets and a sensitivity to overburdened taxpayers. Working full time at the bakery, Dirksen took advantage of his delivery responsibilities by holding impromptu group discussions on the issues of the day. He later marveled at the worth of those occasions: "We settled all these problems to our deep satisfaction in a way that would have made a deliberative body like the United States Senate green with envy." Earning a reputation as a "fiery orator" and a "human dynamo," Dirksen enjoyed a successful stint on the city council. Nonetheless, his unsatisfied ambition encouraged his efforts to run for national office: "I wanted to be part of the nation's hub. I felt it was and would continue to be the political hub of the whole wide world."[16]

Dirksen's friends in the American Legion marveled at his ability to resolve conflict through his extemporaneous speaking ability. At a 1928 Legion convention in Louisville, Kentucky, "rowdy" delegates threatened the productivity of the conference. Dirksen quieted the crowd with an off-the-cuff speech about the meaning of the American Revolution. An onlooker exclaimed, "Who is that man? He should be in politics!" Indeed, Dirksen had been planning a campaign for a seat in the U.S. House of Representatives. With its mix of agricultural and industrial bases, Illinois's Sixteenth Congressional District tested his ability to balance conflicting interests. To manage the competing constituencies that characterized his district, he capitalized on the fact that Abraham Lincoln had represented the area in Congress as a Whig in the 1840s. From the beginning of his political career, Dirksen believed he held a special claim on Lincoln's reputation, and he would often rely on the hero's legacy as he carved out his own position on the important issues of the day. In 1930 he entered the GOP primary as a virtual unknown against the wealthy and established Republican House incumbent, Rep. William Edgar Hull. Despite these obvious handicaps and in the face of friends who scoffed at his impudence, Dirksen entered the race with a fountain of energy and a boundless determination to win the election.[17]

Try as he did, Dirksen failed to win the support of his district's most important newspapers. The *Peoria Star* conceded that he enjoyed the ability to make a speech but argued that "the suggestion that he should be sent to Congress would be on a par with sending a schoolboy." He also hemmed and hawed on the issue of prohibition, telling the voters, "I would abide by the people's wishes and whenever the Sixteenth District gives me a mandate I'll vote as they wish." Perhaps most damaging was a flyer that Hull's supporters distributed in the heavily Catholic Bureau County. Declaring that "Dirksen is a member of the Ku Klux Klan," the handbill arrived in voters' mailboxes on the eve of the election. Dirksen maintained later that the charge was an "unmitigated falsehood." There is no evidence to suggest that he was a member of the KKK, but Pekin's reputation for unbridled nativism must have contributed to the resonance of the charge and Hull's 2,000-vote majority in Bureau County. Despite the seemingly insurmountable obstacles blocking his bid for the nomination, Dirksen went to bed at 2:00 A.M. on the night of the primary with a forty-four-vote lead. In what his local paper called a "dazzling race that thrilled his friends and amazed his opponents," he eventually lost by just 1,100 votes.[18]

The narrowness of the outcome marked him as a politician for the future. Though he had lost thirty pounds in the campaign, the indefatigable Dirksen began stumping for votes in 1932 the day after his defeat. Having achieved name recognition in the previous campaign, he focused on the economic dislocation of the Great Depression. He emphasized his youthful vigor and his willingness to revisit traditional Republican approaches to the unprecedented problems of the times. He reversed field and backed the repeal of prohibition in order to create jobs for his district. While the sixty-six-year-old Hull portrayed himself as a regular Republican and committed supporter of President Herbert Hoover, the desperate conditions of the Great Depression inspired Dirksen to buck party doctrine and advocate lower taxes and federal relief for the unemployed. Dirksen won the 1932 primary with 52 percent of the vote.[19]

Even though his district normally went Republican, Dirksen faced a slew of handicaps as he worked up a strategy for winning the general election. Primarily at issue was his association with the intensely unpopular Hoover and the ridiculed policies of the Republican party. Dirksen exercised his pragmatism and distanced himself from the Hoover campaign: "With unemployment increasing, with banks popping throughout the country and with business stagnant, what could we say in behalf of Herbert Hoover . . . that would have any appreciable political effect?" Dirksen's efforts to win the favor of Democrats and independents smarting from the effects of the depression without alienating GOP regulars climaxed ten days before the general election when Hoover visited Peoria, the industrial hub of the Sixteenth District. Though close to 75,000 came to see the president speak, Dirksen noted that most were "sedate and reserved." Desperate to avoid a loss of the thousands of votes that would have resulted from a strong endorsement of Hoover's anemic leadership, Dirksen resorted to a meaningless speech lauding the George Washington Bicentennial.[20]

Dirksen reaped the benefits of his efforts on election day, carrying his district by 23,000 votes. After the campaign he noted the irony of Franklin Roosevelt's similar margin over Hoover in the Sixteenth District. Dirksen called the odd result an "exhibition of impartiality" and criticized those who held that the minority should pursue a "doctrine of regularity carried to a vicious extreme. I do not believe that such a political gospel appeals to the citizenry." Despite belonging to a party that would be outnumbered 318 to 117 in the House, Dirksen expected to go to Washington to promote positive legislation for his constituents. To him the crisis of the times demanded "the exemplification of citizenship and Americanism rather than partisanship." Though a fundamental part of his upbringing, Dirksen's pragmatism in the 1932 election was primarily driven by the widespread perception that Hoover and the Republican party had failed to address the baleful effects of the Great Depression.[21]

Because he and Louella decided that she should stay in Pekin with Joy, Dirksen left for Washington alone. Arriving by train at Union Station, he could hardly contain his satisfaction and remembered later "what sheer exhilaration it was for a country boy to see the illuminated dome of the Capitol . . . for the first time in his life!" Before his inauguration, he attended the lame-duck Congress to learn the House rules and master its procedures. Capitol Hill proved a satisfying outlet for Dirksen's healthy sense of ambition: "When I got my first dose of Congress . . . and I was called Honorable, and invited to dinners without having to pay for them, and people came saluting me in my office, I thought, 'This is for me.'" Early on he established a reputation for hard work. He sought the advice of a rising star within the party, Joseph Martin of Massachusetts. Dirksen later remembered, "I did the wise thing by cultivating Joe Martin." Dirksen followed the crux of Martin's counsel for the remainder of his legislative career: "Take the assignments you can get and work at them. Perfect yourself in committee work, and in due course you'll start up the ladder. Study the rules. Those who know the rules know how to operate in the House."[22]

Dirksen first engaged the modern presidency as a freshman Republican responding to the rapid-fire experimentation of Franklin Roosevelt's New Deal. Though his conception of the presidency as an institution changed over time, in 1933 Dirksen endorsed the expansion of its boundaries and responsibilities to meet the "cataclysm[ic]" problems of the day: "No one will contend that . . . we cannot find men with sufficient vision and knowledge to fabricate feasible and practical and constitutional measures for the relief of business, agriculture, banking, transportation, and other enterprises." In that spirit, though voting against the Tennessee Valley Authority, the Securities Exchange Act, and the Reciprocal Trade Act, Dirksen supported key New Deal measures such as the National Industrial Recovery Act, the Federal Emergency Relief Act, and the Agricultural Adjustment Act. In 1935 he voted for the Social Security Act and sharply criticized the Supreme Court for striking down the White House's recovery program. "Constitutionality," he insisted, "is no match for compassion." Even though Dirksen displayed consistent opposition to the New Deal's cultural programs, he endorsed many of Roosevelt's economic policies. In fact, Clyde Weed has concluded that Dirksen belonged to a group of insurgent and progressive Republicans from the West who were often at odds with the more conservative eastern wing of the party.[23]

Like many of his midwestern Republican colleagues, Dirksen resented what he considered to be the arrogance of the eastern establishment. While many congressmen wore formal morning suits with tails to events like the State of the Union address, Dirksen donned his "banker's gray" and proudly referred to himself as an "ordinarily attired lowbrow." At times he displayed a curious mixture of disdain and fascination for the pretentious habits of the East. He wrote a detailed letter to Louella describing a "swanky" dinner party hosted by Rep. Hamilton Fish (R-NY). After cocktails and hors d'oeuvres, the guests entered the dining room in order of seniority. Dirksen struggled to identify the successive courses but expressed a childlike fascination with the Blue Bristol deep finger bowls in which the ice cream was served: "Those deep finger bowls are funny. You dip your finger in the water and start rubbing it around the edge of the bowl and it sounds like a sweet sounding bell."[24]

Intrigued as he was by his colleagues' social ostentation, Dirksen winced at the internationalist inclination of the eastern seaboard. He echoed the isolationist sentiments of the Midwest and voted consistently to curb the president's increasing control of the nation's foreign policy. In a 1938 letter to Louella, Dirksen expressed dismay at the threat of another world war, in part because of the "regimentation and dictatorship" it would mean for American life. He had voted for each of the neutrality acts and against the Lend-Lease Act, but his isolationism peaked in August 1941 when he voted against the extension of the 1940 Selective Service Act. Thereafter Dirksen became something of a reluctant internationalist. In September 1941, just six weeks after he voted against the extension of selective service, he denounced isolationism as inappropriate to the challenges of the times. In part, his speech was a clarion call for support of the presidency in a time of national crisis. While he gave measured support to Roosevelt's handling of the Far East situation, the basic thrust of his remarks backed the presidency and sought to unify the nation behind the commander in chief: "To disavow or oppose that policy now could only weaken the president's position, impair our prestige, and imperil the nation."[25]

Though he supported the president's handling of the war, Dirksen began to criticize the White House for usurping authority that traditionally belonged to Congress. Interestingly, Dirksen's solution was not to roll back the president's powers but to increase the expertise of congressional staffs to oversee a swelling executive branch. In April 1943 *Fortune* featured Dirksen's efforts to check the "constant growth of the executive power and a diminution of the legislative power" by streamlining committee work and adding experts to congressional pay rolls. According to Elliot Rosen, Dirksen's criticism of a distended presidency reflected the "misgivings . . . of Main Street." Though he approved of the New Deal's efforts to ameliorate the conditions of the depression, Dirksen began to reject the centralization of power and the steady push toward an "omnicompetent government."[26]

In 1944, acting on the support from many of his midwestern Republican colleagues, Dirksen launched a brief campaign for the White House. He lambasted Roosevelt's efforts to broaden executive power. Pledging to "wage an earnest campaign to stem that idealogy [sic] which we refer to as the New Deal," Dirksen denounced the court-packing plan and supported the constitutional independence of the Supreme Court. He also lashed out at the bureaucratization of the government, its "moral

obtuseness," and its efforts to promote a "doctrine of collectivism."
Dirksen maintained that the depression triggered the "march toward
centralization" and that World War II accelerated the nationalization of
America's political life. By contrast, his vision for America after the war
was to return responsibility to state and local jurisdictions to stunt the
"impersonal" and "fallible" federal government. Admitting later that he
was "aiming rather high" and that he was mostly angling for the GOP's
vice presidential nomination, he withdrew from the contest before the
convention without the pledged support of any delegate.[27]

Though Dirksen's abortive campaign for the White House had attracted the support of many midwestern Republicans, his actions in Congress suggested he was anything but a party stalwart. After Roosevelt's
death, he supported Harry Truman's efforts to broaden the scope of federal power through the 1946 Employment Act, the Federal Employee
Loyalty Act, anti–poll-tax bills, and the Veteran Emergency Housing
Act. Most important, Dirksen provided the administration with consistent support for its anticommunist foreign policy. A trip to Europe at
war's end convinced him that "certain ideologies" and the "selfish grasping of power for economic advantage" had freedom by the throat. He
appreciated the president's solicitation for his advice and consequently
voted for the United Nations, the Truman Doctrine, and the Marshall
Plan.[28]

Just as Dirksen's stature and prominence as a responsible Republican
legislator grew to its highest level, he suffered a career-threatening illness. He first thought that the fuzziness in his eyes was caused by chronic
fatigue, but after consultations with an array of doctors, it was discovered that he suffered from degeneration of the retina, believed to be
caused by a malignancy. He cut back his schedule, but his eyesight remained so poor that his Capitol Hill secretary and Louella had to read
his speeches for him to memorize. He received regular shots that wracked
his body and caused him to "sweat like Billy-be-damned." Nothing
worked. In early 1947, as a last resort, a Johns Hopkins specialist advised the removal of Dirksen's left eye in order to contain the cancer. On
the way to the procedure, Dirksen sought the advice of another doctor
and decided against the operation. His specialist at Johns Hopkins
seemed surprised and asked Dirksen whom he had seen. "The Big Doctor
up there," Dirksen pointed, "the One up there, the Doctor in the sky."[29]

Dirksen's boldness did nothing for his eyesight. By early 1948 he decided to retire from the House in order to devote his every energy toward recuperation. At the end of the session, prominent figures in the press and on both sides of the aisle praised his House career. Speaker Sam Rayburn (D-TX) spoke for many: "If they are going to send Republicans to Congress, let them send the Everett Dirksen kind." Before leaving the nation's capital to convalesce on the Eastern Shore, he asked for and received an appointment with Truman. The president told Dirksen he should not have quit, and in appreciation of Dirksen's support for White House foreign policy programs, he praised his efforts: "We need fellows like you."[30]

Dirksen left Washington fearing that his political career was finished. Clearly he hoped to return, telling political adviser Harold Rainville that he considered retirement an "interlude" undertaken "only by consideration for my family and my physical welfare." Uncertain of what lay ahead, Dirksen fell back on the constants in his life: his family, his faith, and his home. His whole persona was reflective of small-town middle America. Though congressional life on the margins of the nation's political establishment had captured his imagination and left him hungry for more, he spoke deferentially of Pekin and its prominent role in forming his character: "Everything by way of human attribute has a chance for better anchoring . . . in a small town, better than the hurly burly of a metropolitan center. Life is pristine, it's simple." Buoyed by an unshakable faith in the American Dream, Dirksen had long relied on the notion that "if a man devoted an equal amount of time, energy, and concentration to any business or profession, I felt he would be bound to succeed." But at age fifty, with a successful House career cut short by a grave illness, he faced a future he could not control.[31]

To get away from the pressures of Washington, the Dirksens rented a cottage on the Chesapeake Bay. While Everett fished and worked in his beloved garden, Louella "read to him hour after hour, day after day." Ever so gradually his eyesight improved. To the Dirksens, a "miracle" was occurring. Louella held that Dirksen "was healed by God because he was still needed for work in the service of our government." Republican leaders appeared to agree and invited Dirksen to Albany to advise the presidential campaign of New York governor Thomas Dewey, who was running against Harry Truman. In light of his improving eyesight and with a keen determination to participate in the nation's political affairs, Dirksen accepted.[32]

An early Dewey supporter, Dirksen had fought Illinois's more conservative and isolationist Republicans for control of the state's convention delegates. In return, he expected a prominent role in the Dewey administration, perhaps as secretary of agriculture or even vice president. Despite his unbending allegiance to the GOP, Dirksen's ambivalent interaction with its eastern wing continued. The friction was as much social and cultural as it was political. At the Albany strategy session, the bourbon-drinking Dirksen would night after night needle the easterners about the dainty techniques necessary to prepare their dry martinis. Finally, a frustrated and patronizing John Foster Dulles enlightened his more parochial colleague from the Midwest: "Everett, anyone who knows anything about the requirements of a good martini knows that you do not bruise the gin and the vermouth."[33] By the end of the election cycle, though heartened that his vision was improving, an annoyed Dirksen left the lackluster Dewey campaign to crusade for the party on his own.

Such intraparty divisions contributed to Truman's shocking victory. In addition to winning the White House and regaining the Congress, the Democratic party swept Illinois. Adlai Stevenson won the governorship, and Paul Douglas, a liberal economist from the University of Chicago, captured a seat in the Senate. Having lost control of Congress and having been beaten in the race for the White House for the fifth consecutive time, Republicans were understandably downcast. Believing that Dewey lost the election with his hands-off campaign, his acceptance of the New Deal reforms, and his unwillingness to emphasize the un-American ideas of liberal Democrats, many Republicans resolved to eschew the "me-tooism" of the GOP's eastern establishment and fight back harder than ever before.[34]

Events conspired to present the Republicans with a golden political opportunity for the 1950 midterm elections. At home, Truman's domestic program, comprising an aggressive civil rights program, national health insurance, and increased agricultural controls, ran into a thicket of congressional protest and fell prey to an undeclared coalition between Southern Democrats and conservative Republicans. Critics charged the White House with promoting a socialistic program at home at the height of the cold war. In foreign policy, a rash of setbacks even before that summer's communist invasion of South Korea threw the administration on the defensive and shattered the bipartisan commitment to the containment policy. In rapid succession the Soviet Union exploded the atom bomb, China fell to the communists, and former New Dealer and suspected communist Alger Hiss was convicted of perjury.[35]

Recovering in his Pekin home and dabbling in a local law firm, Dirksen began to plan his return to political life. Local party leaders urged him to consider a campaign against Scott Lucas, Dirksen's old friend from the American Legion and Truman's new majority leader in the Democratic Senate. Former House colleague Sen. Karl E. Mundt (R-SD) encouraged Dirksen's efforts and gave him the names of several prominent backers from Illinois who were eager to support a Dirksen bid. Retirement had served Dirksen's political interests well for the 1950 senatorial campaign. First, his declining health and forced departure earned him the accolades of influential figures on both sides of the aisle that legitimated his candidacy. Second, he was untouched by the Democratic landslide of 1948. Third, he had the opportunity to begin his campaign early, a crucial advantage for any political figure who needs statewide name recognition in a U.S. Senate race. For most of 1949 Dirksen delivered speeches and plotted campaign strategy. In September, with the active cooperation of Louella and Joy, he announced his candidacy and launched a rigorous "get-acquainted" campaign to introduce himself to a wide array of Illinois voters.[36]

Dirksen was driven by what one supporter called "almost inhuman energy." He knew that Lucas and the Democrats would fight hard to keep their Senate seat, and he pledged "so long as there is a breath in me, I will carry the battle to them on every issue of socialism and freedom I know." Early on, he had a distinct advantage. While Dirksen, "like a brakeman on a relief shift, hopping here and there about the state," barnstormed through Illinois warning against the spread of an "ideological virus," Lucas was stuck in Washington, tied to Truman's legislative agenda bottled up in the Senate. Pundits were quick to emphasize the frenetic pace of Dirksen's campaign. Fourteen months before the election, one reporter complained that the candidate's only opening for an interview was at a 7:30 breakfast. With a ruddy face and an unruly shock of wavy, gray hair, Dirksen was blessed with a deep-throated, resonant baritone ideal for stump speaking. Hefty but incredibly vigorous, the shabbily dressed Dirksen presented a striking contrast to the handsome and urbane Lucas, who was often criticized in the local press for his aloofness and his overcommitment to his golfing "cronies" in the senatorial establishment.[37]

Both sides agreed that the election was a midterm referendum on the Fair Deal. Harry Truman worked aggressively to salvage the seat of his majority leader. Asked by the press in January 1950 about his strategy for the midterms and his potential role in the Dirksen-Lucas campaign, Truman asserted, "I will do everything I can to help him come back."[38] Illinois Democrats sought Truman's assistance with a vengeance. Jacob M. Arvey, Cook County Democratic chairman, stressed, "Of course we need him," and Paul Powell, the campaign director of Illinois's Democratic State Central Committee, pointed to Lucas's inevitable association with the Truman White House: "If the senator should be defeated it would be a repudiation of the Fair Deal program . . . throughout the nation."[39]

Despite their common backgrounds and some shared experiences in their formative years, Lucas and Dirksen by 1949 held irreconcilable political beliefs. But at the outset Dirksen ran against the Fair Deal's expansion of the New Deal more than he campaigned against Lucas. Facing only token opposition in the Republican primary and leaving organizational issues to his trusted associates, Dirksen focused his energies on the numerous vulnerabilities of the opposition. Lucas sensed that the Dirksen campaign would wage a "tough battle" for his seat and admitted to a friend that his commitments in Washington angered some supporters and required him to "go back and mend my political fences." Lucas knew that Dirksen's backers would make "him the whipping boy in the nation." Nonetheless, his early strategy was to showcase his experience, his Senate leadership, and his impact on the controversial issues of the day. Lucas's tactics played into Dirksen's hands, for he had hoped all along to make the election a midterm appraisal of Truman's Fair Deal.[40]

Dirksen's campaign had significant problems of its own. Lucas's aides prepared a 400-page dossier of Dirksen's House record, "The Diary of a Chameleon." Calling Dirksen "a man of the greatest insincerity and hypocrisy," the Lucas camp concluded that their opponent "has literally stood for nothing." To Lucas, Dirksen was forever reassessing his position on defining issues. While he had been a consistent isolationist until 1941, Dirksen converted to internationalism in the months just before World War II. Though he had supported the basic thrust of Truman's foreign policy, Dirksen after 1948 backtracked and rebuked the administration's diplomatic commitments.[41]

Supported by more than a few journalists, Lucas charged Dirksen with discarding his principles and currying the favor of Col. Robert McCormick, the controversial owner of the *Chicago Tribune* and Illinois's most prominent isolationist. The majority leader worked the issue relentlessly, declaring that "no newspaper in the state of Illinois can tell Scott Lucas what to do on the floor of the Senate. I wonder if my opponent can come in here and say the same thing." Although Dirksen admitted to visiting McCormick before announcing his candidacy, he insisted that "there was no deal." As early as 1949 Dirksen braced himself for the onslaught that he knew would accompany his attacks on policies he had previously supported. In his private notebooks he explained his flexibility on the issues: "Swift world—only fools and the dead don't change minds."[42]

On the campaign trail Louella Dirksen made her husband's bid for the Senate a team effort. During his House career, she had struggled to overcome her self-acknowledged "small-town timidity." Even though she was determined to spotlight Dirksen as the "principal actor on his own political stage," she was both active and productive behind the scenes. In his Senate campaign she sometimes directed campaign adviser Harold Rainville to alert friendly newspapers in advance of a Dirksen appearance. More publicly, she traveled with her husband on the stump. In any given week the Dirksens might spend five nights away from their home in Pekin. Louella favored simple, dark suits, ones that did not "show the soil." Meals on the road consisted of milk and coffee from a thermos and perhaps a boxed lunch of chicken prepared by their supporters. Often she would drive, leaving Dirksen time to rest or to work on his upcoming remarks. Joy pitched in as well. She took dictation, ensuring that the campaign kept up with its mounting correspondence. This team effort, made up primarily of Rainville and Dirksen's family, enabled the candidate to deliver 1,200 speeches in the course of the nonstop campaign, and in the process, to wear out three Dodge sedans.[43]

After shoring up the regular Republican vote, Dirksen focused his energies on the one million registered Illinois voters who had failed to cast a ballot in 1948. His criss-crossing of the state was primarily an effort to win their support: "In that group lies the answer. Who are they? Where are they? We must find out and have them express themselves." Dirksen's handlers played hillbilly music to attract the young to his political rallies. But organizational matters and campaign gimmickry interested Dirksen only tangentially. Delivering speeches at county picnics and answering questions afterward sparked his engines. For it was in this environment that he could wave his arms wildly and rely on his oratorical gifts to focus on the scourge that threatened the freedom of the republic. Even during nonpolitical remarks, Dirksen rarely passed up the opportunity to blister the Democrats. Asked at a January luncheon about the election's key issues, he pointed to three themes that would dominate his campaign: first, "a creeping socialism" at home; second, "wasteful, fantastic spending which leads to national bankruptcy"; and third, an "expensive, inconsistent, ineffective foreign policy which has resulted in the progressive communization of Asia and the liquidation of our freedom."[44]

Journalists and political pundits highlighted foreign policy and subversion from within, in part because Dirksen and Lucas promoted two distinct roles for America to play at home and abroad in the postwar world. Though he had strongly supported the Marshall Plan as a "gamble" worth taking, Dirksen by 1950 was an enthusiastic critic of America's Europe-first foreign policy and its postwar drift to unchecked internationalism. Lucas backed Truman's internationalist foreign policy, underlining its importance in "winning the peace" as well as its investment value: "The dollars we appropriate come home to roost in Illinois and other states because our friends abroad must use those dollars to buy supplies we produce." In a clear philosophic difference, Dirksen argued that the increased taxes necessary to pay for the Marshall Plan swelled the power of the state and eroded freedom at home: "Thousands of millions of our dollars have been poured down rat holes. What shall it profit the United States to save the whole world and lose its own freedom?" Responding to Lucas's assertion that "our country is doing fine," Dirksen played on the tumult of the times and exercised his oratorical prowess: "That's wonderful. Debt is going up and coal piles are going down, spending is going up and farm prices are going down. We are confining the Reds in Europe while they have run us out of Asia. Socialism is marching at home and freedom is retreating. By next June we will be in the hole to the tune of $5.5 billion and maybe more."[45]

Like Richard Nixon in his 1950 anticommunist campaign against Helen Gahagan Douglas, Dirksen pointed to subversion from within to explain America's foreign policy setbacks. While he engaged in his share of public red-baiting (he said that Lucas had "cuddled communists"), he also worked behind the scenes to heighten the political pressure on the majority leader to make clear his position on radicalism at home. Karl Mundt wrote Dirksen in late March 1950 and reported that Lucas was planning to sit on Mundt's antisubversion bill in order to protect Truman, who wanted to present Congress with his own, slightly less aggressive, piece of legislation. Sensing the anticommunist temper of the times, Mundt noted that Lucas was in "deep water," and he encouraged Dirksen to "make a lot of hay" by ratcheting up the pressure on Lucas to act on the bill.[46]

Dismissing the Republican charges of creeping socialism as mere "propaganda," Democratic party regulars focused on post–World War II economic issues and the continuing vitality of the New Deal legacy. Harry Truman energized party workers when he traveled to Illinois in May to bolster the Lucas forces. Advertised as a "nonpolitical" swing through the Midwest, Truman's trip was intended principally to attack the Republican "obstructionists" who were holding up his program. Refreshed by his contact with the people and recalling the success of his whistle-stop campaign of two years before, Truman assailed the "undemocratic elements in our society." He called for the repeal of the Taft-Hartley Act and the enactment of both the Brannan plan for increased agricultural controls and a program of national health insurance. Before concluding, Truman praised his majority leader and identified the importance of his reelection, leaving the platform only after symbolically holding aloft Lucas's right arm. From the White House, Truman wrote Lucas privately and emphasized again his importance to the administration: "I need you—your country needs you."[47]

While Truman and Vice President Alben Barkley came to Illinois to campaign for Lucas, celebrated Republicans crossed state lines to stump for Dirksen. Perhaps most notable was Joseph McCarthy (R-WI). Against the backdrop of the Korean War and in light of several dramatic spy cases, the anticommunist issue maintained its resonance throughout the election season. McCarthy, speaking in the early fall to a German-American society in Chicago, pilloried Lucas and the Fair Dealers. Distinguishing between loyal Democrats and the "commiecrats" in power, McCarthy called for Dirksen's election so that Republicans could "kick the perfumed pinks and punks out of our State Department."[48]

Embittered by McCarthy's tactics, Illinois Democrats nonetheless continued their strategy of pairing Lucas with the president. Hundreds of Chicago billboards showed Truman holding Lucas's hand aloft, over the caption "Keep America Prosperous, Secure, and Free." With the assistance of friendly newspapers, Dirksen altered his strategy and began to criticize Lucas more directly. One influential daily described the majority leader as Truman's "parrot," a cog in the Washington establishment who was unable to "afford any independent thoughts." Later in the summer Lucas distanced himself from two of the most unpopular aspects of Truman's program, the Brannan agricultural plan and national health insurance. Dirksen pounced on his opponent's "frantic search for votes" and described his waffling as "moral and political cowardice." Lucas's backtracking may have disillusioned his liberal supporters and deadened their resolve to promote his reelection. Dirksen leaped at Lucas's hedging. Still reeling from the charges that he had abandoned his own commitments for cheap partisan gain, he recorded in his notebooks that the "senator changes faster."[49]

Dirksen picked up the pace of his already frenetic campaign in the summer months. No audience was too small for the challenger. The *Saturday Evening Post* published a photograph of a dapper Dirksen sporting a wide tie with an elephant design as he entertained a group of Illinois farmers and their sons in front of the Hartsburg post office. Head tilted back, chest puffed out, with one hand stuffed in his buttoned coat pocket and the other on the arm of a potential supporter, Dirksen stumped for the kind of votes he would need to oust the Senate's majority leader. In public speeches he stayed on the attack. Full of "bunglers, blunderers, and stupid policymakers," the Democratic opposition, he suggested, had chosen to ignore the interests of the American heartland. Dirksen's diction was aggressive and belligerent, and he insisted that the election was nothing less than an opportunity to clean the Democrats out "from cellar to garret so that this country and its policy will represent not a viewpoint that comes from the Kremlin, but from the hearts and from the firesides of the American people."[50]

Lucas failed to appreciate Dirksen's progress. Though he criticized Dirksen's "off-again, on-again behavior" in his private correspondence, he refused to confront his opponent's charges. He wrote a supporter that "no one is paying any attention to him. I refuse to dignify the candidate from Pekin. . . . My reputation in Illinois is pretty well established and there isn't anything that McCarthy or Dirksen can do to tear it down." In contrast to Dirksen's combativeness, Lucas on the stump was measured and restrained. He was content to let his record speak for itself, and he sought to portray himself as the methodical majority leader responsible for filtering out the rancor from the divisive discourse of the day. Responding to the attack that the Democrats had failed to defend American troops in the field, Lucas insisted, "We are not going to let ourselves be stampeded by extremists on the other side."[51] At almost every opportunity, he defended the status quo.

Perhaps because Lucas refused to rise to Dirksen's challenge, October found Illinois strangely quiescent. A man from the southern town of Pinkneyville concluded that "nobody's very mad," and James Hill, Dirksen's campaign manager in Springfield, worried that "we're getting the silent treatment." Dirksen redoubled his efforts to shake the voters' apathy. At a catfish fry in Vienna, the Dirksen car was accompanied by two carloads of supporters and a pickup truck outfitted with a pair of booming speakers. Unshaven farmers came in from the fields to hear Dirksen rip the Democrats and promote what one reporter called his "fighting campaign of evangelical Republicanism." Starting slowly and softly, Dirksen eventually whipped the crowd into a frenzy with attacks on Democratic foreign policy, the lack of preparation that led to war in Korea, and a sarcastic imitation of President Truman's 1945 reference to Josef Stalin: "I like old Joe—he's a very decent fellow." By the end of his tirade the coat was off, the tie unknotted, the hair unkempt, and the audience exhausted.[52]

As the election neared and the candidates continued to wage a mid-American battle for the future of the nation's foreign policy, pundits declared the race too close to call. Most agreed that the Democratic dominance of Chicago's Cook County offset the regular Republicanism of downstate Illinois, and in the opinion of one journalist, "The un-fettered citizenry . . . decide[s] the election on the issues and the personal appeal of the candidates." No one could have predicted the election-eve scandal that shook Lucas's hold on Cook County. Despite the pleas of Lucas and other party leaders, Sen. Estes Kefauver (D-TN) brought his Special Committee to Investigate Organized Crime in Interstate Commerce to Chicago when two Cook County investigators were murdered in a twenty-four-hour period. As the unlucky Lucas lay bedridden with a severe case of bronchitis, Dirksen denounced the "star chamber" sessions of the

Kefauver committee and demanded public disclosure of the testimony. Just five days before the election the *Chicago Sun-Times,* a liberal daily that ironically endorsed Lucas's reelection, published the testimony of Daniel "Tubbo" Gilbert, a captain in the Chicago Police Department who was running for Cook County sheriff. Gilbert, whose salary was listed at $9,000, admitted that his overall assets totaled $360,000. Ridiculed as the "richest cop in the world," Gilbert was a confessed gambler who bet on local elections. In 1950 he brought Chicago's Democratic machine to a grinding halt.[53]

Discouraging election-eve news from Korea hindered the Democratic cause as well. Despite American successes in the war earlier in the summer, voters in downstate Illinois cited Korea as a primary issue of concern for the 1950 election. Lucas argued consistently that his brand of internationalism promoted peace and prosperity. War in the Pacific, however, undermined the message on his flyers: "To restore peace! To Maintain Prosperity! Retain Scott W. Lucas." To the charge that Truman had left the United States unprepared for the communist invasion of South Korea, Lucas retorted, "We have the bomb. We know how to use it and we know where to use it, and when we do, we will use it where it hurts." Just one day before the election, Lucas's veiled threat took on a more terrifying meaning. Gen. Douglas MacArthur reported to Truman that isolated pockets of Chinese communists had moved across the Yalu River, a development that even the confident MacArthur described as a "matter of the gravest international significance." Though the Chinese delayed the brunt of their offensive until the end of November, Pentagon officials made it clear before the election that America's fighting men would not be home for Christmas and that the United States faced a widespread war in the Pacific.[54]

Though the war ate away at Truman's opportunities to campaign for the party, he delivered a boisterous preelection speech in St. Louis. He attacked isolationism and argued that a reversal of the administration's foreign policy agenda would enable communist imperialists to "gobble up the rest of the world." Truman's remarks included a last-minute effort to jump-start Lucas's floundering campaign. He equated Republican isolationism with "national suicide" and pointed to Dirksen ("one of them right here in Illinois") and his midwestern GOP colleagues as a threat to the republic's survival.[55]

In the end, however, Dirksen enjoyed too many advantages for Lucas to overcome. The challenger's oratorical prowess and folksy appeal combined with the voters' emerging fear of a protracted war in Korea, Lucas's stand-offishness, Truman's increasing unpopularity, and Gilbert's testimony to ensure a convincing victory for Dirksen. He won widespread support from the Illinois voters, notching victories in 82 of the state's 102 counties. He energized the electorate; in 1950 over 3.5 million Illinois voters went to the polls, just 300,000 shy of those who had voted in the presidential election of 1948. Lucas's Cook County advantage never materialized. Though Dirksen lost the urban Chicago vote by almost ten percentage points, he won 68 percent of the suburban Chicago vote and carried the county as a whole. With his hold on downstate Illinois secure, he won the 1950 election by the comfortable margin of 300,000 votes.[56]

Before the results had been announced, the Dirksen forces started the celebration in Pekin. His home, replete with a "walk in" sign, was "packed like the proverbial can of sardines." Supporters set off red flares in his front yard, and after a fifty-car parade through the streets of Pekin, Dirksen's partisans lifted him to their shoulders to wave for the cameras. To Sen. Robert A. Taft (R-OH) he exclaimed, "I guess we broke their backs this time!" In Chicago a teary and exhausted Scott Lucas finally read a written concession. Democratic County Chairman Jacob Arvey cited trouble in Korea, the treatment of Gilbert, and isolationism as the primary reasons for the Lucas defeat.[57]

In a postelection interview with *U.S. News and World Report*, Dirksen deftly overlooked the Gilbert scandal and attributed the scale of his victory to superior organization, an energized electorate, and the issues of communism and an ever-increasing tax burden. Dirksen's analysis complemented his statement to Illinois voters on accepting Lucas's congratulations. Dirksen resorted to near-apocalyptic language to describe his victory and the political climate of the times: "In an hour of danger, an intuitive sense puts the people back on the beam of Freedom. . . . With their own eyes they could see the socialist pattern which has been readied for our country. They saw the ugly head of communism within the citadel of government." The scope of the Democratic defeat, made much worse but not caused by the findings of the Kefauver committee, obscured the ultimate meaning of the Dirksen mandate as he entered the Senate to begin his long and influential career.[58]

For Dirksen personally, upsetting Lucas represented the fulfillment of a long-held ambition and marked the return to public life he so desperately craved. He revealed a penchant for changing his mind on important issues, a political style he would cultivate and come to perfect, first as the junior senator from Illinois and second as the minority leader of his party. Despite his policy reversals and his appreciation for the inevitability of change, Dirksen throughout emphasized "freedom" and "liberty," themes that inspired his consistent promotion of Americanism, his disdain for subversives and radicals, his instinctive aversion to a planned economy, and his scorn for any sort of liberal social agenda. Dirksen's nebulous conception of freedom and his vision of a simpler, more traditional America dominated the character of his public discourse for the rest of his career.

Taking advantage of a Washington atmosphere that columnist Joe Alsop described as a "drunken beach picnic with a vast tidal wave sweeping in from the horizon," the Republican party cut the Democratic majority from twelve to two in the Senate and from ninety-two to thirty-five in the House. The 1950 elections finished the Fair Deal. Though Joe McCarthy's recent biographers have argued that he was not nearly as influential in the 1950 elections as he claimed to be, there was no doubt that the midterm entrenched his rough-and-tumble style in the nation's political culture. Richard Nixon's victory in California, coupled with Dirksen's reestablishment of the Midwest as a bastion of solid Republicanism, signaled the GOP's temporary move away from the eastern seaboard. Conservative dailies like the *Chicago Tribune* celebrated a "victory for America" and predicted that the freshman Republicans would go to Washington with a "mission to rescue the country from the hands of the fools and traitors in both parties who have been dominant all these years."[59]

Speeches, letters, and editorials from a variety of voices revealed the on-going party split that had crippled the GOP in the 1948 election. Having recovered from that debacle to win a wide array of local elections in the 1950 midterms, Dirksen and his fellow conservatives were still groping for a message that would distinguish the GOP from the Democrats without alienating independent voters necessary to win the White House. Fundamentally, the Republican party was struggling to establish a national position on the New Deal reforms and the nation's commitment to a bipartisan policy of global containment. The power of the presidency, its rightful role and appropriate responsibilities, was the core disagreement between Dirksen's midwestern Republicanism and the more moderate politics of the GOP's eastern seaboard. The 1950 election did not resolve these differences and thus foreshadowed the 1952 convention in Chicago. There and then the two great wings of the GOP joined in a fierce and unrelenting battle for the heart and soul of the Republican party.

Herbert Hoover wrote Dirksen after the campaign, calling the results "magnificent." Dirksen insisted that "we accomplished something for America on election day." Scott Lucas, back home in Havana, no doubt would have disagreed but was civil enough to send along a handwritten "Dear Ev" letter congratulating his opponent and urging him to rise above the paralyzing squabbles of purely partisan politics: "While you are a Republican and I am a Democrat, we are Americans first, and I wish you well in an office that carries heavy responsibilities in these trying and turbulent days." Enjoying a respite in Miami, Florida, Dirksen stiffly acknowledged Lucas's "gracious note and . . . good wishes. I shall make every endeavor to live up to the responsibility which membership in the United States Senate entails." After a week's vacation, the Dirksen team (he rarely referred to himself as "I"; it was still "we") settled their affairs in Pekin and moved to Washington for the start of the Eighty-second Congress.[60]

As a member of the House, Dirksen had rented a room at the Mayflower Hotel. But with a six-year Senate term and his wife and daughter moving with him to Washington, he decided to rent a two-room apartment from the Berkshire on Massachusetts Avenue, N.W. Louella managed the home and took dictation from her husband in the evenings in order to save him time. Twenty-two-year-old Joy drove him to the Senate at 8:30 every morning and worked as an unpaid receptionist in his office. In Washington Joy made numerous friends among the "congressional children." She became particularly close to Mary Baker, daughter of Howard Baker Sr., a congressman from Tennessee. As Illinois princess for the 1951 Washington Cherry Blossom Festival, Joy needed an escort. Mary set her up with her brother, Howard Baker Jr., just back from military service in Korea. Joy and Howard became inseparable.[61]

Dirksen returned to Washington determined to make his presence felt. He wrote in his notebooks that November 7 was an "epic day" and that the GOP was obligated to reverse the "drool, drivel, and deceit" that was rotting away the body politic. Eager to "capture the citadel," Dirksen insisted that the only way to take the White House in 1952 was to fight the Democrats at every turn. Relentless and combative, he stressed that the "duty of the opposition is to oppose." He interpreted the slightest retreat from principled partisanship as a betrayal of those Americans who were disgusted with a bloated government out of touch with the common man. The basic flaw in the Democratic party was the "extension of centralized power" through a distended presidency. Most of Dirksen's early thinking assumed the existence of a leviathan executive that ate away at the liberties of the middle American. His self-defined mission was to reverse executive usurpation and return power to Congress and to the people.[62]

Because Dirksen was a freshman Republican ignored by the Democratic White House, the first two years of his Senate career were his least productive, in terms of both legislation proposed and measures enacted. Nonetheless, the issues he championed, the rhetoric he employed, and the political battles he waged mirrored the conflict and consensus within the Republican party. Despite the frustrations he encountered, his first years in the Senate were ultimately fruitful. Though his critics saw him as a self-satisfied blowhard, GOP conservatives admired his endless energy and his ability to inspire party regulars from the rostrum. In early 1951 Robert Taft helped elect Dirksen as chairman of the Republican Senatorial Campaign Committee. In this capacity, he won the loyalty and affection of his Republican colleagues, gained name recognition across the nation, and began to appreciate more fully the issues that divided the party.[63]

Though he objected to the Democratic concentration of executive power, Dirksen believed that the essential appeal of the Republican party was its commitment to restoring solvency and sanity to a federal government that had careened out of control. His every policy position radiated from the core assumption that the central government had eaten away at individual liberties. He corresponded regularly with conservative Republican Robert E. Wood, president of Sears, Roebuck in Chicago. When Wood suggested to Dirksen that the Senate enact a "reasonable cut" of the Truman budget, Dirksen responded, "My interpretation of a reasonable cut is cutting it to the bone." His early speeches encouraged the government to embark on an austerity campaign. Dirksen railed against federal aid to fund public health units, insisting that the Congress make "sure we do not spend and authorize over our heads, and thus jeopardize the fiscal integrity and solvency of this country." To Dirksen, a control-laden central government led directly to corruption and inefficiency and ultimately to the damnation of a democratic society. He endorsed government "frugality," because a proliferation of federal programs eroded traditional freedoms and made the people dependent on an alien bureaucracy.[64]

While Dirksen focused primarily on domestic issues, more senior Republican senators pointed to the overriding importance of crafting a GOP foreign policy position. Bogged down in Korea, the Truman administration moved quickly to implement its European defense plan, a tactic that suggested to suspicious Republicans that the White House was neglecting its responsibilities in Asia in favor of its Europe-first foreign policy. In a meeting with congressional leaders, Truman asked for an additional appropriation of $16.8 billion to send ground troops to Europe, the initiation of universal military training, and the imposition of wage and price controls to dampen inflationary pressures in the economy. Taft called Truman's proposals "the most important question before Congress." He worried that a troop commitment to Europe would overheat an economy already running at capacity and that the attendant wage and price controls would create a military state at odds with traditional notions of American liberty.[65]

Dirksen joined the fray and railed against a White House that had overstepped its bounds. In a March 26 speech to the Mortgage Investment Bankers, "The State of the Union," Dirksen bared his disdain for a powerful presidency and the creeping one-worldism of a socialist monolith. He pointed to the Korean War, a "garrison state," and "malfeasances and malfeasances" before suggesting that middle America suffered from an "anxiety that liberty be liquidated by . . . forces in our own land." The common denominator, he typed in bold, was the "CONSTANT GROWTH OF THE EXECUTIVE POWER." He listed a litany of presidential dictates that offended his notion of constitutional government: an undeclared war in Korea, increased power to levy tariffs through reciprocal trade agreements, the newly established custom for the White House to present a national budget to the Congress, and a "peacetime concentration of power." The end result, Dirksen bellowed, was "THE RETREAT OF LEGIS-LATIVE POWER." In his eyes, congressional abdication of its authority paved the way for totalitarian dictators like Franco, Mussolini, Hitler, and the European socialists to choke off the democratic impulse. Truman's plan to send more troops to Europe was just another step down the slippery slope to socialism.[66]

Republican critics of Truman's European defense policy fell short of defeating the White House, but their criticism of an all-powerful executive resonated with the public. When Truman dismissed General MacArthur on April 11 for insubordination, the GOP intensified their attacks on the president. Republicans had long idolized the general. In 1932 MacArthur, then under the command of Herbert Hoover, cleared the Bonus Army, which many Republicans believed to be full of radical agitators, out of Washington. While Franklin Roosevelt and America's high command focused first on winning the war against Nazi Germany, MacArthur lobbied for the geostrategic importance of Asia and eventually oversaw America's victory in the Pacific. His aggressive and uncompromising plans for winning the Korean War won favor in the GOP because many Republicans were sharply critical of Truman's strategy of a limited war and the possibility that political considerations in the United Nations might ultimately dictate American foreign policy. Much of the nation exploded in outrage at the president's decision to relieve MacArthur. At a Los Angeles medical school, students hung Harry Truman in effigy. The *Chicago Tribune* ran a front-page editorial entitled "Impeach Truman," and William Jenner (R-IN), from the well of the Senate, called for the president's impeachment.[67]

Dirksen's reaction to MacArthur's firing, though somewhat more temperate than Jenner's, was reflective of the conservative GOP caucus. Though he did not question the president's right to relieve his commanding general, he ridiculed Truman's decision as "summary and captious." Dirksen never approved of MacArthur's formula for winning the war, but he praised the general for having a plan and rebuked the administration for its lack of foresight. Ultimately, however, Dirksen never overcame the inherent contradictions of a belligerent but penny-conscious isolationist seeking political gain from an explosive issue that had electrified the people. Though he blistered the administration for appeasing the Reds in Eastern Europe, he winced at the "small and devious" minds in the State Department, an agency that in his mind threatened the sovereignty of the people and "takes the dollars out of their pockets, and takes their sons from their bed and board, and puts them in uniform."

MacArthur's firing encouraged the GOP to conduct a reexamination of American policy in the Far East. Without the White House or even a congressional majority, Dirksen and his Republican colleagues had little control over foreign policy. But the senator's short-sighted proposals reflected the midwestern GOP's inability to propose a more effective policy than Truman's. In the 1950 campaign Dirksen had criticized the Democrats for abandoning Chiang to the Chinese communists and had lashed out at appeasement of any kind, but he also had regretted the president's decision to move north of the thirty-eighth parallel. He ripped into the British Foreign Office for "trying to find a modus vivendi with the Soviet Union" but fought the wage and price controls the administration argued were necessary to carry on a limited war in Korea.[68]

Though he professed disgust at the weakness of the administration's foreign policy, he worried that the Marshall Plan and other foreign aid programs threatened the essential solvency of the country and diminished the self-respect of the recipient. In short, he sought to fight communism on the cheap without the strong arm of the central government and without Western allies. He never articulated his ideas as clearly as Taft and other party leaders. But Dirksen's strident, almost absolutist, speeches were consistent with the conservative GOP caucus. Dirksen and his anti-Truman colleagues stymied themselves with a partisan and bellicose rhetoric that far outpaced any sober awareness of America's limited means to effect a worldwide policy for the containment of communism or the liberation of captive nations.[69]

Dirksen was more comfortable in the area of budget politics. He warned against the inflationary pressures of increased spending and the attendant devaluation of the dollar in international markets. He held that federal expenditures represented the "real root force" behind inflation: "It's like holding one's hand on a teakettle lid and stuffing up the snout while forgetting to turn off the gas. The result will be an explosion." Dirksen employed his fiscal conservatism to justify votes against soil conservation programs, increased funding for the Voice of America, and Truman's foreign aid program. He insisted that the administration created "perpetual pensioners" with its recovery plan and that it was ultimately impossible to "buy friendship and good will with American dollars." Though Truman insisted that cutting the program would jeopardize European recovery when success was in sight, Dirksen introduced and crusaded for an unsuccessful amendment that would have slashed

$500 million from the foreign aid bill. He grounded his argument on nothing less than the "salvation of the United States" and charged that the Truman administration's spending guaranteed national suicide.[70]

Only Dirksen's commitment to an unfettered market overran his disdain for inflation. From his position on the Banking and Currency Committee, he questioned the need for wage and price controls and worked, again unsuccessfully, to have them eliminated. To Dirksen, rent control resulted in housing shortages that retarded the development of a free society. His eagerness to do away with the controls at the height of the Korean War, however, undermined his call for the federal government to dampen its inflationary spending. Though he clearly argued that the one fundamental question in America "is the preservation of our free economic system within the framework of a free government," his inconsistencies on the important issue of inflation revealed another crippling contradiction in his early thinking.[71]

As 1951 wore on and the Republican party readied itself for another shot at the elusive White House, it became increasingly difficult to separate policy positions from political posturing. In this latter area Dirksen was more prominent and more influential, in part because of his role as chairman of the Republican Senatorial Campaign Committee. More important, Dirksen's Midwest conservatism launched a bitter attack on the more moderate Republicanism of the eastern seaboard. Most Republicans agreed that the rampant corruption in the Truman administration and the White House's efforts to broaden and expand the New Deal reforms were issues on which there was a broad degree of party consensus. But before uniting for the general election campaign, Republicans of all persuasions prepared for the internecine warfare that had become a debilitating ritual performed once every four years.

Foreign policy was at the crux of the conflict. Dirksen's militant isolationism represented one side of the argument. Throughout the year he downplayed the need for allies, once suggesting that if recipients of Marshall Plan assistance continued to trade with communist countries, the United States should "forget about them and not worry about their destiny any longer." On countless occasions he asserted that European nations should make more sacrifices and depend less on the American aid that was promoting a "lavish, paternalistic, and socialistic system." New York governor Tom Dewey, the party's standard-bearer for the past two elections, disagreed. Returning from an overseas trip, he lambasted those Republicans like Dirksen who advocated a reappraisal of the Marshall Plan: "When we no longer have allies, we are lost. If we are strong enough, and stop belly-aching, and build up our allies, we may be strong enough to avert a third world war."[72]

More fundamentally, the two wings of the Republican party clashed over the extent to which the GOP should commit itself to a bipartisan foreign policy of collective security. After Dewey's defeat, Arthur Vandenberg's death, and the souring of the Korean War, most midwestern Republicans held that bipartisanship expanded the powers of the presidency and insulated him from justifiable criticism that he might receive in the wake of setbacks abroad. Dirksen believed that Dewey's unwillingness to criticize Truman more vigorously had contributed to the 1948 GOP debacle. To Dirksen, "a party worthy of the name can develop a program of its own and stand by it and carry it through without depending on the party on the other side."[73]

Gen. Dwight Eisenhower, World War II hero, commander of North Atlantic Treaty Organization (NATO) forces, and prospective candidate for the presidency, later remembered that he would have renounced any intention to run for the Republican nomination had Taft and the midwestern wing of the GOP pledged itself to the bipartisan principle that "collective security is necessary for us in Western Europe." Taft refused to make such a sweeping commitment. Eisenhower, whose unannounced candidacy had already received the support of Governor Dewey, concluded that "isolationism was stronger in the Congress than I had previously suspected." Just as important, Eisenhower worried that Taft was set on "cutting the president, or the presidency, down to size."[74] Because fears of a leviathan executive were at the heart of the GOP's disgust with the New Deal and the presidencies of Franklin Roosevelt and Harry Truman, Ike could not publicly endorse the modern presidency and campaign for its preservation from the start. Indeed, he would on occasion highlight the extravagances of his predecessors and promise to tame executive usurpation by returning the legislative initiative to Congress. But a careful reading of Eisenhower's private papers reveals that he was determined to use the White House to make good on the nation's commitment to global containment. While Dirksen hoped that the GOP would spearhead the return of presidential power to Congress and the people,

Eisenhower was determined to consolidate executive authority and entrench the White House as the principal political agent in cold war America.

Eisenhower's announcement that he was a Republican intensified interest in his candidacy. Dirksen was unimpressed. He saw Eisenhower as a pseudo-Republican propped up by the moneyed power of the eastern seaboard. The freshman from Illinois surprised no one when during a September television interview he sided with Taft. Whatever their differences on specific issues, the two men agreed that the Republican party had to wage a wide-ranging and principled attack on the welfare statism of the Democratic party in order to win the White House. At party conferences Dirksen supported Taft without mentioning his name and in the process attacked the softness of Dewey's 1948 campaign: "There must be leaders who will boldly state the Republican viewpoint and not be deterred by any prospect of defeat."[75]

In mid-November 1951 Taft rewarded Dirksen's loyalty by naming him the preconvention manager of the Taft campaign in Illinois. Some observers pointed to the fact that Taft had not appointed any other manager for a particular state and suggested that his primary interest was to avoid a delegation that might support Dirksen as a favorite-son candidate. David S. Ingalls, chairman of Taft's campaign committee, furthered that impression by asserting that Dirksen's appointment ensured Taft's "decisive grip on the Midwest and greatly enhances the Ohioan's chances for victory on the first ballot." Later in November Taft corresponded with Dirksen, writing, "I have so many things to thank you for that I don't know where to begin." He appreciated Dirksen's repeated endorsements, his willingness to organize political appearances in Illinois, and his eagerness to "look after affairs in Illinois." He praised Dirksen's work on the Republican Senatorial Campaign Committee and looked forward to a get-together in the new year, when Taft could explain his strategy for the upcoming campaign.[76]

Dirksen's first year in the Senate ended with a personal milestone. Just before Christmas Joy married Howard Baker. The groom remembered his conversation with Dirksen, late in the summer at the family's rented home on the Chesapeake Bay, about the couple's plans. According to Baker, "I didn't ask him, I told him." Even so, the conversation was pressure-packed, mostly because Dirksen "was the most formidable character I'd ever met. He was deeply moved. I'm sure he knew. He listened, and I ran out of things to say." What Dirksen, consumed with his duties in the Senate, did not know was that Joy and her mother had already planned the details of the wedding. The couple, who would move to Brentwood, Tennessee, was married in Pekin's First Presbyterian Church. A blinding snowstorm hit Pekin the day of the wedding, and Senator Dirksen, who could now afford a Ben Gingiss full-dress coat, directed traffic in front of the church and at the reception in nearby Peoria.[77]

Back on Capitol Hill at the start of the new congressional session, Dirksen reaffirmed his strong commitment to the conservative and antibipartisan wing of the Republican party. In January he wrote his personal friend Earl Beling, stating that his primary reason for his early endorsement of Taft was to keep the Midwest intact before the convention. To Dirksen, Taft was "truly courageous," a man who "knows full well that the country is confronted with a crisis which can be solved only by forthright and militant action." In the Senate Dirksen angled to secure more legitimacy for his conservative beliefs. In response to the vacancy created by the death of Kenneth Wherry (R-NE), he moved to the Committee on Rules and Administration and took a place on the Senate Elections Subcommittee. This body was investigating William Benton's (D-CT) resolution to oust Joseph McCarthy from the Senate. In short, Benton sought to punish McCarthy for his scurrilous antics in Maryland's 1950 Senate election. McCarthy had traveled to Maryland to campaign against Democratic incumbent Millard Tydings. Angry that Tydings had the temerity to question the truthfulness of his anticommunist crusade, McCarthy distributed doctored photographs that showed Tydings meeting with Earl Browder, a leader of the American Communist Party. Because Wherry had been a steadfast McCarthy ally, Dirksen's membership on the subcommittee did little to change the balance of the investigation; nonetheless, he did begin a period of reflexive support for McCarthy that solidified throughout the year.[78]

In early February Dirksen delivered his annual Lincoln Day address to Illinois's Republican Women's Organization. As he did in many of his speeches, he started slowly, hammering away at themes on which most Republicans could agree. America under Truman was heading "into the land of state socialism." Increasing taxation "stifled all initiative," and Truman's undeclared war in Korea, a "fool's war," was indicative of the "complete destruction of constitutional government." He expected a Republican administration to establish a foreign policy in the "best interest of the American people." By the time he emphasized that "this country is at the crossroads of its existence," his speech had hit a crescendo. Republicans had lost in 1948 because "there was no real choice presented," and "we were all things to all people." To Dirksen, the party had an obligation to offer "the people of this country the opportunity to choose the right way from the wrong way." He championed Taft's candidacy and stressed that "this victory must be gained by a Republican who will campaign without compromise, who will attack the Roosevelt-Truman-Hiss administration in all of its weaknesses, not just part of them."[79]

Because of Korea and the administration's plan to increase troops to Europe, relations between Truman and the Republicans in Congress were already frayed when the president seized the nation's major steel mills in early April. Dirksen and his GOP colleagues exploded in outrage. Responding to calls for Truman's impeachment, Dirksen acknowledged that a full-scale trial was "time consuming" and that a conviction was unlikely. But he agreed that Truman had acted capriciously and arbitrarily, and he took umbrage at the executive's elastic application of "inherent powers" during times of national emergency. To Dirksen, Truman's decision to nationalize the mills was symptomatic of the president's disregard for the separation of powers established in the Constitution. It reminded him, he told his constituents, of the White House's diabolical scheme to wage an undeclared war in Korea. "ONE MAN POWER . . . in an atomic age," Dirksen wrote in his notebooks, "is not a happy thing to contemplate."[80]

The negative nature of Dirksen's early political style dictated his response to foreign policy initiatives as well. His distaste for every element of Truman's leadership led him to buck the administration's sincere efforts to repair its bipartisan foreign policy. In March 1952 he was one of only ten Republicans who voted against the Japanese Peace Treaty, which formally ended World War II in the Pacific and established bilateral security alliances with the Philippines, Japan, Australia, and New Zealand to contain the spread of communism in East Asia. The architect of the treaty was John Foster Dulles, now a GOP adviser to the State Department. Truman appointed the New Yorker in part to answer those critics in the GOP who had charged that bipartisanship applied only to the administration's European policies. Dulles worked closely with William

Knowland (R-CA) and H. Alexander Smith (R-NJ), two of the GOP's most consistent critics of the administration's East Asian policies. Based on Dulles's "active collaboration" with the Republican Senate, the treaty represented the first phase of a new bipartisanship between the White House and Capitol Hill.[81]

Calling the treaty "the work of one man," Dirksen rejected the views of those who lauded Dulles's cooperation with the Senate. He justified his vote against the treaty by pointing to Japan's invasion of Nationalist China before World War II, the uncertainty of the costs of the pact, and the possibility that an unreconstructed Japan might abandon its partnership with the West and turn communist. But chiefly he used the occasion to ridicule Truman's failed leadership in the Korean War and the growth of an unchecked presidency that had overstepped its constitutional bounds. To Dirksen, the "Senate of the United States has very little authority in . . . the Orient." He voted against the treaty in part to block the continuing surrender of American sovereignty to the United Nations and the attendant expansion of the presidency in the field of foreign policy.[82]

Taft's own foreign policy views mirrored Dirksen's. Though Taft had given grudging support to the post–World War II internationalism of Arthur Vandenberg, the senator's illness and death, Truman's victory in 1948, the Korean stalemate, and the very real need to establish his own positions for the upcoming election encouraged him to reappraise the nation's cold war commitments. In A Foreign Policy for Americans, Taft echoed Dirksen when he rattled off the foreign policy disasters overseen by the Democratic party. The Ohioan admonished Truman for his unconstitutional expansion of the power of the presidency and worried about communists working in the State Department. He favored a policy that guaranteed American interests first and noted a sinister parallel between expensive foreign aid programs abroad and New Deal planning at home.[83]

Dirksen was focusing on the election as well. He rarely dampened reports that his support for Taft was meant in part to increase his attractiveness as a vice presidential candidate. On one occasion Dirksen suggested that he was plotting for the presidency, the institution that he had been bashing and mauling since his run for the Senate. He told his supporters that he was for Taft "unless and until something happens to take him out of the race." If a stalemated convention lost its way, he acknowledged, "I am here to serve." Taft did his part to keep Dirksen in the tent.

In early June his headquarters announced that Dirksen would deliver the nominating speech at the Chicago convention. Several days later 6,000 Illinois Republicans attended the state convention in Springfield. A cymbal-playing band kept conventioneers awake through the night. On the floor of the National Guard Armory temperatures exceeded 100 degrees, but Dirksen, who delivered an energetic speech against Truman and Illinois governor Adlai Stevenson, helped line up fifty-nine of the state's sixty delegates for Senator Taft.[84]

Nothing that summer, however, matched the emotional intensity of the national convention. At state conventions everywhere, but especially in the delegate-rich South, both camps fought bitterly for the votes necessary to win the nomination. Having at least read about the unresolved controversies and the malicious accusations dividing the two sides, Republican delegates arrived in Chicago already on edge. When Taft reached Midway Airport, Dirksen was there to greet him. Taft spent most of the convention's early days at the Congress Hotel, insulated from the teeming press of people.[85] As the Ohioan's closest ally in Illinois, however, Dirksen spent his time on the convention floor keeping the troops committed to a vote for Taft on the first ballot. With so many delegations contested, the atmosphere surrounding the 1952 convention was contentious from the start.

Howard and Joy Baker were visiting Dirksen in his hotel suite when Taft arrived for a midafternoon strategy session on July 9. Taft asked Dirksen to give a speech backing the Ohioan's claim for contested GOP delegates from Georgia. At first Dirksen declined, reminding his friend that he was slated to deliver the nominating speech the following evening. Taft insisted. He told Dirksen that the nominating speech would be inconsequential without the Georgia delegates. After Taft left, Dirksen retired to his private quarters, not to prepare a last-minute speech but to catch a nap before the frenzy began in earnest. At 6:00 P.M. he and Baker left for the International Amphitheater. Poised to give perhaps the most memorable speech of his entire career, Dirksen had no notes and no manuscript. When the delegates reconvened that evening at 7:30, the convention hall was thick with tension. Order was temporarily restored for a rendition of the Lord's Prayer, but soon thereafter the rowdiness exploded. Dirksen mounted the platform and began mildly, telling the audience that he hoped for party unity and that he would support whoever won the nomination. He admonished the delegates not to "permit passion and momentary hysteria to set a roadblock in the path of what looks like certain victory in November."[86]

But the crowd's unruliness continued. As Dirksen spoke on behalf of Georgia's pro-Taft delegates, bedlam broke out in the depths of the galleries. Three times his speech was interrupted by shouting from the floor. Ohio's delegates pumped their fists and shouted encouragement, while members from the East did their best to show their disapproval of Dirksen's remarks. He warmed to the challenge. Deep into his speech he asked delegates from New York and Pennsylvania to raise their hands. He then pointed a finger at Dewey, who was standing in the aisle with a tight-lipped smile, and recalled the failures of the last two presidential elections: "Reexamine your hearts before you take this action. . . . we followed you before and you took us down the path to defeat!"

Pandemonium erupted. One reporter wrote that a "howl rose from the delegates on the floor and swept through the spectators in the galleries." Several fights broke out among pockets of onlookers. William Cloon, an alternate from Michigan who was overcome by the commotion, fell from his chair and fainted. When Stanley Tretick of United Press International rushed to photograph Cloon, he was pushed to the floor by a delegate, slugged in the back of the head, and finally removed from the hall by two policemen. The anti-Dewey melee lasted close to one full minute. Dirksen, himself the recipient of boos and catcalls, sipped from a glass of water and made a weak attempt to restore the convention to order: "I assure you, I had no intention of setting off such a demonstration."[87]

Dirksen later told Washington columnist Drew Pearson that he lashed out at Dewey because he saw the New York governor sauntering up and down the aisle with a can of beer during his speech. But the record shows that Dirksen had long harbored a deep-seated distaste for Dewey's suave and sophisticated brand of Republicanism. Moreover, he deeply believed that the only way to strip the White House from the Democrats was to tear into the opposition at every opportunity and roll back the prevailing assumption that an interventionist foreign policy orchestrated by a swollen executive branch was in the national interest. Dirksen held that the election was nothing less than a battle for the Constitution. Time and again he pointed to what he called "the unconstitutional, undeclared war in Korea," and he never wavered from his argument that unchecked authority corrupts the democratic fabric and that the "wise men who wrote the Constitution must have known something about lust for power."[88]

Although he may not have planned his attack on Dewey or have been prepared for the outbursts that followed, Dirksen was convinced that the American people deserved a clearer choice than the Dewey-Eisenhower wing of the GOP afforded. Despite his best efforts, most of the contested delegates went to Eisenhower, and by the end of the evening it was clear that the general had the nomination secured. Thursday night was reserved for nominating speeches, and Dirksen delivered an impassioned, yet not nearly as divisive, address for Taft. He referred to the Korean stalemate and asserted that in these trying times Taft had "helped to stay the steady advance of the juggernaut of socialism." The GOP needed Taft's experienced commitment to the party not only to win but also to govern, to renew America's two-party system, and to reverse without compromise the Democratic party's "evil political witchery." At the end of Dirksen's speech, even though Eisenhower's nomination was virtually ensured, Taft's supporters poured into the aisles and sang "Onward Christian Soldiers," the "Battle Hymn of the Republic," and "God Bless America" in a thirty-two-minute demonstration.[89]

Dirksen's performance at the convention revealed the depth of the geographical and ideological divisions plaguing the Republican party. Eastern papers were especially critical. The *Washington Post* called the proceedings "democracy in the raw" and asserted that millions of Americans were "appalled by the crudeness with which the Old Guard struggled to keep the party in its grip." The *New York Times* agreed, blistering Dirksen's "entirely unwarranted attack" on Governor Dewey and chiding the senator for his disapproval of "a truly moral war." Many Eisenhower supporters were slow to forget Dirksen's tirade against the more moderate wing of the party. Knowing that the general's advisers were meeting at the Blackstone Hotel to discuss a running mate to complete the ticket, Taft called Eisenhower to suggest Dirksen. Gov. William Beardsley of Idaho put an end to the discussion: "After what he said at the convention, I wouldn't wipe my foot on that fellow!"[90]

Though many easterners were critical of Dirksen's antics, he won plenty of support from conservative Republicans. In addition to the praise from the *Chicago Tribune*, influential Republicans affirmed his leadership. Sen. Hugh Butler of Nebraska pledged his support for the Eisenhower candidacy but wrote to "congratulate" Dirksen on his anti-Dewey speech: "Regardless of losing the nomination, Ev, you did a job that needed being done in reading Dewey out of the party. . . . He is thru." Herbert Hoover came to the same conclusion, emphasizing that Dirksen was "the one who emerged from the Convention as the leader of our kind of Republicans. Some day we may be able to stop the left-wing domestic and misdirected foreign policies. At present, we are headed in uncharted waters."[91]

Dirksen could not help but brood over the disappointment of Taft's defeat. Not until July 21 did he declare his support for Eisenhower's candidacy, and even then he insisted that the bulk of his efforts would be directed at winning Republican control of the Senate. Dirksen's role as chairman of the Republican Senatorial Campaign Committee forced him to action and encouraged him to reconcile conflicting views within the party. Though he would long endure the reputation of an uncompromising defender of Old Guard Republicanism, his service to the party as committee chairman ultimately made possible his rise to the minority leadership by the end of the 1950s. From Washington he sent out over 91,000 letters asking past contributors for financial support. On two campaign tours he traveled through twenty-five states, speaking on behalf of a wide array of candidates and seeing firsthand the differences between eastern and midwestern Republicans.[92] Most important, his fellow Republicans appreciated his speech-making abilities, and the favors he did for them would serve as crucial leverage for the future.

Eisenhower made Dirksen a formal part of his campaign team and invited the senator to Denver for a strategy session with his advisers. Not until two days before the conference did Dirksen accept Eisenhower's summons. Before arriving in Denver late in the evening on August 1, he gave a disaffected speech to the American Legion in Chicago. He ignored the general's candidacy and in strident terms denounced Truman's European policy of collective security, the very issue that had motivated Eisenhower to run for the presidency. On arriving in Denver and meeting with reporters, Dirksen turned more conciliatory. Nonetheless, he acknowledged the tension of the situation by admitting that he would be "obviously a little less than human if I didn't feel a little frustrated and disappointed." His feelings aside, he insisted that "I shall work for the ticket from top to bottom, and I make no exceptions."[93]

Though he was in Denver for only sixteen hours, Dirksen's two meetings with Eisenhower seemed productive. Photographers captured an awkward handshake, both men keeping their distance. But two days later, at a luncheon with Illinois Republican leaders, Eisenhower won favor with his audience by emphasizing that when he fought the Democrats, "there will be no padding in my gloves." Moreover, he stressed that his administration would respect the separate powers of the White House, Congress, and the courts. In a private meeting, Eisenhower gave a similar assurance to Hugh Butler, who later wrote to Taft encouraging the Ohioan to campaign vigorously for the ticket. Butler was delighted that Eisenhower respected the independence of Congress and committed his administration to regular and meaningful meetings with the leaders on Capitol Hill: "If he does, we'll be alright [sic]. He said he would never do as Truman has done, spring suggestions without first clearing with Congress."[94]

Dirksen was a vital link between the two rivals. In a letter to Dirksen that he wanted passed to the nominee through Sen. Frank Carlson (R-KS), an early Ike supporter, Taft detailed a list of conditions he wanted resolved before he met with the general. Taft worried that a conference with Eisenhower would be "used (with pictures) to prove that I have now been converted to the general's principles. I don't want it made to look as if I were . . . abandoning my friends to the purge that so many Eisenhower supporters seem to plan for them." The assurances Taft demanded were stringent and specific. In order for him to meet with Eisenhower and campaign for the ticket without reservations, Taft expected the general to fill his cabinet with "approximately half" of the Ohioan's supporters. Despite Dirksen's efforts to get the two rivals together for a Constitution Day gathering in Chicago, the Eisenhower camp delayed a formal response to Taft's ultimatum.[95]

For Dirksen the campaign continued. While most of his efforts were directed at winning Republican Senate seats, he pounced on every opportunity to criticize Governor Stevenson, the Democratic nominee for the presidency. When asked about Stevenson's charge that Eisenhower's crusade was tarnished by his association with Senators William Jenner, John Bricker, and Joseph McCarthy, Dirksen, quick on the trigger, remarked, "Just how well does he think his associates look—Alger Hiss, Dean Acheson, the Americans for Democratic Action, and the lavender lads of the State Department?" Though a committed anticommunist, Stevenson had filed a deposition for Hiss during the first trial in 1949. Dirksen's salvo, in the opinion of the New York Times, represented "the first clearly

identifiable blow" in making the convicted perjurer a 1952 campaign issue. No matter where he was, Dirksen ripped into Truman and the
growth of administrative tyranny. In Maine he bemoaned the administration's arrogance and asserted that the "president acts as if he owns
the government. It isn't his. It's yours."[96]

Despite Dirksen's best efforts, the campaign as a whole was floundering, largely because Eisenhower had made a slow start. Near the end of
August Butler wrote a strictly confidential letter to Carlson, insisting that
the "campaign is NOT going over." He hoped for a prompt meeting between Eisenhower and Taft; "otherwise . . . we are going down to defeat." Dirksen agreed and wrote the Nebraskan that "unless they begin
fighting they cannot make the campaign scour." Republicans across the
nation breathed a sigh of relief when, on September 12, the two antago-
nists met for breakfast in New York at Eisenhower's headquarters in
Morningside Heights. Eisenhower acceded to many of Taft's demands,
and in return the Ohioan promised an energetic effort for the ticket.
James Patterson has concluded that the conference "represented a grand
step toward unifying the party."[97] For Dirksen, the truce was indispensable as he worked to elect a Republican Senate.

If by "fighting" Dirksen had meant hard-nosed attacks on the Democrats for their blunders in Korea, their corruption in office, and their promotion of communists in government, then he did his share of brawling
in the 1952 campaign. His speeches, especially his assault on the "lavender lads" of the State Department, were reflective of those conservative
Republicans who hit the Democrats the hardest. McCarthy referred to
"Alger—I mean Adlai" Stevenson and predicted that if a loyal Democrat
would "smuggle me aboard the Democratic campaign special with a
baseball bat in my hand, I'd teach patriotism to little Ad-lie." McCarthy
and Jenner targeted former secretary of state and war hero George C.
Marshall, Jenner claiming that Marshall, Eisenhower's mentor in the
army, was a "front man for traitors." Richard Nixon, Eisenhower's running mate, pitched in as well. He described Stevenson as "Adlai the ap-
peaser," a Ph.D. graduate from "Dean Acheson's cowardly college of
Communist Containment."[98]

Though he spoke on behalf of all Republican candidates, Dirksen
cooperated most closely with the conservatives. At a Fiftieth Ward Republican victory dinner on September 19 Dirksen defended McCarthy's
charges against Marshall. The crowd roared its approval when Dirksen

asserted, "There is rebellion in the air." Responding to McCarthy's claim that Marshall had engineered in China a "conspiracy so immense," Dirksen concluded, "Joe McCarthy was essentially on good ground, and don't let anyone kid you about it." Dirksen finished the evening by appealing for McCarthy's reelection to the Senate, whipping up more fervor when he cited the need to rally behind the Wisconsinite against "eastern money and propaganda."[99]

Though Dirksen traveled as far afield as New England, his campaign for a Republican Senate met with less success in the East. After his attack on Governor Dewey, Rhode Island Republicans revoked an invitation for Dirksen to speak on behalf of the party, concluding the "prejudices" he created would hurt the local candidates. The *New York Times* underscored the party discord that the senator had perpetuated, writing in late summer "that Republican organizations in parts of the East believe their Senate candidates would not be helped by appearances by Mr. Dirksen." After wiring Sen. Margaret Chase Smith (R-ME) and requesting dates and places that she could speak for the party, Dirksen ignored her reply and chose not to schedule her appearances. Already angered by the extent to which Dirksen and Eisenhower had supported McCarthy's reelection bid in the Midwest, the author of the Declaration of Conscience sensed that she was being pushed to the margins of the GOP and grew increasingly suspicious of Dirksen and his priorities for the party.[100]

Despite the geographical and ideological cleavages that continued to separate Dirksen from the eastern wing of the party, his service as chairman of the Republican Senatorial Campaign Committee solidified his reputation as a dedicated party regular who was willing to sacrifice time and energy for a higher cause. Butler testified to Dirksen's importance, writing, "I don't see how we can get by out here in Nebraska without you making one or two more appearances. . . . These fellows won't settle for anyone but you or Taft." Sen. William Purtell (R-CT) expressed his "deep appreciation" for Dirksen's "constant helpfulness." Barry Goldwater, who won a surprise election that year in Arizona, credited Dirksen, whom he called his "political godfather," with suggesting and inspiring his bid for a Senate seat.[101]

By the end of September Dirksen was confident that Eisenhower would win the presidency and carry the Congress. Though the GOP failed to win the eight seats he predicted earlier in the election season, they gained control of the Senate with a paper-thin margin of one seat.

Given the divisions that had wracked the party for twenty years and in the aftermath of the contentious Chicago convention, both Eisenhower and Dirksen had reason to be proud of their accomplishments. For Republicans in the Senate, it remained to be seen what kind of president Eisenhower would make. Most appreciated his professed intention to show greater respect for the coordinate responsibilities of the separate branches of government. Just how his administration would handle the prickly issues of the budget, the New Deal reforms, Korea, and America's commitment to collective security remained pure speculation. Although Taft hoped that the general would turn out to be more conservative than his eastern advisers, he worried that "we may get another New Deal administration which will be a good deal harder to fight than the Democrats." Replying to a letter from Hoover after the convention, Dirksen insisted that the conservative "cause is not lost and we must keep religiously at it."[102]

2. "A Foot . . . in Every . . . Camp"

When Dwight Eisenhower entered the White House in January 1953, his greatest political challenge was to accept the basic responsibilities of the modern presidency while at the same time bridging the ideological and regional divide that had plagued the Republican party since the New Deal. To this task Eisenhower brought a formidable array of personal skills, including extraordinary powers of persuasion, an engaging personality, and a keen insight into the motivations of the people around him.[1] Widely considered a political novice, Eisenhower in World War II excelled in the most political of all responsibilities, balancing the clashing agendas of Britain's Field Marshall Bernard Montgomery and America's Gen. George C. Patton while holding the alliance together in its pursuit of common goals. Eisenhower brought the same conception of leadership to the White House. Above all, he sought to create a unified team, a collection of leaders focused on formulating and executing the policies that constituted the mandate he received from the voters in November 1952.

Everett Dirksen and Robert Taft retained highly ambivalent feelings about Eisenhower, his version of Republicanism, and his appreciation for party leadership. Remembering his vehement support for Taft in Chicago, Dirksen recalled that he had no idea what Eisenhower "would think of me." Politically, the president-elect irritated the party's conservative wing with a number of his cabinet appointments. Most obnoxious was Eisenhower's decision to tap Martin Durkin, a plumbers' union president who had supported Adlai Stevenson for the White House, as secretary of labor. Taft spoke for many conservatives when he argued that the Durkin appointment represented "an affront to millions of union members and officers, who had the courage to defy the edict of officials like Mr. Durkin that they vote for Stevenson." The *Chicago Tribune* sensed a more sinister motive, holding that Eisenhower and his liberal advisers were plotting a "continuance of the New Deal under a different name." Even though Durkin hailed from Illinois, the Eisenhower transition team chose not to confer with Dirksen before the appointment, suggesting that the president-elect either was ignorant of the customs of senatorial courtesy or had sensed and accepted the gulf that separated him from the conservative Republicans.[2]

Though the Durkin appointment was a political disaster, the president-elect won some important victories that narrowed the GOP's ideological and geographical divides. Taft's eventual decision to serve as majority leader represented a prominent addition to the Eisenhower team and was an early vindication of the general's leadership style. Winning Dirksen's loyalty was not so easy. The senator's early obstinance challenged Eisenhower's persuasive abilities and tested the goodwill he hoped to instill in those close to the administration. Though Eisenhower appreciated Dirksen's importance to the Republican Senate (party leaders had appointed him to the Appropriations, Judiciary, and Government Operations Committees) and Dirksen respected the general's popularity, the two treated one another with a standoffish acceptance reflective of the conflict and consensus that had defined the Republican party in the early 1950s.

In an April speech to the state chamber of commerce, "Big Government—The Road to Tyranny," Dirksen argued that Eisenhower should first contain and then roll back a "labyrinthian wilderness" where "capricious and arbitrary" federal bureaucrats jeopardized the nation's freedom. Even as Dirksen argued for a smaller federal government and a less intrusive president, Eisenhower entered the White House determined to protect the powers of the modern presidency and to put a Republican stamp of approval on the responsibility of his administration to direct an interventionist foreign policy.[3] Dirksen's and Eisenhower's competing conceptions of the institutional presidency represented the core ideological conflict between eastern and midwestern Republicanism. If Dirksen were ever to join Eisenhower's team, he would have to accept the central place of the executive branch in America's political life and abandon the notion of legislative governance that defined his 1950 campaign and his early Senate career.

Though there were early grumblings from the GOP's more conservative senators about the administration's reluctance to overturn the New Deal, Eisenhower enjoyed relative quiet from Republican critics during his first months in office. The truce ended in March, when the Foreign Relations Committee reported out Eisenhower's nomination for ambassador to the Soviet Union, Charles E. Bohlen. Despite the committee's unanimous support for the nominee, Bohlen's impeccable pedigree as a cosmopolitan eastern internationalist made him a natural whipping boy for hard-core conservatives. Suave, sophisticated, and independently wealthy, he entered the Foreign Service in 1929 after graduating from Harvard College. Even more damning than his pampered eastern lineage, Bohlen had served as an interpreter for Franklin Roosevelt at the Yalta conference and during his confirmation hearings refused to repudiate the president's wartime decisions. For the most conservative Republicans, Yalta represented the immoral appeasement of the Soviet Union and the bitter fruits of a capricious and arbitrary executive acting without the consent of Congress.[4] The GOP had repudiated Yalta in its 1952 platform, and to Eisenhower's harshest critics, his nomination of Bohlen signaled his sinister intention to ignore the tenets of real Republicanism.

Initially concerned about Bohlen's "family life" (standard 1950s code for homosexual inclinations), Secretary of State John Foster Dulles eventually declared Bohlen a good security risk. Joe McCarthy would not be deterred. He announced that the State Department was covering up a confidential file that contained ruinous information about Bohlen's personal indiscretions. Eisenhower went to the wall for his nominee. As commander of NATO, he had befriended Bohlen in the late 1940s when the latter was serving as minister to France. To Ike, Bohlen was the natural choice. He spoke Russian fluently, he was familiar with many of the Soviet leaders, and he could hold his own in the regular vodka-drinking contests that defined Kremlin culture. Eisenhower refused to release the contents of the file to the Senate and in a March 25 news conference gave the nominee his ultimate endorsement: "I have known Mr. Bohlen for some years. . . . I have played golf with him. I have listened to his philosophy. So far as I can see, he is the best-qualified man for that post that I could find."[5]

McCarthy attacked Dulles's integrity, but a more restrained Dirksen focused on Bohlen's work at Yalta for Democratic presidents. After praising Eisenhower's "great character," Dirksen asked, "If we are going to disavow Yalta, how can we accept the architect? . . . 'Chip' Bohlen was at Yalta. If he were my brother, I would take the same attitude I am expressing in the Senate this afternoon. . . . I reject Yalta, so I reject Yalta men." Bohlen, like many of the more internationalist Senate Republicans, understood the crux of the conflict, for he realized that his opponents were primarily "attempting to subvert the president's constitutional prerogative in foreign capitals." Taft's own support of Bohlen ensured his confirmation, but the "rough and tumble" Senate debate leading up to the 74-to-13 vote (eleven Republicans including Dirksen went against the president) bared the rift within Republican ranks. Eisenhower chafed at the party disunity. He had earlier written in his diary that Dirksen had "been the model of cheerful and effective cooperation." But after the Bohlen vote the president added Dirksen to his list of the "most stubborn and essentially small-minded examples of the extreme isolationist group." Even so, Eisenhower decided that winning the loyalty of five or six of the McCarthyites was the most effective way of "reduc[ing] to impotence" the splinter group in the Senate.[6]

The Bricker amendment complicated Eisenhower's early efforts to co-opt a handful of conservative Republican senators without accepting a diminution of the presidency. Until 1953 Ohio's John Bricker (dubbed "Honest John" by his admirers) had endured a relatively inconsequential Senate career. Bricker's most noticeable physical features included a shock of white hair and bright blue eyes. Though he took great pride in his virtuous lifestyle, Bricker would on occasion enjoy a highball or smoke a pipe. He was quiet and reflective, and his few passions included the Cincinnati Reds and the Ohio State Buckeyes.[7] Innocuous as he appeared, Bricker emerged as a Senate player in early 1953 when he introduced a broadly backed amendment that would have stripped the presidency of recently assumed foreign policy powers.

Like many conservative Republicans, Bricker resented the constitutional provision that declared international treaties the "supreme law of the land." He and his supporters were disgusted with the ways in which World War II treaties and executive agreements had appeased communism, accelerated the legislative retreat, and enabled the UN Charter to quash the rights of the sovereign states. On January 7, 1953, the senator introduced a constitutional amendment that limited a president's prerogative to enter into executive agreements. In its most controversial provision, the amendment declared that "a treaty shall become effective as internal law in the United States only through legislation which would be valid in the absence of a treaty." Sixty-two senators, including Dirksen and forty-six other Republicans, cosponsored Bricker's resolution.

The amendment was an unmistakable threat to Eisenhower's commitment to the modern presidency. Hoping to talk Bricker out of pressing for his amendment on the Senate floor, Eisenhower refused public comment. In his private correspondence he showed some appreciation for the conservative critique of Roosevelt's and Truman's executive activism and agreed in principle to an amendment that ensured that no treaty would violate the Constitution. He opposed, however, the essence of Bricker's amendment, which he argued would "cripple the executive power to the point that we become helpless in world affairs." Dirksen disagreed wholeheartedly with the president. Eager to protect the economic and social freedoms that in his mind had been jeopardized since the end of World War II by an invasive federal government, Dirksen hoped to weaken the presidency. Blaming Yalta for almost every postwar setback, Dirksen once suggested that the president should be required to go to Congress to ask permission to make specific foreign policy decisions at summit meetings like Yalta. Dirksen made clear his intent to "circumscribe the executive" and to restore legislative vitality as the best way to preserve representative government.[8]

In early April Dulles and Attorney General Herbert Brownell testified before the Judiciary Committee. After making a twenty-five-minute statement in which he admitted his apprehension about abuses of presidential power but warned of a retreat into an isolationist shell, Dulles faced two hours of "calm and even-tempered" questioning led by Dirksen. The following day, when Brownell argued that the amendment would upset the balance of powers established by the Constitution, Dirksen emphasized that Bricker's efforts grew from a "new and revolutionary era" in which UN agencies like the International Labor Organization (ILO) sought to prescribe terms and conditions for employers. An amendment that protected Congress and the traditional responsibilities of the states was the best way to "bind in organic law safeguards against these eager men and women and their fanciful brains."[9]

Eisenhower continued to promote his notion of teamwork, but Bricker's refusal to weaken the heart of his amendment irked the president. "I am quite concerned," he confided to Brownell, "about the complete readiness of the Republican party to tear us apart." Though Eisenhower failed to beat back Bricker and his supporters, he did achieve a Senate delay. Taft and the president worked with friendly allies to ensure that the amendment would not be debated on the floor until the spring of the coming year, but William Knowland reported a "strong feeling . . . in the Republican conference" and made it clear to the White House that the issue would hound the administration for months to come.[10]

Dirksen also crossed swords with Eisenhower on the issue of federal spending. Early in the year the senator cited the public's "mass impatience" with the White House and announced his intention to push the president to both balance the budget and cut taxes during his first year in office. While both Dirksen and the White House agreed that military spending should be cut as soon as peace in Korea could be restored, Dirksen thought Congress, if it "show[ed] a little guts," could slash domestic spending and move toward a balanced budget. When Clement Atlee, Great Britain's Labor opposition leader, suggested that the United States accept a truce in Korea on communist terms and argued that Republicans like McCarthy wielded as much foreign policy influence as Eisenhower, Dirksen denounced the British as ungrateful mendicants who gobbled up American dollars and intruded in American business. In addition to calling Atlee a "discredited statesman" and an "intellectual pygmy," Dirksen vilified the foreign aid program and predicted its demise: "I am not so sure that we have not been 'played for a sucker' on some occasions. I think the time has come, as our people are asking for tax relief . . . to keep some of these American dollars at home for the benefit of our own people."[11]

Though not denouncing Eisenhower as he would a Democratic president, Dirksen was clearly frustrated at the president's unwillingness to make deeper cuts in spending. In his early debates with the White House, whether over Bohlen, the Bricker amendment, or the budget, Dirksen emphasized that traditional notions of American freedom began and ended at home. By contrast, Eisenhower held that budget and tax cuts had to be balanced against security interests and the potential for Soviet aggression. In his private correspondence the president lamented that the *Chicago Tribune* and its readers appealed to man's natural fear of failure and that the "welfare and security of the United States are pitted against the narrow-minded, selfish, and completely reactionary views of Colonel [Robert R.] McCormick."[12]

Dirksen angered the president again in early June when he introduced a successful rider to a bill that called for the United States to cut off funding for the United Nations if Communist China were admitted. Eisenhower made clear to reporters his commitment to keeping the Chinese

communists out of the UN, but he winced at the effect Dirksen's rider
would have on the president's ability to direct the nation's foreign policy.
After Dirksen left on a fact-finding mission to East Asia for the Appropriations Committee, Eisenhower called the Republican congressional
leaders to the White House for an impromptu meeting. Holding that it
was inappropriate for the United States to issue such an ultimatum to the
UN, Eisenhower insisted that the nation could not cut itself off from the
rest of the world and abandon the organization that represented "the
hope of the world for creating eventually an association in which laws
could replace battlefields." Republican congressional leaders bent to
Eisenhower's will, agreeing to shelve the Dirksen rider and instead substitute a nonbinding resolution that prohibited Communist China from
UN membership. The eastern press lauded Eisenhower's leadership. One
daily described the incident as the "first time he had met such an issue
head on."[13]

Dirksen continued to nip at Eisenhower's heels. Before he left on his
East Asia tour to investigate mutual security and foreign aid, Dirksen
again assaulted the budget. He told his colleagues, "I wish the record were
an infinitely more impressive and better one." He and Warren Magnuson
(D-WA) made no speeches and held no press conferences during their
journey; nonetheless, the national media suspected that the two were engaged in "a new attack on foreign aid spending." Returning to the Senate, Dirksen moved to slash Eisenhower's budgetary requests for foreign aid. During the authorization debate he voted for an unsuccessful
amendment to scale back the mutual security program. Dirksen's strident speeches gave rhetorical substance to the votes he cast on his return
from Asia. He contended that past efforts to support the Europeans with
economic aid resulted in "neutrality or indifference" and noted that in
many countries Americans were "the objects of a large amount of ill will."
In Asia, where Dirksen tended to be slightly more generous, the senator
showed a sophisticated appreciation for nationalist forces and used an
anti-imperialist argument to justify reduced support for French Indo-
china. Lacking Dirksen's subtlety, the *Chicago Tribune* pushed for an immediate end to foreign aid. Asserting that Eisenhower was addicted to
the "same New Deal clichés" as his predecessors, the conservative daily
insisted that the "expenditures of tens of billions in foreign aid has accomplished nothing save to force American taxpayers to bear unwarranted burdens." Dirksen echoed the sentiments of the GOP's conservative

wing when he declared that "we shall not be on this road for ten years if the junior senator from Illinois has anything to say about it."[14]

Taft was counting on a major cut in the president's program, and he advised the White House through the Washington press corps to prepare a liquidation program for foreign aid. Eisenhower refused to yield, despite relentless pressure from the party's conservative wing. His brother Milton remembered that the principal reason he had run for the White House was that "he believed in mutual security." During a legislative leaders' meeting at the White House, Eisenhower bristled at the suggestion that funds would have to be cut. When it was suggested that the GOP reduce economic aid but restore the military appropriation, Eisenhower emphasized the importance of the program to American security: "To cut it would be like ripping off one wheel of a wagon, and . . . to confine our program to purely military activities would be . . . the most expensive way of ensuring security."[15]

As the Appropriations Committee marked up Eisenhower's mutual security bill and Dirksen hinted that cuts could total $1 billion, the president worked feverishly to save the substance of his program. Robert Taft, his most important conservative ally in Congress, had just been diagnosed with cancer and would die by the beginning of August. Eisenhower neither trusted nor respected William Knowland, the GOP's new majority leader. More politically vulnerable than he had ever been, Eisenhower was forced to turn to Dirksen and to woo his former antagonist into the administration's camp. The president probably never knew that Dirksen's off-the-record notebooks on mutual security belied his tempestuous and irresponsible speeches. In his notes Dirksen acknowledged that the program was "likely to be with us a long time." Moreover, he understood the ill effects of diatribes, like his own, on the nation's allies: "Careless words. Speeches and remarks in Congress and responsible officials of the U.S. find their way to all corners of the earth. This is delicate business. There should be caution." Dirksen's notes implied that a part of him hankered after a more responsible Senate role. Eisenhower knew of Dirksen's legislative expertise in budget politics and the respect he commanded in conservative circles. Ike's July 23 diary entry after a breakfast meeting with Dirksen revealed the senator's importance to the administration's more moderate program: "I asked him to be the 'verbal leader' of the middle-of-the-road philosophy in the Senate. Regardless of the formal leadership, he would be the man to take on all attackers, the champion who would put on the armor and get on the white horse and take on the fight."[16]

Courted constantly by Eisenhower and driven by a more subtle and sophisticated understanding of world politics than he shared with the public in his speeches, Dirksen in late July reversed his position on foreign aid and defended the president's program. When conservatives questioned his motives, Dirksen insisted that he was "accountable only to himself and his constituency. The senator from Illinois has the courage ... to go along with the president when he thinks it is in the national interest." Speaking against a flurry of amendments that would have crippled the mutual security program, Dirksen abandoned his earlier attitude and argued that as the world's greatest military leader, Eisenhower was entitled to the support of his own party in the Senate.[17]

During the three-day debate Eisenhower sent Dirksen a letter showering him with praise and encouraging him to stay the course: "I have heard glowing reports of your impact on the MSA appropriation. ... I am not in the least surprised that you have taken so positive and forthright a position of leadership. ... I am highly pleased with what you did." After all efforts to restore cuts made in the House were defeated and the Senate appropriated $6.7 billion, Eisenhower beamed with pride at his own leadership and Dirksen's support when he told his cabinet, "I got Dirksen in. He stood up for us and did a good job despite all the pressure on him." The *Chicago Tribune* deplored Dirksen's betrayal, describing the senator as the administration's "principal defender" in the battle. In terms of the part of Eisenhower's foreign policy program that meant the most to him and in view of the heavy odds in Congress that he overcame to tilt the Republican party toward a more internationalist position, the mutual security appropriation for fiscal year 1954 was perhaps the most significant initial accomplishment of his presidency.[18] Though neither the president nor Dirksen fully trusted one another, and though Eisenhower remained piqued over the difficulties the senator could generate, their cooperation on mutual security showed that Dirksen at least had the capacity to support the administration in difficult times.

George Reedy, legislative assistant for Senate Minority Leader Lyndon Johnson (D-TX) and a shrewd observer of the upper house, described Dirksen as an ambitious man on the move with a "foot or a finger in every possible camp." Never detached from his partisan responsibility to build on the paper-thin Senate majority, Dirksen overlooked his earlier disagreements with the White House and hitched himself to the president's popularity. When former president Harry Truman charged his successor with sacrificing national security for the sake of a balanced budget, Dirksen responded with a well-placed barb: "I am sure the country prefers to rely on the wisdom of the man who commanded the invasion of Europe than on the artillery man from Independence." Eisenhower returned the favor. In a September speech to Republican women in Chicago, with Dirksen on the platform, the president described him as "a very great associate of mine." While he exaggerated wildly when he portrayed Dirksen as "absolute in his devotion," Eisenhower nonetheless showed an increasing appreciation for the senator's importance to the White House.[19]

But several of Dirksen's more reckless speeches toward the end of 1953 prefigured issues that would distance him from the president. Though he always blamed Truman for the communists "studded" in government, Dirksen's eagerness to clean out "one of the most riotous, reckless, scandalous administrations in the history of the Republic" from his place on Joe McCarthy's Permanent Investigations Committee hinted at the conflict that would soon erupt between legislative and executive authority. His travels around the country in his capacity as chair of the Republican Senatorial Campaign Committee tested his attachment to the White House as well. During a Los Angeles speech, Dirksen's reference to McCarthy evoked fifteen seconds of sustained applause from an otherwise docile audience.[20] Dirksen's position in the Republican party was more complicated than it had been earlier in the year. By December the conservatives and the White House were both vying for his allegiance as the GOP struggled to establish its identity with a president in the Oval Office.

Like many Republicans, Dirksen deplored the president's initial indifference toward the responsibilities of political patronage. Just before the Inaugural in January 1953, Dirksen recalled that with a Democrat in the White House he would go to the postmaster general, "hat in hand, and in a voice that was frail and faltering and filled with entreaty," to ask for a third-class postmaster in Bugville. With Eisenhower in the White House, Dirksen expected to reap the rewards of political victory: "I will walk in; I will say, 'I don't want a postmaster; what I want is a new post office, and I would like to have it ready for business two weeks from next

Tuesday." Because Eisenhower believed that patronage demeaned the presidency and was characteristic of an unsavory leadership style he associated with his Democratic predecessors, he found its incessant demands "a constant annoyance." When GOP leaders expressed their dissatisfaction with the way Eisenhower handled patronage, the president could barely control his irritation. Even to the GOP's congressional leaders he complained that his greatest problems seemed to come from his own party. Citing patronage as just one example, Eisenhower asked the leadership how the Republicans "were able to hold a party together through all these years." Had they been more courageous, the leaders might have reported that patronage had always been the foundation for party unity. Eisenhower's view was different, and more similar to Roosevelt's than he would have liked to admit. As political scientist Sydney Milkis has shown, the president was just as likely to appoint his own nonpartisan supporters as he was to anoint long-serving foot soldiers from the GOP ranks. More committed to the modern presidency than to regular Republicanism or local party politics, Eisenhower infuriated congressional Republicans who had hoped to wipe out the New Deal bureaucrats that staffed the federal government.[21]

Washington insiders from both sides of the aisle marveled at Eisenhower's growing decisiveness as party leader. George Reedy pointed to the White House's more determined efforts to "crack down on dissident elements in the Republican party." At least in public, even Dirksen appeared to have softened. Earlier he had called on the administration to clean up the federal government and roll back a bloated bureaucracy, but in early 1954 Dirksen praised Eisenhower's "competence." Eisenhower was forced to move slowly, Dirksen allowed, because "the inheritance of iniquity was too great." Eisenhower reciprocated, writing in his diary that Dirksen "seems radically to have changed his attitude toward international affairs and is now seemingly disposed to go along with the administration as its supporter and lieutenant." If Dirksen's support continued, Eisenhower predicted, "he may well soon become the most effective man . . . in the Senate."[22]

It appeared as if an increasingly practical Dirksen had dropped his conservative mantra and taken up the administration's nonideological brand of Eisenhower Republicanism. While the vast majority of his Republican colleagues were sharply critical of the president's farm program and its secretary of agriculture, Ezra Taft Benson, Dirksen backed the administration's proposals and commended Benson. Most Republicans feared that Benson's commitment to a flexible price support system, overturning the Democratic policy of a 90 percent fixed parity rate for crops, would cost the party its majority in the 1954 midterms. Dirksen favored the White House plan because it tackled the troubling issue of skyrocketing surpluses and began to restore the principles of supply and demand by ensuring an open market for farmers and consumers.[23] The apparent harmony between Eisenhower and Dirksen obscured a festering conflict that divided the two Republicans for the rest of the year. The crucial issue remained the appropriate balance of power between the president and Congress. Though he had shown signs of acceding to Eisenhower's expertise in the realm of foreign policy, Dirksen's decisions were based primarily on deference to Eisenhower rather than on a principled acceptance of a more powerful presidency. Moreover, the senator remained committed to the dual responsibility of Congress to oversee the executive and to restore legislative activism in the domestic arena.

In January 1954, after months of frustrating and fruitless negotiations with the White House, John Bricker and his Senate allies brought the Ohioan's constitutional amendment on treaties and executive agreements to the Senate floor. Though the Republican congressional leadership advised the president to put his weight behind the measure for the sake of party unity, Eisenhower redoubled his efforts to kill any meaningful proposal. He resented the section of the amendment that validated a treaty or executive agreement only if it could be passed on its own in Congress or state legislatures and endorsed by the courts. Privately, he described the amendment's supporters as "our deadly enemies" and bemoaned the crusade as a "stupid, blind violation of the Constitution by stupid, blind isolationists." Though most GOP senators backed Bricker and contributed to the two-thirds vote necessary to send the amendment to the states for ratification, Eisenhower's firm opposition won him the votes of several northeastern internationalist Republicans who had earlier cosponsored the resolution.[24]

Dirksen's support of the amendment was never in doubt. As a member of the Judiciary Committee who had heard hours of testimony on its language, Dirksen moved to block the president's capacity to upset the nation's social and economic traditions through treaties or executive agreements. In the floor debates on the amendment and its many substitutes,

Dirksen pointed to the postwar explosion of international agencies that jeopardized the sovereignty of the people. He hoped to reverse a creeping one-worldism, and he articulated a traditional notion of American exceptionalism when he pointed to the machinations of the ILO: "They ought to hang a sign on the door reading 'men working,' because they are working early and late, day and night, and they are cooking up a dish." When opponents suggested that no liberties had yet been lost, Dirksen thundered, "Do we have to wait until the horse is stolen before we lock the stable?" While Eisenhower feared that the amendment would cripple the executive's ability to conduct the nation's foreign affairs, Dirksen held that its provisions would overturn "a lawmaking power which completely bypasses the Congress."[25]

Bricker and his supporters suffered a bitter defeat when, on February 26, 1954, they fell one vote shy of the two-thirds necessary for victory. With the vote standing at 60 to 30 and only fifteen Republicans having voted for the White House, a tipsy Harley Kilgore (D-WV) was rousted from a nearby tavern to cast the decisive vote against the amendment. No matter how he had won, Eisenhower was relieved. Sensitive to intraparty divisions that the amendment exposed, the president moved to patch up his differences with the congressional GOP in time for the midterm elections. In his first meeting with the legislative leadership after the final vote on the amendment, Eisenhower began by emphasizing that there was room for differences in the party but that he hoped Republicans could unite their forces in order to pass his program. Frustrated by the divisiveness that the amendment generated, Eisenhower bared his impatience: "I'm getting jumpy on the shortness of time."[26]

The president's focus on his legislative program was distracted, however, by what he called another "sideshow," coming just on the heels of the Bricker debate.[27] The White House had long endured an awkward relationship with Senator McCarthy, who was determined to continue his anticommunist crusade no matter who was in the White House. Dirksen found himself in the middle of the fray. Eisenhower continued to coax him into the White House's camp, but Dirksen kept his distance. He counted himself as one of McCarthy's few friends in the Senate, served as his colleague on the Government Operations Committee, and jealously guarded the right of Congress to oversee the executive.

Eisenhower approached the McCarthy issue with monumental delicacy. In the 1952 campaign, at the behest of Dirksen and other party regulars, he had endorsed a straight Republican ticket. In McCarthy's home state of Wisconsin he went so far in a campaign speech to delete a paragraph that supported his old mentor and McCarthy target, George C. Marshall. Once in the White House, Eisenhower hoped to keep his hands off McCarthy without surrendering executive prerogative. He and Secretary of State Dulles accepted McCarthy's aggressive snooping into the State Department's International Information Agency and the Voice of America. Though deeply disturbed by McCarthy's attacks on Dulles's integrity and the ability of the president to choose his own foreign policy team, the White House remained tight-lipped during the Bohlen nomination fight. Even when McCarthy, from his position as chairman of the Government Operations Committee, tried to negotiate a secret agreement with a Greek shipowners' group to stop its trade with Communist China, Eisenhower ignored the truculent Wisconsinite. At every turn he refused "to get in the gutter" with McCarthy.[28]

Ike's approach was excessively passive, but the president justified his inaction with a well-articulated conception of the limitations of presidential leadership. Having announced his party affiliation just eight months before the election, Eisenhower hoped to assure his many detractors of his regular Republicanism. While the civil libertarian in him rejected some of McCarthy's more noxious methods, he was nonetheless a committed anticommunist who had campaigned on the issue and who hoped to clean up the corruption besmirching the nation's capital. Most important, Eisenhower predicated his early leadership style on mending the rifts that divided the party. "A leader's job," he wrote in his diary, "is to get others to go along with him in the promotion of something. To do this he needs their good will. To destroy good will, it is only necessary to criticize publicly."[29]

McCarthy showed no such restraint. Never known for his self-discipline, McCarthy began to career even further out of control after Eisenhower's election. As chairman of the Government Operations Committee, he lashed out at "homos" and "pretty boys" in a supposedly patriotic crusade to cleanse the nation of its traitorous elements. Always partial to liquid refreshment, McCarthy boasted to friends and foes alike that he downed a fifth of bourbon every day, and he regularly carried a bottle of whiskey in a beat-up briefcase that he said was full of "documents." McCarthy was most dangerous when his colleagues (like Dirksen) on the committee forfeited their responsibility to attend hearings and thus paved the way for the chairman's one-man inquisitions. In committee he was ruthless and he was savage, and his pathological disregard for the truth enabled him to slander any convenient target.[30] Fully aware of McCarthy's threat to the republic, Eisenhower nonetheless hoped to ignore the senator into insignificance.

Ike was eager to avoid a "pissing contest with that skunk," but when McCarthy launched an investigation of the army's Signal Corps engineering laboratories in Fort Monmouth, New Jersey, he challenged Eisenhower's honor as an army man and spurred the president to action. Until January 1954 McCarthy kept demanding, and the army kept denying, open access to the security files of the Fort Monmouth employees.[31] Primarily at issue was a conflict between the Senate's right to oversee the executive and the White House's assumed prerogative to protect itself and its employees from congressional scrutiny on the grounds of national security.

A flurry of White House appeals secured McCarthy's temporary cooperation in the Fort Monmouth affair. Still convinced that the administration was indifferent to the threat of internal subversion, however, an unreconstructed McCarthy quickly turned his attention to the case of an army dentist commissioned and promoted at Camp Kilmer, New Jersey. Under a heavy barrage of questions and accusations, Irving Peress, who had never signed a loyalty oath, employed the Fifth Amendment to answer Chairman McCarthy's suggestion that he had once belonged to the Communist Party. After the army gave Peress an honorable discharge and promised an internal investigation, McCarthy exploded in outrage and moved to expose the left-wing rot in the armed services. In mid-February he called World War II hero Brig. Gen. Ralph W. Zwicker, Camp Kilgore's commanding officer, to testify. McCarthy was the only senator in attendance at his committee hearing, and he assailed the witness, describing Zwicker as a man with "the brains of a five-year old" who was not "fit to wear" the uniform of the U.S. Army. The general, McCarthy insisted, would be back to testify again. Secretary of the Army Robert T. Stevens jumped into the fray and protected Zwicker and other McCarthy targets from the senator's de facto one-man committee. He ordered Zwicker to refuse future subpoenas, a decision that enraged McCarthy and prompted one of the most famous meals in American political history.[32]

On February 23 Stevens and Republican subcommittee members McCarthy and Karl Mundt attended a luncheon hosted by Dirksen. Immediately flustered when he saw scores of reporters waiting outside of what was to have been a confidential meeting, Stevens never regained his composure. After dining on the Senate delicacies of fried chicken, head-of-lettuce salad, and coffee, the principals got down to business. At the conclusion of the two-hour meeting, Stevens buckled before a hostile McCarthy and a coaxing Dirksen. He agreed to allow Zwicker to continue his testimony and promised to release "the names of everyone involved in the promotion and honorable discharge of Peress." McCarthy and his Republican supporters had won a total victory. Even though Dirksen had played "good cop" during the luncheon, one reporter credited him with having played the "key role" in Stevens's "surrender." Dirksen gave weight to that impression when after the meeting he mumbled dejectedly, "It seems like I'm always going around this place with an oil can."[33]

The White House was not so impressed. After the media denigrated the president's leadership and portrayed the "chicken luncheon" as the capitulation to McCarthy that it was, Eisenhower worked to limit the damage Stevens had created. When personal friend and army colleague Lucius Clay suggested to Eisenhower that Dirksen had "played the leading role" and "double-crossed" Stevens, the president gave Dirksen the benefit of the doubt. He called his chief troubleshooter on the Republican right to the White House and urged him to consider a change in the committee rules that would require a majority to issue subpoenas, thus blocking McCarthy and his aides from holding unannounced, one-man hearings.[34]

McCarthy refused to sign a statement written by Dirksen and the president's staff that endorsed Stevens's leadership and that promised to treat all future witnesses with respect. At Eisenhower's insistence, Dirksen returned to the White House and helped write a face-saving statement for Stevens to deliver to the media: "I shall never accede to the abuse of army personnel [or to] them being brow-beaten or humiliated. From the assurances which I have received from the members of the subcommittee, I am confident that they will not permit such conditions to develop in the future."[35] Though the primary conflict between Congress's right to know and the White House's duty to protect itself remained unresolved, the immediate crisis passed because of the president's timely leadership and his successful efforts to secure Dirksen's cooperation.

Dirksen visited the White House twice in early March. Taken together, the meetings revealed the push of Eisenhower's ongoing efforts to solicit Dirksen's loyalty and the pull of the Republican Senate's frustration with the president's party leadership. In the first meeting McCarthy was still very much on Eisenhower's mind. Three days before, Eisenhower had phoned Brownell's office for clarification of the president's capacity to shield his staff from congressional subpoenas. Though their breakfast session covered a wide array of issues, Eisenhower and Dirksen spent most of their time discussing the ways in which the latter could encourage Republican members of the McCarthy committee to attend the hearings and keep McCarthy under control.[36]

Later that afternoon Dirksen, in his capacity as chairman of the Republican Senatorial Campaign Committee, attended a cabinet meeting on that fall's midterm elections. After outlining electoral strategy and detailing the strengths and weaknesses of various candidates, Dirksen again launched into a lecture on the importance of patronage to a party's success at the polls. He stopped only briefly to apologize for perhaps speaking out of turn but emphasized that he was "scolded for it around the clock." For Dirksen, patronage, "judiciously placed" and "expeditiously spent," was the "motive power" in the party system. He suggested that every senator have a patronage expert working in the office and underscored the importance of lower-level appointments: "Real patronage is *in the field*. Much more so than an ambassador or a man who comes to D.C. A $3,200 job is most pleasing to county chairmen." After Eisenhower had cut in to stress the importance of moving delicately and adhering to civil service regulations, Dirksen barreled forward. "Some people," he added, "say second and third class are not important, but they are. It's where people call for their mail. They gossip at the post office, and Democratic postmasters are right out front for all to see, tipping their hats."[37]

No matter how irritating for Eisenhower, patronage problems paled in comparison to the dilemma that McCarthy had become for the White House. While avoiding any public mention of his target, Eisenhower worked behind the scenes to degrade McCarthy's influence. He told the legislative leaders that he appreciated the right of Congress to investigate but warned, "We can't defeat communism by destroying the things in which we believe." In part because he could not trust Majority Leader Knowland to rein in McCarthy by himself, Eisenhower continued his courtship of Dirksen. Over the telephone the two men again discussed ways to revise the committee's rules to limit McCarthy's antics. Privately the president wrote that he "despise(d)" the Wisconsinite's scurrilous methods, but he continued to insist that his hands-off approach was the most appropriate strategy. Most frustrating to Eisenhower was that the McCarthy issue diverted the GOP's attention from the president's legislative agenda: "We have sideshows and freaks where we ought to be in the main tent with our attention on the chariot race."[38]

The White House kept the heat on McCarthy. On March 10 Eisenhower decided to cut the senator from the team, telling aide Wilton B. Persons, "If he wants to get recognized any more, the only way he can do it is to stand up and publicly say, 'I was wrong in browbeating witnesses, wrong in saying the army is coddling communists, and wrong in my attack on Stevens. I apologize.'" One day later, at White House instigation, the army released a detailed chronology that plotted McCarthy's and chief assistant Roy M. Cohn's efforts to secure favors for G. David Schine, private in the army and member of McCarthy's committee staff. McCarthy responded to the allegations by arguing that the army was using Schine to cover up its communists and to blackmail the senator into derailing committee business. The magnitude of the charges and countercharges resulted in the creation of a special congressional committee to investigate the Schine affair.[39] In reality, more than Schine was at stake. Ultimately, the McCarthy imbroglio and the televised hearings that followed displaced the uneasy truce the White House and the conservative GOP had maintained regarding the separation of powers and the appropriate responsibilities of the executive and legislative branches. The Government Operations Committee's Permanent Investigations Subcommittee, minus McCarthy and plus another Republican to take his place, presided over the Army-McCarthy hearings.

Dirksen found himself in an awkward position. He had always backed McCarthy. Aide Harold Rainville remembered that Dirksen was the senator's "strongest defender" in committee hearings and party discussions. Further, Dirksen judged McCarthy a valuable campaigner who bolstered the GOP's electoral appeal. But Dirksen was also sensitive to Eisenhower's entreaties. Essentially a traditionalist and a patriot who had served in the armed forces, Dirksen believed in the army's basic integrity and its fundamental soundness as a loyal American institution. Moreover, he bristled at Cohn's efforts to win favorable treatment for Schine. Wedged between McCarthy and the army, Dirksen tried unsuccessfully to forge a compromise. Because he believed both sides were guilty of the charges, he proposed to scrap the hearings in favor of a dual resignation, Cohn's and that of the army counsel, John G. Adams.[40]

While Dirksen hoped to avoid the hearings for the sake of party unity, Eisenhower edged toward a more assertive role as GOP leader. He continued to believe that the issue acted as a brake on his legislative program, but McCarthy's attack on the army forced Ike to defend the modern presidency, which was at the heart of his moderate program. "The Republican Party," Eisenhower wrote in his diary, "has got once and for all to make up its mind whether to follow the ludicrous partnership of the Old Guarders and the McCarthyites, or whether it is going to stand up behind the administration and the middle-of-the-road philosophy."[41]

Dirksen dawdled. As preparations for the hearings continued, Eisenhower increased his efforts to win Dirksen's loyalty. He called the senator's office to ask permission to refer to him as "my good friend" in an innocuous message of congratulations to the Alpha Organization. No doubt Dirksen appreciated the endorsement of the popular president, but to his constituents he defended McCarthy. In an April 9 speech at the annual Gridiron dinner, Dirksen teased the president and played down the divisiveness plaguing the GOP. Contrary to critics who suggested that Eisenhower spent too much time playing golf and was inattentive to his duties, Dirksen joked, "Ike is on the ball, on the ball every day. If he can't make the front page, he can make the sports page. We'll settle for either." To those who characterized the GOP as a fractured party, Dirksen admitted only to a "calculated confusion," a conscious ploy to defuse Democratic attacks.[42]

Dirksen played a limited role in the day-to-day preparations for the Army-McCarthy hearings. On a trip to visit Joy and Howard Baker in Knoxville, Tennessee, he recruited the committee's counsel, Ray H. Jenkins, although no evidence suggests that Dirksen was angling for any particular outcome to the conflict. Determined that his committee would serve as "umpires in a neighborhood baseball game," Karl Mundt gaveled the proceedings to order on April 22. Millions of Americans were glued to their television sets. In the early stages of the hearings, with McCarthy and the army skirmishing over countless points of order, Dirksen contributed little to the fanfare. His behavior was consistent with his purely practical belief that the hearings jeopardized the party unity necessary to win a congressional majority in the midterm elections.[43]

Mundt had promised the president that the hearings would last a week, once the principals were in place and the rules of procedure were established. Early on, however, it was clear that the drama might stretch well into the summer. Just five days after the hearings had begun, Eisenhower was sickened by the display. "The Army-McCarthy argument, and its reporting," he wrote personal friend Swede Hazlett, "are close to disgusting. It saddens me that I must feel ashamed for the United States Senate." Periodicals like *Time* and *Newsweek* wrote about little else, and Walter Lippmann described the proceedings as "our national obsession."[44]

Despite the heavy attention paid to the hearings, Dirksen and Eisenhower tended to other business. In a private conference with Gov. William Stratton (R-IL), Eisenhower reported that he had not yet given up on Dirksen. He described the senator's "good ability," pointed to their consistent interaction, and suggested that his greatest weakness was that he had "never before played on a team." One day later Dirksen took Joseph Meek to the White House for a political conference. A committed conservative, Meek was running for the U.S. Senate seat of Paul Douglas (D-IL) and was anxious for the president's endorsement. Worried that Meek might prove problematic if elected, Eisenhower highlighted Dirksen's instinct for cooperation and praised the senator for having "carried out some extremely difficult assignments." On leaving, Dirksen coopted the president's own language, assuring Eisenhower that Meek "is a team player." Wary of allying himself with the conservative cause, Eisenhower refused to make any significant contribution to Meek's flagging candidacy.[45]

Several weeks later Eisenhower reported to his cabinet another instance in which Dirksen had cooperated with the White House. At an earlier meeting between the two, Eisenhower discussed John Foster Dulles's troubles with the Republican Congress. No one doubted the power of Dulles's legalistic intellect or his tireless support for the administration, yet his supporters and detractors alike were irked by his preachy manner. The son of a Presbyterian minister, the crusading Dulles manifested a confident self-righteousness that dogged him for his whole career. Many people found Dulles tiresome and boring. A popular saying described the dour secretary as "Dull, Duller, Dulles," and Winston Churchill mocked him by calling him "Dullith" behind his back. When Eisenhower asked Dirksen for his suggestions to improve his secretary's relations with Congress, the senator proposed a series of informal dinners at Dulles's Washington home. After another off-the-record meeting with Eisenhower on mutual security, Dirksen pointed to the effectiveness of these occasions. The dinners, Dirksen argued, were "more important than committee hearings." The president urged the rest of his cabinet to experiment with Dirksen's suggestion: "Choose from one or both sides of the aisle. Get the right people, get the help of a friendly senator."[46]

In the meantime, the Army-McCarthy hearings dragged on. Correspondence from influential GOP contributors showed that the proceedings were crippling party spirit, and in early May Dirksen moved to shorten the drama. If only to free his committee to jump-start its own investigations, McCarthy too hoped to limit the hearings. Dirksen suggested that the public hearings include the testimonies of only Secretary Stevens and Senator McCarthy; all other witnesses could be heard in executive session, and the McCarthy committee could pursue its unrelated responsibilities. The three Republican members agreed with the Dirksen proposal. The Democrats, however, balked at Dirksen's move, mostly because it would have terminated an event that was damaging GOP prestige. Chairman Mundt cast the deciding vote against the proposal after he learned that Secretary Stevens, whom McCarthy had berated during his testimony, objected to any setup that would have been more lenient to the other principals.[47]

Made with the tacit support of a White House that hoped McCarthy and his advisers would humiliate themselves on national television, Stevens's decision to continue the hearings opened the door for the controversy that highlighted the gulf between Eisenhower and the GOP's conservative wing. The balance of power between Congress and the administration was at the heart of the conflict, and the testimony of army counsel John G. Adams brought this unresolved issue to the fore. According to Adams, White House officials had advised him in a mid-January confidential meeting to construct a detailed chronology of Cohn's requests of favors for Schine. Adams's testimony undermined the army's claim that it had acted without any assistance from the administration, and senators from both sides of the aisle peppered Adams for more information concerning his meeting with White House officials. Under orders from the White House, Adams refused to expand on his earlier testimony.[48]

For the only time during the hearings, Everett Dirksen took center stage. Calling the committee's decision to continue the hearings "one of my greatest regrets in my legislative career," he testified about a January meeting in his office attended by Adams and White House aide Gerald Morgan. Dirksen's testimony supported both the army's and McCarthy's allegations while also casting doubt on the White House's professed independence. The senator remembered Adams detailing Cohn's extraordinary efforts to secure favorable treatment for Schine, but Dirksen also recalled Adams's attempt to obstruct the committee's investigation: "Mr. Adams came to my office for the purpose of enlisting my influence to kill those subpoenas and to stop them." Dirksen, it seems, had already concluded that both sides were to blame, and his unsuccessful attempt to stop the hearings derived from his commitment to preventing "the demoralization of the armed services and the development of dissident spirit in this country." Other committee members wanted more evidence, but the testimony they sought conflicted with the administration's dogged determination to shield its conduct from congressional scrutiny.[49]

Eisenhower was well prepared for the battle over executive privilege. In March he had directed the attorney general's office to write a memorandum of precedents that detailed the president's right to protect his staff from congressional subpoena. In early May he told Henry Cabot Lodge that he "would be astonished if any of my personal advisers would undertake to give testimony on intimate staff counsel and advice. The result would be to eliminate all such offices from the presidential staff. In turn, this would mean paralysis." On May 14 the White House directed counsel for the army Joseph N. Welch to object to any question that probed any meeting involving a presidential adviser. A weekend hiatus did not calm the storm. In a May 17 White House meeting with the congressional leadership, Majority Leader Knowland insisted that Congress had the right to subpoena administration officials. Eisenhower balked and claimed blanket protection for the White House: "Let me make one thing clear. Those people . . . who are my confidential advisers are not going to be subpoenaed. Their jobs are really a part of me, and they are not going up on the Hill."[50]

Back in committee, Adams made the president's position public. He read a letter Eisenhower had written to the secretary of defense that prohibited any departmental employee from testifying about any meeting in which a presidential adviser participated. Like most of the committee members, Dirksen was dumbfounded. Eisenhower's order challenged his belief in the right and the duty of Congress to oversee the White House and, in this particular instance, prevented a full disclosure of evidence necessary to render final judgment. He continued his criticism of the president in a hard-hitting speech to his Illinois constituents. In "Congress vs. the Executive," Dirksen gave some recognition to the importance of a president's confidential relationship with his staff. But, he insisted, "Congress ... can subpoena any person in the executive branch including the president, if it so desires." The committee failed to overturn Eisenhower's directive. Though the hearings continued until June 17 and eventually resulted in McCarthy's self-destruction, Dirksen's role diminished. At the conclusion of the hearings he side-stepped his previous efforts to stymie their progress. Instead, he lamely praised the fact that the proceedings had reached millions of viewers and had rejuvenated the "crusade against communism and subversion and disloyalty."[51]

Although Dirksen must have been relieved that the hearings were over, the Senate's campaign against McCarthy was just beginning. Two days before the end of the hearings, Sen. Ralph Flanders (R-VT) introduced a resolution to strip McCarthy of his committee chairmanship. Few if any insiders considered the seventy-three-year-old Flanders much of a player. He shunned the spotlight and proved quirky enough as a legislator to be tarred by some as a liberal and by others as a conservative. Despite his quiet demeanor, Flanders loathed Joe McCarthy. Even though he was a fervent anticommunist, Flanders was distressed over America's tarnished image abroad in the wake of McCarthy's ongoing antics. Senate support for Flanders, however, failed to materialize. Neither the Republican leadership, which wanted to put an end to the party's internal bloodletting, nor the Southern Democrats, who jealously guarded the Senate's seniority system, backed Flanders's effort to depose McCarthy. Unbowed and unbroken, Flanders introduced a substitute resolution that condemned McCarthy for having brought the Senate into disrepute. With 500 visitors waiting outside and 1,000 packed into the galleries, ninety senators listened as Flanders introduced and defended his resolution. McCarthy, Flanders insisted, "has an habitual contempt for people. ... Unrebuked, his behavior casts a blot on the reputation of the Senate itself."[52]

The atmosphere was electric and, given Dirksen's strong belief in McCarthy, created the conditions for one of his most passionate Senate speeches. He spoke for over an hour, and according to James Reston, delivered "perhaps the most significant and certainly the boldest" speech on McCarthy's behalf. For the most part, he held the attention of his audience. When he referred, however, to McCarthy as a "humble" senator, the galleries broke into fits of laughter. The thrust of his remarks was directed at Flanders. His resolution, Dirksen argued, was tainted by the support of left-wing groups who functioned outside the margins of the American political tradition. "The Communist Party," Dirksen bellowed, "has gone into bed with Senator Flanders, and the CIO too, to liquidate a member of the Senate." To Dirksen, the Flanders resolution threatened the protective cloak of senatorial traditions and jeopardized the very existence of conservatism. With his "voice shifting from a whisper to a roar," Dirksen insisted that no conservative "will be safe in this body if we ever take this action, because all they need, if they disagree with you, is to get one man like the senator from Vermont—honorable as he is—to put the brand upon you and with a censure resolution to condemn you." When he finished, an emotional McCarthy stood and shook his hand. He later presented Dirksen with a handsome gold clock bearing the inscription, "To Everett McKinley Dirksen: Who on This 30th Day of July 1954 Represented a High Moment in the Conscience of Man."[53]

Debate on the Flanders resolution was so intense that the Senate voted to create a special committee to investigate charges that McCarthy had tarnished the upper house. In the meantime, Dirksen dived headlong into his duties as chairman of the Republican Senatorial Campaign Committee, a position, he estimated, that required 35 to 40 percent of his time. Dirksen was uniquely qualified for the role. His efforts to cooperate with the White House without betraying his conservative friends frustrated Eisenhower but kept him in good stead with the conflicting factions in the party. When Eisenhower loyalist Bertha Adkins criticized Dirksen in a private meeting with Ike in late July, the president summarized the mixed results of his many attempts to secure the senator's loyalty. Dirksen, Eisenhower told Adkins, "tries to be too many things to too many people. For example, if he were sitting here at this moment, he'd agree to absolutely every word being said. At the end of last session, he led the fight for me and we won victory. Yet he seems kind of subtle about things." Still, in his correspondence with Dirksen, Eisenhower praised his conservative troubleshooter: "I feel deeply indebted to you for the fine work you have done in a number of instances when I have called upon your help."[54]

In part because he wanted to maintain the perception that he was above politics, but also because he was irritated at the factionalism plaguing the GOP, Eisenhower campaigned sparingly in 1954. In general, he left the stumping for Vice President Richard Nixon and for "workhorses" like Dirksen. Most of his colleagues were grateful for Dirksen's efforts on their behalf. In a tight campaign, Dirksen's speaking ability was in high demand. Leverett Saltonstall (R-MA) was a committed Eisenhower Republican who was ready to vote for McCarthy's censure. Dirksen nonetheless backed his candidacy. "The reports of your meetings in Massachusetts were superb," Saltonstall wrote Dirksen. "Thank you also for the nice boost. I hope things come out well here but it's going to be close." Even though John Sherman Cooper (R-KY) was a liberal internationalist and a heavy underdog in a normally Democratic state, Dirksen trekked to Kentucky and campaigned for Cooper in a snowstorm.[55] Dirksen's efforts to secure a Republican congressional majority prompted him to value the party's heterogeneous vitality over a rigid set of ideas, and the stumping he did for a wide array of candidates counted as strategic favors for future use.

Dirksen's loyalty to the party was put to its sternest test in New Jersey. Clifford Case, a liberal Republican who backed the Eisenhower program and promised to vote against McCarthy as chairman of the Government Operations Committee if he were elected, won the party's nomination. Angry conservatives looked to Dirksen to buck Case's candidacy and "save the country" from a Republican party dominated by "the CIO and ADA elements." When Dirksen attended a White House luncheon and announced that "[Case] is our candidate and it is our duty to get him elected," embittered conservatives flooded his office with over 2,000 letters. Dirksen's loyalty to the party outweighed any sympathy he may have had for Case's detractors. "I have a duty," he told a Republican audience, "to assist him in every possible way, and I know that my colleagues in the Senate will expect me to do my full duty in that respect."[56]

Though he fought hard for every Republican nominee, Dirksen's stump speeches suggested that his drift toward a more cooperative relationship with the White House was more apparent than real. In these speeches he cajoled his listeners and pleaded for a Republican majority. He held that a Democratic victory would force the president, "hat in hand," to lobby for his program before a hostile Congress. But Dirksen's diatribes also revealed contrasting conceptions of the GOP. While Eisenhower promoted a middle-of-the-road Republican agenda and emphasized the importance of reaching across the aisle to fashion a bipartisan foreign policy, Dirksen depicted the Democratic opposition as a corrupted pariah exiled from power by a redemptive Republican party. In a Los Angeles speech to a "militant throng of Republican women from all parts of the Union" (i.e., the National Federation of Republican Women), Dirksen saluted the "preserving mothers" for protecting the American republic as "the greatest moral, spiritual, and political force in the land." He pictured a Republican elephant fitted with a vacuum cleaner in front and a rug beater behind, equipment appropriate not only for his audience, he noted, but for a party that had committed itself to "cleaning up the mess which we found in the government household." Without referring to McCarthy by name, he endorsed the dirty but supposedly necessary work the senator had undertaken for America's freedom. "Seeking out the wreckers and destroyers, the security risks and homosexuals, the blabbermouths and drunks, the traitors and the saboteurs is no picnic," he spewed, "especially when one senses the nausea which goes with the fact that American citizens . . . were permitted to infiltrate under the prior administration."[57]

In the six weeks leading up to the election, Dirksen delivered forty-three speeches in twenty states. He predicted that the party would win five Senate seats and add to its majority. He must have been disappointed when the Democrats picked up two seats on election day to win control of the Senate. But given the fact that a stagnant economy and growing unemployment blunted the GOP appeal, the narrow defeat was not disastrous. Eisenhower, who campaigned vigorously for the party in the days leading up to the election, interpreted the results as a rejection of rigid conservatism. In a postelection meeting with Lucius Clay, he described the Republican right as "the most ignorant people now living in the United States" and began to organize an effort to modernize the GOP: "The Republican party must be known as a progressive organization or it is sunk. . . . I think far from appeasing or reasoning with the dyed-in-the-wool reactionary fringe, we should completely ignore it, and when necessary, repudiate it." He pointed to McCarthy and Colonel

McCormick and concluded, "Their thinking is completely uncoordinated with the times in which we live."[58]

Dirksen's take on the election was different. Though he was far too astute to criticize Eisenhower or the White House, he suggested that McCarthy could have led several defeated Republicans to victory if party leaders had called on him to campaign more extensively. Dirksen's personal support for McCarthy peaked in a special postelection session to debate and vote on the censure proposition. The special committee recommended McCarthy's censure on two counts. First, in his position as chairman of the Government Operations Committee and head of its Permanent Subcommittee on Investigations, he had abused General Zwicker. The second count was even more serious. The special committee concluded that by refusing to answer a committee subpoena in the previous Congress, McCarthy showed contempt for the Senate and blatant disregard for the legislative process.[59]

The Senate began its debate on the special committee's report on November 8. Constituent mail flooded Senate offices. In a letter to Ohio's John Bricker, one voter described McCarthy as a "fearless and selfless American" doing his duty against almost insurmountable odds: "With all the stupid, irritating, and obviously communist-inspired heckling throughout the days, months, and years, who can blame Senator McCarthy for losing his temper and striking out. . . . And deserving a vote of confidence for his stand on the matter is Senator Everett Dirksen." From the glaring lights of the Senate floor, McCarthy resorted to the thuggish standards of behavior that delighted his most avid admirers. He insisted that the proceedings showed how the Communist Party "has now extended its tentacles" to the Senate, and he irresponsibly attacked Flanders as the Communist Party's "unwitting handmaiden."[60]

Within days of McCarthy's outburst, rumors swirled around the Capitol that Dirksen the conciliator was working up a milder version of the final resolution. Several factors prompted Dirksen's attempt to salvage McCarthy's Senate career. First, he was one of very few senators who considered the Wisconsinite a personal friend. Second, he believed in the righteousness of anticommunism and adhered to the traditionalist midwestern variety of Republicanism that lashed out at all things alien. Most important, he feared that McCarthy's censure would jeopardize legislative oversight and continue the executive's endless encroachment on Congress. "I put Senator McCarthy aside for the moment," he told

NBC's *Meet the Press*, and "think of it in terms of curbing the freedom of a senator in pursuit of his investigatory power. Once you put a limit on it, where do you stop?"[61]

Whatever his motives, Dirksen moved to save his friend from the wrath of the Senate. When McCarthy entered Bethesda Naval Hospital with an elbow injury on November 17, Dirksen attacked those members who wanted to continue the proceedings without the defendant. Noting that McCarthy had been harassed since his 1950 speech in Wheeling, West Virginia, Dirksen, with a rising voice, insisted that "this is a time for compassion. There is fever, and there is pain." Despite a ten-day recess, Dirksen knew that the vote was imminent and that "this thing was all cooked and ready." Desperate to soften the resolution, he went to McCarthy's hospital room with a bottle of bourbon and a proposed letter of apology to retiring Sen. Robert Hendrickson (R-NJ), whom McCarthy had once described as "a living miracle in that he is without question the only man in the world who has lived so long with neither brains nor guts." When McCarthy showed more interest in Dirksen's bourbon than in the apology that might have helped his cause, the Illinoisian told his colleague, "I'm your friend and your lawyer, and you ought to pay attention to me." The two talked for several hours, but still McCarthy would not sign. "I don't crawl," he told Dirksen. "I learned to fight in an alley. That's all I know."[62]

There was nothing left to do but vote. In the 67-to-22 vote for censure, Republicans divided evenly, 22 to 22. Senate GOP leader Knowland and Dirksen voted against censure, but the final tally revealed yet again the split that continued to hamstring the Republican party. Eisenhower was frustrated. Acknowledging that some senators voted for McCarthy in order to protect the Senate's right to oversee the executive, the president pledged his efforts to establish the GOP as the nation's majority party and rededicated his administration to "get every Republican committed as a moderate progressive." Dirksen wrote McCarthy after the vote, lamely suggesting that his friend and colleague "should be quite happy" that the "pressure is over" and the resolution was not more severe. He added that he was "quite sure the general will not like it."[63]

At the end of 1954 Dirksen was as estranged from the Eisenhower White House as he had ever been. Despite endless entreaties from the president, Dirksen held his ground and continued to advocate a more nationalistic and conservative Republicanism than Eisenhower could accept. Even though he voted with Eisenhower on 82 percent of important roll-call votes in the Eighty-third Congress, Dirksen kept his distance from the White House on the most critical issues. The only hint that he was prepared to betray the conservative cause and endorse the modern executive was his eventual decision to back the administration's mutual security program.[64] With the president determined to mold a more modern Republican party by shunning the far right and Dirksen apparently ready to carry on his own anticommunist, heavily partisan style of politics, it was clear that the next two years would prove pivotal, not only to Dirksen's career but also to the future direction of the GOP.

Compared to the tumult and controversy of the year before, 1955 was quiet and uneventful for the national GOP. Nonetheless, that year proved to be a watershed in Dirksen's eventual decision to edge toward a national leadership role within the party and in the Senate. At the beginning of the Eighty-fourth Congress he was still smarting from McCarthy's censure. In a Senate speech he told his colleagues, "I trust . . . that I shall not lack restraint and violate a rule of the Senate, and thus invite censure." But Dirksen was also looking to distance himself from McCarthy. He moved off the Government Operations Committee and focused his energies solely on the Appropriations and Judiciary Committees. Though he always spoke fondly of McCarthy, Dirksen acknowledged that "I'd go crazy if I had another like him to defend."[65]

Early in 1955 Dirksen sent mixed messages to the White House. Though he praised the president's State of the Union address and continued his practice of deferring to Eisenhower on national security issues, he also repledged his support for the Bricker amendment. In a series of speeches commemorating Lincoln Day in the Midwest, Dirksen did little to affirm Eisenhower's leadership. He joined McCarthy, George Malone (R-NV) and Utah governor J. Bracken Lee at a Chicago rally for conservatives. Seventeen hundred people attended the one-day conference, whose theme was "What shall the Republican party do in 1955 to preserve the republic, and itself?" Vendors hawked red, white, and blue "I'm for McCarthy" buttons. From the podium Dirksen made a feeble attempt to "salute and applaud" Eisenhower's defense of Formosa in the brewing Quemoy-Matsu crisis. His support for the White House "won a light patter of applause." The crowd roared its approval of Dirksen's promotion of the Bricker amendment and his praise of the McCarthy committee's "great job" of alerting the people and ferreting out communists. Dirksen's anticommunism outpaced his civil libertarian sensibilities: "I have no doubt that some injustices were done . . . , but . . . when you have a sinister destructive force that stalks through the country . . . you can't find refuge in a lot of brittle legalisms."[66]

As hysterical as Dirksen's speech was, his remarks were far more tepid than those of his colleagues. Dirksen was the only speaker to give even grudging support to Eisenhower's leadership. In fact, Governor Lee's disenchantment with the White House drove him to propose a third party tethered to conservative and isolationist ideals. Calling Lee's idea "just nonsense," Dirksen recoiled at the prospects of a protest party. Lee's speech awakened Dirksen's commitment to the vitality of the two-party system and focused his attention on the national GOP and on the popular successes of Eisenhower's middle-of-the-road leadership. In a March interview he made clear his ultimate commitment to the White House. Speaking of Eisenhower, Dirksen insisted, "He is our president. He has done a good job. . . . I think it's my responsibility as a Republican to go along in every case where it does not require a forfeiture of conviction. . . . He is our party chief."[67]

Rumblings about a third party were not the only factor pushing Dirksen into the Eisenhower camp. Until 1955 Dirksen had acted as a virtual mouthpiece for the *Chicago Tribune,* his rhetoric often mirroring the language found in the daily's editorial pages. But on January 19 Colonel McCormick underwent complicated abdominal surgery from which he eventually died in early April. Along with Taft's death and McCarthy's censure, McCormick's demise meant that many of Dirksen's personal and political ties to the party's Old Guard had been severed. Significantly, Dirksen opted not to eulogize McCormick from the Senate floor.[68]

Even though his speeches continued to emphasize traditional notions of spirituality and the force of the human will to combat the complexities of the nuclear age, Dirksen no longer shied away from a realistic appraisal of America's obligations and responsibilities in world affairs. The senator provided yeoman service to the administration on the prickly issue of foreign aid. Angry at his critics who were "trying to make political capital out of something they don't know anything about," Eisenhower depended on Dirksen's support. In May Eisenhower and Sen. Styles Bridges (R-NH), ranking member of the Appropriations Committee, asked Dirk-

sen to travel to Asia and the Middle East in order to evaluate the foreign
aid program. Eisenhower invited Dirksen to the White House before he
departed. Dirksen brought with him a letter praising the "patient and
diligent" work of Charlie Willis, the president's chief assistant on patronage. Though he had been sharply critical, Dirksen admitted that
"handling patronage matters is a thankless job which would tax the pa-
tience of a saint," and he concluded that "Charlie has done a superb piece
of work under a good many handicaps and deserves a resounding pat on
the back." Eisenhower asked Dirksen to extend his personal greetings to
the heads of state. He told the senator that he thought the foreign aid
program was succeeding but that he was "sure there were mistakes being
made and he would be glad to hear about them."[69]

Dirksen returned to the United States in July, just in time to debate
and vote on the administration's foreign aid appropriation. The stakes
were high. Eisenhower was traveling to Geneva for a high-level summit
meeting with the Soviet Union, and the president's defenders in Congress
were determined to bolster his international prestige by prevailing on
foreign aid. With great rhetorical flourish, Dirksen sprang to the administration's defense. He acknowledged that foreign aid "connotes a giveaway or welfare program" but argued that "this is the most selfish program I know of. . . . It is not a giveaway program. . . . We are doing it for
the greatest, most blessed, most prosperous country on God's footstool."
In case anyone had overlooked his conversion, the former ultranational-
ist cried, "I remember the day when I used to attack this program. I did
it with a good deal of verve and vigor. I take it back. Publicly and privately, I take it back."[70]

Southern Democrats and conservative Republicans were stunned. A
red-faced William Jenner "yelled his way" through a prepared response.
While Dirksen and other supporters held that Eisenhower's aid program
was an inexpensive way to promote the nation's security, Jenner proclaimed that the reductions he sought went "to the heart of the congressional power over the purse strings. . . . The program is choking to death
with funds." And just to make clear his disillusionment with Dirksen's
metamorphosis, Jenner concluded, "Somebody in the cloakroom told me
he heard a whirling sound. I am sure that was Colonel McCormick turning over in his grave when the senator made that statement."[71]

After the Senate beat back all attempts to reduce the White House's
foreign aid package and provided the president with a "clear-cut victory,"

Dirksen again allied himself with Eisenhower when he and eighteen Republican senators endorsed his Open Skies proposal. Minority Leader Knowland and Bridges chose not to comment on the president's plan, which would have called on the United States and the Soviet Union to exchange their military blueprints. Though the proposal never came to pass, Dirksen's support for a policy that in the words of the *New York Times* "caught the imagination and kindled hopes of people everywhere" showed the extent to which he was reevaluating his rigid and unnegotiable anticommunism of years before.[72]

Though Dirksen had not yet announced his candidacy for reelection, it was clear that he was tying his political future to the president's popularity. Whether he realized it or not, Dirksen the opportunist was edging toward a more reflexive endorsement of the modern presidency. Even if the ideological significance of his acrobatics escaped him, he was acutely aware of the electorate's unbroken affection for Eisenhower. In August 1955, polls gauged the president's popularity at 76 percent, higher than his approval rating had ever been. Dirksen continued to defend the McCarthy committee, but he gave more emphasis to the peace and prosperity that Eisenhower had promoted. After McCarthy recklessly asserted that Eisenhower had appeased communism, Dirksen retorted that he "thoroughly disagree[d]" with this assessment. Just three days after a severe heart attack crippled the president and threw the election into disarray, Dirksen told reporters, "Duty is the shining, iridescent word the president learned at West Point. He knows and will know where his duty lies."[73]

In early October Dirksen went home to Pekin to announce his candidacy. He asserted that his primary goals for a second term included the pursuit of peace, the promotion of national security, and the maintenance of fiscal solvency. He was popular enough among the party activists in Illinois that no one stepped up to challenge him for the GOP nomination. Nonetheless, he had taken significant strides away from the conservative bloc and toward the White House. Old Guard Republicans continued to mumble criticisms about Eisenhower's leadership, many using his illness as an opportunity to stir up intraparty conflict. Dirksen, however, did not engage in this skirmishing. Instead, he pledged his commitment to Eisenhower's second term. When Eisenhower returned to Washington from Denver in November, Dirksen joined twenty-eight of his Republican colleagues (Knowland and Bridges were again notable exceptions) in welcoming the president back to his political duties and endorsing his middle-of-the-road Republicanism.[74]

In December 1955 Dirksen wrote, "I take pride in the fact that [Eisenhower] has considered me as one of his top troubleshooters in the Senate. I have said very little about it because I recall my conversation with the president in which he asked me to serve in this capacity without asking any glory or headlines for such service."[75] Previously Dirksen had played down his relationship with Eisenhower because he sought to protect his prestige as a conservative Republican. But by 1956 the political climate had changed, and Dirksen intensified his efforts to associate his candidacy with Eisenhower's leadership. He even so opted the president's rhetoric. Before, he had laced his speeches with such language as "militant," "cutting it to the bone," and "tyrannical," but in 1956 he emphasized "moderation," "unity," and "harmony."

Though Dirksen had declared his allegiance to the administration, he and the president continued to differ on the Bricker amendment. "Sick to death" of the amendment, Eisenhower told his press secretary James Hagerty, "If it's true that when you die the things that bothered you most are engraved on your skull, I am sure I'll have the mud and dirt of France during the invasion and the name of Senator Bricker." Dirksen no longer went public to emphasize his differences with Eisenhower but instead worked in early March to simplify the amendment's language and to present a proposal acceptable to the White House. On March 5 he authored a resolution that sailed out of the Judiciary Committee by an 11-to-2 vote. The crux of the Dirksen resolution read, "A provision of a treaty or other international agreement which conflicts with any provision of this Constitution shall not be of any force or effect."[76]

Dirksen insisted in his private correspondence that "nothing is done to restrict or hamstring the president's authority to negotiate treaties or international agreements." He emphasized, however, that he was creating legislative machinery to ensure that the Senate would have the opportunity to examine treaties and executive agreements to establish that they did not contravene the Constitution or jeopardize the liberties of the people. Moreover, he argued that the amendment would stunt the baleful effects of the United Nations in the several states and block any unintended consequences emanating from the proliferation of executive agreements. Newspaper reaction to the Dirksen amendment was decidedly mixed. Though the proposal won the favor of some midwestern dailies still concerned about presidential power, the *New York Times, Washington Post,* and *Chicago Sun-Times* objected to the amendment.[77]

Dulles echoed concerns about the scope and meaning of Dirksen's language. He wrote Eisenhower, concluding, "I have never known any legal document which could be fairly interpreted by taking each of its provisions separately. Our Constitution is a framework of government."[78] If he could keep the amendment off the Senate floor through behind-the-scenes maneuvering, Eisenhower saw no reason to mount another campaign against the resolution. Minority Leader Knowland, never a White House confidant, did little to assuage the administration's concerns. In legislative meetings at the White House he emphasized the importance of restoring the constitutional balance between the president and Congress. Suggesting that the Democratic leadership might throw the amendment on the floor to embarrass Eisenhower, the *New York Times* wrote of a "political time-bomb ticking away in the closets of the U.S. Senate." Dulles grew frustrated with the president's reluctance to take a stand. He told Eisenhower that he was unwilling to "preside silently over the liquidation of the treaty-making power and the capacity of the president to conduct foreign affairs." More politically astute than his secretary, Eisenhower expressed his reluctance to "make a direct challenge which would seriously disrupt party lines." When in June the White House won Bricker's promise to postpone Senate consideration of the amendment until after the November elections, a minor crisis had passed and Eisenhower maintained his hold on the GOP.[79]

Despite Dirksen's sincere hope that the amendment would pass the Senate and fulfill the 1952 Republican platform pledge that "no treaty or agreement with other countries deprives our citizens of the rights guaranteed them by the Federal Constitution," he expressed no public quarrel with the postponement. Meanwhile, Dirksen devoted most of his rhetorical and political efforts to consolidating his alliance with Eisenhower. Calling for a "crusade for Ike," the senator pointed to the "peace, progress, and prosperity" of the Eisenhower years and described the economy as "stabilized, not built on the broken, bruised bodies of Americans who haven't come back. It hasn't had to depend on war." He commented on his private meetings at the White House in an effort to calm concerns about the president's health: "I've never seen him look better. They've taken the excess fat off him. I wish I could do it."[80]

More important, Dirksen continued to provide much-appreciated political support for the White House on the controversial issue of foreign aid. His arguments reflected the maturation of his views and a growing inclination to give the administration more latitude to execute its foreign policy. He told Illinois voters that mutual security "diminish[ed] the possibility of a peripheral conquest with us in it." In 1956 the cause was complicated by a bitter debate over an administration plan to provide American fighter planes for Yugoslavia, a communist country striving for independence from Soviet Russia. Minority Leader Knowland told Eisenhower he could see nothing that "would ever separate Yugoslavia from Russia." Eisenhower chafed at this exaggerated anticommunism, which he equated with a form of isolationism: "A country like ours that is founded on democratic principles must rely on persuasion alone. We have no chance to persuade anyone if we cut ourselves off from them."[81]

Eisenhower's efforts to win Knowland's support failed. Not surprisingly, the White House turned to Dirksen. Secretary Dulles gave him a secret memorandum to read to the Appropriations Committee to ensure that funds for Yugoslavia were left intact when the foreign aid bill reached the Senate floor. Knowland's opposition, however, was irreversible. He entered an amendment that would have prohibited the shipment of any military equipment to Yugoslavia and then upstaged the White House by leaving the minority leader's seat at the front of the Senate floor "to make it clear that on this amendment I do not speak for the administration." Dirksen declared that the Knowland amendment would tie Eisenhower's hands and be "interpreted as a vote of no confidence in the president." Moreover, he embraced the substance of the administration's argument, holding that "it is necessary to pry some of the satellites loose from international communism." Even though the amendment passed 50 to 42 and the *Chicago Tribune* called him "Tito's senator" and accused him of abandoning his Illinois constituents, Dirksen gained more than he lost. His support of Eisenhower's position on Yugoslavia cemented his relationship with the White House at a crucial time. He later remembered, "I got calls more frequently for help from 'The Chief.'"[82]

Dirksen's electoral strategy was clear. He would attach his political fortunes to Eisenhower's popularity and ride the crest of the wave to victory in November. Dirksen's handwritten notes from the 1956 campaign underscored his approach. "Women, wives, and mothers" profited from "prices within the paycheck," and Americans everywhere benefited from the peace and stability that the Eisenhower administration had promoted. The former firebrand even adopted the president's more moderate style, praising his "manners," his commitment to avoiding "name-calling, threats, and bombast." Dirksen redoubled his efforts to tie his candidacy to Eisenhower's popularity and gave even shorter shrift to local Illinois politics when it was discovered that Republican state auditor Orville Hodge had embezzled over $1.5 million from the state treasury.[83]

Dirksen's Democratic opponent, state legislator Richard Stengel, played into the senator's strategy. Rather than associating Dirksen with local Republican corruption, Stengel tried to discredit Dirksen's claim that he was one of the president's most valuable backers. Stengel traveled to Pekin and attacked Dirksen's record. He described Dirksen as a "diehard, reactionary, isolationist, antipresident, antiprogress candidate." Stengel capped his speech by arguing that if "this is a record of supporting the president, then it was written with an ax." Despite a limited campaign in which he actively endorsed only those Republicans committed to his program, Eisenhower countered Stengel's strategy by emphasizing Dirksen's importance to the White House. At the conclusion of the legislative session Eisenhower sent Dirksen a personal letter meant to bolster his chances for reelection. "In your case," Eisenhower wrote, "I have been especially pleased by the way you have responded when I personally called on you for special help in important legislation. . . . I hope the people of your state will give you the opportunity to continue your service in the United States Senate." At a speech in Peoria on farm issues, Eisenhower, exaggerating slightly, again praised his "good friend" Dirksen and urged his reelection: "He's a tough fighter, and I ought to know. These last four years, every time I have asked his help he has given it wholeheartedly."[84]

Dirksen took on an active role at the 1956 GOP convention in San Francisco. His service as chairman of the Civil Rights Subcommittee foreshadowed the prospects and pitfalls of his Senate leadership on the civil rights issue. Washington columnist Drew Pearson had written that Dirksen was an integral part of an unofficial, bipartisan bloc on the Senate Judiciary Committee that bottled up civil rights legislation. Dirksen's solicitation of support from Southern Democrats on key issues like the Bricker amendment and the McCarthy censure gave some credence to the impression. Though he was neither a progressive nor a visionary, Dirksen was nonetheless far ahead of the Eisenhower administration on the issue of civil rights. As early as 1953 he had introduced admittedly mild legislation to establish a Federal Commission on Civil Rights and to encourage, through grants and federal aid, southern states to slacken their discriminatory practices.[85]

Clarence Mitchell, chief congressional lobbyist for the National Association for the Advancement of Colored People (NAACP), declared that his organization was depending on Dirksen to steer any and all civil rights legislation through the landmines of the Judiciary Committee. From San Francisco Dirksen suggested that the GOP would endorse the Supreme Court's 1954 ruling on desegregation in public schools and take steps to ensure its implementation. On that score he criticized the Democratic platform, calling it an "equivocal nothing" and declared that "it sounded like the old song about 'Hang Your Clothes on a Hickory Limb, but Don't Go Near the Water.'" Dirksen insisted, "We're dealing with the Constitution here, and if it's going to have any meaning, you're going to have to go near the water. A decision by the highest court in the land just can't go floating around in the air. Sooner or later it has to be enforced."[86]

But Eisenhower shrank from Dirksen's pledge. Because he hoped to crack the Democratic South in the 1956 election and because he believed that laws did little to change the hearts of men, the president insisted on a milder civil rights platform. Holding that "in this business he was between the compulsion of duty on one side, and his firm conviction, on the other, that because of the Supreme Court's ruling, the whole issue had been set back badly," he told Attorney General Brownell that he wanted language that avoided any endorsement of the decision. More sympathetic to Dirksen than the president was, Brownell argued against Eisenhower and eventually won the compromise phrase that "the Republican party accepts" school desegregation. In the face of an ordered retreat, Dirksen was loyal to the end. Though the GOP platform was only a cosmetic improvement over the Democratic language, Dirksen praised it as a "much firmer" commitment to the cause of civil rights.[87]

The exigencies of the campaign discouraged any break from the Eisenhower team. As it was, Brownell traveled to Illinois and campaigned for Dirksen on the issue of civil rights. Honing his more moderate political style, Dirksen welcomed the support of the GOP's eastern establishment and even invited former antagonist Thomas Dewey to Illinois. "As conclusive proof that political wounds rarely do more than break the skin," Dewey accepted. The backing of former GOP foes, however, was virtually meaningless compared to the unqualified endorsement he won from the White House. Aside from Eisenhower's support, Dirksen's greatest political asset continued to be his speech-making. One reporter described the effect: "The words flow smoothly, easily, steadily, and soon fall into a rhythm that is mildly hypnotic. . . . Not a man to back away from sentimentality, no matter how sticky, Dirksen expresses himself in terms that might seem purple to a Victorian female audience."[88]

As election day approached, Dirksen's greatest fear was a low Republican turnout. He had wisely avoided local political issues, but the scandals, according to one GOP stalwart, had the "Republican party in trouble. . . . The Illinois situation is deplorable. The attitude of many of the leaders is so callused and warped that they cannot be viewed as much help." As it turned out, Dirksen's concerns were exaggerated. Eisenhower won his cherished mandate, claiming 58 percent of the vote and taking all but seven states. In Adlai Stevenson's home state of Illinois, Eisenhower drubbed his opponent and amassed a 60 percent majority. After an anxious early evening in which solidly Democratic Cook County announced its returns, Dirksen won handily. Though lagging behind Eisenhower, Dirksen's 54 percent majority and his plurality of nearly 360,000 votes were impressive. The voters vindicated his high-wire act of balancing party factions against each other while finally casting his lot with an immensely popular president.[89]

"Delighted" with the results, Eisenhower wrote to enlist Dirksen's support for his second term. In his first four years, with minimal support from Dirksen, Eisenhower had overcome efforts by Bricker and McCarthy to reverse the powers of the modern presidency. That accomplished, he looked to improve the health and vitality of the Republican party. Long concerned over the future of the GOP, Eisenhower ran for reelection primarily because "I still have a job of re-forming and re-vamping the Republican party." Though it was by no means clear that the fickle Dirksen would go to great lengths to support a president whom the Constitution had just made a lame duck, Eisenhower's successful efforts to win the senator's loyalty served as a model example of what he might achieve as he worked in his second term to create a modern and unified Republican party organized around a powerful presidency.[90]

3. "We Can Always Count on Ev"

Having beaten back the isolationist tendencies of the conservative Republicans and steered his party to accept the foreign and domestic responsibilities of the modern presidency, Dwight Eisenhower embarked on a crusade to remake the GOP into a moderate and responsive governing institution shorn of the ideological rigidity of decades past. He emphasized as much on election night in 1956, when he told his supporters that "modern Republicanism looks to the future. . . . As long as it remains true to the ideals and the aspirations of America, it will continue to increase in power and influence for decades to come."[1] Shortly after the election Eisenhower set about the task of winning the congressional support necessary to achieve his most important objectives while at the same time improving the party's vitality for the future. Having lured Everett Dirksen away from the GOP's most conservative ranks, Eisenhower hoped to win the senator's total commitment to the administration's agenda.

Two weeks after the election Dirksen called the president from his Washington office. Eisenhower had sent a congratulatory wire to Dirksen, adding that he initially had been concerned by Stengel's early-evening lead. Dirksen explained that Democratic Cook County returns were counted first and that the downstate results provided him with his comfortable majority. Still, Dirksen must have realized that he ran far behind Eisenhower in Illinois. Grateful for his timely and enthusiastic support, Dirksen told the president to let him know if he could do any "chores" for the White House. Not one to pass up hard-earned political capital and knowing that Dirksen was an influential member of the Judiciary Committee, Eisenhower suggested that the senator press for the early confirmation of William Brennan to the Supreme Court.[2]

Dirksen's reelection signified his increasing importance in the Republican Senate. He gained seniority on the Appropriations and Judiciary

Committees. With the retirement of Eugene Millikin (R-CO), the GOP lost its chairman of the Republican Conference, and when Minority Leader William Knowland hinted to party intimates that he might retire from the Senate in 1958 to run for the California governorship, it was clear that the GOP's Senate hierarchy was in the midst of an important shake-up. Before Knowland made his intentions official, Dirksen's most important ally among the conservatives, New Hampshire's Styles Bridges, scrambled to add the Illinoisian to the Senate leadership. Realizing that the mild-mannered and moderate party whip, Leverett Saltonstall, occupied the position of Knowland's likely successor, Bridges convinced his Massachusetts colleague to leave his post to chair the Republican Conference. Bridges and Knowland then nominated Dirksen to serve as the GOP whip, and despite the protestations of several Republican liberals, he was elected. That same day Knowland announced that he would not be a candidate for reelection in 1958.[3]

Besides being the early favorite to replace Knowland as minority leader, the sixty-one-year-old Dirksen enjoyed a position of influence in the policymaking body of the Republican Senate. As Knowland's chief assistant, Dirksen was perfectly placed to gauge the strengths and weaknesses of the Californian's leadership style. Moreover, he served as acting floor leader when Knowland was home campaigning. Most important, Dirksen attended Eisenhower's weekly meetings with the legislative leaders of the Republican Congress. Along with Bridges, Knowland, Saltonstall, and the leaders of the Republican House, Dirksen crafted party strategy and assessed the progress of the administration's legislative agenda. While he had earlier served as chairman of the Republican Senatorial Campaign Committee and had undertaken various other efforts to improve party unity, Dirksen's election as GOP whip propelled him into a formal position of leadership in the Washington political establishment.

Eisenhower's gradual disinheritance of the Republican right sparked a last-ditch fight for the heart and soul of the GOP. Having won a landslide reelection victory at the polls, the president enjoyed the initial advantage against his party rivals. A key member of Eisenhower's White House team, however, opened the door for congressional conservatives to challenge the president. Eisenhower submitted his budget for fiscal 1958 on January 16, five days before the inauguration. He gave substance to his centrist rhetoric by proposing increased expenditures in the areas of resource development, welfare programs, school construction, and foreign aid. But that very day Secretary of the Treasury George M. Humphrey held a press conference in which he undercut Eisenhower's ambitious agenda. With the president's approval, Humphrey made public a letter to the White House bemoaning the budget's $2.8 billion increase and its drag on the nation's free economy. To reporters Humphrey was less restrained; inviting Congress to cut the budget wherever possible, the secretary warned, "If we don't [reduce expenditures] over a long period of time, I will predict that you will have a depression that will curl your hair."[4]

Coupled with the support Humphrey won from conservatives on both sides of the aisle, his grandstanding defined the lines of intraparty conflict that would hamstring the GOP through 1957. Eisenhower never overcame the central contradiction of modern Republicanism. Though he wanted to sever the party from its negative image and lure it to the center of the political spectrum, the president refused to abandon his commitment to balanced budgets and smaller government. Still at issue was the GOP's relationship to the modern presidency. While the battle over the budget and funding for mutual security were inextricably intertwined, Eisenhower would have to solidify the GOP's position on civil rights and negotiate the role of the presidency in overcoming the most glaring contradiction of the nation's democratic promise.

Foreign policy crises flared up as well. The year's first political controversy began before the inauguration and stemmed from unrest in the Middle East caused by the Suez crisis of 1956. Gamal Abdal Nasser, an Arab nationalist, had secured power in Egypt and moved to nationalize the Suez Canal. Nasser's scheme infuriated oil-starved France and Britain, whose private companies owned the canal and secured the easy passage of vital economic resources. Israel saw Nasser's ambition as a threat to its national security and, with French and British support, attacked Egypt just before the 1956 election. A Soviet- and American-backed UN resolution condemned the invasion, which eased the tension and achieved a partial withdrawal of the principal belligerents. The French and the British, however, had suffered an irreparable loss in prestige, and the resulting power vacuum encouraged Eisenhower to act in order to prevent potential communist aggression in the area.

On New Year's Day Eisenhower presided over a bipartisan legislative leaders' meeting at the White House. He outlined an initiative to enable the United States to use military and economic aid to thwart communist infiltration in the Middle East in the wake of the Suez fiasco. On January 5 he addressed a joint session of Congress to ask for approval of his

Middle East resolution. In order to "give courage and confidence to those who are dedicated to freedom and thus prevent a chain of events which would gravely endanger all of the free world," Eisenhower asked for $200 million in military and economic aid to be dispersed at his discretion. In addition, he requested the power to deploy U.S. armed forces to the region to block any "overt armed aggression from any nation controlled by international communism." Eisenhower's proposal signified an important amalgamation of the president's power to control the nation's cold war foreign policy.[5]

In his meetings with GOP legislative leaders, the president pressed for an early and favorable congressional endorsement to what became known as the Eisenhower Doctrine. Admittedly "anxious," Eisenhower emphasized, "Of course I want you to be careful. But after the debate is exhausted, I hope the pressure is on." Even though Barry Goldwater (R-AZ) had already made public his distaste for any resolution that would increase the executive's warmaking authority at the expense of Congress, Dirksen assured the president that his resolution would pass without "any real difficulty." More privately, Goldwater honed in on the key element of change that characterized the evolution of the Republican party since 1950. He telephoned adviser Stephen Shadegg and hit at the heart of the matter: "Now, goddamn it Steve, . . . I just can't see how I can go for it. I hate like hell to start out voting against the Boss, but Christ, we criticized that action in Korea. We've criticized similar actions all along. . . . Who determines what the emergency is? Who says how many boys?"[6] With the popular and internationalist Eisenhower at the helm, and with conditions in the Middle East presumably ripe for further communist aggression, Republicans debated the meaning of further abandoning their historical and ideological opposition to the executive's assumed prerogative to manage unilaterally the nation's foreign policy.

Right-wing Republicans intensified their opposition to the resolution. Jealously guarding the power of Congress to declare war, Indiana's William Jenner objected to any plan that gave the White House "arbitrary powers of our national resources" and a "blank check power to the president for the use of American Armed Forces." Aside from his constitutional scruples, the isolationist Jenner feared an "irreversible" American "subordination to the rulers of the new world state." Having become an outspoken advocate of Eisenhower's foreign policy, Dirksen took the floor to rebuke his Republican colleague. He accepted Eisenhower's January 5 argument that the Soviet Union had designs on the Middle

East and that the United States had a vital interest in giving economic and military support to friendly nations in the region to preserve a fragile peace. He endorsed the Eisenhower Doctrine and the expansion of the president's responsibilities, not because he sought to abdicate congressional power but because the exigencies of the cold war demanded flexibility to respond quickly and with a variety of means to halt communist aggression. Ever the pragmatic realist, he chided his opponents for their high-minded ideals and insisted that "when the blood starts running, their arguments on the Senate floor will sound empty and vapid indeed."[7] Though his contribution to the administration's 72-to-19 victory was not pivotal, Dirksen's support of the Eisenhower Doctrine reflected the congressional GOP's increased willingness to accept the foreign policy standard of an activist and modernist presidency established by Democrats Franklin Roosevelt and Harry Truman.

Though heartened by his success with the Eisenhower Doctrine, the president ran into more trouble with conservative Republicans when he tried to revitalize the nation's mutual security program. Until 1957 he had operated on the premise that the United States could eventually scale down its foreign aid program in favor of increased trade with its allies. In that vein the administration had worked to reduce tariffs, hoping that the infusion of private capital in Third World countries would bolster their economic and political institutions. The Suez crisis, however, forced Eisenhower to revisit these assumptions, and he concluded that the most vulnerable nations received only a fraction of the resources they needed to stunt potential communist belligerence. By 1957 Eisenhower had decided that the nation needed to revise the mutual security program. He therefore requested the creation of a Development Loan Fund of $2 billion spread over a three-year period. Rather than relying on private capital, Eisenhower's new plan stressed government-to-government, long-term loans at favorable interest rates to Third World countries. A bold departure from the established program that stressed trade over direct loans, his proposal called for a $4 billion appropriation and continued military assistance to neutrals like India and Yugoslavia. Even though he sensed that his prospects of winning congressional approval were "approximately nil," Eisenhower identified his mutual security program as an administration priority.[8]

On May 21 Eisenhower addressed a joint session of Congress. His remarks amplified his appeal of two weeks before to the legislative leaders. In that closed-door meeting he had ridiculed the appeal of "building a fortress and retiring in it." Eisenhower maintained that "this is not a static world. It is extremely dynamic, marked especially by the growing force of nationalism which I consider to be even stronger than communism. . . . We can't wage peace just from the pulpit." In his nationally televised speech to the joint session, he emphasized the danger of the nation's turning its back on the growing number of countries achieving their independence in the wake of disintegrating empires. "We simply cannot afford," he maintained, "to blight the hopes of . . . the free peoples who turn to the free world for help in their struggle for economic survival. Should we do so, these peoples will . . . be driven toward communist or other totalitarian solutions to their problems."[9]

Part-time speechwriter Emmet John Hughes remembered Eisenhower's appeal as a "hopeful omen." But key Republicans balked at the president's request. On the same day that Eisenhower delivered his speech to the Congress, Bridges scorned foreign aid in a Chicago speech. "I am beginning," he declared, "to be a little fed up with the global do-gooders who want to see us spend the hard-earned dollars of American citizens in support of a worldwide welfare state." Eisenhower was furious. He called Bridges to the White House and excoriated the man he recognized as the most senior and respected Republican in the Senate: "I think my party ought to trust me a little bit more when I put not only my life's work, but my reputation and everything else, on the line in favor of this." Trying to calm the president and explain his remarks, Bridges insisted that he was opposed only to that part of the program that allocated funds to neutral nations like Yugoslavia, India, and Indonesia. Eisenhower had none of it. Maintaining that his greatest political goal was to "put the Republican party together" in the pursuit of "moderate government," he argued that "if we were to become a garrison state, we would not have freedom. . . . And I want to wage the cold war in a militant, but reasonable, style where we appeal to the people of the world as a better group to hang with than the communists." One day after Eisenhower's speech and his attack on Bridges, Dirksen addressed the issue. Not wanting to anger the conservatives, he allowed that it might be possible for Congress to cut Eisenhower's program. But he remained in the president's corner. Mutual security, he held, was "justified on the ground that it makes a distinct and vital contribution to the security posture of the United States."[10]

Though the final appropriation votes on his program would not be taken until later in the summer, Eisenhower realized that Congress and its constituents "inevitably linked" the costly policy with a bloated budget. Conservative Republicans eagerly exploited the opportunity Secretary Humphrey had provided when he predicted a depression induced by too much federal spending. A wavering Eisenhower failed to endorse his modern Republican budget when in a press conference two days after the inauguration he expressed "complete agreement" with "the thought behind the secretary's statements." Minority Leader Knowland joined the fray when he went public with his belief that $1 billion could be cut from the White House budget. McCarthy agreed, maintaining that Eisenhower's budget "far outdoes" President Truman in "his wildest spending spree." Dirksen's conservative constituents contributed to the uproar. Arthur Welton wrote to "protest against the utter incapacity of this administration and apparently the Congress also to stop spending so much money like a drunken sailor." Welton ripped into Dirksen for supporting Ike, telling the senator, "You have lost my vote forever."[11]

By joining the chorus for spending cuts, Democrats exacerbated Eisenhower's vulnerable political position. With the Democrats "ready to claim to be the economy party," Eisenhower hunkered down and looked to key congressional allies for help. Without cutting his ties to stalwart conservatives like Knowland and Bridges, Dirksen provided the White House with welcome support. At White House meetings, when other Republicans were arguing that "it is unquestioned that the budget must be cut," Dirksen suggested that as it stood the Eisenhower program "left little room for finding any substantial cuts." Minority Leader Knowland reported that the administration's 1958 budget had touched a nerve in the country and "the mutual security appropriation would be the thing to suffer most." Dirksen held that "reckless cutting can ruin the budget," and though he would not rule out responsible reductions, insisted that Republicans should approach the volatile issue with a "scalpel, not a meat ax."[12]

As the intraparty budget debate continued, some conservative Republicans jumped at the chance to impugn Eisenhower's moderation. Goldwater established a reputation as the most articulate of the president's conservative critics. Tall, fit, and dashing, the Arizonan was a gregarious and amiable man who nonetheless began to tear into the White House at every opportunity. His hardening conservatism and his grassroots appeal among GOP activists contrasted neatly with Dirksen's steady support of

Eisenhower's moderate version of Republicanism and his growing preference for establishment politics. While Ike grew increasingly appreciative of Dirksen's eagerness to battle in the Senate trenches for the administration's program, he grew equally disillusioned with Goldwater's tendency to fire right-wing salvoes out on the hustings. In April Goldwater took the Senate floor and castigated the president's leadership. He held that until the White House released its 1958 budget he had supported Eisenhower's political agenda. The budget, however, convinced Goldwater that the administration had abandoned its earlier commitment to "cut spending, balance the budget, reduce the national debt, cut taxes—in short, to live within our means and allow our citizens the maximum personal benefits from their economic endeavors." Goldwater lashed out at the "faulty premises" of modern Republicanism and ridiculed "this splintered concept of Republican philosophy." Comparing Eisenhower to his profligate predecessors, the Arizonan maintained that the White House "was demonstrating tendencies to bow to the siren song of socialism."[13]

With the headline "Senator Rips Ike Backdown on Economy," the *Chicago Tribune* gave Goldwater's speech front-page coverage. And the next day's editorial concluded that Goldwater spoke for those Americans who "are fed up with the defeatism in Congress which suggests that there is nothing that can be done" to cut the White House budget. Holding that foreign governments "have been on the gravy train more than a decade," the *Tribune* promoted a budget ceiling of $55 to $60 billion: "No other people is being sweated in such unmerciful fashion to satisfy the insatiable pretensions of the politicians. . . . We want the government off our back. We want to keep what we earn and spend it as we, not government, not Congress, not Mr. Eisenhower, please. It is up to Congress to deliver." Measured by this standard, Dirksen failed his more conservative constituents. Though he rejected the label of "modern Republican," he continued to criticize those party members who were working to sabotage the White House budget.[14]

Just as the furor over the budget died down, Dirksen found himself in the middle of another controversial issue of even greater national importance. Nonviolent African-American protests like the 1955 Montgomery bus boycott and the explosion of racist white citizens' councils in the wake of the Supreme Court's 1954 desegregation ruling forced Eisenhower to push for civil rights legislation. Though never sympathetic to the overwhelming prejudice and danger facing blacks in their daily lives, the White House introduced what Eisenhower believed to be a moderate civil rights bill to protect the right to vote. Specifically, the measure would have established a civil rights division within the Justice Department, created a federal Civil Rights Commission with subpoena power to force state and local officials to testify and to open their records for federal inspection, and, most contentious, granted the Justice Department authority to intervene by federal court injunction on behalf of citizens whose civil rights had been breached or threatened.[15] As the Republican whip and a senior member of the Judiciary Committee, Dirksen was perfectly positioned to serve as the administration's point man on civil rights.

When southerners flocked to Capitol Hill to belittle the proposed bill as the creation of a "federal Gestapo," Dirksen joined with the attorney general to enact a bill protecting the civil rights of all Americans. Noting that federal law enabled the attorney general and the secretary of labor to cooperate in the prohibition of interstate commerce profiting from child labor, Dirksen insisted that southern efforts to hamstring the federal government in the field of civil rights "makes a mockery" of America's democratic ideals. Like Eisenhower, Dirksen maintained that the proposed bill was moderate in scope. "But this much we must do," he admonished, "or else we become the target for effective propaganda by a brutal and godless ideology which can in truth proclaim to all the world that with one hand we seek to bring the benefits of freedom to a whole area of the world, while on the other hand those freedoms are snatched away at home."[16] As in foreign policy, the exigencies of the cold war at home spurred Dirksen into accepting a more powerful presidency than Republicans of earlier generations had deemed advisable.

In the hands of unfriendly Southern Democrats, the civil rights bill languished in the Judiciary Committee through the spring and early summer. When the legislation finally made its way to the Senate floor in July, Southern Democrats attacked its provisions with a vengeance. Most vehement was Richard B. Russell's (D-GA) diatribe. A long-standing bachelor with few intimate friends, Russell had given his life to the Senate. His only conspicuous indulgence was smoking, and he normally puffed his way through three packs a day. Kind and gentle by nature, Russell was wholeheartedly opposed to civil rights, and he was unafraid to break with his preferred style of behind-the-scenes politics to lash out at the bill's supporters. "If you propose to move into the South," he thundered, "you may as well prepare your concentration camps now, for there are not enough jails to hold the people of the South who will today oppose the raw federal power to forcibly commingle white and Negro children in the same schools and in the same places of entertainment." Dirksen took the floor to defend the bill. Emphasizing that its provisions merely enforced the Fourteenth Amendment and safeguarded the rights of all citizens, he underlined the essential moderation of the measure: "Seldom in my long legislative experience have I seen . . . so many ghosts discovered under the same bed, but I am confident that if the civil rights bill is enacted the heavens will not be rent asunder, the waters will not part, the earth will not rock and roll, and we will go on."[17]

Ironically, Russell's speech may have been more meaningful for what he omitted. He attacked Section 3, which he held gave the attorney general the power to promote the desegregation of public schools, and lashed out at a portion of Section 4, which authorized trials by federal judges to punish those who offended the civil rights statutes, but he left important parts of the bill open for debate. Given his retaliatory speech aimed at Russell's defiance, Dirksen was committed to enacting the whole of the administration's legislation. But on the day after the Senate confrontation Eisenhower undercut any chance the White House might have had for more meaningful legislation. In response to a reporter's question about whether the White House might shelve Section 3 of the bill in favor of legislation geared solely to protect the right to vote, the president wavered: "I was reading part of that bill this morning, and there were certain phrases I didn't completely understand. So before I made any more remarks on that, I would want to talk to the attorney general and see exactly what they do mean." Holding that Eisenhower's performance "was a stunning confession of ignorance," biographer Stephen Ambrose argues that his "admission was an open invitation to southern senators to modify, amend, [and] emasculate his bill."[18]

As the Justice Department crafted a response to Russell's diatribe for Dirksen's use on the Senate floor, Eisenhower betrayed the White House bill. While underlining his commitment to voting rights, the president met with Russell and reminded his guest that "I have lived in the South, remember." Dirksen conceded the battle to the southerners and Eisenhower but declared that the war was far from over: "It is not going to be stopped. It may be stopped now, but it will roll." The issue, Dirksen insisted, was that "we are dealing with human beings. Though their color is black, I cannot imagine for a moment that they were not endowed with a spirit and a soul, just as is every other human being under the canopy of God's blue heaven." Despite Dirksen's exhortations, the Senate voted Title 3 out of the bill by a margin of 52 to 38. Though he commented to White House secretary Ann Whitman on retaliating against those Republicans who voted against the administration, Eisenhower made clear in private correspondence that he "had no objection to the elimination of Section 3 from the bill."[19]

Hoping to legitimate his claim as a national statesman but believing that the compromise bill would precipitate an unbreakable Senate filibuster, Majority Leader Lyndon Johnson added a jury trial amendment to the voting rights section of the bill. Eisenhower Republicans resisted this provision, for they knew that white juries in the South would clear any white violator of a black's civil rights. Even so, southerners profited from a strange alliance with liberal Democrats to push for the amendment. Labor leaders had long despised the ways in which hostile federal judges responded to disputes by issuing injunctions forcing workers back on the job without the benefit of a jury trial. When Johnson promised that the civil rights amendment would include a requirement for a jury trial in criminal contempt cases involving unions, labor leaders like George Meany of the American Federation of Labor (AFL) and John L. Lewis of the United Mine Workers of America (UMWA) pressured liberal Democrats to back the Johnson plan.[20]

At the White House Dirksen told Eisenhower and the legislative leaders that Johnson's amendment would weaken the power of the executive to protect the voting rights of all Americans. He wrote Roy Wilkins of the NAACP and asserted that in the face of southern intransigence, "it becomes the clear responsibility of the federal government to carry out this obligation." Promising Wilkins that he would "vigorously oppose" any jury trial amendment, Dirksen maintained that "an acceptable bill . . . is long overdue." After Johnson and the Democrats added their amendment to the civil rights bill by a 51-to-42 margin, Vice President Richard Nixon derided the "vote against the right to vote," and a "bitterly disappointed" and "damned unhappy" Eisenhower thought seriously about vetoing the watered-down bill that failed to protect the basic civil rights of black Americans. The president admitted to his cabinet that the setback was "one of the most serious political defeats of the last four years, primarily because it was such a denial of a basic principle of the United States." He told the legislative leaders that "if we fight them, we cannot only do something for civil rights, but we can break up their coalition. They will have to take the blame for defeating this. . . . When someone tries to hit me over the head with a brickbat, I start looking around for something to hit him with." Dirksen, however, wanted the bill. He advised Eisenhower that the best chance for an improved bill would come at the House-Senate conference, "when responsible people . . . act on it. We must ask for more than we expect to get. We must take a few bites at the cherry."[21]

House negotiators won a minor concession. The conference agreed to jury trials only when a judge's sentence exceeded a $300 fine or forty-five days in jail. After Strom Thurmond (D-SC) broke the Senate filibuster record by speaking for twenty-four hours and eighteen minutes and the Senate passed the amended legislation, Eisenhower on September 9 signed the bill into law. Few civil rights proponents were happy with the legislation. The 1957 bill did very little to guarantee voting rights and absolutely nothing to protect or promote the desegregation of public schools and public facilities. Though describing his subject as a "great and good man," Stephen Ambrose criticizes Eisenhower's "hesitancy" and "confusion" in the field of civil rights. Eisenhower, Ambrose concludes, "passed on to his successors the problem of guaranteeing constitutional rights of Negro citizens."[22]

One political figure who gained immensely from the experience and who would be looked upon in the future to correct neglected wrongs was Everett Dirksen. He waited while Southern Democrats sat on the bill and slowed its progress to a crawl in the Judiciary Committee. He watched helplessly as Eisenhower abandoned the White House bill and cut deals with influential southern senators. Though he was by no means the most important principal and saw himself as merely the administration's spokesman in the Senate, Dirksen hamstrung himself by speaking out so clearly in the early stages of the debate. In the future, he kept his thoughts to himself and thus retained more flexibility as legislation snaked its way through Congress. Despite the obvious frustrations of having to support a gutted bill, no one could overlook one basic fact: the U.S. Congress had passed civil rights legislation for the first time since Reconstruction. Those who voted for the bill had proved that if the conditions were right, civil rights legislation could make it through the labyrinthine thicket of congressional politics. Moreover, the bill established the Civil Rights Commission and a Civil Rights Division in the Justice Department to study the issue in the future. With valuable lessons learned and with monitoring mechanisms established, a disappointed Dirksen looked to the future to achieve "something that is probably a divine force."[23]

Eisenhower suffered other important defeats before Congress adjourned for the summer. Conservatives from both parties continued to criticize the president's budget, his commitment to "Social Security, unemployment insurance, health research by the government, assistance where states and individuals are unable to do things for themselves." In the end Congress passed a budget that cut $4 billion from the White House's original package. Minority Leader Knowland did little to support the administration's requests for increased appropriations. Less disastrous for the White House was the final vote on the president's mutual security program. Though Congress cut his original proposal by one-third to $2.7 billion, they granted Eisenhower's request for a Developmental Loan Fund to foreign countries. The president lashed out at those who worked to cut the program as "still stupid enough to believe in the concept of 'Fortress America'"; nevertheless, congressional acceptance of the Developmental Loan Fund created the machinery necessary to promote economic development in the Third World.[24]

Dirksen supported the president at every turn. Eisenhower was especially appreciative of his backing of the administration's innovative foreign aid policy. Calling Dirksen's assistance "exceptional" and "further evidence of [his] devotion to our nation's good," Eisenhower praised his "forthright" and "effective" contribution to the mutual security debate. After Congress adjourned, Eisenhower wrote Dirksen again, concluding that "each year you seem to deserve congratulations even more than the year before."[25] To the White House, Dirksen had proven that his loyalty outpaced a mere eagerness to be reelected. Most important, the political controversies that dominated Congress in 1957 revealed Dirksen's increasing commitment to an activist presidency responsible for addressing the needs of the day.

The session was not without personal loss. In early May Joseph McCarthy died, thus cutting one more personal tie that Dirksen had with the Republican right. Alienated from the reporters and political figures who before his censure gave him the attention he craved,

McCarthy drank uncontrollably and suffered from acute hepatitis and cirrhosis of the liver. Dirksen stayed with McCarthy to the end, accompanying his body to his colleague's home in Appleton, Wisconsin, for burial. He corresponded with McCarthy's wife, Jean, telling her that he hoped she would be "sustained in carrying on the work which Joe initiated and so courageously advanced." In a Senate speech to honor McCarthy's memory, Dirksen recalled "his courage to pursue the enemies of the Republic. . . . It takes courage for a man to stand up with his chin in the air, when he knows there is an organized effort to destroy what he is trying to do in the interest of the Republic. . . . That is the courage to follow through, to ask no quarter, and to give no quarter."[26]

Jean McCarthy was delighted with Dirksen's speech. She wrote immediately, asking the senator to pass along a picture she could save to show her young daughter, Tierney, when she grew older and asked about her father's friends. Dirksen complied, writing Jean that "a wonderful thing it will be to have a bound volume of comments, letters, and documents to provide not only comfort, but to give [Tierney] an appreciation of the esteem [in which] Joe was held by his friends."[27] Though vituperative anticommunism had waned in the years after McCarthy's censure, it was clear that Dirksen maintained his loyalty to the Wisconsinite and continued to believe that their efforts to root out radicals and subversives had served the national interest.

For Eisenhower, his 1957 troubles did not end with the adjournment of Congress. Just before the president left for his summer vacation in Newport, Rhode Island, Arkansas governor Orval Faubus flouted federal law by using the state's National Guard to prevent court-ordered desegregation of Little Rock's Central High School. Face-to-face negotiations with Faubus fell through; and after a white mob refused the president's order to desist and disperse, Eisenhower, with the greatest reluctance, sent paratroopers to Little Rock and federalized the Arkansas National Guard in order to protect and promote the orders of the court. Russell referred to the soldiers as "Hitler's storm troopers," but throughout the crisis Dirksen embraced the modern presidency and supported Eisenhower's efforts to "assert the power of the federal government."[28]

Already under attack, Eisenhower's political prestige suffered its greatest reversal when the Soviet Union launched the world's first man-made satellite, *Sputnik*, into orbit. The Soviet achievement rattled the nation's psyche and forced a reassessment of every American institution. Americans feared that they were vulnerable to an unprovoked nuclear strike and that the Soviets had leaped ahead of them in missile development and production. For Eisenhower, the aftermath of *Sputnik* proved to be the greatest political challenge of his second administration. Senate Democrats like Lyndon Johnson and Stuart Symington (D-MO) lambasted the president for his complacent leadership and smug self-satisfaction with the status quo. Though they had already capitalized to some extent on a stagnant economy and the early stages of a painful recession, prominent Democrats jumped at the chance to patch up their differences over civil rights and repair their party's political prestige. Johnson's legislative assistant George Reedy wrote his boss that only by dramatizing the *Sputnik* affair could his party overcome the "integration issue" that had united the GOP and "chew[ed] the Democratic party into pieces." On top of his political problems, Eisenhower in late November suffered a minor stroke that generated more doubts about his physical fitness.[29]

The second session of the Eighty-fifth Congress began with Eisenhower still reeling from the setbacks of the previous year. In the face of aggressive Democratic attacks on his leadership, the Republican party overcame much of its previous squabbling and united behind the administration's legislative agenda. As Democrats abandoned their economy crusade and called for increased spending to overtake the Soviets in missile production and to jumpstart the economy, Eisenhower committed his administration to the containment of federal expenditures. He soft-pedaled fears of Soviet superiority and argued that excessive spending on infrastructure, even during a painful recession, would result in debilitating inflation and a future depression. For these tasks, he found a useful ally in Dirksen, who continued to provide unwavering support for the administration. In so doing, Dirksen was unquestionably preparing for the minority leadership election in January 1959. Despite Eisenhower's apparent vulnerability, the president was still the nation's most popular Republican. By associating his efforts with Eisenhower's leadership, Dirksen was trying to overcome lingering beliefs on both sides of the aisle that he was at heart an Old Guard Republican wary of the president's centrist achievements.[30]

When Democrats like Sen. J. William Fulbright (AR) criticized Eisenhower for leaving the country "fat and immobile" from a steady diet of "sugar-coated half truths," Dirksen jumped to the president's defense. Comparing Eisenhower to Lincoln and the troubles he faced from

Congress during the Civil War, Dirksen praised the president for "very calmly" giving "direction to the ship of state" in troubled and turbulent times. When the contents of a supersecret National Security Council report (commonly known as the Gaither Report) were leaked to the press, Democrats pressed for its release. The study affirmed their own conclusions and argued for increased spending on military programs and defense shelters. With congressional pressure mounting, Dirksen nevertheless gave a ringing endorsement of executive privilege when he maintained that Eisenhower "not only has the authority to withhold the Gaither Report, but also has done the wise and discreet thing in so doing."[31]

Dirksen must have felt relieved when on February 1 the United States finally launched a successful satellite into orbit. He derided the "emotional binge" the Democrats and the press corps had fueled and asserted that "it is time we recover our emotional balance and look upon reestablishing our domestic tranquillity." Ironically, he ridiculed "the spectacle of witch hunting in every nook and corner of the executive branch of government." The former McCarthy supporter engaged in an apparent role reversal when he chided the Democrats for being "unable to present a program of their own" and thus for opting to diminish the White House for cheap political gain.[32]

Dirksen's most important support for Eisenhower in the months leading up to the minority leadership election came when he defended members of the White House team against charges of political ineptitude and ethical misconduct. As part of his agenda presented to the Congress, Eisenhower asked for legislation that would ease controls on acreage allotments and reduce price supports for staple products. Though Eisenhower's proposal reflected his commitment to avert inflationary pressure on the economy, Democrats and Republicans alike insisted that the administration's agricultural program showed the president's callous indifference to the American farmer in the depths of a persistent recession. Secretary of Agriculture Ezra Taft Benson served as the most convenient target for the president's critics. Despite hailing from the Midwest, a slice of the agricultural heartland where Eisenhower's program was especially unpopular, Dirksen defended Benson against his attackers. Dirksen's relative unconcern for the plight of the nation's farmers may have derived from the fact that, unlike many of his midwestern colleagues, neither he nor his family had made their living off the land. Whatever his motivation, Dirksen's stubborn support for Eisenhower's beleaguered secretary of agriculture jeopardized his standing with his downstate Illinois constituents. Nonetheless, he pushed on. At a legislative leaders' meeting at the White House, Dirksen backed Benson and insisted that "it [is] high time to stop this business of 'going after Ezra.' "[33]

Focusing primarily on national politics, Dirksen left local Illinois issues to trusted subordinates like Harold Rainville and spent more time with Eisenhower. Sensing that the Democratic program was little more than an effort to win political capital before the midterm elections, Dirksen urged Eisenhower to veto Democratic legislation. "Keep the blue pencil handy," he suggested. "It's good for the country." Despite his aversion to spending his way out of the recession and his increased willingness to veto Democratic bills that busted the White House budget, Eisenhower refused to cut his mutual security program. Especially in this area, Dirksen continued to provide yeoman service to the White House. When Knowland again expressed his belief "that there were some cuts to be made," Dirksen disagreed, saying, "I'm always optimistic." Dirksen took his advocacy to his constituents. Midwestern Americans had long been suspicious of the value of spending money abroad. But the former isolationist argued that the United States had a 20,000-mile free-world perimeter to defend and that military and economic assistance to prop up embattled allies and noncommunist nations "always looked to me like a good investment in survival for the defense of our country and all the free institutions that have been woven into the life of this nation." In the end Congress appropriated $3.3 billion for mutual security, all but $600 million of Eisenhower's request.[34]

Eisenhower's greatest personal loss of 1958 was the forced resignation of Sherman Adams, the White House chief of staff with the formal title of assistant to the president. Even though Adams was more of a gatekeeper than a policymaker, most insiders who encountered him despised him and deemed him more machine than man. His behavior was short to the point of rudeness, and his rock-solid face rarely betrayed any emotion. Eisenhower prized Adams's unflinching fidelity, but the New Hampshire native was cold even to his boss. Once Ike painted a portrait of Adams and presented it to his friend. The only gratitude Adams could muster before he left the room was, "Mr. President, thank you, but I think you flattered me."[35]

By 1958 Adams's problems were legal as well as personal, and his attackers were swarming. In June a House committee alleged that Bernard

Goldfine, a New England textile manufacturer and longtime friend of Adams, had used his relationship with the chief of staff to secure favorable treatment from the Federal Trade Commission and the Securities and Exchange Commission. For his services, the allegations went, Goldfine presented Adams with expensive gifts, including a fur coat intended for his wife. Not surprisingly, Democrats tore into Adams and demanded his resignation. Influential Republicans also joined the fray. In a White House meeting Knowland called the situation a "serious problem." Visibly irritated, Eisenhower jumped to Adams's defense. "Here's a man who's absolutely honest," he insisted. Maintaining that there was a "hell of a difference between a gift and a bribe" and that Adams "shouldn't be stampeded," Eisenhower told the leaders that he "hope[d] no one is ever hesitant to stand up and speak to his offic[ial] conduct."[36]

But as the furor increased and the House investigation intensified, Republicans called for Adams's resignation. Many of them were up for reelection and especially sensitive to any ethics charge that might taint the party. But Adams's severest GOP critics, such as Knowland, Goldwater, and Roman Hruska (NE), were also the party's most conservative legislators. The Republican right had especially disliked Adams. He had ignored their patronage requests, and, most noxious, he shielded Eisenhower from conservative ideas. In the opinion of one conservative journal, he succeeded in "alienating and affronting practically every Republican leader" with whom he came into contact. The Adams fiasco became a severe test of loyalty to Eisenhower. Just days before the mounting pressure forced Adams to resign, Dirksen continued to defend him. In a Milwaukee speech he "went to great lengths" to champion Adams's importance to the administration. In the process, Dirksen won Eisenhower's "undying gratitude."[37]

The Adams debacle combined with lingering distrust over the health of the economy (the recession technically ended in late summer) and fears about a weakened defense posture to put the GOP in a precarious political position for the 1958 midterms. Party leaders pondered ways to combat the "defeatism" and "complacency" that plagued GOP workers in the trenches. One month before the election Dirksen and other congressional leaders joined Eisenhower at the White House to create a "crusading spirit in Republican ranks." It was to no avail. Just two years after winning a second term to the White House, Eisenhower's Republican party suffered its worst congressional defeat since the dark and dreary days of Roosevelt's New Deal. The 1958 midterm election was nothing less than a "political landslide," one in which the GOP lost a total of thirteen Senate seats. The party entered the 1959 legislative session with fewer House members than at any other time since 1937. The disaster provoked widespread criticism of the president. Goldwater wrote Nixon, bemoaning Eisenhower's lack of "interest" in the future of the GOP. Already focusing on the meaning of the midterm in relation to the 1960 presidential election, political pundits depicted Eisenhower as an aging lame duck almost desperate to retire to a simpler, less stressful life on his Gettysburg farm.[38]

In the wake of the 1958 election disaster and in anticipation of the 1960 presidential campaign, Republicans of all persuasions angled to direct the identity and mission of the GOP. A defining episode became the January 1959 struggle for the minority leadership of the Republican Senate, one of the first and most important instances in which Washington Republicans with competing visions vied for party leadership. Eisenhower hardly mourned Knowland's retirement, mostly because he found him to be dour, obstreperous, and incredibly difficult to control. Never known for his finesse, Knowland (described by his detractors as "subtle as a Sherman tank") crossed the administration at critical times. The president once confided to a friend that "it is a pity that his wisdom, his judgment, his tact, and his sense of humor lag so far behind his ambition." Eisenhower once criticized the minority leader for having "no foreign policy except to develop high blood pressure." Later Ike charged him with advocating a preventive war to liberate Communist China. At times appreciative of Knowland's committed service to the party, the president bared his true assessment of the Californian when he responded privately to the latter's attempt to rush Eisenhower into a decision regarding his availability for the 1956 campaign. "In his case," Eisenhower confided, "there seems to be no final answer to the question 'How stupid can *you* get?' Why he has to talk about such things I wouldn't know—unless he's determined to destroy the Republican party."[39]

Dirksen's loyalty to the administration was no longer a question. By late 1958 he had committed himself so completely to the White House that several conservative Republicans toyed with the possibility of backing the more doctrinaire Goldwater for the minority leadership. While conservative Republicans winced at Dirksen's drift to the left, liberal GOP senators never trusted what they believed was the expediency that drove his new-found moderation. Eisenhower aide Bryce Harlow told Ann Whitman that the Republican liberals would rather work with an "avowed" conservative, such as Bridges. Unlike Dirksen, who was "sometime conservative, sometime liberal," Bridges "at least keeps his word."[40]

Calling for fresh congressional leadership to inject the party with a dose of much-needed progressivism, liberals pointed to the disastrous results of the recent election. Conservative Republicans, like Ohio's John Bricker and former minority leader Knowland, had fared especially badly, but the liberal Republican Nelson Rockefeller provided, in their opinion, the party's only ray of hope by winning New York's gubernatorial election. Rockefeller's victory over Averell Harriman invigorated the progressive wing of the party and vaulted the New Yorker into the 1960 presidential election as a prospective candidate and opponent of Vice President Nixon. Rockefeller did little to quiet rumors that his real ambition lay in the Oval Office. On election night 1958 he told the press that he "was really interested" in running for the White House. More than his lofty aspirations bothered mainstream Republicans, however. Because of his family's prodigious wealth, Rockefeller's pampered and polished image was a menace to those Republicans who worked to identify the party in terms other than the moneyed interests of the eastern establishment.[41]

Having earlier served in the Eisenhower administration as special assistant to the president, Rockefeller eventually resigned that post because he saw a rudderless Eisenhower as drifting from crisis to crisis. Promising to satisfy his state's neglected infrastructure and human services, Rockefeller's program of deficit-financing contrasted to Dirksen's vision of government's limited role in society. New Jersey's Clifford Case spoke for many liberal Republicans when he criticized Dirksen for not promoting "the kind of program that our group collectively does . . . in schools, in health, in education, in urban renewal, unemployment compensation benefits, and all the rest." Others asserted that the GOP is "a gone goose unless we change the public conception of it voiced in the last election."[42]

Liberal Republicans cringed at the idea of Dirksen as minority leader long before they came up with a standard-bearer. For his part, President Eisenhower remained above the fray as combating groups of Republicans fought to give ideological direction to the GOP. The president's neutrality, however, did not mean that he ignored the intraparty split. Ann Whitman described December 15, 1958, as one of the White House's "worst" days, in part because GOP progressives had just announced their intention to challenge Dirksen for the party leadership. White House aides feared that the liberals would "polarize" the party by provoking a fight for Knowland's position. Though Eisenhower chose not to side with one group or the other, he indirectly endorsed the front-running Dirksen by encouraging all interested parties to avoid an open split that would blunt the GOP's ability to beat back an emboldened Democratic party with heavier majorities in both houses of Congress. Anti-Dirksen Republicans chafed at Eisenhower's directive to avoid all-out conflict; along with weeklies like the *New Republic,* liberal GOP senators argued that a clean party fight would give much-needed vitality and energy to Republicans across the nation. Kentucky's John Sherman Cooper echoed the frustration of many liberal Republicans when he criticized the president's desire for an amicable settlement of the dispute: "We disagree wholly with that. We think [the battle] will help the party."[43]

The president ultimately failed in his half-hearted efforts to prevent a party fracas, but the record shows that the prudent Eisenhower never involved himself directly in the GOP's senatorial caucus. Conferring privately with Eisenhower at the White House, Majority Leader Johnson asked the president who his counterpart would be in the next Congress. Eisenhower replied that he had chosen not to get involved but wondered if Johnson had any suggestions. The Texas Democrat again attempted to drag Eisenhower into the Republican row by naming the candidates with whom he could and could not work. White House notes of the meeting show that the president's only reaction was to emphasize a "close cohesion on the Republican side in matters avoiding excessive expenditure and [that he] would urge close cooperation with Senator Johnson in this field."[44]

On December 30 at 10:00 A.M. ten liberal Republicans caucused in the office of George Aiken (VT) to select their leadership slate for the upcoming election. A well-respected senior Republican, Aiken was the prohibitive favorite. Totally unpretentious (he wore his suits shiny blue, and he lived in a small and sparsely furnished apartment near Capitol Hill so that he could walk to work), Aiken radiated a relentless independence and an instinctive eagerness to take an unpopular stand. He turned down his nomination "because I knew there would be times when I would not agree with the position which the party as a whole was taking." GOP progressives soon settled on John Sherman Cooper as a compromise candidate. Dapper and bespectacled, Cooper was a man whose cosmopolitan tastes bewildered a layer of his Appalachian constituents and flattered those eastern Republicans who preferred martinis and operas to bourbon and college athletics. Bookish from an early age, the fifty-eight-year-old Cooper graduated from Yale University (where he joined Skull and Bones) and attended Harvard Law School before serving as ambassador to India in the early years of the Eisenhower administration. Like Dirksen, Cooper considered himself an Eisenhower Republican. Writing to his Republican colleagues, he pledged to strengthen the party and to create a "sound and constructive program" by promoting "full expression within the conference."[45]

Dirksen appeared undaunted by the liberals' efforts to overturn an election that many observers had before seen as a fait accompli. Privately, however, Dirksen expressed concern about the liberal defiance and moved to strengthen support for his candidacy. Perhaps in an effort to lure the administration into the conflict on his side, Dirksen told Nixon's office that the opposition hoped to push Rockefeller into the 1960 presidential election. To the press, Dirksen downplayed the importance of intraparty politics and displayed his usual confidence and buoyancy. About Cooper's aspirations, Dirksen said simply, "We are doing our work quietly and, I think, effectively."[46]

Dirksen's work combined the cajolery and compromise that would mark his Senate leadership for the rest of his career. While Cooper had yet to complete a full term in the Senate, the smooth-speaking Dirksen had won the loyalty and appreciation of Republican senators by traveling around the nation and stumping on behalf of a wide array of GOP candidates. In this regard, Dirksen distinguished himself from the rigid and stodgy Knowland, who in 1956 made a campaign visit to Connecticut without ever mentioning the imperiled candidacy of Prescott Bush, a moderate Republican and committed supporter of President Eisenhower. In one instance Dirksen's loyalty to his colleagues won him the vote of a Republican who shared little of his agenda. Described by the Washington press as a "maverick" and a "populist," William Langer (ND) found himself in deep political trouble during the primary battle for the 1958 nomination. Breaking unwritten party rules that discouraged intervening before a nominee had been elected, Dirksen traveled to North Dakota to stump for Langer. Dirksen's new ally kept him informed of Cooper's tactics and during the election sat next to the Illinoisian and marked his ballot DIRKSEN in capital letters for all his colleagues to see.[47]

As the liberals trumpeted their cause on the Sunday morning talk shows, Dirksen (working largely by telephone) quietly called in his political debts. In order to convince Republicans of all persuasions that he was more eager than his predecessors to absorb ideas at odds with his own, Dirksen offered to allocate committee appointments more evenly and to accept a liberal as his assistant leader. This tactic appeared even more appealing when some of Dirksen's conservative supporters expressed their opposition to the concession. His formal proposal to change the GOP's Senate rules guaranteed a major committee assignment to every senator, regardless of seniority. This reform not only spread prestige and influence more evenly around the caucus, but it also ensured that as minority leader he would be the primary arbiter of prized committee seats. Though he lost the vote of North Dakota's Milton R. Young because of his staunch support of the unpopular Benson, his overall commitment to the White House served him well. Other factors worked in Dirksen's favor once the matter found its way to the privacy of the Republican cloakroom. One variable was the relative weakness of his opposition. Cooper was a self-described Burkean who at times would subordinate the interests of his constituents and loyalty to his party in favor of his conscience as an elected representative. Characterizing his fellow Kentuckian as the "epitome of goodness, compassion, and virtue," one Frankfort newsman explained that Cooper "had perfected his Jesus image."[48]

Though Dirksen may not have been the ideal candidate, even some of Cooper's supporters questioned the Kentuckian's ability to defend Republican interests against the parliamentary skills of Majority Leader Johnson. An affable man with a keen intellect and progressive instincts, Cooper would have been "eaten up" in the heat of Senate debate, speculated one supporter. Twenty years later Clifford Case admitted that Cooper would have struggled in the leadership, mostly because "his ability to be himself might have been somewhat compromised if he had taken on the responsibility of attempting to lead and draw together people on least common denominator propositions." Dirksen's expertise on the floor won him the respect of some of his GOP detractors. Describing Dirksen as "well informed and a tremendously hard worker," Margaret Chase Smith admitted that "he is a polished speaker and excellent parliamentarian and clever tactician on the Senate floor. But his greatest strength is perhaps his flexibility."[49]

Republicans were desperate for an effective leadership to bolster the Eisenhower administration in the face of increasingly harsh Democratic attacks. Knowland, according to many people, had failed in this regard, thus making it imperative that the remaining survivors in the Republican Senate choose a leader able to work closely with the administration against the opposition. Florida Democrat George Smathers remembered Majority Leader Johnson leading Knowland "around by the nose." While Democrats like Smathers chuckled at their good fortune, Republicans hankered for a floor leader who could spar with Johnson but make a deal at the end of the day. Such a man they found in Everett Dirksen, who was able to match Johnson's mix of anger, flattery, and intimidation on the Senate floor before joining the majority leader for a whiskey during the cocktail hour.[50]

Most important, liberal Republicans proved too willing to sacrifice the qualities that made their party different from the Democrats. Mindful of those conservatives recently retired by the voters and eager for a more authoritative voice in the party councils, GOP progressives appeared to mainstream Republicans as nothing other than New Deal Democrats on the other side of the aisle. Clifford Case gave substance to the impression, telling reporters that "we are making our party, seek to make it a . . . truly representative American party, and I don't care at all whether it is the same as another party may be." Dirksen effectively distinguished himself from his opponents by underscoring his own strengths as a candidate for minority leader: "I am Republican, period—no tags, no labels, no qualitative adjectives."[51]

An array of factors, therefore, resulted in Dirksen's victory, won on the morning of January 7, 1959, by a margin of 20 to 14. His party service, his commitment to regular Republicanism, his parliamentary skills, and his willingness to compromise with his critics combined to realize Dirksen's aspirations and propel him to the minority leadership. For the GOP, Dirksen's victory over Cooper foreshadowed Richard Nixon's 1960 nomination and the triumph of mainstream Republicanism over its more progressive and conservative varieties. For Dirksen personally, his election to the minority leadership capped a process begun as early as 1955. Until then backing the president only in fits and starts, Dirksen thereafter tied his political future to the Eisenhower presidency.

Moreover, his selection fulfilled an unmistakable ambition that had driven his efforts from the beginning of his political career. Corresponding with his staunchest supporters in the Republican caucus, Dirksen called the results "energizing" and "heartening," hoping in the end to "merit that feeling of trust."[52]

Along with Charles Halleck's election as minority leader of the House, Dirksen's rise to national prominence changed Eisenhower's relationship with the Republican Congress, a transformation that had some effect on the public policy of his final two years as president. The administration's primary mechanism for dealing with the Congress had always been regularly scheduled Tuesday morning meetings at the White House. Seeing these gatherings as an onerous burden that had to be borne, Eisenhower rarely looked forward to these occasions and was often seen doodling or drawing on the agenda in front of him. Mistaken by his critics as an utter indifference to public policy, Eisenhower's apathy was primarily a function of his tempestuous relationships with former Republican leaders William Knowland and Joseph Martin. Knowland was particularly bothersome. Sherman Adams once observed that "It would have been difficult to find anyone more disposed to do battle with much of the president's program in Congress" than the humorless Californian.[53]

With Dirksen and Halleck at the helm, the atmosphere brightened and the tempo accelerated. It was not uncommon for Dirksen to laugh and joke with the president over a cartoon before the meetings came to order. More important, Eisenhower spoke openly with Dirksen both about the problems of leadership and about ways to invigorate the Republican Congress.[54] Never before had Eisenhower found the weekly meetings so enjoyable and productive. At the close of a January 1959 session Eisenhower told the leadership, "These meetings are getting so good we'd better allow more time on the schedule!" In part, the fighter in him relished the opportunity to strengthen the GOP while beating back the heavily favored Democrats in the legislative arena. But just as important, Dirksen and the Republican leaders gave the White House indispensable advice on political strategy. Every week they weighed the potential effects of a presidential veto. Here and there Dirksen would lecture administration officials on ways to enact the White House program. To take one of many examples, Dirksen in February supported White House aide Bryce Harlow's efforts to pass controversial mutual aid legislation: "Bryce is right. There has to be a sustained effort, built up week after week. Start with the Joint Chiefs' statement and build the book. The country still thinks it is a giveaway. We sold it in Illinois—Caterpillar in terms of jobs."[55]

White House aides sensed the president's improving spirits. One reported, "We can always count on Ev to push our program—once it's been fought for and agreed upon. This we could never do in Knowland's case." Later in the year Sen. Thruston Morton (R-KY) told Drew Pearson that "Ike now enjoys the Tuesday morning GOP leadership meetings because he finds Halleck and Dirksen much easier to work with than Martin and Knowland." Dirksen surprised his critics by giving the liberals a voice in those legislative conferences at the White House. At his first leadership meeting on January 13, new Minority Whip Tom Kuchel (CA) sat silently until Dirksen prompted his progressive assistant for his views on party strategy and the budget process.[56]

Outside of White House meetings Eisenhower commended Dirksen's defense of the administration on the Senate floor and during his sessions with the Washington press corps. Knowland had seen himself as an independent spokesman of the Republican Senate, but Dirksen defined himself as the White House's primary defender in the Senate. Eisenhower savored the difference. The language in his letters to the minority leader made clear the president's appreciation for Dirksen's efforts. In January he congratulated Dirksen for a floor speech supporting Vice President Nixon: "This is the kind of combative spirit and teamwork I like. Our party will do fine as it generates more of both." When Democrats criticized Eisenhower's leadership, Dirksen was there to support him. On one occasion the president wrote Dirksen that "when there is need for a telling statement, I know of no one who does a better job than you do. . . . You do credit to the Senate's finest traditions of oratorical power!" Eisenhower sometimes joked that Dirksen attacked the opposition with too much fervor. "Please watch your blood pressure," he admonished. "I value your cooperative efforts in this business of government too highly not to urge you to keep yourself fit."[57]

Dirksen was more than a mere spokesman for the White House. He continued to play an important role in the nuts and bolts of controversial legislation. Though after the 1958 elections Eisenhower had targeted the containment of federal spending as his most important political goal, the eventual enactment of the Landrum-Griffin labor bill in September 1959 proved to be the GOP's greatest legislative achievement of the year. The

McClellan committee's public exposure of rampant racketeering in several prominent unions generated enough attention to make some sort of anticorruption labor bill inevitable. With their heavy majorities, Democrats were confident of crafting legislation that appealed to their working-class constituency. Hoping to bolster his reputation as a national leader, presidential aspirant Sen. John F. Kennedy (MA) proposed legislation that would protect union finances and ensure workers the right to vote secretly for union officials.[58]

Despite Kennedy's early momentum and the public's fervor for a labor bill, Dirksen called the Democratic bill a "halfway" measure. In addition to the provisions stipulated in Kennedy's bill, the White House sought legislation to outlaw blackmail picketing and to prohibit secondary boycotts. Kennedy and the Democrats saw these additions as antilabor proposals and fought to push the original bill through the Congress. Dirksen worked to slow its passage. By resorting to a Senate rule that forbade committees to meet without unanimous consent while the Senate was in session (usually beginning at noon), Dirksen frustrated Democratic efforts to hold Labor Committee hearings on the bill.[59]

When the committee did meet, Dirksen thwarted the legislation's progress in other ways. To delay the formation of a quorum, he and other Republicans would wait until the last Democrat appeared before arriving at the committee hearing. After Kennedy spoke for the bill, Dirksen turned to a stack of materials he had brought to the hearing and announced, "Well, we've been considering legislation in the Judiciary Committee that has a bearing on this legislation, particularly as it affects the Northwestern Railway. I have here a history of the Northwestern Railway, which I want to place in the record, if the chairman will permit." He then proceeded to read until noon, when the bell rang and the committee had to adjourn for the opening of the legislative day. His parliamentary scheming aside, Dirksen's most extraordinary gift was to fight to the finish for his political goals without provoking animosity or bitterness from opponents he might need as allies in the future. According to an observer who witnessed the spirit of Dirksen's gamesmanship, "Kennedy was laughing and everybody was broken up. It was just preposterous business." Dirksen's delaying tactics combined with public opinion and what historian R. Alton Lee calls Eisenhower's "superb leadership" to produce a tougher bill that included restrictions on secondary boycotts and gave states more flexibility and leverage to regulate their unions. Happy with the work of his legislative leaders, Eisenhower remembered Landrum-Griffin as "a definite improvement on the legislation previously existing."[60]

If he was satisfied with the results of labor legislation, Eisenhower was devastated by the Senate's 49-to-46 decision to block his nomination of Adm. Lewis L. Strauss to be secretary of commerce. An angry Eisenhower told Ann Whitman that the Senate had disgraced itself and that "this was the most shameful thing that had happened since the attempt to impeach a president many, many years ago." Still bitter ten years later, Eisenhower above all resented the fact that two Republicans (William Langer and Margaret Chase Smith) "deserted" the White House and refused to confirm the nomination: "For neither one of them have I ever had the slightest use since then." Though he had put himself in charge of defending Strauss against a number of attackers, Dirksen made clear after the vote that he bore no hostility for Smith or Langer. He and Majority Leader Johnson emphasized that the parties should put the controversy behind them and get on with the important business of enacting legislation in the national interest.[61]

For Dirksen, the most important development of his first year as minority leader occurred not with any one piece of legislation but with the creation and maturation of a leadership style reflective of the political consensus of the times. Within the GOP conference he emphasized inclusion and participation. Employing well-developed skills of cajolery and persuasion, he pursued party rapport at the expense of a personal agenda. His efforts were not lost on his colleagues. George Aiken, known for his crusty independence and one of the primary leaders of the anti-Dirksen drive, asserted the "Republican side of the aisle has functioned with more harmony this year than I have ever known it to do."[62]

Outside the Republican caucus Dirksen became an integral part of the nation's political establishment. As minority leader, he developed a highly complex but mutually beneficial friendship with his Democratic antagonist, Lyndon Johnson. Dirksen and Johnson interacted daily, both on and off the Senate floor, as the two were responsible for scheduling the legislative agenda and pursuing the interests of their parties. Johnson's legislative assistant George Reedy remembered that the encounters were often unplanned and rarely formal. In fact, the two politicos so understood each other that nods, snorts, and grunts often composed the whole of their conversations. As Reedy recalled, "One of the characteristics of a really good rather than merely capable politician is their capacity to come up with large-scale, complex plans without one single word on paper and practically nothing spoken except 'hello.' It's quite an act, and that's one act at which Dirksen and Johnson were masters."[63]

By the late 1950s both Dirksen and Johnson were centrists, each respectful of the other's efforts to balance the ideological extremes of the Republican and Democratic parties. In his November 1958 meeting with Eisenhower, Johnson emphasized his eagerness to work with Dirksen but expressed "concern" that the Republicans might elect the more conservative Goldwater to the minority leadership. In March 1959 Dirksen stood by as Eisenhower reached across the aisle for bipartisan support from Johnson and House Speaker Sam Rayburn (TX) in the midst of a cold war crisis in Berlin. Without minimizing divisions in the Democratic party upon which he might later capitalize, Dirksen played the centrist's part when he rebuked the more liberal Democratic Advisory Council's (DAC) criticism of Rayburn and Johnson for cooperating with the White House. While the DAC bemoaned the foreign policy consensus of the Eisenhower era, Dirksen praised Rayburn and Johnson for supporting the establishment's conception of the national interest as "the type of thing which makes America great, statesmanship, standing above party politics."[64]

Dirksen's instinct for the center and his apparent fascination with consensus politics extended to the domestic arena. It was no coincidence that just three months after his election as minority leader he began a friendly correspondence with former president and longtime political antagonist Harry Truman. And in October Dirksen clipped a newspaper article that reported Paul Douglas's frustration with Johnson's unwillingness to pursue a more liberal program. Dirksen sent the article to the majority leader, along with a short note of support: "My colleague speaks of being 'watered down to your level.' Nice people, what!" In private correspondence at the end of the 1959 legislative session, the two men exchanged letters that revealed their mutual admiration. First Dirksen wrote Johnson, emphasizing the obligations of and limits to partisanship in the legislative arena: "We have fought—gently—I hope, but always with understanding. We have asserted our various party causes, but always in good grace. We have shared a high mutual pride in the Senate." Johnson immediately replied, underscoring his respect for Dirksen's leadership: "Of the leaders with whom I have served, there have been none who can wield the partisan stiletto with quite the gusto and the zest that you do. But even though the stiletto cuts deep, it never stings." More important than the protestations of a deepening friendship, these two letters expressed a shared belief that a functioning Senate must prove able to both honor and absorb partisan differences.[65]

By 1960 the minority leader's prestige as a national leader had soared dramatically. Political pundits applauded Dirksen's and Johnson's jousting on the Senate floor, a "duel with political daggers, smilingly pulled away just as they are about to pierce the opponent's hide." Dirksen was sixty-four years old and, in the opinion of one journalist, reflected the contradictions of a masterful thespian playing conflicting roles simultaneously: "His expensive clothes [are] invariably disarranged. The fingernails on his large farmer's hands are neatly manicured and his white hair is artfully rumpled. Since he shed forty pounds last year, his face has lost much of its pinkish roundness; now it is burdened with folds of flesh, particularly under the eyes." Those who knew Dirksen best appreciated that he was more than a showman. Rising at 5:30 every working day, he used the early morning hours to draft speeches and to master the endless reports that formed the basis for important legislation.[66]

As Dirksen's reputation brightened in Washington and on the eastern seaboard, his stature dimmed to some degree among his more conservative Illinois constituents. A. M. Kennedy, day managing editor of the *Chicago Tribune,* wrote columnist Walter Trohan about a potential Dirksen feature: "If you and Willard regard Dirksen as a stinker, I would rather pass up a story on him. I'm sure your judgment is correct, and I have no desire to butter up the guy. Could we settle for Goldwater?" By contrast, the *New York Times* regarded Dirksen as "one of Washington's most delightful attractions for sophisticated sightseers." His mesmerizing oratory remained his most striking quality. "He needs," wrote the *Reporter,* "but open his mouth and the great rolling spherical phrases begin to bubble out. . . . Like a mighty pipe organ, he has merely to regulate the wind volume to achieve awesome effects. With his back turned to the Senate press gallery, his barest whisper is clearly audible in its farthest reaches." Though Dirksen employed a number of oratorical techniques, journalist Rowland Evans Jr. remembered that none was more effective than the drink of water. As Dirksen's speeches drew to a close and he summarized his arguments, Evans recalled that he "would take a long, slow drink of water, and then he'd hit them with the punch line.

He used the glass of water for periods, commas, colons, semi-colons, and dashes, and he did it beautifully."[67]

Though he sensed that 1960 was likely to be a "rugged and spirited" session in anticipation of the upcoming presidential campaign, Dirksen continued to function well within the confines of a Washington political establishment that included the principal leaders of both parties. Dirksen invited Johnson and Eisenhower to his fourteenth annual birthday party, a gathering that the *Washington Evening Star* called "the party of the year" because the "glittering assemblage" included senators from both sides of the aisle, foreign ambassadors, members of the White House staff, cabinet members, and union leaders. Eisenhower dropped by on his return from Augusta, and when he arrived, Dirksen suggested to Johnson that "it would be nice for both of us to meet him." The three strode in, Eisenhower in the middle, joking that "birthday parties should be bipartisan."[68]

Despite their genuine efforts at conciliation and cooperation, Johnson and Dirksen had their party priorities to pursue. Since the opening of the Eighty-sixth Congress Republicans and Democrats disagreed most often on budgetary politics. Johnson and the Democrats promoted a more aggressive federal approach to public works, health care for the aged, and defense procurement; Eisenhower and the Republicans just as doggedly sought to contain deficit financing and the attendant weakening of the dollar. As usual, Dirksen gave Eisenhower needed support. Before, he had edged to the center of the political spectrum as the White House absorbed the New Deal reforms into the nation's political economy, but he now cast himself as the principal defender of Eisenhower's "belt tightening" against an antagonistic Democratic Congress infected by "spenderitis." Eisenhower's move to the right after the 1958 elections made easier Dirksen's job of backing the president against his partisan opponents.[69]

Though Johnson and Dirksen clashed most noticeably on economic issues, the two continued to collaborate on matters that transcended party affiliation. When Dirksen traveled to Houston in January 1960 to speak at a GOP dinner, he went out of his way to praise Johnson as a "fair, highly skilled, reasonable, completely cooperative, competent leader who has ever appreciated the fact that reasonable men can cooperate for the benefit of the nation." The two men interacted most conspicuously on civil rights legislation. Under increased pressure from African Americans still denied fundamental freedoms, the Eisenhower administration worked with legislative leaders in both parties to pass a moderate bill that would protect the right to vote. Johnson wanted to enhance his prestige as a national leader in preparation for a probable run at the White House, but neither Johnson nor Dirksen wanted to tear their parties apart on a volatile issue during an election year.[70]

The two leaders cooperated to sidestep the Senate Judiciary Committee and to put civil rights legislation on the Senate floor. When the Senate was debating a minor bill over funding for a Missouri school district, Johnson surreptitiously opened the floor for amendments. Ready for his cue, Dirksen jumped at the chance and introduced the Eisenhower administration's civil rights bill. Southerners decried the "political trick," but Dirksen, praising Johnson's "courage and his fidelity to commitments," explained that the strategy derived from a September 1959 gentleman's agreement he had with Johnson to debate civil rights in the early stages of the second session of the Eighty-sixth Congress.[71]

Though the two worked together on procedural matters, they disagreed sharply over the scope and meaning of the bill. In short, Dirksen wanted a tougher bill than Johnson thought the South could accept. Hammered out with the help of Attorney General William Rogers, the Dirksen legislation sought to impose new criminal penalties for blocking court-ordered or court-approved segregation; to define as federal crimes the bombings of schools and churches, offenses punishable by $5,000 and five years imprisonment; to preserve federal election records for three years and grant the Justice Department the power to investigate; to endorse the *Brown v. Board of Education* decision and grant complying schools technical assistance; to provide federal assistance to servicemen's children seeking to continue their education in areas where public schools were closed because of desegregation disputes; to establish as a statutory agency Eisenhower's committee for creating equal job opportunities under federal contracts; and to impose a federal "referee" plan to protect the right to vote.[72]

Johnson bristled at the scope of the Dirksen proposal. Though he wanted a bill, angry southerners pressured the majority leader to protect them from what Russell decried as the "onrushing federal juggernaut" of election supervision: "The insidious campaign to harass the southern people and to destroy the southern way of life is being pressed against us from all sides." Southerners particularly disliked the administration's endorsement of the *Brown* decision and its intention to provide assistance to desegregating schools. When Dirksen moved to have the Supreme Court ruling entered into the *Congressional Record,* Sen. James O. Eastland (D-LA) thundered, "That's crap. That's tripe. I don't want the *Record* cluttered with such crap."[73] With his range of motion constricted by the inflammatory rhetoric of his southern colleagues, Johnson favored a watered-down House bill that omitted the provision endorsing *Brown* and giving aid to complying schools.

Southerners expressed their objection to any bill by staging a regional filibuster. Hoping to tire the anti–civil rights contingent, Johnson imposed twenty-four-hour sessions for the Senate. He also wanted Dirksen to settle for less than his initial proposal. At first Dirksen refused, but the rigors of the continuing filibuster increased the pressure for a compromise. Sleeping on cots between frequent quorum calls, senators ate breakfast in their offices and changed into fresh shirts brought by their wives. Minority Whip Kuchel called the scene "skid row." Dirksen wrote Roy Wilkins, emphasizing that through the "grueling" effort he hoped to "win a substantial victory." But just as he had done in 1957, Eisenhower lowered the ante. On the same day that Dirksen wrote Wilkins, the president told the legislative leaders that "protecting the sanctity of voting" was his highest priority: "The educational grants . . . were something he had accepted but had not ever deemed essential."[74]

Sensing even before Eisenhower's announcement that he did not have the votes for the original proposal, Dirksen began to cooperate more closely with Johnson on compromise legislation. A liberal bloc of northern Democrats and Republicans voted for cloture to shut off the debate; but holding that their support of the doomed proposal would only fortify the position of the extremists, both Johnson and Dirksen voted against the liberal motion. As the debate continued, the two leaders maneuvered to prevent the introduction of controversial amendments to the compromise legislation. This effort required Dirksen to vote against provisions he had earlier supported, but he "stressed that this agreement was necessary in order to assure any bill at all."[75]

A whittled-down bill focusing almost wholly on voting eventually passed the Senate by a vote of 71 to 18. Dirksen reported Eisenhower's satisfaction with the bill, and the president praised his legislative leaders (especially Dirksen) for their determination to enact voting rights legislation in an election year. Dirksen commended Johnson for his cooperation. Though liberals like Sen. Joe Clark (D-PA) derided the law as "only a pale ghost of our hope of last fall" and Sen. Jacob Javits (R-NY) described the result as "very disappointing," the *New York Times* credited Johnson and Dirksen and concluded that the achievement was a "major milestone on the road to an America in which our reality will more nearly coincide with our basic ideals."[76]

For the rest of the session Dirksen provided Eisenhower with unbroken political support. Only once did the president and his staff express any recorded disappointment with his leadership. In early July Republican senators of all persuasions informed the president that political pressure from home in an election year would prevent them from voting to override Eisenhower's veto of what he deemed to be an inflationary bill increasing federal wages. Dirksen told the president that "one must accept the facts as they actually are, and that based on polls . . . it would be impossible . . . to support the veto." An angry Eisenhower accepted the assessment but told Dirksen and Thruston Morton that "maybe it would be better for the boys on the Hill to impeach him." To his staff he was even more critical. He was "disgusted with the Republican leadership; . . . he does not know why anyone should be a member of the Republican party." Ann Whitman wrote that aide Bryce Harlow "says Dirksen is so tired he is lethargic. . . . Even . . . his speech is affected to the point where you cannot understand him."[77]

Eisenhower's flare-up over the case of federal salaries was the exception rather than the rule. Given the halfhearted and haphazard support he had won from William Knowland, the president prized Dirksen's important promotion of the administration's agenda. Dirksen's speech introducing Eisenhower to the 1960 GOP convention in Chicago revealed the immense transformation that his previous critic had undergone in the eight years of his administration. The Senate minority leader praised Eisenhower's foreign policy, his commitment to world peace and individual freedom. Not surprisingly, Dirksen applauded Eisenhower's "resolve to preserve the solvency of this nation." But he also affirmed the president's conception of a powerful executive charged with the promotion of a modern Republicanism that absorbed but contained the New Deal's expansion of government responsibility: "Finally, he was ever mindful of human needs. So often he uttered the sentiment once expressed by

Lincoln that 'the legitimate object of government is to do for a community of people whatever they need to have done, but cannot do at all, or cannot do so well for themselves, in their separate and individual capacities.' "[78]

After the convention Dirksen gave GOP nominee Richard Nixon solid but unspectacular support. Unlike those on the hard right of the party, Dirksen chose not to criticize Nixon's efforts to soften intraparty differences through his secret meeting with Governor Rockefeller three months before the election. Goldwater called the Nixon-Rockefeller rendezvous a "surrender" and "the Munich of the Republican party." Based on the political style of inclusion and moderation that he pursued after his election as minority leader, Dirksen must have approved of Nixon's attempt to unify the divergent cores of the GOP. Though he made few headlines in the weeks leading up to Nixon's narrow defeat by the Democratic ticket of Kennedy and Johnson, Dirksen employed his pointed sense of humor and showcased the politics of gentility that he had learned to master in a speech to his colleagues in the waning moments of a special postconvention session of Congress: "I wish our distinguished compatriots who seek higher political office everything good—up to a point. I have always been amazed to see what a difference sixteen blocks can make. I extend to the senators the warm hand of fellowship. We want to keep them here. It would be lonesome without my distinguished friend the majority leader, and my distinguished friend from Massachusetts."[79]

For Dirksen, the flood of letters his colleagues sent after Congress adjourned testified to the success of his leadership in the final two years of the Eisenhower presidency. After the 1958 debacle Dirksen and House Minority Leader Halleck proved to be crucial agents in "winning battles for Ike in a Democratic Congress." John Sherman Cooper applauded Dirksen's "magnificent record," and Leverett Saltonstall described him as "always patient and cooperative, and never with any loss of temper or seeming haste." Dirksen won praise from GOP conservatives as well. Karl Mundt held that the "considerable success which we have had in turning back the enemy . . . is attributable to your energetic, consistent, and brilliant leadership of our party." Wallace Bennett (R-UT) wanted to give Dirksen a gold medal for leadership: "I am only sorry that we Republicans didn't have sense enough to give you this job a long time ago."[80]

As these kudos imply, Dirksen developed and honed a highly successful and personal style as minority leader of the Republican Senate. In short, he worked to absorb as many divergent views as possible when discussing party policy with the president. This pursuit of inclusion necessarily meant that he played the center against the party's ideological extremes. Sometimes this meant that he edged toward the liberal wing of the GOP. In one case, for example, he vouched for compromise labor legislation that Goldwater "condemed [sic] . . . for its inadequacies." In other cases, however, he turned more conservative. In civil rights he dropped the fight for a legislative endorsement of the *Brown* decision and the pursuit of federal grants for desegregating schools. His pursuit of the possible could be merciless. In August 1959 Clarence Mitchell came to Dirksen's office to lobby for a civil rights bill that included Section 3 of the 1957 proposal. The minority leader told Mitchell "that they were up against a tough situation and that they would have to take what little bread they could get."[81]

Dirksen's emphasis on politics as the art of the possible buttressed the "liberal consensus"[82] that shaped Washington politics from the 1950s through the early 1960s. Although the national politics of the time delayed the resolution of issues important to conservatives and liberals outside the inner circle, the Washington establishment operated on a shared set of assumptions about the appropriate role of government in post–World War II America. In this sense, Eisenhower's most important political achievement was to put a Republican stamp of approval on the New Deal reforms and the nation's commitment to a policy of worldwide containment. Though he ultimately failed in his effort to remake the Republican party in his own image, Eisenhower achieved a significant political victory by winning Dirksen's unwavering support for the administration's agenda and his acceptance of a powerful presidency. Dirksen's interaction with the Kennedy administration would reveal whether his commitment to the modern presidency was primarily a function of his personal loyalty to Eisenhower as the era's most popular Republican or derived instead from a changed perception of the office and its role in the American political economy.

Everett Dirksen in the 1920s. (EMDC)

Joe McCarthy campaigned for Dirksen in 1950. (EMDC)

Dirksen on the hustings, 1950. (Guy Pasquarella, *Saturday Evening Post*)

Election night in Pekin, November 7, 1950. (EMDC)

Dirksen and Dwight Eisenhower, August 6, 1956. (DDEL)

Dirksen defeated Kentucky's John Sherman Cooper for the minority leadership, January 7, 1950. (EMDC)

Charlie Halleck, Eisenhower, and Dirksen at the White House,
September 14, 1959. (EMDC)

Lyndon Johnson, Dirksen, and Eisenhower at Dirksen's January 5, 1960, birthday party. (*U.S. News and World Report,* Library of Congress)

John Kennedy and the congressional leadership, March 2, 1961. (JFKL)

Dirksen and the suprapartisan establishment at opening day for the Washington Senators, May, 1963. (EMDC)

A somber Dirksen at Kennedy's funeral, November 25, 1963. (*Look*, JFKL)

Johnson and Dirksen at the inaugural luncheon, January 20, 1965.
(Yoichi R. Okamoto, LBJL)

Dirksen in a familiar pose for his impromptu press conferences.
(*Look*, EMDC)

Johnson and Dirksen, eyeball to eyeball, March 31, 1966.
(Yoichi R. Okamoto, LBJL)

Dirksen, Johnson, and Majority Leader Mike Mansfield, October 3, 1966.
(Yoichi R. Okamoto, LBJL)

Johnson checking on Dirksen at Walter Reed Hospital, May 12, 1966.
(Yoichi R. Okamoto, LBJL)

Congressional leaders from both parties caucus in Dirksen's Senate office.
(Senate Historical Office)

Johnson worked feverishly to keep Eisenhower and Dirksen in the administration's camp at the height of the Vietnam War. Here Eisenhower occupies the seat of honor at the White House.

Dirksen in his study at Broad Run Farm near Leesburg, Virginia.
(Senate Historical Office)

Like Johnson, Dirksen was a constant
user of the telephone. (*Look*, EMDC)

4. "He Is My President"

John Kennedy's inauguration changed Everett Dirksen's political career forever. Elected Republican Senate leader just two years earlier, Dirksen represented the conflicting interests of thirty-six GOP senators without the luxury or burden of a popular president fashioning party policy. While Richard Nixon lost to Kennedy by a whisker in the presidential election, the Democrats continued their dominance in the Congress and entered 1961 with majorities of 263 to 174 in the House and 64 to 36 in the Senate. With pundits asserting that "the Republicans are about to become a minority party," Dirksen struggled to keep the GOP from the margins of the nation's political life.[1] His greatest challenge was to ensure that he and the party remained relevant to America's political culture in the face of an agonizing failure to win the White House and a second consecutive drubbing in the congressional elections.

Fortunately for Dirksen, he got along well with John Kennedy. The two had served together in the House and in the Senate, and though they often found themselves on opposing sides of political issues, they respected one another's abilities and enjoyed their times together. Never an ideologue, Kennedy admired Dirksen's malleability. He and George Smathers (D-FL) agreed that "Dirksen was the greatest speaker either of us had ever heard. . . . Both of us heard Dirksen make the best speech for the Marshall aid plan that was ever made in the House and both of us heard Dirksen make the best speech that was probably ever made against the Marshall aid plan when he got to the Senate." Kennedy was close enough to Dirksen to solicit the minority leader's advice after the 1960 Democratic convention. Sensing that his voice was weakening and not likely to endure the rigors of the upcoming campaign, candidate Kennedy asked Dirksen for some assistance. "You keep talking off your vocal cords," Dirksen counseled. "I've been watching you. You need some

143

exercises. You have to throw your voice down to your diaphragm." Dirksen advised Kennedy to hire a voice teacher, and he later marveled at the Democrat's improvement: "By golly, that's what Jack did and he never had any trouble after that."[2]

Robert Kennedy remembered that "Everett Dirksen liked President Kennedy a great deal" and emphasized that the White House bartered patronage and the prestige of the presidency for Dirksen's cooperation during moments of crisis and controversy. Observing that Dirksen was the "most powerful" man in Congress, Sen. Stuart Symington (D-MO) asserted that Kennedy's efforts to cultivate an alliance with "a strong and powerful and highly thought of Republican senator was very much to his own benefit." Most Kennedy loyalists suggest that the president controlled Dirksen and dictated the terms of their relationship. By contrast, journalist David Broder recently recalled that Dirksen "patronized" Kennedy and "didn't take him seriously as a political player. You had the sense that Dirksen thought he could toy with Kennedy in a way that he never would have flattered himself that he could toy with Lyndon Johnson." An understandable reluctance to see his words used against him discouraged Kennedy from writing Dirksen, but the president telephoned the Senate Republican leader frequently. The Illinoisian appreciated Kennedy's personal efforts to maximize their cooperation, remembering that "there was one nice thing about it: every time you carried the torch for him, he would call you up almost immediately to thank you without any intervening operator." On several such occasions Dirksen responded to Kennedy's greetings with "Yes, Jack," only to be reprimanded by Louella for his inappropriate informality.[3]

Dirksen also developed a productive relationship with Johnson's successor as majority leader, Montana's Mike Mansfield. The tempestuous Johnson was blustery and demanding; by contrast, Mansfield was quiet and contemplative. Before he entered politics in 1942, Mansfield had taught Latin American and Far Eastern history at Montana State University. As a senator he never wavered from the completely unpretentious and professorial style he had projected as a teacher. He smoked a pipe and dined every morning with the most reflective GOP senator, Vermont's George Aiken. Despite his laconic personality—he preferred to answer complicated questions with a simple yes or no—Mansfield was determined to work closely with his Republican counterpart. Mansfield regularly deflected praise and attention to Dirksen and cooperated at every turn. He referred to his "intimate" friendship with Dirksen and recalled the multidimensional nature of the minority leader's personality. Though Dirksen "never avoided a press conference" and "did a good deal . . . of acting on the floor of the Senate," he did a "good deal less acting in the back rooms when we met to discuss the potentials."[4]

Dirksen's personal relationships with Kennedy and Mansfield would count for little, however, if the minority leader could not command the support of his party in the Congress. In a postelection strategy session at the White House, Dirksen and House Minority Leader Charles Halleck complained to President Eisenhower that Nixon's defeat meant that the GOP had no viable forum for promoting party doctrine. At the same time, both leaders appreciated the opportunity that Kennedy's victory presented for their personal advancement and emphasized to Eisenhower that as congressional leaders they expected to represent the GOP's "center of gravity" for the foreseeable future.[5]

Even though he privately worried that Dirksen and Halleck would ignore the input of other party leaders, Eisenhower suggested that they continue their weekly press conferences during congressional sessions. Before taking questions from the media, Dirksen and Halleck attended regular meetings with the chairman of the Republican National Committee (RNC) and with other GOP congressional leaders. At these sessions the participants hammered out statements that were often responses to White House domestic policy proposals. After the leaders caucused, Dirksen and Halleck would meet reporters and cameramen for a wide-ranging press conference. Networks edited the film for the evening news. On one level, the production was little more than a "creation of the television age" that "provided a regular forum for articulating the political philosophies of the party out of power." By trying to control the flow of information, the GOP congressional leaders were also working to block the emergence of independent and more ideological Republican organizations, given that the Democratic Advisory Council, in their minds, had undermined Democratic unity in the Eisenhower years.[6]

Tom Wicker of the New York Times dubbed the production the "Ev and Charlie Show." Cartoonists like Herblock lampooned the vaudeville act, portraying Dirksen with a sad, sagging face, and unkempt hair and Halleck with a puffy profile. One caption read, "In ten thousand words or less, Ev—is it true that you're verbose?" Never the closest of associates, Halleck and Dirksen fought each other for the limelight. The effect, observed one GOP insider, was the "increasingly evident irritation between Everett and Charlie" and "a serious image problem for the party." Liberal Republicans lambasted the production for ideological reasons. Sensing that Dirksen and Halleck represented only a narrow band of GOP thinking, Jacob Javits (R-NY) proposed a more representative shadow cabinet to tap into "the best minds in the party" and to generate an "imaginative, creative force . . . to mold and guide our thinking in the critical years ahead." Conservatives vented their own frustrations. Describing Dirksen and Halleck as little more than "able technicians," the *National Review* held that the GOP's congressional leadership was unable to revitalize and redirect the party "towards ordered freedom in the machine age." Dirksen had not the "remotest idea how to handle President Kennedy" and his "photogenic stewardship." In the estimation of the *National Review*, the end result was an unprecedented accumulation of power in the executive.[7]

More sympathetic journalists appreciated that the two leaders were working to "find the elusive but important distinction between opposition and obstruction." Halleck bristled at the treatment he received from "the smart-assed reporters that kept trying to ridicule us." William Knowland shared Halleck's contempt for the media. David Broder remembered that during press conferences "you would see the color start to come up from the base of [Knowland's] neck and his whole face would get red. It didn't take much to set him off." From his standpoint, Dirksen loved the attention. Always at home on the stage, he treasured his role as party showman. He developed mutually beneficial relationships with Washington reporters who valued his copy and kept him in the news. He showed an appealing ability to laugh at himself and shrugged off the gibes and digs from unfriendly critics. Early in the history of the show, Dirksen appeared on stage with an enormous pair of black horn-rimmed glasses that covered the bags under his eyes. He told the press corps that they were his television spectacles. Prompted by a question, he stuck his fingers through the frame and, referring to his producers and the president's celebrated daughter, said, "They say they make me look young—and I have a vanity. Of course I can't expect to look as good as Caroline."[8]

Asked if the constant criticisms from the press bothered him, Dirksen insisted that "it doesn't offend me at all, any more than when you refer to some of those great duos in American life, like corn beef and cabbage, ham and eggs, the Cherry Sisters, and Gallagher and Shean." Even so, he could hardly ignore the relentless grumbling from his party colleagues. Although these critics expressed their frustrations with Dirksen's and Halleck's weekly antics before the camera, every Senate Republican supported Dirksen's leadership. Essentially, the dissatisfaction that both liberal and conservative Republicans articulated reflected the intraparty conflict that had existed in the GOP even before Dirksen's election to the Senate in 1950. An astute observer of ongoing party skirmishes, Dirksen saw his "first responsibility" as absorbing the differences within the caucus "to develop a degree of unity and cohesion . . . to make a militant phalanx."[9]

Dirksen's command of the GOP caucus was even more remarkable when one considers the party's fragmented leadership structure. Senate Democrats consolidated power in their floor leader, who typically chaired both the Democratic Conference and the Democratic Policy Committee, but Senate Republicans distributed authority among the floor leader, chairman of the Republican Conference, and chairman of the Republican Policy Committee. Until Dirksen emerged as minority leader, the most influential GOP senators had often chaired the GOP's Policy Committee.[10] Beginning in the Kennedy years, Dirksen employed his unique personal skills to achieve his most important goals and to ensure that he was the most prominent and respected Republican in Washington.

At the same time, he continued to win open support from former critics who had doubted his commitment to a unified party. Margaret Chase Smith told an audience that Dirksen "is more personable and gets more response from Republican senators than Senator Knowland ever did. Dirksen is much more thoughtful and adjustable to current needs. His whole attitude is one who realizes one must give in order to get." Wallace Bennett (R-UT) resented Knowland's attempt to run a "one-man show." Dirksen, by contrast, practiced inclusion by relying on personal skills that escaped his stodgy predecessor. Carl Curtis (R-NE) once recalled that Dirksen "never seemed to be in a hurry. If I went to see him with something I was concerned about, or meant a great deal to my state, he never put you off. He would stand there and listen and hear you clear out before he opened his mouth." Dirksen continued to give up favored committee assignments in order to ensure that his colleagues achieved the prominence necessary to win reelection. When John G. Tower (R-TX) won a special election in 1961, Dirksen fulfilled a personal promise and gave "a deeply grateful" Tower his own seat on the Banking and

Currency Committee, a move that he expected "will be both fruitful and beneficial to Texas." One border-state Republican called Dirksen a "great conciliator" and pointed to Dirksen's oratorical skills as a method by which he built up precious capital for later favors: "I never wanted anybody to come in from outside the state to speak when I was a candidate, because I knew the issues better than they did. But with Dirksen, he could come in and convince everybody that he understood the problems of the state. He'd studied them."[11]

To be sure, leadership had its perquisites. He settled into a Capitol Hill office that commanded a magnificent view of the Washington Monument and was just steps from the Senate chamber. During Dirksen's tenure, the walls were adorned with portraits of Lincoln and multiple clocks with rows of lights to remind him of what was happening on the floor. Compared to the carved mahogany doors and glittering chandeliers in Johnson's various offices, which some people called the Taj Mahal, Dirksen's quarters were notably spare. Because every politician knows exactly how much space his rival has, Dirksen must have bristled at Democratic extravagance.[12] Even so, he used his modest office and his fun-loving personality to build up goodwill in the Republican caucus.

Dirksen's responsibilities as minority leader crammed his schedule and prevented him from traveling as much as he had earlier in his career. In Washington he promoted after-hours socializing to keep his outnumbered troops together. Dirksen had joined the Congressional Country Club outside Washington after being elected Republican whip in 1957. As minority leader, he used his membership to organize cocktail parties for the senatorial caucus, and on occasion, for their spouses. He and Louella had always enjoyed drinks in the evening. Dirksen explained to a reporter that "we have a standing rule in our family. My wife sticks to champagne and I prefer a fellow by the name of Jonathan Daniels." Thanking a Senate colleague for a Christmas gift, he wrote that "champagne is Mrs. Dirksen's favorite vegetable." The social gatherings he organized, therefore, were merely an extension of an instinctive preference for informal meetings at the cocktail hour and were designed to inspire esprit de corps in the ranks. "You'd be surprised," he maintained, "at the amount of goodwill [the parties] produced. You'd be surprised at how chummy they get at a party with a drink in their hands."[13]

On Capitol Hill Dirksen cordoned off a private section of his office and named it the Twilight Lodge. Similar to Sam Rayburn's famous

Board of Education, the Twilight Lodge served as Dirksen's bar where he entertained Senate colleagues with drinks at the close of the legislative day. The most distinctive feature in the Twilight Lodge was a clock with each hour replaced with the number five. According to Tower, "No matter where the hands stood, it was always after five o'clock and time for a drink." Dirksen's aides John Gomien and Oliver Dompierre mixed the drinks. Dirksen himself was partial to bourbon, but he provided other beverages. After concluding the formal business of the day, Dirksen would tell his colleagues, "Boys, the bar is open." Tower recalled that Dirksen would "have a few drinks and talk—about marigolds and such—and on about the fourth drink he'd come around to the issue." One Senate staffer remembered that "he drank a lot, but he wasn't an alcoholic." Apparently always under control, Dirksen was representative of a Capitol Hill milieu where "drinking was a social convention, almost a ritual." Notwithstanding the "social coloration," the activities at the Twilight Lodge were meaningful in their own right. According to one scholar, "The underlying logic was the building and maintenance of legislative coalitions."[14]

In early January 1961 Dirksen addressed the GOP caucus on being reelected minority leader. His remarks recalled the theme he had emphasized when he and Halleck left a strategy session at the White House with Eisenhower. Dirksen told reporters that the GOP intended to embark on a course of "responsible and constructive opposition" to Kennedy's domestic program. While the party would cooperate in passing legislation "in the national interest," the line would be drawn whenever the Democrats proposed measures that led to "reckless and irresponsible spending." Dirksen echoed these comments when he addressed his GOP colleagues. Because the 1960 election was so close, Democrats could not meaningfully speak of a mandate. The message, Dirksen insisted, was that "there was no real desire for a change." The Republican strategy would be to "dedicate ourselves to the national well being without guile or rancor, without frustration or bitterness. . . . Where we honestly differ from the administration, we should seek to modify policies and proposals."[15]

Dirksen's nonadversarial conception of the opposition differed markedly from Robert Taft's. Dirksen promised to work with the White

House to secure legislation in the national interest and to offer alternative bills when the two sides disagreed; Taft simply declared that "the business of the opposition is to oppose. Minority leaders . . . have no responsibility for presenting a program. Their role is one of opposition and criticism." Dirksen based his own strategy on the belief that "in time[s] of national crisis, the minority party should meet the challenge of the time and embrace the opportunity to render unselfish and loyal services to the country." According to Dirksen, the feverish emergencies of the cold war encouraged and even required interparty cooperation at defining times. But even during the height of World War II and the Korean War, Taft and his supporters never wavered in their commitment to principled criticism of the party in power. Interestingly, Dirksen in 1950 agreed with Taft and argued that the "duty of the opposition is to oppose."[16] But by 1961 he had been co-opted by an establishment that celebrated pragmatic compromise and ridiculed ideological obstinacy. Dirksen's cooperative approach marked a fundamental change in the GOP's interpretation of the opposition and the party's role in national politics.

Essentially, the Dirksen-Halleck plan marked the seamless continuation of the suprapartisan interaction between Eisenhower and Democratic congressional leaders Sam Rayburn and Lyndon Johnson, especially in the field of foreign policy. Although ideologues in both parties disagreed with and fought the politics of the status quo, the Washington establishment survived the Eisenhower-Kennedy transition intact. Dirksen's strategy of cooperation and constructive opposition dampened the intraparty conflict between GOP liberals and conservatives that might have exploded had he sought any other course. Kennedy's pursuit of Dirksen's support underscored the president's own commitment to the politics of foreign policy at the expense of an ambitious domestic agenda that would have fractured the Democratic party. Moreover, the codependent relationship that Kennedy maintained with Dirksen increased the latter's prominence in the national arena and provided the minority leader with ample opportunities to confound his critics and frustrate his friends in the years ahead. Most significant to the history of the modern Republican party, Dirksen's relationship with Kennedy affirmed the tenets of the modern and activist presidency, even when a Democrat occupied the White House.

Dirksen's strategy for collaborative opposition placed a premium on positive personal interaction with the Kennedy administration. Though he was the most senior Republican on the Judiciary Committee, Dirksen handled Robert Kennedy's nomination for attorney general with the delicate care of one committed to remaining in the good graces of the new administration. He objected to the youthful Kennedy's lack of experience and sensed that the president's brother might not have the administrative expertise to run the Justice Department; nevertheless, Dirksen upheld the president's entitlement to "pick" his "official family" and in Kennedy's hearings before the committee looked at the nominee and remarked, "I could almost say my friend Bob."[17]

After visiting Dirksen's office in February, White House aide Mike Manatos reported that the minority leader "was most cordial and assures me that he will cooperate with the administration to bring about needed legislation." Dirksen underlined one quid pro quo for his constructive attitude. According to Manatos, Dirksen made clear his interest in GOP patronage positions that would provide him with the necessary links to government agencies and enhance his prestige in Washington politics. At a more conspicuous level, Dirksen benefited from the president's popularity. When Kennedy hosted a purely social bipartisan leadership luncheon that started off with a round of martinis, Dirksen (without discussing the beverages) chose to detail the affair to his Illinois constituents in a radio-television broadcast.[18]

Dirksen's cooperation with the White House did not mean that he acted as Kennedy's Republican leader in the Senate. Outside the realms of cold war crises and political protocol, Dirksen enthusiastically embraced his role as a partisan fighter. He remained wedded to traditional GOP ideas such as a balanced budget, a limited role for the federal government in the nation's social and economic affairs, and strident opposition to communist expansion. Although he acknowledged that Kennedy's inaugural address was "inspiring" and "a very compact message of hope," he claimed that the president's agenda for a New Frontier would require new and unwanted taxes: "Look at education—two-and-one-half billion—a billion for this, a billion for that, a billion for something else. Three to five billion for public works. You haven't got any budget balance left. You'll be deeply in the red."[19]

Despite his opposition to the legislative thrust of the New Frontier, the record shows that Dirksen maintained open lines of communication with the Kennedy White House. Philosophically, the two men were more similar than distinct. The fiercely pragmatic and nonideological Kennedy emphasized the importance of "getting the country moving again," but his early domestic agenda was only a modest departure from Eisenhower's commitment to absorbing and containing the New Deal reforms without jeopardizing the budget. Dirksen admitted as much when he allowed that "thus far there has been a greater adherence to the middle of the road than I anticipated when I first went through that platform." In fact, Dirksen's language mirrored the consensus rhetoric of the times. He lectured the Republican faithful that "there should be no defeatism. Let's go right down the middle of the road. . . . We know that if they push the New Frontier too far we will be ready to push it right back."[20]

Because of Dirksen's temperamental affinity for the new administration, he proved responsive to Kennedy's idealism and respected the president's early popularity. In a March meeting of the Republican congressional leadership, Dirksen reported on his meeting with Sargent Shriver, Kennedy's designee to head the Peace Corps. The session was primarily informational, enabling Dirksen to clear up points of confusion and relay the explanations to his colleagues. Rep. Charles B. Hoeven (R-IA) argued that the party should mount an uncompromising attack on the Peace Corps, concluding that "this is a Kennedy program and . . . a pilot project indicates Republican approval of the program." Dirksen condemned Hoeven's hard-shell attitude: "Republicans cannot and should not take a negative approach to this program. . . . It does have appeal to young people, as well as the churches."[21]

Dirksen's sympathy for the Peace Corps represents one of those rare occasions when he went out of his way to challenge a fellow party leader on behalf of Kennedy's domestic agenda. Much more common was his steady cooperation in the realm of foreign policy. Kennedy assiduously courted Dirksen's support, inviting him to join the president's party at the Washington Senators' opening-day baseball game and arranging personal briefings for the minority leader at the White House. For Kennedy, these occasions served to keep Dirksen informed of foreign policy developments and aware that the White House relied on a bipartisan approach to the policy of global containment. On one occasion he showed the minority leader a letter from French president Charles de Gaulle, emphasizing that the views of America's allies often complicated issues and discouraged otherwise attractive courses of action.[22] Even though Dirksen was rarely asked to contribute to the making of foreign policy, these meetings signaled that he was a trusted and privileged member of the

Washington establishment. Moreover, his private interaction with Kennedy enhanced his prestige in the GOP caucus and made him a key disseminator of information to his Republican colleagues.

Kennedy's pursuit of Dirksen's cooperation paid immediate dividends in the aftermath of the Bay of Pigs fiasco in April 1961. In a plan begun under President Eisenhower, the Central Intelligence Agency (CIA) trained a group of Cuban exiles to invade their homeland and overthrow Fidel Castro, a revolutionary with radical communist leanings. Though the scheme was developed in another administration and was badly flawed from its inception, Kennedy made himself more vulnerable to criticism by calling off American air cover designed to protect the exiles as they landed on the Cuban beachhead. In addition to briefing Eisenhower at Camp David and former vice president Nixon at the White House, Kennedy called a bipartisan legislative meeting as a way to control the political damage the Cuban disaster precipitated.

Dirksen backed Kennedy and urged a "proper kind of restraint . . . on the part of the loyal opposition." Moreover, he gave a ringing endorsement of the modern presidency's pattern of taking increasing responsibility for the development and execution of foreign policy: "Since foreign policy is under his direction, I do not like to get wires crossed; I like to maintain that position of support where foreign matters are involved. . . . We recognize the role of the president . . . and we have averred over and over in the course of these sessions that we mean to support him when a decision has finally been made." In his meeting with Nixon, a distraught Kennedy laid bare his relative indifference to his domestic agenda and implied that Dirksen's support in times of crisis meant far more than his consistent disapproval of the New Frontier at home. "It really is true," Kennedy insisted to his former rival, "that foreign affairs is the only important issue for a president to handle, isn't it? I mean who gives a shit if the minimum wage is $1.15 or $1.25, in comparison to something like this?"[23]

By early May the GOP leaders were eager to lash out at the White House for the Bay of Pigs failure. But at a Gettysburg meeting Eisenhower cautioned Dirksen and Halleck to maintain their statesmanlike restraint. He downplayed the importance of a wide-ranging investigation. "Don't go back and rake over the ashes," he warned, "but see what we can do better in the future. . . . I would say the last thing you want is to have a full investigation and lay this out on the record." Dirksen's reluctance to heed the call on both sides of the aisle for a congressional investigation protected the Washington establishment and widened the gap in foreign policymaking between the president and the foot soldiers on Capitol Hill. Dirksen believed that if Congress had to get involved, any effort at oversight should be conducted by "a few men of knowledge and discernment" who might conduct "a quiet investigation" and report to the president.[24]

Although GOP elites rallied behind Kennedy in the wake of the Bay of Pigs, they stepped up their criticism of his domestic policy agenda. Dirksen continued to doubt the existence of any mandate that might threaten the status quo and reported to Eisenhower that "not one of the Kennedy proposals have [sic] generated any enthusiasm on either the Democratic or the Republican side nor can we find any evidence of real support for the Kennedy program by the American people." To Dirksen, the administration's adoption of "welfare statism" and deficit spending was a poor imitation of the agendas pursued by former Democratic presidents: "It may be called the New Frontier, but the Kennedy program is the old New Deal taken out of an old warming oven. It was hot stuff twenty-five years ago but time has passed it by."[25]

In Washington, meanwhile, Dirksen qualified his support of Kennedy's foreign policy. Showing understandable signs of discomfort as leader of the loyal opposition, he drew an imaginary and disingenuous line between his principled politics of suprapartisan statesmanship and the brass-knuckled brawling that GOP backbenchers encouraged. He admitted that some Republicans resented his defense of the administration and that his course might not have been rigorous enough to "assuage" these hard-liners. He then resorted to his rhetorical skills in order to keep the administration's troubles in the news without betraying his supposed commitment to back the president "in a world that is filled with fear and madness." Dirksen insisted that he would be neither "venal" nor "narrowly partisan," that he would not "take the situation in Laos and assail the administration for timidity." He would muffle the "blundering incompetence" of the Bay of Pigs, and he would avoid any reference to the recent erosion of American "prestige" abroad. Instead, the minority leader accepted his cold war role "to uphold the hands of the president and the commander in chief . . . to manifest to all the world that this is still a united country even though the decision may not accord with the views that we have expressed before."[26]

Dirksen's posturing was by no means a ringing endorsement of the popular president's leadership, but his public statements were a sharp departure from the GOP's savage attack on Harry Truman's handling of foreign policy crises in the early 1950s. Politically, the minority leader's slap at the White House achieved two goals. First, Dirksen insulated himself from critics who charged that he was little more than a Republican mouthpiece for the administration. Second, he let Kennedy know that his cooperation was conditional and would be contingent on the president's popularity and his commitment to the Cold War consensus that had dominated national politics since the latter half of the 1940s.

Despite his thinly veiled support of the administration, Dirksen used the international emergencies of the day to argue against an ambitious social and economic agenda. To the minority leader, the rash of troubles abroad and the overriding necessity of a balanced budget left little space for domestic programs close to the hearts of liberal Democrats and Republicans. "We have so many crises in far-away places," Dirksen insisted, that "emphasis will have to be on guns. We are going to put some emphasis . . . on ways the domestic budget and so-called welfare items can be trimmed in view of the delicate international situation."[27] Dirksen cast himself in the role of a committed patriot dedicated to protecting the nation's security. He conveniently used troubles abroad to fight against a liberal social agenda that he had long found repugnant. More important to the history of the GOP, Dirksen's accession to an arms buildup muted debate on Capitol Hill and undermined Eisenhower's warning to guard against the rise of a military-industrial complex. Not less than six months after Eisenhower left the White House, GOP congressional leaders sacrificed Ike's most challenging legacy to the party and the country. This was a self-serving political decision that would eventually expose the glaring contradiction between the GOP's ostensible commitment to fiscal responsibility and the reality of ballooning defense expenditures.

Kennedy was more concerned about the politics of the here and now, and he was grateful for Dirksen's support in troubled times. Dirksen and Halleck stood in the president's corner during the second major international crisis of 1961. Beginning in 1959 Soviet premier Nikita Khrushchev had threatened to sign a separate peace treaty with East Germany. Such a course would have halted the flow of refugees from the East to the West but also would have enabled the Soviets to cut off Western access to Berlin, which lay in the East. In the minds of many Americans, capitulation to the Soviets on the issue of Berlin would result in an irreparable loss of the nation's prestige and would send a signal of rank timidity to its European allies. Khrushchev intensified the pressure during a Vienna summit meeting with Kennedy, who, like Eisenhower, refused to negotiate Western access to Berlin. Instead, Kennedy mobilized 120,000 reservists, requested more funds for national defense, and promoted a widespread fallout shelter program. With Soviet and American armies occupying the same city and squared off against each other, the threats and counterthreats generated one of the most explosive crises of the cold war.[28]

Before the crisis reached its fever pitch, Dirksen had worked behind the scenes to ensure that the situation received adequate national attention. After an extended briefing for congressional leaders at the White House, he leaked information to the *Chicago Tribune* revealing the seriousness of the issue. Later he teamed up with the midwestern daily to criticize Kennedy for softness on the Berlin issue. By highlighting intraparty disagreements across the aisle, Dirksen's jockeying probed Democratic vulnerabilities over the crisis and pointed at the same time to the GOP's loyalty and patriotism. Republicans were especially critical of Majority Leader Mansfield, who argued that the West should press for nothing more than a guarantee of Berlin's status as a free city. Most obnoxious to the GOP was the implication that the hard-fought victories of World War II might be frittered away in a diplomatic free-for-all. After they were convinced that the president had stiffened his resolve, Republican leaders Dirksen and Halleck pledged Kennedy their "complete" support, but they warned the White House to cut its domestic programs to offset increased defense expenditures.[29]

Khrushchev escalated tensions by cordoning off East Berlin with a concrete wall. Even though the Republican leaders suggested that Kennedy and the Democratic leaders in Congress had invited the communists to seal the border in order to defuse the crisis, Dirksen and Halleck backed the administration's acceptance of the wall and underlined the importance "for this nation's officials to speak with one voice of strength and determination." The party in power, however, had wavered under pressure. "We can only wonder," the two minority leaders mused, "what the world thinks when President Kennedy correctly announces we are going to stand firm on our Berlin commitments only to have important Democratic spokesmen make statements which are at variance with that policy."[30] In later years Dirksen came to perfect the technique of exposing rifts between the president and congressional Democrats over divisive foreign policy issues.

Later in the summer Dirksen and Halleck sharply criticized the State Department. Though Undersecretary of State Chester Bowles enjoyed only marginal prestige in administration circles and made little progress with his proposals, the patrician New Englander promoted a policy that would have granted equal UN representation to Communist China and to Nationalist China. Dirksen discarded the expectation that such a move would enable the United States to play Russia's and China's rival ambitions against one another. Instead, he maintained that America would suffer an incalculable loss of prestige and urged the White House to cease its practice of "playing Russian roulette" with America's China policy. Dirksen and Halleck gave substance to their rhetoric by introducing a congressional resolution opposing the UN's recognition of Communist China. In July both the House and the Senate passed the resolution by unanimous votes. The two leaders later heard of a White House shake-up that would have removed the embattled Bowles from the State Department. The liberal and effete Bowles was a threat to Dirksen's version of the containment consensus and to Kennedy's preference for men of action. The undersecretary resisted the move and succeeded in achieving a delay until November, but Dirksen made it clear that Bowles's ideas on China policy were unacceptable: "We know that Mr. Bowles was recently scheduled to be fired but was not. We do suggest, however, that he either be completely muzzled or removed from the china shop of diplomacy lest he break something really costly."[31]

By exaggerating the extent of the White House's reevaluation of its China policy and by scapegoating one of the State Department's most liberal members, Dirksen and other GOP supporters of Nationalist China stifled the New Frontier's remaining sources of dynamism and innovation. Though Dirksen had fulfilled his pledge and stood with the president in times of international crisis, the minority leader discarded almost every creative idea and discouraged any alteration of the foreign policy status quo. In short, Dirksen provided one of the "countervailing forces . . . which made new initiatives in China policy difficult." To a more sympathetic reporter, the overall effect of the GOP leaders' efforts "has been to stiffen the president's stand."[32]

As the first session of the Eighty-seventh Congress drew to a close,

Dirksen faced a difficult decision regarding his political future. Though he was now at the height of his political power, his health had suffered badly from the endless hours he had logged on Capitol Hill. In July he was hospitalized for eight days with an ulcer, and he used that time to "iron out all the aches and pains which have been accumulating over the year." Citing his declining health and their lack of time together, Louella mounted a private campaign to secure Dirksen's retirement from public life: "For the first time in our married life I strongly opposed his running again. In fact, I had fully made up my mind that I was going to put my foot down. I would not permit him to run for reelection."[33]

Moreover, Dirksen worried that his time away from Illinois dimmed his appeal with the voters. Writing privately, the minority leader noted that "the home folks clobber me to come back." But his connections to the Washington establishment tempered any resentment the voters may have harbored. Eisenhower boosted Dirksen's chances for reelection when the former president traveled to Chicago and spoke at a $100-a-plate testimonial dinner for Dirksen's campaign. Though he departed from the prepared text that Dirksen's office had provided him, Eisenhower praised the minority leader as a "great leader" and the "statesman" from Illinois. In his most partisan speech since leaving the White House, Eisenhower assailed the Kennedy administration for its indifference to the freedom of the individual and ridiculed the "towering waves of conflict that create the cleavage between the factions and divisions of the party now in power." Six days later Dirksen returned home to Pekin and overruled his wife's objections by announcing his bid for reelection. In a maudlin speech, in which he explored his love of gardening and the "majesty of the universe," the sixty-five-year-old Dirksen insisted that little had changed since his first bid for public office in 1927. He was, he insisted, "just a baker boy who found out long ago that you can't fool the people."[34]

The most intriguing aspect of Dirksen's evolving relationship with Kennedy was that the two men interacted at a number of different levels. To most Americans, Dirksen was little more than the loyal leader of the opposition. In the election year of 1962 the nation's pundits expected "a long and bitterly fought political match" as the two parties worked to distinguish themselves from one another and to accumulate as much political capital as possible. Dirksen savored the attention he received as the GOP's partisan leader in the Senate. He ripped into Kennedy's State of the Union address with characteristic gusto. Especially obnoxious was the president's request for standby authority to cut income taxes to pull the country out of recession. Dirksen bristled at this presidential grab at congressional power, arguing that the proposal "appears as a request for Congress to surrender its authority . . . and would seem to be a movement in the direction of centralized executive power." Overall, the speech reminded the homespun Dirksen of a "Sears Roebuck catalog with all the old prices marked up."[35]

Dirksen continued his rhetorical assault when he referred to the administration's increased budget as "heading us forward to the Leviathan state." The New Frontier, he charged, "has turned out to be nothing more than a bright ribbon wrapped around the oldest and most discredited political package on earth—the centralization of power." In a rare political speech outside Washington, Dirksen traveled to Kennedy country in Boston and pilloried the White House for violating traditional notions of American liberty: "The trend today . . . is toward power and control. . . . Let it then be emphatically and unequivocally said that control is the essence of socialism."[36] But behind closed doors Dirksen continued to pursue a more cooperative and symbiotic relationship with Kennedy, especially on the cold war foreign policy issues that to the establishment outstripped other concerns in their vital importance to America's political life.

When Kennedy called a bipartisan leadership meeting to discuss the crisis in Laos and the potential involvement of American troops, Dirksen referred to a Republican National Committee newsletter attacking the president's equivocation as little more than meaningless political posturing. "In essence," Dirksen emphasized, "it was clear that the Republicans fully supported the president's position." Just one week later he reported to the Republican Policy Committee that President Kennedy hoped members of Congress would not "get too talkative" about the deteriorating situation in Laos and Vietnam. Veteran Capitol Hill observers correctly sensed that Kennedy's pursuit of Dirksen's cooperation blunted potential criticism from GOP ranks. One journalist noted that it was widely held in Washington that "Dirksen is Kennedy's minority leader."[37]

The president was astute enough to cooperate with the Republican opposition in order to build up capital for future use. In early January

Dirksen scheduled a confidential breakfast meeting with Kennedy. Eisenhower had asked Dirksen to intervene on behalf of Sherman Adams, his former White House chief of staff who was under intense investigation by Robert Kennedy's Justice Department. Kennedy and the lawyers at Justice were probing the relationship between Adams and Bernard Goldfine, the Boston textile manufacturer whose gift of a vicuna coat had forced Adams to resign his post in 1958. Goldfine now claimed that Adams had received "more than $150,000 in cash over the period of about five years." Though an acute and terminal case of arteriosclerosis made Goldfine an unreliable witness, a trail of cashier's checks seemed to substantiate the charges. According to the secretary of the Senate, Bobby Baker, who heard the story from Dirksen, Eisenhower called the minority leader and reported that Adams's wife (whom Baker referred to as Mrs. Jones in his book) feared her husband was on the verge of committing suicide. An "embarrassed" Eisenhower reluctantly telephoned Dirksen and asked him to get a commitment from Kennedy: "I'd like you to ask President Kennedy, as a personal favor to me, to put the Jones indictment in the deep freeze. You have the authority to advise him he'll have a blank check in my bank if he'll grant me this favor."[38]

Dirksen told Baker that he and Kennedy strolled into the Rose Garden to make the deal. Back in the Oval Office the president called his brother and ordered him to kill the indictment. Dirksen remembered a heated telephone exchange, which ended when Kennedy told the attorney general: "I'm president. If you can't comply with my request then your resignation will be accepted." From his Senate office Dirksen wrote to Eisenhower informing him that he had seen Kennedy "about one of your former staff members. . . . I believe everything is in order." A grateful Eisenhower replied in kind: "I am particularly indebted to you for following through."[39]

Little that occurred between Dirksen and Kennedy in 1962 can be seen outside the context of the midterm elections. Though he flatly and repeatedly denied the charge, Dirksen made his positive interaction with the ebullient and popular president a cornerstone of his reelection bid. On its face, his strategy seemed misguided. After UN ambassador Adlai Stevenson decided not to enter the race, Chicago's Democratic machine nominated Rep. Sidney Yates as Dirksen's opponent. From the beginning Yates ran as a full-time supporter of President Kennedy. According to *Congressional Quarterly,* Yates voted with the administration 97.5 percent of the time, a score that tallied second in the House among committed supporters of the White House agenda.[40]

Dirksen's codependent relationship with Kennedy irked a number of influential Republicans and Democrats. Paul Douglas resented the president's high regard for Dirksen. The liberal Illinois Democrat remembered that as early as 1960 Kennedy had told him that "Dirksen was about the best Republican Senate leader that we could expect." In February Douglas's office called to apprise the White House of Dirksen's tactics and to criticize the administration for granting the minority leader plum patronage appointments in an election year. According to a sympathetic Kennedy staffer, "Dirksen is making a show in Illinois—describing himself as a Kennedy man. This is making it very difficult for Sid Yates."[41]

Dirksen expended endless energy balancing his contradictory roles of party leader and loyal supporter of the president in times of crisis. One perceptive observer argued that "the tactics that win him Senate acclaim cost him support as national GOP leader." The heavy Democratic majority in the Senate and the president's continuing popularity encouraged "conciliation and cooperation" at the expense of "uncompromising partisanship." Rather than standing on a set of principled and articulated ideals, Dirksen relied primarily on instinct to determine his position on developing issues and unpredictable events. On one occasion he joked with reporters that he flipped a coin to decide on a course of action. On one side of what he called his "electric decision processor" was the inscription "go ahead, do it"; the other read, "the hell with it." Dirksen maintained that "ever since this equipment was installed, I've wasted much less time in making up my mind." Though his actions were not as chaotic and random as he implied, there was no blueprint for his leadership. He continued to write his own speeches, making him "probably . . . better versed in the details of more legislation than any other senator." His days, however, were grueling. They often ran from 5:30 A.M. to 10:30 P.M., with occasional time out in the evening to take in an episode of *Tales of Wells Fargo* or *Bonanza*.[42]

In spring 1962 Dirksen solidified his position as an almost indispensable member of Washington's political establishment. He moved with the greatest of ease from a partywide effort to discredit liberal Democrats for their "surrender" foreign policy to hobnobbing with the president at a social occasion to providing him finally with the pivotal support necessary to pass a measure deemed critical by the White House. Conservative Republicans like Barry Goldwater had long been tarnished by their refusal to condemn the ideals of the John Birch Society, a group led by Robert Welch that grew in importance in the early 1960s. Welch and his followers charged that Eisenhower was a communist and that liberalism was little more than a treasonous plot engineered by power-hungry Democrats and unwitting Republicans to lead the United States into the company of communist countries. Mainstream dailies and journals like the *New York Times, Life, Newsweek, Look,* and the *Saturday Evening Post* ran articles denouncing the extremism propounded by the Birchers. Kennedy's Justice Department targeted the society as "a matter of concern."[43]

Increasingly uncomfortable with any ideology outside the mainstream, Dirksen played dumb on the issue: "I have no comment on the John Birch Society. First, I know nothing about him. I have never seen a John Bircher in my life. I have no idea what they're achieving. I've seen some of these things in the press. That's about as far as it gets." But when twelve Democratic members of the House sponsored the book *The Liberal Papers,* Dirksen pounced on the extremism of the opposition. The minority leader ridiculed their conclusion that the United States should recognize Communist China and East Germany, demilitarize West Germany, and begin to disarm Western Europe. Taken together, the manifesto could have been titled *Our American Munich.* Dirksen continued, "Chamberlain surely never did as much for Hitler as is proposed here under the name of liberalism to be done for Khrushchev and Mao."[44]

Dirksen's efforts won him praise from conservative corners. In addition to the *Chicago Tribune, Human Events* congratulated the minority leader for drawing attention to the Democrats' "soft underbelly" and the publication "which has shocked the country." Dirksen sought to marginalize and tarnish the Democratic left. "We have heard much of 'thunder on the Right,'" he insisted. "Will we hear less now that 'surrender on the Left' is with us?"[45] Coupled with the administration's attack on the John Birch Society, Dirksen's assault on the authors of *The Liberal Papers* bolstered mainstream politics by ensuring yet again that the ideological extremes in both parties canceled each other out.

One week after excoriating the Democratic left, Dirksen entertained President Kennedy at a Capitol Hill cocktail party. The occasion was the opening of a new reception room across the corridor from the Senate chamber, and Kennedy stopped by for about twenty minutes to build up goodwill from members on both sides of the aisle. The party kicked off at 5:00 P.M. Shortly thereafter seventy senators "manfully downed bourbon, scotch, and martini and Manhattan cocktails" as a "fog of cigarget [sic] smoke dimmed the glow of the big chandelier." Meanwhile, Wayne Morse (D-OR) took the floor of an empty Senate chamber and objected to the revelry. Dubbed the "Five O'Clock Shadow" by reporters who disliked his late-afternoon speeches, Morse insisted that "millions of Americans think that drinking in the Capitol constitutes desecration." After Lyndon Johnson greeted Kennedy "with the politician's handclasp, right hand clutching the right hand and left hand firmly grasping the victim's upper arm," Dirksen welcomed the president and warned him that "Wayne Morse is on the floor assailing the iniquities of drinking in the Capitol." According to one observer, a visibly grateful Kennedy "didn't even look toward the bar." Instead he stepped into the empty Senate chamber, waved at a grinning Morse, and called out, "That's the way it was when I left the Senate!"[46]

Kennedy's social call on Capitol Hill coincided with a bitter Republican debate on the president's proposal to bail the UN out of its latest financial crisis. He asked the Congress for authority to buy half of a $200 million bond issue as a way to ease the immediate pressure on the international organization. Dirksen coauthored a bipartisan Senate compromise that not only would have enabled Kennedy to buy the $100 million but that also would have granted him the authority to lend the nation's share of the bonds back to the UN, at rates of interest and terms of duration to be set by the White House. Not surprisingly, the GOP's most conservative senators drew on the party's historical contempt for an unchecked presidency and balked at giving Kennedy this kind of latitude. Moreover, there was widespread disenchantment with opening the U.S. Treasury to the United Nations. Goldwater termed the plan "the most complete surrender to the Executive I've seen in my ten years in Congress," and Homer Capehart (R-IN) warned against giving Kennedy a "blank check." The Chicago Tribune reported that at a heated Senate Republican conference the announced opposition was two to one against the measure.[47]

The New York Times argued against the resurgence of "a new nationalism and isolationism" that would have eroded America's international prestige and imposed "additional burdens for free world defense upon us." Conservative Republicans, however, blanched at the fiscal power that Congress was surrendering to the White House. Bourke Hicken-looper (R-IA), who had become the chairman of the Policy Committee after the death of Styles Bridges, offered a substitute bill that would have limited the duration of the loan to three years at an interest rate determined by the open market. Dirksen took the floor in dramatic fashion to rebuke his GOP colleagues. He argued that the Dirksen-Mansfield compromise gave the Congress a more detailed agreement than they had ever required of Eisenhower. To those who bemoaned the cost of the loan, Dirksen answered, "Who would raise questions about $100 million? Why, we spend more than that on lipstick in this country in one year. . . . This is not a financial question. This is a moral question. We must stand up and be counted in our generation. It does not make any difference what the mail back home says to us." The bottom line, he roared, was that "I haven't forfeited my faith in John Fitzgerald Kennedy. I'm willing, as always, to trust my president, because he is my president."[48]

John Pastore (D-RI) praised Dirksen for delivering "one of the finest speeches ever delivered in the Senate." An elated Kennedy, who admired the work of any political maestro, privately referred to Dirksen's efforts as "damned good. Sid Yates is screaming." The normally critical *Chicago Sun-Times* lauded Dirksen as the "leader of the loyal opposition." Another asked if it were possible for Kennedy to "campaign in Illinois for the defeat of a man who proved to be such a valuable ally." Republicans, however, were not so pleased. Though Dirksen won twenty-two of thirty-three votes from his side of the aisle, one national Republican noted two weeks after that Kennedy "has certainly got Dirksen's number. Ev goes down there to a foreign policy briefing and he comes out with stars in his eyes." In a pointed and sarcastic editorial, "Hard Luck, Sid," the *Chicago Tribune* ridiculed Dirksen's eagerness to sell out the traditional conservative condemnation of a power-hungry executive for cheap political gain: "In such a fashion did our hero arrive, when men of little faith were deriding the virtuous U.N. and denying their peerless leader. . . . The final moments of the debate . . . were marked by a declaration of faith in our president from Everett McKinley (we repeat, McKinley) Dirksen." Dirksen remembered that some of his Illinois constituents sent newspaper reports from his speech with "shame" scrawled across the top.[49]

Kennedy rewarded the minority leader by inviting him to accompany the president's party to the Washington Senators' opening-day baseball game four days after the Senate's debate on the UN loans. A happy-faced Dirksen sat just behind the president, who warmly greeted the minority leader on his arrival. Newspapers throughout Illinois ran pictures of Kennedy's encounter with Dirksen at the Capitol Hill cocktail party, Dirksen's attendance at the baseball game, and the Dirksens' entrance at a formal White House reception for Congress one day later. By then, Yates and Douglas were exasperated. The little-known Yates had had to plead for a photo opportunity with the president of his own party, but Dirksen received free advertisement from his position as minority leader and the politics of conciliation he pursued. To top it off, *Time* ran an article, "The Ev Show," applauding Dirksen's leadership and his commitment to the national interest. The widely read weekly concluded that the minority leader's "qualities of flexibility, political shrewdness, willingness to compromise, and above all the realization that times and events do change, have made him the most effective Senate Republican leader in years."[50] Dirksen basked in the adulation of a national press that affirmed his place in the center of Washington's political establishment.

Having secured his reputation as a national statesman, Dirksen moved to shore up his standing among conservatives and regular Republicans who looked to the minority leader to provide a coherent opposition to Kennedy's New Frontier. A constituent wrote and emphasized that "we expect him to get Kennedy and not play footsie with him." The *National Review* bemoaned the "collapse of the GOP" and asked, "Has ever so much power been accumulated in the presidency?" Though Dirksen had just promoted the power of the presidency, he and Halleck indicated to Eisenhower that they agreed with the conservative journal. Bryce Harlow wrote the former president that the GOP leaders "count heavily upon your expression of concern over bloat throughout the executive branch." Eisenhower hammered away at the theme in May when he met with reporters in place of Dirksen and Halleck. He detailed his belief that freedom in America would not be taken away in a calculated and coherent assault manned by the opposition. Instead, he feared a "steady erosion of self-reliant citizenship, and in excessive power concentration, resulting from the lodging of more and more decisions in an ever-growing federal bureaucracy."[51]

In June Dirksen relied on a series of articles by Willard Edwards in the *Chicago Tribune* to discredit those individuals in the State Department who were pressing for a more sophisticated and flexible foreign policy. He reported to the Senate that Walt W. Rostow, chairman of State's Policy Planning Council, had submitted a draft of a report, "Basic National Security Policy," to the White House. An academic from the Massachusetts Institute of Technology, Rostow was a committed cold warrior. Once a Rhodes scholar, the ebullient Rostow was known for his relentless enthusiasm and his unswerving commitment to ideas that whipped through his mind at a breakneck pace. Kennedy once remarked that "Walt can write faster than I can read." Rostow's academic background aggravated traditional Republicans like Dirksen, who distrusted intellectuals of all stripes and persuasions. In the *Tribune* articles Edwards reported that Rostow had argued "that the Soviet Union and its Communist masters are 'mellowing'; that Russia is becoming a mature state; that if we are only nice to the Soviets they will drop all of their suspicions of the free world and peace will finally bloom." Rostow's report offended Dirksen's hard-line view that the "only times we have ever gotten anywhere with the Soviet Union—the only times the Soviet Union has ever mellowed—have been when the United States was tough." To Dirksen, Rostow's naive interpretation of American foreign policy bore a striking resemblance "to the fuzzy thinking of the late and lamented 'Liberal Papers.'" In revising a draft completed after Edwards's articles and Dirksen's Senate speech, Kennedy's foreign policy team dropped "a certain mellowing" from the position paper.[52]

Though not a member of the Foreign Relations Committee, Dirksen attended the three-hour grilling Rostow received less than a week later. Calling the meeting "round number one," he added, "I want to see the document." He was respectful of presidential prerogative throughout the committee hearing. Nonetheless, he scoffed at Rostow's academic background and mocked his apparent willingness to impose utopian theories for the future on the realities of foreign policymaking in the here and now. He asked Rostow, "How do you disassociate your opinions, convictions that you have had and that you uttered as a professor and as a planner, and how do you shuck them all to one side now when you start working with a strategy document?" He was especially piqued at Rostow's and the administration's apparent eagerness to contemplate major foreign policy changes without consulting Congress. *Human Events* shared Dirksen's indignation. The journal lashed out at Rostow's reliance on executive privilege and the "arrogance of the administration in withholding the details of this master plan."[53]

Despite his penchant for a more zealous partisanship in anticipation of the upcoming election, Dirksen never lost the respect and acceptance of the most prominent figures in the Washington political establishment. In August retiring senator Prescott Bush took the floor and led a round of tributes to the minority leader. Much to the dismay of Dirksen's Democratic opponents, Majority Leader Mansfield delivered the second salute and underlined Dirksen's importance to the Senate and to the Washington elite: "Everett, I am honored and grateful that you sit across the aisle from me. You are a tower of strength as a collaborator in the leadership of this body. For thirty years you have served your party faithfully and brilliantly. But for thirty years you have served your country more." A livid Douglas fired off a copy of Mansfield's remarks to the White House, asserting that "this has gone all over Illinois and has done immeasurable damage to Congressman Yates."[54]

Yates endured another setback in September when a statesmanlike Dirksen, sporting a jungle of tangled hair, appeared on the cover of *Time*. Describing Dirksen as a "big-handed, big-boned man with a lined, cornfield face and graying locks that spiral above him like a halo run amok," the popular weekly emphasized the minority leader's importance to the administration. One Democrat (later named as Bobby Baker) maintained that "I like Sid Yates. But my party would be in a hell of a mess— Kennedy would be in a hell of a mess—if Dirksen got defeated." A White House staffer (later identified as Larry O'Brien) more or less agreed: "Who could dislike Dirksen? He gets his arm around your shoulder and, well, he's a total pro, able, cute, and clever." Dirksen took advantage of the free advertising by having 200,000 reprints copied for his Illinois constituents.[55]

Even as he gloried in the kudos, the opportunistic Dirksen continued his practice of "cannonading the New Frontier." His chief target was Cuba, and the thrust of his remarks was directed at reports that the Soviets had delivered military equipment and personnel to the island. While the Senate was in session, Dirksen deplored the administration's "inaction," but he also appealed to all Americans "to unite in a calm, considered approach to meet this problem." Describing himself in his correspondence as "virtually a captive" in Washington, he accepted the administration's view that the Soviet military aid was defensive in nature and not a threat to the vital interests of the United States. But once on the hustings and outside the circle of the Washington establishment, he pilloried the administration and seemed to agree with Goldwater's assertion that the Cuban situation was "one of the best issues" for the GOP in 1962.[56]

When the Senate finally ended its session, an anxious Dirksen immediately flew to O'Hare Airport in Chicago to begin campaigning. After just three hours of sleep, he launched a tour of the downstate districts in order to patch up relationships with constituents who deemed him a prisoner to Washington. That first morning he invited reporter David Broder to join him and his pilot on the campaign trail. It was, Broder recalled, "one of the most vivid days in my whole life as a reporter." Dirksen made five stops that first day. He catnapped and read on the campaign charter and ingested a "diet of coffee, cigarettes, and chewing gum mixed in about equal portions" to keep him going. Most remarkable to Broder was the fact that Dirksen delivered five separate speeches without a single note. The only material he carried with him was a marked-up copy of the 1960 Democratic platform that he used to lambaste Kennedy's record.

On the stump Dirksen drifted between moments of self-promoting statesmanship and bare-knuckled brawling. He blamed Kennedy for the Bay of Pigs, arguing that his decision to call off the second and third air strikes was responsible for "the dismal record." For dramatic effect he quoted the platform's commitment to Cuba's freedom and independence. Then he asserted that "she has been taken over, lock, stock and barrel by the Soviet Union. They are also building bases for missiles [which he pronounced 'mizzles'] potentially capable of striking any part of the United States. If that is not a colossal failure, I do not know the meaning of failure." Though he laced his remarks with references to Cuba, no two speeches were the same. "He was so exhausted," Broder recalled, "that he'd climb back on that little plane and literally before the plane could take off he'd nod off. He was going purely on nerve and backbone and just delivering absolutely marvelous speeches."[57]

In what Rowland Evans Jr. called the "best and the last one-man political vaudeville show on the election circuit," Dirksen assailed the New Frontier without attacking the popular president. He made his friendship with Kennedy and his place in the suprapartisan Washington establishment central themes in his reelection bid. To one audience Dirksen referred to Kennedy and purred, "He has been my friend for fourteen years. He calls me to the White House. He sits in the rocker. I tell him what I think from the bottom of my heart and I think that's why he keeps on asking me back." But he also used his relationship with Kennedy to score political points against the Democratic party. His voice finding its rhythmic cadence, Dirksen hammered away on the issue of Cuba: "It was that good man, President McKinley, of humble heart and gracious spirit, who liberated the sunny little island of Cuba sixty-four years ago. And now what do we see? That bearded dictator Castro and his Russian motor torpedo boats, with launching pads on them. And they have builded [*sic*] missile sites on the land. Oh, I know whereof I speak. I know because they told me so at 1600 Pennsylvania Avenue."[58]

Mindful of the disadvantages that he would have to overcome, Yates focused on the economic issues of the New Frontier. His assaults on Dirksen's conservatism were relentless: "He is the original 'no' man. On medical care under Social Security, on the $1.25 minimum wage, on federal aid for depressed areas, on emergency public works, on aid to education, on housing—you name it, he voted no, no, no, and no again." But even as his campaign picked up momentum, Yates realized his best chance was to attach his candidacy to Kennedy's popularity. In order to portray himself as an important ally in the administration, Yates and his supporters on numerous occasions appealed to the White House for a Kennedy visit to Illinois.[59]

On October 19 the president flew to Chicago to campaign for Yates. Raucous crowds gave him a "roaring welcome," and "school children screamed themselves hoarse. It was the kind of welcome reserved for rock n' roll singers." That evening, well aware that it was entirely possible that the Soviets had armed Cuba with ready-to-fire surface-to-surface nuclear missiles, he attended a $100-a-plate dinner at the Sheraton Blackstone Hotel hosted by the Cook County Democratic Committee. He endorsed Yates without attacking Minority Leader Dirksen. Robert Kennedy later recalled that the "president did not want to become so personally involved that it would antagonize Dirksen." Kennedy's tepid speech merely recited a litany of domestic policy positions that Yates supported and the minority leader opposed. That evening American reconnaissance confirmed the offensive nature of the Soviet nuclear weapons, and National Security Council adviser McGeorge Bundy called Kennedy staffer Kenneth O'Donnell in Chicago to tell the president to cut short his campaign trip. White House press secretary Pierre Salinger informed the press that Kennedy was suffering from a head cold, and under these pretenses the president returned to Washington to oversee the American response to the cold war's most dangerous crisis.[60]

Once he decided on the limited military action of a blockade to prevent the Soviets from adding to their nuclear arsenal in Cuba, Kennedy called the congressional leaders back to Washington for an emergency briefing. The Dirksens were in a hotel on the campaign trail when the call came in from the White House. "Well, Mrs. D.," Dirksen told his wife, "you're taking over the campaign. That was the president. He wants me back in Washington. He's sending his plane for me. It's urgent." At the meeting, Dirksen teased a stone-faced Kennedy: "That was a nice little speech you gave for Sid Yates in Chicago. Too bad you caught that cold making it." Kennedy stuck to the business at hand. He emphasized that he was neither consulting Congress nor asking for their advice but was merely informing the leaders of a course of action he and his advisers had already charted.[61]

After briefings from the CIA, the Pentagon, the State Department, and the NSC, Kennedy outlined his plans for a blockade. Richard Russell (D-GA), chairman of the Senate Armed Services Committee, favored an invasion. He told the president that "the quarantine will earn bitter statements and a series of incidents could more likely lead to nuclear war than the fait accompli of having done that which we told them we would do." Surprisingly, Senate Foreign Relations Committee chairman J. William Fulbright agreed with the bellicose Georgian. A fuming Kennedy "drummed the arm of his chair." In contrast to two of their most prominent Democratic counterparts, GOP leaders Dirksen and Halleck gave the president's plan their backing. According to one account, Halleck "glared" at Fulbright and declared, "I'm standing with the president."[62]

Though making clear that they had been informed rather than consulted, the Republican leaders underscored to the press their belief that "Americans will support the president on the decision or decisions he makes for the security of our country." Two days later Dirksen and the congressional leaders returned to the White House for a follow-up briefing on the status of the quarantine. In contrast to the earlier meeting, the tone of this encounter was more civil and businesslike. Dirksen argued that Khrushchev's request for an early summit meeting between the two leaders was "useless" unless ground rules could be established that guaranteed positive results. Kennedy concurred. As the meeting drew to a close, Dirksen emphasized that some members were "anxious" about being stuck in Washington at the height of the congressional campaign. Kennedy agreed that the leaders could travel to their home states and districts but warned that they would remain on an eight-hour alert pending further developments.[63]

Nothing could have highlighted Dirksen's importance to the suprapartisan Washington establishment more than an international crisis and Kennedy's decision to dispatch air force jets to fetch him and other GOP leaders for urgent briefings at the White House. Nevertheless, the minority leader took no chances on his reelection bid. On his way home from the airport after his return and in the presence of a newspaper reporter, Dirksen whispered loudly to his wife that Kennedy wanted him to stay longer in Washington. Dirksen pointed to the upcoming election, but the president had presumably scoffed, "What are you worrying about, Ev? You've got it in the bag." Reports of this alleged conversation dominated newspaper coverage in the days leading up to the election.[64]

An angry Yates called the minority leader's report of his exchange with Kennedy an "outright contemptible lie." Dirksen soft-pedaled, telling reporters, "I was having a little private conversation with my wife, and somebody overheard it." Nothing in the record verifies his rendition of the story, but despite Yates's frustration, an otherwise occupied White House did little to deny Dirksen's assertion or to boost the Yates campaign in its final days. The Chicago Democrat endured a final blow on the day before the election when Majority Leader Mansfield announced that he and Dirksen would travel together to international trouble spots before making a report to the White House. Not surprisingly, Dirksen won reelection by 200,000 votes. With the sharpest of political instincts, he drifted between his roles as an indispensable leader of the loyal opposition to partisan critic of the administration's liberal machinations and back again to defender of the White House in times of trouble before the closing of the polls on election day.[65]

Safely reelected, Dirksen in 1963 began to distance himself from the White House. He told his colleagues that "my greatest pride has been that we did develop a cohesive force which made itself effectively felt on all matters of major importance in the national and international field." The ideological fissures in the GOP caucus prevented principled opposition to the New Frontier and encouraged some cooperation with the White House; nevertheless, the minority leader worked to distinguish his troops from the party in power. He reversed an earlier position and reported to his colleagues that he planned to call for a bipartisan Senate committee to investigate the Bay of Pigs fiasco. To the press, he overturned his earlier penchant for introducing substitute legislation for New Frontier proposals. "If the basic concept is bad," he insisted, "you are under no obligation to come along with an alternative. You just reject it out of hand."[66]

In February Dirksen wrote his colleagues and suggested the topics for "hard-hitting speech[es] on the Senate floor." Before, Dirksen had taken pride in his commitment to a bipartisan foreign policy; now he emphasized that "we are . . . moving into a period when we should come to grips with the failures of the New Frontier," and he gave special attention to the "deterioration in our relations with other countries." The GOP criticism of Kennedy culminated in a series of Lincoln Day speeches that pointed to the administration's breakdown in the realm of foreign policy. The invective was sharp and pointed enough to inspire the *Washington Post* to ask, "Does politics still end at the water's edge?" Sensing that Dirksen was drifting outside their sphere of control, the White House considered ways to woo "liberal Republicans who may not be really enthusiastic with the hand-in-glove game now going on between the swami from Illinois and the Southern Democrats."[67]

Despite ongoing rumblings of dissatisfaction with the "Ev and Charlie Show," Dirksen and Halleck continued to use the production to oppose the New Frontier. By 1963 it was common for fifty Washington reporters to attend the weekly news conference. One critic noted that Dirksen's participation in the act became an instrumental part of his political persona: "His style may be hopelessly out of date, but when those words come pouring out in measured cadence there is no confusion over the identity of the actor." Dirksen ensured that more than his voice was distinctive. As he explained to one reporter, "If you have some kind of trademark like unruly hair, people get to recognize you." Walt Rostow's wife, Elspeth, pulled alongside Dirksen's chauffeur-driven car one morning when she was returning from Andrews Air Force Base and he was presumably headed into the Senate. She saw Dirksen in the back seat consciously running his fingers through his hair in order to create its "tousled, halo look. He was doing this so skillfully," she recalled, "that I suspected many years of practice."[68]

After his reelection Dirksen used the "Ev and Charlie Show" to condemn the White House. One of his favorite targets was the administration's ongoing efforts to secure a nuclear test ban treaty with the Soviet Union. He ridiculed the "parade of concessions" and bemoaned the erosion of American prestige that the negotiations incurred. But even while the GOP intensified its partisan opposition to the Kennedy administration, an unparalleled national crisis was brewing that soon commanded the bulk of the establishment's attention. With little direction from the White House and no organized resistance on the streets to capture the collective attention of the American people, Congress made no progress on civil rights in the first two years of the Kennedy administration. Besides nominating federal judges with racist records, the White House had opted not to send any significant legislation to the Congress. Dirksen and the GOP fared no better. In February, when he recited a series of New Frontier failures that deserved public attention, Dirksen sidestepped the issue of civil rights. But in spring 1963 the charismatic chairman of the Southern Christian Leadership Conference (SCLC), Martin Luther King Jr., planned to highlight systematic racial discrimination in the American South by organizing massive demonstrations in its most segregated city, Birmingham, Alabama.[69]

Led by public safety commissioner Eugene "Bull" Connor, local white leaders overreacted and played into the hands of the protesters. In addition to arresting King for violating a city ordinance banning demonstrations, the Birmingham police threw as many as 2,000 children in jail. Connor's most despicable act was to direct local firemen to turn their high-pressure hoses on the demonstrators. From the comfort of their living rooms, Americans watched television footage of water slamming into victims, driving them against walls, and ripping off their clothing. Connor then ordered attack dogs to the area. When one officer held a group of white hecklers at bay, Connor bellowed, "Let those people come to the corner, sergeant. I want 'em to see the dogs work. Look at those niggers run." Kennedy echoed the reactions of millions of outraged Americans when he reported that photographs of the snarling attack dogs made him "sick."[70]

One administration official who used Connor's atrocities to jump-start his flagging political engines was Vice President Lyndon Johnson. Though Kennedy respected Johnson's political abilities, the White House relegated the former Senate giant to the sidelines and used him primarily for ceremonial purposes. Johnson was in a funk, and he was battling feelings of personal inadequacy when the legislative conundrum of the civil rights crisis rejuvenated his career and sparked his creative genius. Before the crisis, calculations of partisan gain had dominated both parties' efforts to tackle the problem. In an early June telephone conversation with Kennedy adviser Theodore Sorensen, Johnson dismissed these considerations and argued for a suprapartisan approach. To Johnson, the chaos and hatred in Birmingham resembled a foreign policy emergency that required the full power of the Washington establishment: "If this is not warfare, I don't know what is. . . . They're arresting them by the thousands; they're killing them by the dozens." To protect the president from the inevitable Southern Democratic filibuster and to produce the best bill possible, Johnson suggested that the White House "get the Republicans in on this thing."

The key was Dirksen. The administration had to do whatever was necessary to keep him on board; otherwise, he and archsegregationist Richard Russell "will be sitting around next Sunday with a mint julep. . . . I'd make a book with him instead of Russell making it with him. Didn't I turn every moral force in this country loose on him?"[71] Johnson's assessment transformed the administration's approach to civil rights. By establishing Dirksen and the centrist core of the GOP as fundamental partners, the Kennedy White House redoubled the consensus politics of the time and committed the suprapartisan Washington establishment to a resolution of the nation's greatest domestic crisis since World War II. Marginalized even further were both the liberal faction, who wanted a more sweeping bill, and the archconservative/segregationist faction, who recoiled at the prospect of an intrusive federal government arrogant enough to direct the social mores of the several states.

Kennedy joined the fray with a televised speech to the nation on June 11. That same day he federalized the Alabama National Guard and forced the state's grandstanding governor, George Wallace, to permit the lawful desegregation of the University of Alabama. Kennedy's speech marked the first time any president used the bully pulpit to speak on behalf of civil rights for all Americans. He underscored the moral dimension of the matter and asked his audience, "If an American, because his skin is dark, cannot eat lunch in a restaurant open to the public, if he cannot send his children to the best public school available, if he cannot vote for the public officials who represent him, if, in short, he cannot enjoy the full and free life which all of us want, then who among us would be content to have the color of his skin changed and stand in his place?" In his remarks he touched on the omnibus legislation he would introduce to the Congress. True to the administration's new policy of involving Dirksen and the GOP in the deliberations, he invited the Republican leaders to a White House meeting before delivering his speech.[72]

Majority Leader Mansfield maintained the momentum when he called a private meeting in Dirksen's office to discuss the prospects for a bipartisan civil rights bill. The two leaders agreed on a bill to extend voting rights based on completion of the sixth grade; extend indefinitely the life of the Civil Rights Commission; continue and expand the desegregation of all public schools and community facilities; and give statutory authority to the vice president's Fair Employment Commission. The only area of disagreement was the White House's request for a public accommodations clause. Dirksen intimated that he could not support this provision in the bill, especially if it were justified by the interstate commerce clause rather than by the Fourteenth Amendment, which had been a Republican party principle in the post–Civil War era of Reconstruction.[73]

After visiting Kennedy at the White House, Eisenhower wrote Dirksen and underscored his "conviction that the race question has become one that involves the conscience of both the nation and the individual." The former president held that he would "support the enactment of any legislation that seemed to me applicable, proper and constitutional." Dirksen concurred. Though he pledged to back a limited bill, he left a bipartisan White House meeting several days later and reported that he would oppose legislation that outlawed segregation in private businesses, accommodations, facilities, and services. The minority leader maintained that the proposed legislation would be a violation of the Constitution's protection of private property and asserted, "I don't believe such power resides in the Fourteenth Amendment or in the commerce clause." Moreover, as columnist Arthur Krock argued, Kennedy's civil rights legislation represented an "incalculable expansion of executive power." Though in this instance Dirksen did not articulate the traditional Republican fear of an overassertive White House, it was clear that enforcing the legislation would arm the presidency with "discretionary powers over private property and individual freedom."[74]

Despite the setback, Mansfield never abandoned his commitment to working with Dirksen. He wrote Kennedy, "It is better to secure passage of as much of the administration's legislative proposals on civil rights as is possible, rather than to run the very real risk of losing all in an effort to obtain all." Knowing that final passage of the bill would require the sixty-seven Senate votes necessary to invoke cloture over a certain Southern Democratic filibuster, Mansfield underlined the importance of "complete cooperation and good faith with respect to Senator Dirksen. If that does not exist, the whole legislative effort . . . will be reduced to an absurdity." Dirksen had already told Mansfield that "his power to persuade these key Republicans . . . will be lost if the impression develops that the Democratic party is trying to make political capital." The two men agreed, therefore, to introduce a joint bill that included the provisions with the exception of the public accommodations clause. Other senators would offer the administration's complete proposal separately, and the committee hearings and lobbying efforts would determine which bill had more appeal.[75]

Despite the urgency of the situation, Kennedy's civil rights legislation stalled in the House. Dirksen seemed unruffled. "If this is the issue of the century," he remarked, "let's let it go along for a while." Liberal Republicans chafed at Dirksen's apparent indifference. In an editorial, "Will Lincoln's Party Measure Up?" the *New York Herald Tribune* pointed to Dirksen and complained, "The Republican voice in this crisis has been neither strong nor convincing. Republicans have conferred inconclusively, talked endlessly, and some have played partisan politics with a great national tragedy."[76]

On Capitol Hill, the civil rights debate did not take place in a vacuum, as Kennedy stepped up his efforts to achieve a nuclear test ban treaty with the Soviet Union. The Cuban missile crisis brought the United States closer to nuclear war with the Soviet Union than at any other time in the cold war. Sobered by a new understanding of the horror of the "new force of war," Kennedy energized the talks with an eloquent speech for a "just and genuine peace" he delivered at American University on June 10. The president announced a new round of test-ban negotiations in Moscow, and he emphasized the shared interests of the superpowers:

"For . . . our most common link is that we all inhabit this small planet. We all breathe the same air. We all cherish our children's future. And we are all mortal."[77]

Dirksen was unreceptive to Kennedy's appeal. He ridiculed the president, asserting that another round of talks was merely "another case of concessions and more concessions to Khrushchev to achieve some kind of test ban treaty." Later he derided the administration's "renunciation of the policy of strength." Undeterred, Kennedy proceeded. After twelve days of talks the American delegation, led by Averell Harriman, and the Soviet delegation, led by Andrei Gromyko, signed a limited test ban treaty that prohibited atmospheric testing. Relative to his other endeavors with the Congress, Kennedy's commitment to his treaty was unparalleled. In this one instance he matched his moving rhetoric with behind-the-scenes jockeying to push the treaty through the Senate. When planning his speech to the nation announcing the initialing of the agreement, he told Secretary of State Dean Rusk, "We got to hit the country while the country's hot. That's the only thing that makes an impression on these goddamned senators."[78]

Dirksen's first reaction was to express "extreme caution and a little bit of suspicion." He underscored the constitutional role of the Senate's consenting to the treaty and pledged to examine "every word and every phrase and every line and every paragraph and every implication . . . to make sure we don't get a pig in the poke." Nevertheless, he promised to be open-minded. He had told his GOP colleagues in January that the failure of the past "does not mean that a treaty may not be contrived." To his constituents, he repeated Kennedy's recitation on national television of the ancient Chinese proverb: "A journey of a thousand miles must begin with a single step."[79]

In late July Dirksen attended a special Senate meeting with Harriman. Thereafter, his language was more restrained and responsible. No longer did he point to "concessions" and the erosion of American prestige; instead, his remaining reservations were more technical. In mid-August he questioned the staunchly anti-Soviet air force chief of staff, Gen. Curtis LeMay. The senator applauded plans for future underground testing and favored a "program of constant readiness," whether or not the Senate passed the limited test ban treaty. Because prestigious Democrats like Russell, John Stennis (D-MS), and Henry "Scoop" Jackson (D-WA) either opposed the treaty or threatened to propose crippling reservations,

Kennedy wanted an unqualified endorsement from Minority Leader Dirksen.[80]

Archconservative dean of the Notre Dame Law School Clarence E. Manion wrote Dirksen and quoted the prophet Isaiah: "We have made a covenant with death and an agreement with Hell." To Manion, the "evil of this treaty with the communists is the basic evil involved in any agreement with militant activated atheism." Liberal Republicans lobbied for the treaty. The *New York Herald Tribune* scolded Dirksen for his reluctance to embrace the treaty and wrote that he "added to the prevalent impression that a lot of the Republican Old Guard have cobwebs behind their eyes." With the conservative and liberal wings of the GOP at one another's throats, no one really knew where Dirksen stood. One Republican senator predicted that "Dirksen loves theatrics. He'll gamble a while and then at the right moment come in with another 'Put your trust in JFK' speech."[81]

The White House was not so sure. A determined Kennedy uncharacteristically told his aides that he would "gladly" sacrifice his reelection on behalf of the treaty. Frederick Dutton of the State Department informed Secretary Rusk that Dirksen "backed and filled" in order to keep the treaty from becoming a "clear-cut accomplishment of the administration useful in '64." Another prominent Republican who had yet to take a public stand on the treaty was former president Eisenhower. Kennedy ensured that he was briefed before the agreement was initialed in July. Even though the Geneva negotiations for a test ban treaty and a self-imposed moratorium on atmospheric testing had started in his administration, Eisenhower expressed serious reservations to Secretary Rusk: "Five years ago, we were fully confident of our own superiority in nuclear science." He feared that now the pact would enable the Soviets to jump ahead in antimissile development: "An agreement would favor them."[82]

Kennedy's margin of support was withering. Fulbright agreed with the president that any effort to propose a reservation from the floor represented the "most dangerous" threat to the treaty. According to Bobby Baker, Kennedy called Dirksen to the White House to cash in on his credit with Eisenhower for squelching the Sherman Adams indictment. "Ike said I had coin in his bank and you say I have coin in yours. . . . I want you to reverse yourself and come out for the treaty. I also want Ike's public endorsement of the treaty before the Senate votes. We'll call it square on that other matter." According to Baker, Dirksen told Kennedy, "Mr. President, you're a hell of a horse trader. But I'll honor my commitment, and I'm sure that General Eisenhower will." The former president sent a letter to Fulbright supporting the treaty.[83]

Less surreptitiously, Dirksen went with Mansfield to the White House to iron out his last-minute reservations. By then other factors pointed to the treaty's passage. Though Dirksen declared that his mail was three to one against the agreement, a September 1 Gallup poll indicated that 63 percent of the nation supported the pact while only 17 percent were opposed. Even in the traditionally isolationist Midwest, 63 percent backed the treaty. Dirksen warned his constituents that the "treaty will be approved by the Senate." The remaining task was to "dispel the fears that have been so freely uttered and have found their way to the front pages." At the White House the minority leader detailed the doubts and concerns of the military, many Republicans, and some conservative Democrats. He was fidgeting with his papers when the president asked, "You got your notes?" Dirksen replied that he did. "Can I have them?" Dirksen handed over a letter of assurance that he had drafted and that he wanted Kennedy to write to the majority and minority leaders. "Okay," said the president, "it will be done."[84]

Armed with the president's guarantee, Dirksen took the floor at 2:00 P.M. on September 11 to endorse the treaty. Earlier in the day he told his GOP colleagues in a closed-door meeting that he would support the agreement that so many conservative Americans found repugnant. To strengthen his reputation as a partisan fighter, Dirksen turned to an array of issues that the GOP could use in the 1964 presidential campaign. These included "weak leadership . . . , a stagnant economy, and foreign policy mess." But after lunch Dirksen played the role of a suprapartisan statesman defending the national interest against heavy odds. Forty-one senators gathered in the usually empty Senate chamber to hear his remarks, and the public galleries filled to near capacity.[85]

He read Kennedy's letter into the *Record* and emphasized the president's promise that "underground nuclear testing . . . will be vigorously and diligently carried forward" and that the "treaty in no way limits the authority of the commander in chief to use nuclear weapons for the defense of the United States and its allies." Then, with great drama, he affirmed the leadership of John Kennedy and promoted the responsibility of the modern presidency to negotiate arms control agreements in the interests of a lasting peace while at the same time monitoring the nation's military preparedness: "I want to take a first step. . . . I am not a young man. . . . One of my age thinks about his destiny a little. I should not like to have written on my tombstone, 'He knew what happened at Hiroshima, but he did not take a first step.'" Though there were days of debate left before the final Senate vote, Dirksen's unqualified endorsement of the treaty ensured its passage by a heavy majority. Kuchel later insisted that Dirksen's speech "changed the outcome" of the vote. Kennedy was delighted. Loyalist Theodore Sorensen wrote that "no other accomplishment in the White House ever gave Kennedy greater satisfaction."[86]

Dirksen's support for the treaty distanced him from the conservative wing of the Republican party. The *National Review*'s Frank Meyer pointed to the neutralization of Laos and the abandonment of a free Cuba and asserted that Kennedy's negotiation of the pact produced a foreign "policy of appeasement, retreat, and inherent weakening of the military stance of the United States." Goldwater wrote that the treaty was "the opening wedge to disastrous negotiations with the enemy, which could result in our losing the war or becoming a part of their system." On the other hand, Dirksen won the acclaim of the nation's establishment. In a press conference on the day after Dirksen's speech, Kennedy praised Dirksen and Mansfield for promoting the "great tradition of American bipartisanship and national interest." The *Christian Science Monitor* wrote, "We doff our hat to Senator Dirksen." The *New York Times* commended "bipartisanship where it counts."[87]

The *New York Times* called for similar cross-party cooperation in the realm of civil rights. The administration's legislation was stalled in the House Rules Committee, and Kennedy's aides fretted about the inevitability of a prolonged Senate filibuster. In the intervening weeks Dirksen had continued his opposition to the public accommodations clause. Civil rights leaders gathered in his office on the morning of the March on Washington to lobby for the bill. Emphasizing his overarching commitment to "independent judgment" and "constitutional responsibilities," Dirksen seemed unmoved by their presence. But the Kennedy administration continued to press their case.[88]

In early November the president invited Dirksen to travel on Air Force One to Chicago for that year's Army–Air Force football game. The deteriorating situation in Vietnam prevented Kennedy from making the trip, but his advisers used the occasion to discuss the bill with Dirksen. Assistant Attorney General Nicholas deB. Katzenbach recalled that the minority leader, though noncommittal about certain provisions, gave his word that a filibuster would be beaten. "Don't worry," he promised, "the bill will come to a vote in the Senate." In Washington Dirksen advocated Kennedy's continued commitment to working through the Washington establishment and the leadership of both parties to achieve his most important goals. Just as important, he proved open to the White House's use of its prestige in the now-constant pursuit of his favor. Dirksen wrote the president that "you missed a good, spirited football game, a big crowd, a lot of impressive pageantry, fine fellowship and a beautiful, sunny day outdoors. Thanks for the invitation and for a smooth, pleasant air trip to Chicago."[89]

By November 1963 John Kennedy was clearly growing into the presidency. Though the first years of his tenure were marked by exaggerated rhetoric and too little progress, the president showed with the passage of the nuclear test ban treaty and with the vigorous movement toward comprehensive civil rights legislation that he could work with both parties and play the political game well enough to achieve his most important goals. Nevertheless, his critics (then and later) insisted that Kennedy sacrificed too much in pursuit of his positive relationship with Dirksen. In essence, they argued that Kennedy's ongoing courtship of the minority leader stunted the momentum necessary to promote a more liberal and activist agenda. The president's sympathizers, on the other hand, maintained that Kennedy's conduct was the necessary price to pay for Dirksen's cooperation in times of crisis. Though Dirksen was rarely reluctant to play on traditional GOP fears of a leviathan executive taking on more and more responsibility, his actions at defining times affirmed the evolving nature of the modern presidency and its tendency to expand enough to meet the problems of the day. In this sense, Kennedy's stop-and-go lobbying efforts to win the minority leader's favor paid handsome dividends.

Not everyone was impressed. Kennedy's liberal detractors wished that the White House shared their penchant for a larger federal government more responsive to the people's needs. These critics, however, overlooked the prevailing circumstances that circumscribed the president's range of political motion. Elected without a majority and well aware of the nation's overriding instinct for the politics of moderation, Kennedy was far too pragmatic and nonideological to embrace such an expansive definition of government's role in American society. Kennedy's relationship with Dirksen testified to his ultimate commitment to be an effective foreign policy president and a national unifier in times of domestic crisis. In short, the president's interaction with Dirksen underscored both the potential and the limitations of the consensus politics of the times.

November 22, 1963, was a day like a multitude of others in the U.S. Senate. After the chaplain's prayer, Symington detailed his daily responsibilities and took exception to a growing number of press reports that held that "senators were loafing on the job." Dirksen and Mansfield discussed the final vote for the administration's foreign aid package. Morse hammered away at an education bill. The horror seemed to come from nowhere. A stunned Dirksen heard the news that Kennedy had been shot from Richard Riedel, the Senate's press liaison officer. In the middle of his Senate speech Morse called for an emergency quorum. Majority Leader Mansfield was so overcome by emotion that he could not formally adjourn the Senate. Dirksen took the floor and shut the Senate down. A shaken group of GOP colleagues followed him to his spacious office to watch the events unfold on television. By 2:30 P.M. their worst fears were confirmed. Kennedy's untimely death cut down his budding presidency and generated an incomparable national crisis that rocked the Washington political establishment.[90]

5. "You're My Kind of Republican"

The murder of John Kennedy threw the nation into grief and shook the political establishment to its core. Before leaving Dallas a stunned Lyndon Johnson took the presidential oath and then hurried back to Washington to survey the situation and create a political strategy for dealing with the tragedy. Most scholars have praised the new president's leadership through an unplanned transition. Indeed, the emotional shock of the assassination played directly into the suprapartisan politics that first Majority Leader Johnson and then Everett Dirksen had perfected in the Eisenhower and Kennedy administrations. Though many Americans greeted the Johnson presidency with uncertainty and trepidation, Dirksen was comfortable with Johnson's political style. The two Senate warhorses shared common cultural roots and preferred bourbon and scotch to the dry martinis of the eastern establishment. The friendship they enjoyed in their Senate years as the leaders of their parties in the late 1950s was the foundation for their political relationship during Johnson's presidency. Dirksen remembered that as Senate leaders, "we learned a sort of common language . . . and we could talk to each other freely at his office or mine, and you could throw in a few expletives that don't always sound good in public." Johnson admired Dirksen's "patriotism." He recalled that "when the nation's interests were at stake, he could climb the heights and take the long view without regard to party."[1]

Johnson was quick to draw on his estimation of Dirksen's commitment to the establishment and his responsibility to the national interest. One day after the assassination, he called the minority leader and commended his instinct to put partisan politics aside. He told Dirksen that "every chance you get to say like you did this morning and let them know you're part of this partnership and your country comes first would be good."[2] Like Eisenhower and Kennedy, Lyndon Johnson identified his

184 EVERETT DIRKSEN AND HIS PRESIDENTS

presidency with a centrist political establishment that abandoned party loyalty and scoffed at a principled set of ideas in times of crisis. Johnson differed from his predecessors, however, in the political style he pursued to achieve his most important goals. Both Eisenhower and Kennedy were reluctant to lobby individual members of the House or the Senate, but Johnson employed the aggressive tactics he had mastered as majority leader to push his legislative agenda through the Congress. He wrote letters, held meetings, and invited important players to the White House for after-hours consultations.

Louella Dirksen, who maintained her ambivalent assessment of Johnson well into the 1970s, remembered that on one occasion she had organized a dinner party that her husband could not attend because the president would not allow him to leave the White House. Though Dirksen supposedly tried to extricate himself on several occasions, Johnson said, "Now, Ev, just another minute or two." What most angered Mrs. Dirksen was that the president was well aware of her party. She ridiculed the pens, buttons, and other presidential memorabilia that Johnson sent home with Dirksen as nothing more than a "domestic peace token from the president for spoiling my dinner party." Dirksen's son-in-law, Howard Baker, recalled another occasion when Johnson called Dirksen at his Senate office and invited him to the White House for a drink. Dirksen felt obligated to decline, telling Johnson, "I'm sorry I can't come down for a drink. Last night I came home late and Louella was mad."[3]

Johnson's favorite tool for politicking was the telephone. He used the phone to cajole, plead, console, praise, advise, agonize, condemn, and tweak. Everett Dirksen was a regular object of Johnson's endless efforts to have his way. Recently opened telephone tapes at the Johnson Library reveal the richness of the president's hands-on political style and provide a more textured view of his personal and political relationships with Minority Leader Dirksen. Johnson used Kennedy's assassination as the political catalyst necessary to pass the Kennedy program and to give substance to the legacy of the fallen president. In the days after Kennedy's funeral, Johnson took to the telephone. In these conversations he was a dynamo who would brook no rebuff. An exasperated Dirksen once complained early in Johnson's tenure that the president "called me up six times yesterday. I can't get any work done because he's always got me on the phone."[4]

The president's first goal was to pass the Kennedy administration's tax

reduction package. Johnson sensed that Kennedy's assassination generated enough goodwill to push the program through the Congress. But
his interaction with Dirksen demonstrates that the president was also
committed to securing the approval of those Americans who questioned
his leadership abilities and who were suspicious of his ascendancy to the
White House. In a late-November phone call Johnson urged Dirksen to
help him pass the tax bill because "if we don't, we're gonna get bad
press." He referred to James MacGregor Burns's recently published book,
The Deadlock of Democracy, and insisted, "If Congress . . . can't pass
a tax bill between January and January, we're in a hell of a shape."
Though he needed Dirksen's support, Johnson gave the minority leader
no time to reply. Instead, he pointed to the advantages of suprapartisan-
leadership: "You'd probably pick up a bunch of Senate seats because
you're running the Senate like I ran it. You're being pretty patriotic and
you've cooperated." Dirksen pledged his commitment. Four days later Secretary of the Treasury Douglas Dillon (a registered Republican) chuckled
when he reported to Johnson that Dirksen's "sorta acting as if he's our
floor manager for the bill." Unlike Kennedy, who almost never sent a
letter of congratulations to a Republican, Johnson from the beginning
praised Dirksen in writing. His cooperative attitude and "loyal service,"
Johnson wrote, put country above partisan affiliation and thus "deserves
the gratitude of all Americans."[5]

Dirksen's willingness to collaborate with the White House advanced
Johnson's political interests. Even at this early stage, however, the Johnson-
Dirksen relationship was more reciprocal than it appeared. Jacob Javits
(R-NY) held that Dirksen "got more from Johnson than Johnson got
from him." Larry Temple, the White House's liaison with the Justice Department, was more measured: "They both had their eyes wide open. I
don't think that Johnson gave away the store and I sure don't think Dirksen was star-struck." At the very least, the president's incessant pursuit
of Dirksen's favor increased the minority leader's prestige and influence
on Capitol Hill. His constant interaction with Johnson made him the primary source of information and analysis when he and his colleagues caucused to devise political strategies. Just as important, Dirksen's relationship with the White House strengthened his standing with key sectors of
his Illinois constituency. Though Dirksen continued to treat his home
state's politics with relative unconcern, his importance to the Johnson
administration translated into disproportionate patronage for Illinois.

White House aide Jack Valenti remembered that "Everett Dirksen peopled commissions with his people more than anybody I ever saw in my life. You couldn't name a commission where there wasn't a Dirksen man on it somewhere."[6]

Johnson's first instinct was to think of Dirksen when a Republican vacancy emerged. Just before Christmas the two politicos negotiated an ambassadorship for William Macomber, who had served in the State Department during the Eisenhower administration. Johnson asked if Dirksen wanted him appointed. Dirksen gave his endorsement, lamely telling Johnson, "Well, he's a damn good guy." With mock irritation, the president snapped, "There's a million Johnson men that are good guys, but he's a Republican, and if we're gonna appoint Republican ambassadors they better be your Republican ambassadors. I'm not gonna be appointing them just out of the skies. . . . Do you want this guy appointed?" Dirksen replied that, yes, he did, and Johnson shot back, "All right, he'll be appointed, period. But don't you think I'm gonna be appointing Republicans around without talking to Republicans. There're all kinds of Republicans." Dirksen agreed, "Yes, sir." Johnson finished the conversation: "You're my kind of Republican. Good-bye." A flabbergasted Dirksen stammered, "Yes, sir."[7]

Even though Johnson nurtured his relationship with Dirksen by showering him with patronage and a sense of political importance that far outstripped the number of votes he commanded, the minority leader was reluctant to toe the Johnson line at the expense of his partisan position in the GOP. Johnson sensed this, and he mixed his flattery of Dirksen with real concern that the minority leader might sabotage his legislative program. There was, however, no question of his importance to the White House. On the defining issue of civil rights, advocates and opponents assumed that only Dirksen could deliver the Republican votes necessary to beat back a Southern Democratic filibuster. Johnson told the NAACP's Roy Wilkins, "You're gonna have to persuade Dirksen why this is in the interests of the Republican party. . . . I'm a Democrat, but if a fella will stand up and fight with you, you can cross party lines."[8]

Still, Dirksen's delaying tactics in the Senate frustrated Johnson. In a telephone call to Eugene McCarthy (D-MN) he emphasized that the Senate had to pass the tax reduction package and turn to civil rights, or the "Negroes are going back to the streets and we're going to have chaos in this country . . . and that just ruins us and we'll have nothing to go to the country on and besides we'll have a big depression." The problem, he believed, was Dirksen. Johnson feared that Dirksen was stalling the program for political gain. The minority leader, he sensed, "wants to go home before the convention and he doesn't ever want to come back. . . . His very interests [are] for us to do nothing. If we can do nothing they can say, 'Well, we had no program.' "[9]

Yet when Dirksen went to the hospital with an ulcer flare-up in early February 1964, a worried Johnson overcame his restiveness and worked to bolster his friend's spirits. When Johnson called, a weary and sedated Dirksen reported, "Well, I'm doing pretty good. That ulcer hit me about midnight." Johnson retorted, "Well, if you would quit drinking that damn Sanka and get on a good scotch whiskey once in a while." Dirksen agreed, slurring, "Well, I think you have a point there." Johnson wasn't finished. "What you need to do is go out and get you about three good half glasses of bourbon whiskey, and then go down to the Occidental and buy a red beef steak and then get you a woman." The sixty-seven-year-old happily married Dirksen could only chuckle. With a drugged Dirksen flat on his back and far from healthy, Johnson could not resist the opportunity to play some politics and discuss an appointment to the Federal Deposit Insurance Commission (FDIC). Settling into his White House responsibilities, the new president saw himself at the absolute center of the political universe. As he most always did, Johnson wrapped up the call: "Go back to sleep now and don't let anybody else call you. I just wanted to wish you well and tell you I was thinking of you and hoping you hurry up and get back."[10]

After Congress passed the administration's tax reduction package in February 1964, the Senate turned its attention to civil rights. A heavy bipartisan majority in the House had approved a broad and progressive bill that would desegregate public facilities and prohibit discrimination in employment.[11] In the Senate, Southern Democrats made clear their commitment to watering down or even killing the legislation through the filibuster. Because Senate rules required a two-thirds majority to beat back a filibuster, and because Democrats from ten southern states were sure to resist any move toward cloture, Dirksen found himself in the pivotal position on Capitol Hill as the Senate faced the nation's most defining social issue since World War II.

House Democrats and Republicans won a pledge from Attorney General Robert Kennedy that the administration would not allow the Senate to eviscerate their courageous but contentious bill. Yet Dirksen had already made clear his reluctance to support the bill's two most controversial provisions. Title 2 would have outlawed segregation in public facilities, excepting retail stores and personal service firms. Title 7 would have established a five-member Equal Employment Opportunity Commission (EEOC) charged with investigating discrimination in employment and bringing suits on behalf of individuals. In his notes early in the debate, Dirksen questioned the restrictive effects of a sweeping investigatory authority and asked, "What protection is afforded to an employer from fishing expeditions by investigators in their zeal to enforce Title 7?" Chief among his worries was the fear that a federal EEOC would overlap with similar state regulatory agencies already established in the North: "Shall we have the federal forces of justice pulling on the one arm and the state forces of justice tugging on the other? Shall we draw and quarter the victim?" Dirksen's initial objections revolved around traditional Republican fears that proliferating executive agencies would jeopardize individual liberties.[12]

Johnson worried that "[Richard] Russell and Dirksen got a deal on cloture." He told Kennedy, "I don't think we can get Dirksen to take with him twenty-five Republicans out of the thirty-five necessary to get cloture." At a meeting of the Leadership Council on Civil Rights (LCCR), Assistant Attorney General Nicholas Katzenbach was more hopeful. He predicted that Dirksen would favor the bill, "since he had never let us down." House Republican William McCulloch, the steely Ohioan who cosponsored the House bill, told a Capitol Hill group supporting the legislation that "he thought he knew Dirksen pretty well and he wasn't sure." Not even Dirksen's aides knew where he really stood on the bill. At a February 20 press conference with Charles Halleck, Dirksen emphasized his opposition to Titles 2 and 7 and reported that "I have no assumption in mind at the present time" for supporting cloture. But he also insisted that he "had an open mind" and was considering a number of amendments to satisfy his objections. He told the reporters that freedom would be his watchword. To underscore his point, he recounted a story that amused the press corps. "I am just like little Johnny," Dirksen insisted, "when the teacher asked him to spell 'straight.' He said, 's-t-r-a-i-g-h-t.'

She said, 'And what does it mean?' And he said, 'Without ginger ale.' And that's the way I take my freedom."[13]

Dirksen's indecisiveness heightened his importance on Capitol Hill. After Democratic whip Hubert Humphrey, who was in charge of the bill on the floor, went on *Meet the Press* and praised Dirksen's patriotism, Johnson called to congratulate him: "Boy, that was right. You're doing just right now. You just keep at that. Don't let those bomb throwers . . . talk you out of seeing Dirksen. You drink with Dirksen! You talk with Dirksen! You listen to Dirksen!" He advised Humphrey that "Ev is a proud man. So don't pull any damned protocol. *You* go see *him*. And don't forget that Dirksen loves to bend at the elbow. I want you to drink with him till he agrees to vote for cloture and deliver me two Republicans from the mountain states." Though he drank himself "damned near blind," Humphrey kept after him and later claimed, "I would have kissed Dirksen's ass on the Capitol steps."[14]

Humphrey pressed him constantly. "Well, Dirk," he would ask, "when do you think we ought to meet and talk over some of your amendments?" Dirksen would often say, "Well, give us a couple more days. It isn't time yet." While the administration and scores of civil rights activists lobbied for early consideration of the bill to stave off street demonstrations that were sure to turn violent, Dirksen stalled. He bristled at their "impatience." He deemed it "unworthy" of the Senate as "a deliberative body if threats of demonstrations and taking to the streets [move] us to hurried and careless craftsmanship."[15] Dirksen knew that he had few of the Republican votes necessary for a successful cloture. His stalling was meant in part to increase the pressure on those Republicans whose support would be essential. By declaring an open mind and an eagerness to make the bill more palatable through the amendment process, he was keeping his options open and was including all factions of the GOP in the writing of the bill.

But Dirksen's wait-and-see strategy also advanced his personal interests. In early April a Chicago newspaper reported that "Dirksen today is at the peak of his powers." A Senate aide held that the basis for his influence was a "jovial, light-hearted manner." But another Capitol Hill staffer was quick to emphasize, "He's got a mind like a steel trap. He's always at least six steps ahead of you." He had been working with his staffers to craft a number of amendments that would address his objections to the bill. And in early April, he began to introduce these amendments without calling them up for floor debate. Cornelius Kennedy, his legislative assistant, recalled later that Dirksen's early amendments "were for educational purposes." The minority leader was simply testing the waters to determine where the various actors stood on the bill. Two of his proposals proved immediately controversial. First, Dirksen suggested the elimination of the EEOC's authority to file suits. Second, he rewrote Title 7 to ensure that the states would preempt federal power in cases of employment discrimination.[16]

Civil rights activists were outraged. To them, Dirksen's amendments would have gutted the bill. Humphrey tried to assuage a group of leaders in his office: "My position is no amendments. But I want to praise Dirksen. He's not trying to be destructive. He's trying to be constructive. There's no chance of getting cloture unless we have Everett Dirksen." But they would not be mollified. Clarence Mitchell, the NAACP's chief Washington lobbyist, wrote Wilkins and reported that "Dirksen's amendments are poison for the most part. . . . Just imagine what kind of FEPC [Fair Employment Practices Commission] Mississippi would set up." Mitchell told Humphrey that "if we let the Dirksen amendment prevail, there will be Negro revolution throughout the country." Even McCulloch was sharply critical. He was angry that Dirksen had introduced the amendments without first consulting him and worried that the proposals would weaken the bill's enforcement provisions. Several days later groups of Catholic, Protestant, and Jewish seminarians began a twenty-four-hour-a-day prayer vigil at the Lincoln Memorial that lasted until the Senate passed the House bill. Though he told Humphrey that he was in no way ready to support a cloture motion, Dirksen must have been impressed by the wide variety of advocates pushing for strong legislation.[17]

Racist southerners lobbied Dirksen as well. He had objected to a bill pending in the Mississippi legislature that would have outlawed the Republican party. Noting the parallel between the Mississippi proposal and the "communist conception of the single-party state," Dirksen held that it was "incomprehensible that a legislative body in the United States could bring itself to vote for a law setting up a one-party take-it-or-leave-it state." Mississippi's House speaker Walter Sillers offered a trade. "You help us kill the civil rights legislation in Congress, and we will kill any legislation which would destroy the Republican party in Mississippi. . . .

There has never appeared any state legislation which is more communistic than the civil rights legislation now pending."[18]

Most of the pressure, however, came from Humphrey and the Republican liberals. On April 21 Humphrey met with Dirksen. The two agreed that the Senate would pass an effective civil rights bill. The minority leader, however, believed that cloture would not be necessary. The southerners, Dirksen suggested, "were running to the end of their rope . . . and the bill would pass largely in its present form." Perhaps sensing that Dirksen was again testing his commitment, Humphrey disagreed. He believed that the filibuster was the only way the southerners could "get themselves off a political hook" and that Dirksen was responsible for delivering twenty-five Republican votes for cloture. After Humphrey further flattered Dirksen, the two men talked about timing. Dirksen wanted to avoid any "repercussions from the bill" during the Republican convention, but he pledged his commitment to secure the votes necessary for cloture. According to John Stewart, a Humphrey staffer close to the negotiations, "It appears that Dirksen is beginning to swallow the great man hook and when it is fully digested we will have ourselves a civil rights bill."[19]

Thomas Kuchel's legislative assistant Stephen Horn appreciated the subtlety of the situation. Dirksen did not yet have the votes. Moreover, he and other Republicans were "anxious to avoid the federal bureaucracy running throughout private enterprise." As negotiations wore on, Dirksen's reservations became clearer and more acceptable to some Democrats. John Stewart later wrote in his journal that the core of Dirksen's objections was "in no way related to the racial problem as such, but to the old fear of so-called big government. If Dirksen can be made to appear the person who attempted to protect the businessman from the evil influences of big government, then he should feel reasonably well satisfied."[20]

Other proponents were more hostile to Dirksen's influence. Andrew Biemiller of the AFL-CIO told Humphrey that he hoped the Democrats would not bend over backward to accommodate Dirksen. Sen. Joe Clark (D-PA) thought that the minority leader was dawdling because he "has no interest in President Johnson's legislative program. He feels that if people are kept involved on civil rights, it will be too late to do much about the Johnson program." When Katzenbach reported that Dirksen remained the pivotal player, Clark bristled, "Let's not kid ourselves, this has become the Dirksen bill! I deplore it, but that's it." The most widely held suspicion, however, was that Dirksen had been planning all along to gut the bill in a private meeting with Johnson.[21]

Humphrey scored a preemptive strike on Dirksen by arriving unannounced at the White House one day before Dirksen's scheduled conference with the president. Humphrey worried that Dirksen would try to persuade Johnson to divide the bill by title and first pursue a cloture vote on the relatively uncontroversial jury trial amendment. Civil rights activists feared that such an action would amount to an abandonment of the more contentious but important provisions of the legislation. White House aide Larry O'Brien told the president that "Hubert would like to get the sleeves rolled up totally with Dirksen on the Dirksen amendments overall and . . . aim for overall cloture rather than cloture on the jury trial amendment." Humphrey's meeting with Johnson secured the White House's commitment to the bill as a whole.[22]

Johnson called Mike Mansfield fifteen minutes before Dirksen's April 29 arrival at the Oval Office. He was irritated at Dirksen's interaction with the Washington press corps. Johnson reported to Mansfield, "I'm gonna tell him that I support a strong civil rights bill. He gave out a long interview of what he's gonna tell me today before he comes which is not like him." Perhaps more to the point, Johnson objected to a Dirksen statement that took issue with the president's handling of one of his dogs: "I don't know what's happening to him here lately. He's acting like a shit-ass. First thing he said he wouldn't treat his dog like I treated mine. . . . It's none of his damn business how I treat my dog and I'm a hell of a lot better to dogs and people than he is." Whatever the source of Johnson's displeasure, one Republican insider reported that Dirksen found the president in a "tough and uncompromising mood. . . . It appears that Johnson threw the ball back to Dirksen rather than letting Dirksen leave it on the White House stoop."[23]

Dirksen now knew that there would be a civil rights bill. His self-defined responsibility was "to make it as workable and as equitable as possible." He sought to improve the bill through the amendment process and hoped that the compromises he won would be enough to gain the necessary Republican votes for cloture. He knew that he would have to secure commitments from a number of conservatives who were reluctant to sacrifice the filibuster's inherent protection of the minority and who were wary of increased federal power through the creation of intrusive executive agencies. Carl T. Curtis (R-NE) told Kuchel that he would "not vote for cloture unless the Dirksen amendments are adopted."[24]

In early May the principals began sifting through Dirksen's proposals. Though Mansfield reported "cautious optimism" to the White House, committed liberals and conservatives objected to the negotiations. Roy Wilkins warned Humphrey that if the administration accepted Dirksen's plans for weaker federal enforcement, there would be "sharp and cynical resentment in the Negro community." Martin Luther King and James Farmer of the Congress of Racial Equality (CORE) predicted mass protests if Congress did not quickly pass the House legislation. Others criticized Humphrey's decision to negotiate in Dirksen's office. Humphrey shot back, "I don't care where we meet Dirksen. We can meet him in a nightclub, in the bottom of a mine, or in a manhole."[25]

Rumblings from the Republican right were even more ominous. Invited to attend the early sessions, chairman of the Republican Policy Committee Bourke B. Hickenlooper (R-IA) stormed out in protest. "I don't know," the Iowan proclaimed, "who the minority leader is speaking for! He is not speaking for Hickenlooper!" Suspicious of "zealous bureaucrat employees," Hickenlooper objected to the establishment of the Fair Employment Practices Commission and deemed its delegated authority "discretionary and coercive." He considered the Dirksen amendments "wholly inadequate." The presidential primaries tangled the situation even further. Barry Goldwater had already made clear his opposition to the bill; the momentum of his campaign complicated Dirksen's efforts to fashion a bill that a vast majority of Senate Republicans could support. Washington insiders reported that Goldwater's Senate supporters were reluctant to isolate him on an issue as volatile as civil rights. Southern Democrats "patted Barry on the back and said, 'You keep winning those elections—it's helping.'"[26]

The White House was seething with frustration. At the expense of every other piece of legislation pushed by the administration, the Senate filibuster had lasted over ten weeks. Johnson and his staff wanted around-the-clock sessions to wear down an aging coterie of southerners. Mansfield balked. In his estimation, such strong-arm tactics were likely to backfire and cost the administration the support of moderate and conservative Republicans who needed to see firsthand the widespread support for a strong civil rights bill. O'Brien disagreed. In a telephone call with the president, O'Brien detailed a conversation with Humphrey: "God Almighty, all the intellectuals you're talking to all day long and changing commas and language . . . for God's sake, you've got the title 'Whip,' and you better just get a whip out. . . . Dirksen will say just before the Republican convention, 'OK, boys, let's have a bill,' and then he'll sneak out of town [and] then we'll have a bunch of things that'll be lined up at the door of the Senate and they're going to try and duck 'em all."[27]

Humphrey heeded their call. Though he and Mansfield refused to lengthen the legislative day, he increased his already intense efforts to push through a bill. He told the LCCR that "people are getting disgusted. . . . Every day we wait for cloture is nibbling away at the bill." Two days after Humphrey took the minority leader out to dinner, Dirksen broke the impasse. Attending the pivotal May 13 meeting with Dirksen in his office were Mansfield, Humphrey, Attorney General Robert Kennedy, Kuchel, and the most influential members of their staffs. Joe Clark was there briefly, but in a prearranged gambit he stormed out when the conversation turned to a proposal to modify Title 7: "It's a goddam sellout," he shouted. Humphrey looked at Dirksen and pleaded for sympathy: "See what pressure I'm up against? I can't concede any more on this point." The minority leader insisted that he was ready to deal and that he was committed to pushing through "as good a bill as . . . quickly as possible." He admitted to slippage among his conservative ranks as a result of Goldwater's primary victories but pointed to specific amendments that might be adopted to win the support of other Republicans.[28]

The essential terms of the compromise reflected not only Dirksen's long-held distaste for overlapping bureaucracies and needless litigation that combined to stifle business activity but also his recognition that entrenched segregation was a moral blot on Abraham Lincoln's vision of a democratic republic. First, Dirksen won an agreement that stripped the EEOC of its authority to file antidiscrimination suits. Though the commission could make recommendations, only the Justice Department had the power to initiate a suit. To Dirksen, this arrangement eliminated excessive litigation without jeopardizing necessary federal enforcement in the South. His proposal also reflected his lingering dislike for ballooning executive agencies like the New Deal's National Labor Relations Board, whose broad enforcement powers had grown through the years and fueled long-held conservative opposition to a power-hungry White House.

Second, Dirksen insisted that local agencies have the first opportunity to enforce federal law. He emphasized that fair employment "starts back home" and that the EEOC must defer to state FEPCs and their commitment to "local spirit." Dirksen's offer mirrored the Republican and conservative Democratic aversion to a paternalistic federal government imposing social justice from faraway places. When Humphrey and the liberals articulated the well-founded fear that southern states would merely create paper FEPCs to avoid federal enforcement, Dirksen gave way and limited the state FEPC's jurisdiction to sixty days, after which a complainant could turn to the EEOC for justice.

Third, the bipartisan group turned to the language of Titles 2 and 7. Though Attorney General Kennedy and the Democrats refused to support Dirksen's suggestion that they add a title that dealt specifically with enforcement powers, the two sides agreed to back Dirksen's second proposal. He insisted that the attorney general file suit only after it was evident that a clear "pattern and practice" of discrimination existed in places of public accommodation and employment. Dirksen thus protected northern and western businesses from intrusive federal agencies without letting the South off the hook. At the close of the May 13 meeting, which capped ten days of exhaustive negotiations, Dirksen emerged and told an expectant media, "We have a good agreement." Humphrey was ecstatic. He told Johnson, "We've got a much better bill than anyone dreamed possible." He also endorsed Dirksen's proposals: "We haven't weakened this bill one damned bit. In some places we've improved it."[29]

Winning enough votes for cloture, however, was still in doubt. Dirksen told the bipartisan leaders that he would distribute copies of the bill to his colleagues for discussion at a party caucus on May 19. He also reported to Johnson that he had drawn the line for Richard Russell, who "gave me no comfort." Dirksen told the Georgian, "You're gonna have to fish or cut bait, 'cause I think we've now gone far enough and I think we've been fair." Johnson congratulated Dirksen: "You're worthy of the land of Lincoln and a man from Illinois is going to pass the bill and I'll see that you get the proper attention and credit." Even so, he referred to potential protests in the South and pressed his friend to round up the necessary votes: "If these schools are out at the end of this month, and we haven't got a bill, we're in a hell of a shape."[30]

Not every interested group was satisfied with the compromise. Joe Rauh, vice chairman of the Americans for Democratic Action (ADA), insisted that Humphrey had "sold out on Title 7." Perhaps sensing that their options were limited, other civil rights advocates were more restrained. GOP conservatives, however, were sharply critical. At the May 19 Republican conference Hickenlooper raged at the intrusive powers that the "gargantuan" bill conceded to the attorney general. Dirksen bristled at the mutiny in his ranks. Immediately after the caucus, he invited the press corps to his office and single-handedly changed the terms of the debate for his party. Endorsing the package he had crafted and embracing the moral pressure that had been building in the country, he started softly and slowly, paraphrasing Victor Hugo's diary: "No army is stronger than an idea whose time has come." Suddenly, he was more animated. In a warning to the conservative rebels, he insisted, "Today the challenge is here! It is inescapable. It is time to deal with it! No one on that floor is going to stop this. It is going to happen."[31]

Dirksen's dramatics gave the leadership the momentum necessary to win a cloture vote. For the rest of the week he met with his Republican colleagues and worked to overcome their objections. Though thrown on the defensive, Hickenlooper would not be deterred. Dirksen's Senate colleagues held that personal acrimony between the two was the primary motivation for Hickenlooper's obstinacy. George Pavlik, Hickenlooper's legislative assistant, wrote his boss that the Dirksen compromise "would go a long way, but not all the way, in meeting your primary objections" to the House bill. But Hickenlooper, easily spotted in the Senate chamber with his red-headed crew cut and his horn-rimmed glasses, would not budge. Hugh Scott remembered Hickenlooper as "explosive and choleric," and he sensed that the Iowan resented Dirksen's central role in the debate: "He was a very prideful person. Certainly all of the public attention and glory was going to Dirksen." Whatever his personal feelings toward Dirksen, Hickenlooper employed traditional Republican rhetoric to condemn the bill. He scorned the "tyrannical abuse by centralized authority" and railed at the bureaucratic "roadrunners checking into every business and the whole economic system."[32]

For the time being, however, Dirksen had weathered the Hickenlooper storm. By May 26 Humphrey and Dirksen had established enough consensus to introduce the latter's substitute. The minority leader promoted "a salable piece of work" that emerged from the negotiating process and insisted, "We have now reached the point where there must be action." Richard Russell was not so sanguine. He pilloried the Dirksen measure and denounced the bill as "purely sectional."[33] Despite Russell's attack, Dirksen sensed that he had led his party to the cusp of a breakthrough on civil rights. Though he and Humphrey did not yet have enough committed votes for cloture, Dirksen, for the first time in three weeks, turned his attention away from the bill and addressed a problem that would come to rival civil rights as the most defining issue of the 1960s.

Lyndon Johnson's intuitive decision to continue his predecessor's foreign policy program was fraught with peril. John Kennedy endorsed America's post–World War II policy of global containment, and the rhetoric he employed at crucial times exceeded Truman's and Eisenhower's. Though Kennedy endorsed different means to contain communist aggression, he subscribed to the bipartisan belief that foreign policy was a zero-sum endeavor in which a loss to the communists anywhere would result in an erosion of American prestige everywhere. Like Kennedy, the new president was most reluctant to challenge the Washington establishment's conception of the foreign policy status quo. As majority leader he had cooperated closely with Eisenhower on foreign policy issues; once in the White House, he instinctively reached across the aisle to include the opposition in the most important decisions of his administration.

Johnson inherited from Kennedy a number of international trouble spots. None was more vexing than Vietnam. Carrying on Eisenhower's commitment to South Vietnamese independence, Kennedy had seen social and political instability threaten the legitimacy of Ngo Dinh Diem's anticommunist government. To check increasing communist infiltration from the north and to deter a growing communist movement in the south, the Kennedy administration endorsed Diem's overthrow as the best way to address the multiple problems of the South Vietnamese people and thus to provide a modicum of political stability in the region. The change in government, however, made little difference, and the situation in Vietnam continued to unravel. In late January 1964 Gen. Nguyen Khanh, a fierce anticommunist but an unreliable political ally, overthrew the provisional government. Shackled to the containment policy and all too aware of an increasing communist presence in South Vietnam, Johnson had little choice but to recognize the Khanh regime. As the communist insurgency intensified, the president increased the U.S. military commitment to South Vietnam. He approved an expansion of covert raids on North Vietnam and authorized guerrilla raids on infiltration trails leading into the south, reconnaissance flights over Laos, and the shelling of military targets in the Tonkin Gulf.[34]

During this time, Dirksen spurred on the White House. In February he placed Vietnam within the framework of America's vital interests. Angry that "one nation after another with smaller populations than most of our larger cities kicks us on the shins and gets away with it," he scolded Johnson for promoting a toothless policy that created "drift and dismay." He told the press that "if Vietnam went down the drain, it could conceivably cost us all of Southeast Asia." He made sure the political stakes remained high. Having entered the Senate just as the United States "lost" China on the watch of a Democratic president, Johnson knew that the Republicans would exploit any perceived weakness in his execution of the containment policy. Besides promoting what the establishment deemed to be the nation's foreign policy goals, Johnson's defense of South Vietnam as a bastion of anticommunism was designed to protect his political flank. When the White House asked Congress for $125 million to fund its military program, Dirksen denounced Johnson's "indecision" on Vietnam, which was "dribbling away both American lives and American prestige in Southeast Asia." Even though he had already been invited to an afternoon conference at the White House, Dirksen on May 26 suggested that Johnson was neglecting his responsibility to involve the GOP in crafting the nation's response to the turmoil in Vietnam: "We've got to have frequent conversations."[35]

After the bipartisan meeting, Johnson worried that events in Vietnam limited his options. On May 27 he called his old mentor, Richard Russell. The president admitted that Vietnam was "deteriorating every day." Russell agreed that the situation there was "the damn worst mess I ever saw." Unlike Johnson's closest advisers, however, Russell counseled caution. When Johnson asked him how significant Vietnam was to America's overall interests, the Georgian stressed that "it isn't important a damn bit." When Russell suggested that the administration look for a credible reason to disengage, Johnson pointed out that his advisers were for escalation and that the United States had to fulfill its obligations to the Southeast Treaty Organization or risk losing international prestige. Even more telling, he sensed that "the Republicans are gonna make a political issue out of it, every one of 'em, even Dirksen. . . . Yesterday before he came he gave out a big statement that we had to get us a program and go after 'em." Later that day Johnson told National Security Adviser McGeorge Bundy, "It looks to me like we're getting involved in another Korea and it just worries the hell out of me and I don't see what we can ever hope to get out of there once we're committed." Johnson was trapped by his predecessors' commitment to anticommunism in Southeast Asia. By attacking the administration for its reluctance to pursue a more aggressive policy, Dirksen tightened the political choke-hold on Johnson and narrowed his options for dealing with the crisis. Because he was unwilling to jeopardize his prized political capital in an election year, Johnson disregarded his instincts against escalation and stumbled his way to the point of no return.[36]

At the time, however, the more pressing issue was civil rights. Proud of his ability to secure the support of 80 percent of his Republican colleagues, Dirksen nonetheless endured the criticism of his more conservative constituents who chafed at his cooperation with liberal Democrats. When conservative critics wrote to condemn his efforts, Dirksen was quick to underline the essential force driving the bill forward: "This is an issue which . . . has a deep moral aspect and there is a duty on the part of Republicans to do their full share if they hope to be worthy of the Republican tradition . . . and Abraham Lincoln." Agreeing with Mansfield that the time had come to seek a cloture vote, he and the majority leader jointly announced that the day of final reckoning in the Senate would be June 9, 1964. The GOP's pivotal California presidential primary was scheduled for June 2, and Goldwater had already informed Dirksen that he intended to vote against cloture. Dirksen delayed the vote to enable Goldwater's allies in the Senate to vote for cloture without jeopardizing his chances for the nomination.[37]

On June 2 Goldwater won the California primary. That same day an exhausted Dirksen developed a heavy chest cold and was unable to go to work. Bourke Hickenlooper, still smarting at the accolades showered upon the minority leader and disdainful of the bill's acceptance of the "capricious power of bureaucracy," used Dirksen's absence and Goldwater's victory to stir up conservative opposition to the bipartisan package.

To Hickenlooper, Dirksen's efforts to amend the bill were nothing more than "frosting on the cake." The Iowan held a series of meetings with conservative Republicans from the West and Midwest, and within a few days he had picked up considerable support for his views. Dirksen's ongoing convalescence enabled the revolt to continue. On June 5 Hickenlooper asked for unanimous consent to consider three amendments to the substitute that would have diluted the bill.[38]

Humphrey worried that Hickenlooper had the votes to deny the leadership the cloture motion it so desperately sought. Dirksen sensed that his rival was weaker than he appeared, but his agreement to accept Hickenlooper's terms suggests that a vote on the Iowan's amendments was the price he had to pay to keep his troops in line. Hickenlooper promised to support cloture after his amendments were voted up or down on June 9. Even though the least important of Hickenlooper's proposals (a revision of the jury trial amendment for contempt of court cases) was narrowly adopted, the leadership defeated the other amendments and overcame the last significant threat to winning the cloture vote. As Robert D. Loevy has observed, "The most important thing the Hickenlooper revolt demonstrated was how essential Everett Dirksen was to getting the required Republican votes for cloture." Only his illness allowed the Hickenlooper movement to start at all, and only his presence could keep the more conservative Republicans committed to the bill.[39]

June 10 dawned hot and sunny in the nation's capital. The Senate convened at 10:00 A.M. for final arguments before the cloture vote, but the public galleries had been packed for hours. CBS's Roger Mudd, who had been covering the Senate for the length of the filibuster, waited for a telephone call from the press gallery to report the vote of each senator on the cloture motion. Before that, however, the principals had their final say. In language characteristic of conservative Democrats and Republicans rankled by an executive branch appropriating more and more authority, Russell bemoaned the bill's "unbridled grants of power to the appointive powers of the government." Adhering to his custom of deflecting attention to individuals who enjoyed it more, Mansfield arranged for Dirksen to deliver the final speech. Weary and wan from his chest infection, he had arisen at 5:30 A.M. to compose his remarks. Though it was not one of Dirksen's better oratorical efforts, his language held the day. Noting that change is the only constant in American culture, he championed the morality of the cause and the need for sweeping legislation: "The time has come for equality of opportunity . . . in government, in education, and in employment. It will not be stayed or denied. It is here. . . . There is no substitute for a basic and righteous idea."[40]

Shortly thereafter, the Senate voted. Members on both sides kept tally sheets to count the votes. Congressmen stood along the walls of the Senate chamber. Critically ill with cancer, Clair Engel (D-CA) was wheeled onto the Senate floor. Though he could not speak even a single word, Engel pointed to his eye to signal an aye vote when his name was called. John Williams (R-DE) delivered the sixty-seventh and last vote needed for cloture. The motion passed by a final vote of 71 to 29. Twenty-seven of thirty-three Republicans voted with Minority Leader Dirksen. It was the most meaningful triumph of his career. His greatest achievement was to ensure that the Senate stood up, accounted for itself, and remained relevant in the face of the most important social movement of his generation. Although Joe Rauh held that Dirksen "was only switching 'ands' and 'buts,'" and that the minority leader "sold out cheap," the compromises he won and the package he crafted were consistent with his Republican heritage and his small-government instincts.[41] Nevertheless, the essential effect of the bill expanded the power of the federal government and embraced the modern presidency and those executive agencies necessary to enforce such revolutionary legislation. Dirksen's eventual decision to stare down all opposition to the bill was the climactic event in his stop-and-go odyssey toward a celebration of the executive branch as the key agent for change in America's political life.

Reaction to Dirksen's achievement was mostly positive. John Sherman Cooper, the liberal Republican who ran against Dirksen for the minority leadership in 1959, wrote Nelson Rockefeller and asserted that the House bill had been much improved by the Dirksen amendments. Martin Luther King praised his "able and courageous leadership." Wilkins wrote a congratulatory note that concluded, "Your key work will receive the credit it deserves." The bill, Wilkins declared, advanced the "cause of human rights and the commitment of a great, democratic government to protect the guarantees embodied in this Constitution." Even more telling, Wilkins wrote the NAACP's Illinois branch to point to Dirksen's "decisive role. I know that many of us have been critical of Senator Dirksen. . . . After all twenty-seven of the thirty-three Republicans . . . voted for cloture when the expectation only two months ago was that we would have trouble getting only twenty-two of them." Johnson added his voice to the chorus of well-wishers. With a twinge of envy, he told Dirksen, "You are the hero of the hour now. They have forgotten that anyone else is around. Every time I pick up a paper it is 'Dirksen' in the magazines. The NAACP is flying Dirksen banners and picketing the White House tomorrow."[42]

Conservatives, however, felt that Dirksen had let them down. A Virginia Republican wrote to Hickenlooper to "ask whether or not Dirksen has lost his mind. He is supposed to be the leader of the opposition but I can't see that he is doing much opposing." W. H. von Dreele was more creative. He wrote a poem for the *National Review* rebuking Dirksen's leadership: "All hail to thee, McKinley! / I sure do like your style. / Whenever you begin, we / anticipate a smile. / I hear the echoes clearly / of Webster and Calhoun. . . . / It's obvious—though older— / you've got a lot to say. / Then why the devil shoulder / The load for LBJ?" More significant for the GOP, likely presidential nominee Barry Goldwater voted against the bill. Though Dirksen worked hard to win the Arizonan's support and told his colleague that "you can't do it [to] the party," Goldwater held that the public accommodations and employment provisions were unconstitutional.[43] Dirksen's failure to lure Goldwater into the fold tarnished the luster on his political triumph, damaged the Republican ticket in 1964, and haunted the GOP for decades to come.

After a bruising intraparty debate, Dirksen searched for an issue to unify the GOP for the upcoming election. Before the Eisenhower administration, Republicans had focused their political ire on the notion of a leviathan executive that abused the rights of the several states and ran roughshod over the liberties of individual Americans. From Eisenhower through the early Johnson years, the core of the GOP endorsed a more powerful presidency. Having promoted the modern presidency and having accepted its role in directing the nation through both foreign and domestic crises, the GOP was forced to spotlight another agent in America's political culture that revealed the inherent evils of big government.

Not surprisingly, many Republicans turned to the Supreme Court. In *Baker v. Carr* (1962) the Court held that unequal apportionment of seats in state legislatures was unconstitutional and could be corrected by federal courts to achieve a one-man, one-vote ratio. Two years later, in *Reynolds v. Sims,* the Court found that bicameral state legislatures had to be apportioned along the lines of one-man, one-vote. Taken together, the Court's rulings threatened the GOP's small-town constituencies in state legislatures. More to the point, many Republicans criticized the Court's meddling in state affairs. Just five days after final Senate passage of the civil rights bill, Dirksen suggested in a GOP caucus that the Court's actions "might well be used as a campaign issue by the Republicans in the upcoming elections." On this issue, he and Hickenlooper agreed. The chairman of the Republican Policy Committee remarked that the Court's decrees "are in conflict with the Constitution and . . . tend to completely centralize former state authority in the federal government."[44]

Many conservatives argued that Dirksen had abandoned their principles on the issue of civil rights, but liberals and moderates were outraged when the minority leader decided to endorse Goldwater for the presidency. Rowland Evans and Robert Novak wrote that Dirksen's "decision killed the last, best hope of the party's liberal-to-moderate forces to stop Mr. Conservative." James Reston argued that "his timing was appalling." Dirksen squelched rumors that he was backing Goldwater in exchange for a nomination to the vice presidency. Though many hoped he would support the candidacy of Pennsylvania governor William Scranton, Dirksen valued a commitment to party regularity and could not overlook the fact that his Senate colleague had done the spadework necessary to win the nomination: "Barry earned his spurs as a Republican. He traveled the length and the breadth of this land year after year for Republican candidates." At one of his meetings with the Washington press corps, he emphasized Goldwater's commitment: "Show me a Republican who has campaigned as hard, then bring me a straw hat, and I'll eat it." Thruston Morton's comment was more pointed. "Ev's not a man to swim upstream," he explained privately, "so he just went the way he had to go. And, in this way, once he decided to go, he grabbed the banner and led the way. Ev's a man who flows with the stream." Goldwater agreed. After Dirksen's announcement, he marveled, "That old boy's got antenna three feet long."[45]

Dirksen also accepted Goldwater's invitation to introduce his nomination at the 1964 Republican convention in San Francisco. Before traveling west, he visited Goldwater's Washington apartment to read the likely nominee the speech he had written. The two colleagues sat in a dim twilight as Dirksen went over what he intended to say. As he finished, he heard Goldwater weeping. Dirksen feared that he had offended Goldwater by referring to him as the "militant son of an immigrant peddler."

Instead, the Arizonan was touched and flattered by the remarks. After Dirksen's San Francisco speech, in which he described Goldwater as a "clear-cut choice" and the leader of a conservative cause whose "tide is turning," Goldwater scribbled a note of thanks: "My prayer is that I will always merit the wonderful words you bestowed on my name today. To a large measure—in fact the largest measure—I was able to hear those words because of you, my political godfather, my friend, and my adviser."[46]

More privately, Dirksen worried about the effect of the Goldwater nomination. Even before his acceptance speech, in which Goldwater stressed that "extremism in the defense of liberty is no vice" and "moderation in the pursuit of justice is no virtue," Dirksen confided to reporter Neil MacNeil that "we've got to control him." He winced at Goldwater's tendency to ignore the subtleties of policymaking: "We have got to stop this hip shooting. It is simply too dangerous in the world as it is." Later that evening Joy Baker and her Pekin friend Richard Stolley, who wrote for *Life* magazine, encountered Dirksen in his hotel suite. A "portrait of total dejection and weariness," Dirksen was slumped in an armchair with a drink in his hand. "I did the best I could for him," Dirksen muttered.[47] Though he and Goldwater were personal friends, Dirksen sensed that Johnson would crush Goldwater and the GOP in 1964; even more important, he must have found fault with Goldwater's disregard for the Washington establishment's politics of conciliation and compromise.

Meanwhile, in Washington, the politics of the election affected Johnson's handling of the situation in Vietnam. Urging an escalation of the war, Goldwater had consistently criticized the president for his restrained response to the communist advances in the south. Overly sensitive to Goldwater's attacks, Johnson was determined to show the voters that he was an ardent but responsible cold warrior committed to defending the nation's interests abroad, and he waited for an opportunity to prove his mettle without heedlessly widening the conflict. The occasion for the president's political posturing came in early August. As part of a gradual escalation of pressures against the north, the White House had ordered the destroyer *Maddox* to the Gulf of Tonkin to engage in electronic surveillance. After some minor skirmishes with North Vietnamese gunboats, the Pentagon sent the destroyer *C. Turner Joy* to the area and positioned the ships close to the North Vietnamese coast in order to provoke an attack that would require a U.S. response. On August 4 the *Maddox* and the *Turner Joy* signaled that they were being shelled.[48]

Though bad weather called into question the veracity of the report, and Congress was never informed of the provocative nature of the American mission, President Johnson used the encounter to justify a military response against the north. He called the congressional leaders to the White House for a foreign policy briefing. When Johnson explained that the retaliation would be in proportion to the attack on the American ships, a hawkish Dirksen urged the president to reconsider: "If I had to do it I would put our references to 'limited' in the deep freeze. It connotes we would be like sitting ducks. We should make it clear we would meet every enemy threat."[49]

Johnson also used the incident to call for a comprehensive congressional resolution that would empower him to take "all necessary measures to repel any armed attacks against the forces of the United States and to prevent further aggression." Though scholars have argued that Johnson's primary intention was to demonstrate his determination to contain communism in Southeast Asia, he was in effect asking Congress for permission to run foreign policy without the participation of Capitol Hill. Essentially, the Gulf of Tonkin resolution most resembled Eisenhower's 1957 Middle East resolution.[50] In effect, Johnson's actions were nothing less than an evolutionary application of the power of the modern presidency to direct the whole of the nation's cold war foreign policy.

Dirksen could not have been an easier sell. Though he hailed from a party that had criticized the executive usurpation of powers delegated to Congress and had joined his GOP colleagues in lashing out at Truman's prosecution of a "one-man war" in Korea, Dirksen backed the president's request for the authority he needed to wage war in Southeast Asia without a formal declaration from the Congress. The rhetoric Dirksen employed to support the Gulf of Tonkin resolution reflected the Washington establishment's disregard for the essential vitality of partisan politics and the appropriate role of the opposition in times of crisis in cold war America. He told his colleagues that Johnson had invited leaders from both parties to the White House to discuss the developing situation: "When we have had our day in court and the decision has been made, we are prepared to abide by the decision to demonstrate to the whole wide world that there is no division between the Executive and Congress."[51]

But Dirksen never challenged the information presented by the White House, nor did he press Johnson to defend his views. He merely encouraged the president to pursue a military response that would be followed by a sweeping congressional resolution. Dirksen told his colleagues that Johnson had gone beyond the call of duty to involve Congress in what he considered to be an international emergency of the first order: "The President could have taken this action on his own right as commander in chief. He does not have to ask Congress about the deployment of troops and submarines." Dirksen was nothing more than a mouthpiece for the administration, and he failed to meet even his own minimal standard for the role of the opposition in a democratic society. His eagerness to wave the flag and defend the free world in "an hour of need" was in part responsible for the Senate's 88-to-2 vote for the Gulf of Tonkin resolution and Johnson's understanding of his authority to escalate the war.[52]

Johnson's victory in 1964 was never in doubt. The scale of his triumph, however, left the GOP reeling. The Republicans lost a Senate seat and entered the Eighty-ninth Congress facing a 68-to-32 Democratic majority. Dirksen wrote Johnson to pass along his "heartiest congratulations on the horrendous thing that happened on November 3." Intraparty feuding stymied the GOP after the election. When Hickenlooper wrote Dirksen that some conservative Republicans "might take some reprisal" on his liberal whip Thomas Kuchel, the minority leader warned against such an attack: "We have enough crosses to bear."[53] In the House, Michigan's fifty-one-year-old Gerald Ford defeated Charles Halleck for the minority leadership. The strident style of Goldwater's campaign, the party's reduced minority in the Senate, and Ford's commitment to revamping the image of the GOP combined to complicate the established patterns of Dirksen's leadership.

The national GOP struggled to remain relevant after Goldwater's crushing defeat. His flirtation with doctrinaire conservatism made him an easy target. Johnson's political dexterity kept the opposition even more off balance in the months after the election. One Republican senator complained, "That damn Lyndon Johnson hasn't just grabbed the middle of the road. He's a bit to the Right of center, as well as a bit to the Left of center. And with Johnson hogging the whole road, Right, Left and center, where the devil can we go except the ditch?" Despite the fallout from the 1964 election and the altered terrain of the American political scene, Dirksen maintained his place at the center of the Washington establishment, as Roscoe Drummond's *New York Herald Tribune* article affirmed: "The GOP Needs Leader—And It Has Dirksen."[54]

Johnson ensured that Dirksen maintained an extraordinary level of national prominence after the Goldwater debacle. Aide Joe Califano remembered that Johnson told his staff, "Remember one thing, always be good to Everett Dirksen, always. He's good to us." Dirksen's close relationship with Johnson was indispensable, but the real reason for his prestige was his prominence in a Washington establishment that shunned strident partisanship. Like Johnson, Dirksen had mastered the mores of the inner circle. White House aide Jack Valenti remembered that Dirksen would call the White House and ask about Johnson. Then he would ask Valenti to relay a message: "Tell him I'm going to sort of cut him up a little bit on the floor tomorrow." After his floor speech, he would call back: "I'd like to see the boss." Valenti recalled that Dirksen knew to arrive through the Diplomatic Reception Room so the Washington press corps would not know he was making yet another call at the White House. Valenti described the atmosphere at these meetings: "Sometimes they'd have a drink together. They would sit and chew the fat, reminisce, tell stories, laugh, and really enjoy themselves. Then they would sit down about a half hour after they arrived and really begin to parley." White House aide Larry Temple suggested that the cocktail hour was the unspoken signal that the legislative day had come to a close and that the establishment could relax its partisan obligations. When drinks were served at the White House, Temple remembered, "Everybody would know that it was off the record by definition, and you could talk among friends."[55]

The vexing issues of the 1960s certainly encouraged Johnson to keep Dirksen in the fold. When the White House turned its attention again to the issue of civil rights, Dirksen occupied center stage on Capitol Hill. As Johnson struggled to prosecute the Vietnam war while sustaining some important defections in his own Democratic party, Dirksen became his crucial foreign policy ally in the Congress. It is little wonder, therefore, that Johnson took Mrs. Dirksen aside at the Capitol Hill luncheon after the 1965 inaugural and told her, "You've got to take care of that man. We need him." Whenever Dirksen went to Walter Reed Hospital for a checkup or medical treatment for one of his many maladies, Johnson put his surgeon general on the case and received up-to-date information on the status of Dirksen's recovery.[56]

Dirksen developed a mutually beneficial relationship with a largely uncritical Washington press corps to keep himself at the center of attention. Just days after Dirksen threw his support behind Goldwater in July 1964, George Dixon of the *Washington Post* stressed that reporters "almost unanimously consider Senator Dirksen a great guy." Instead of buying his own, Dirksen often bummed cigarettes off his favorite journalists, all the while stressing that he was trying to cut down on his steady intake. In the early 1960s reporters mocked him as "the syrupy half of the Ev and Charlie Show," but they prized their relationship with him. Dixon emphasized that Dirksen would often track reporters down to share a piece of news. He created his own ad hoc press conferences and would sit cross-legged on tables and answer questions (many of which he kept off the record) until everyone was satisfied. David Broder remembered that there was a certain routine to Dirksen's sessions with the press. Veteran journalists like William White and Jack Bell stood close to Dirksen while a multilayered ring of senior reporters kept the junior writers on the periphery. The unspoken but unmistakable spacing of the impromptu press conferences would have counted for little if Dirksen had not intentionally whispered his answers to his favorite reporters and left the youngsters begging for morsels from their senior colleagues. Broder had the feeling that Dirksen the showman was playing with the press, that at the peak of his powers he was in complete control and knew exactly how his remarks would be portrayed in the morning news. At the time, Broder was just grateful to be in on the show.[57]

The press was fond of his quick wit and easy sense of humor. When he left Walter Reed in early 1965, he provided an amused core of reporters with a graphic description of his place in the establishment and the politics that he had come to dominate. He said that the surgeon general called to inquire how he liked his suite. "Fine, Doc," Dirksen said, "except for one thing. There's no bar." The nation's number-one doctor asked, "Why does a guy with stomach spasms want a bar?" Dirksen replied, "Because at a bar you can get a shot of bourbon. Don't you know, doctor, there is nothing better for interior sedation?" According to Dirksen, the surgeon general called out, "Nurse, bring the senator some bourbon—THIS HIGH!" Dirksen told his friends that Johnson called him every day, advising, "You stay and get a good rest." Dirksen chided, "I've got a general, a colonel, a major, four sergeants, and four nurses attending me. It's so soft here that if I stay in longer, I'll become a bum. I'll get so soft I won't be able to sharpen up my right hook and left jab to sock the Great Society." When Johnson said not much was going on in Washington anyway, Dirksen retorted, "I've got to get back to work in eight days to save your program, dammit, whether you Democrats want to save it or not."[58]

In early 1965 Dirksen was not joking about Vietnam. Throughout the year he worked to stiffen the president's resolve in Southeast Asia, supported his efforts to maintain a noncommunist government with respect to South Vietnam, and, for political purposes, attacked those on the other side of the aisle who suggested that the United States reverse its growing commitment. For Dirksen, American prestige and honor were at stake. At one White House briefing he asked Bundy and the president about the effects of pulling out of Vietnam. But he never followed up this line of inquiry, and he was too quick to accept the conventional wisdom that defeat in the jungles of Vietnam would damage America's image abroad and endanger the nation's interests in all of Southeast Asia.[59]

On February 10, in the wake of a Viet Cong air strike on an American air base at Qui Non, Johnson held a meeting with congressional leaders to discuss the viability of a reprisal attack. Though Dirksen was celebrating Lincoln's birthday in Illinois and could not attend, he spoke with Johnson by telephone and pledged his support for "continuing action" in response to the bombing. Dirksen insisted, "We have no other choice," except losing "face with the world." Just as important, he publicly highlighted the president's frustration with members of his own party who had expressed reservations. Johnson, Dirksen noted, seemed "very annoyed at the disagreement of some Democratic leaders." Mansfield had urged restraint and the importance of negotiations at the White House meeting. Roscoe Drummond endorsed Dirksen's stance. Hinting that the president's critics were disloyal self-promoters who injured the cause, the columnist praised Dirksen for "rendering an invaluable service to the nation."[60]

Though Republicans like Thruston Morton expected a "great debate" over Vietnam in the Congress, Dirksen discouraged any rigorous examination of the administration's policy. Dwight Eisenhower, still the nation's most prominent Republican, echoed Dirksen. In a meeting with Johnson, the former president pointed to the sanctity of American prestige and the importance of keeping the Indochinese peninsula noncommunist. He "hoped it would not be necessary to use the six to eight divisions mentioned [by Johnson], but if it should be necessary, so be it." To his constituents, Dirksen mocked the possibility of negotiations. He acknowledged that "this is a rough deal in Vietnam." But Dirksen's aversion to appeasement and his unflinching belief that a victory for communism anywhere was a defeat for democracy everywhere conditioned him to maintain that there was no choice but to stay the course. "Negotiation," he emphasized, "is almost as bad as a man painting his front porch when the house is on fire." He was also quick to castigate those "members of the president's own party" who were calling for negotiations. Two weeks later Rolling Thunder, the administration's previously established policy of escalated air attacks on North Vietnam, began in earnest.[61]

Civil rights, however, pushed the administration's escalation of the war from the front pages. Though the 1964 bill overturned established patterns of segregation in public accommodations and places of employment, African Americans throughout the South were still denied the right to vote. In early 1965 Martin Luther King and his Southern Christian Leadership Conference highlighted this injustice through a series of demonstrations in Selma, Alabama. In Selma's Dallas County only 355 of 15,000 black citizens were registered to vote. The rest were denied through a combination of poll taxes and unevenly applied literacy tests that discriminated on the basis of race. King and his followers also chose Selma because they expected Sheriff Jim Clark to react to their peaceful protests with a viciousness and ferocity that would win the sympathy of the nation, the White House, and the Congress.

Clark did not disappoint. In the first two months of the year the Selma police arrested 3,000 demonstrators and hundreds of schoolchildren. Many were beaten and kicked in front of television cameras. On February 10 Clark arrested 165 protesters, turned them on a three-mile forced march out of town, and shocked them with electric cattle prods. Clark beat a woman who had pushed him and punched a black minister on the courthouse steps. A few days later Jimmy Lee Jackson intervened when the Alabama police assaulted his mother and infirm father. The police turned on Jackson and fatally shot him at point-blank range. On March 7, in response to the slaying of Jackson, John Lewis and Hosea William of the Student Nonviolent Coordinating Committee (SNCC) ignored

King's warning and led 600 demonstrators on a march from Selma to the state capital of Montgomery. When the Alabama state police ambushed the marchers and mounted cavalrymen swung bullwhips and rubber tubing wrapped in barbed wire, Johnson and the leadership on Capitol Hill had seen enough.[62]

Without much fanfare, the White House had been drafting a voting rights bill. Attorney General Nicholas Katzenbach shunned the liberal Republicans and negotiated solely with Dirksen, whom the White House again treated as the crucial agent who could overcome the inevitable southern filibuster. Vice President Humphrey wrote Johnson to complain that Katzenbach and his advisers had even ignored Mansfield as they drafted the bill: "We must be very sure that we always work through and with the majority leader on our legislation. He should not have to find out information through the minority leader." Protocol aside, the White House realized that Dirksen was key. Although he had objected to the public accommodations and fair employment portions of the 1964 bill in its early stages, Dirksen was committed to the administration's voting rights legislation that was intended to enforce the Fifteenth Amendment, adopted in 1870 by the Republican party. Like many Americans, he was outraged by the brutality in Selma and told Katzenbach that he would support a "revolutionary" bill to reverse the injustice. Dirksen told his colleagues that the "Republican senators would have to assume leadership . . . because . . . the Democrats would not do so." Legislative aides and lawyers from the Justice Department gathered daily in Dirksen's office to craft the legislation. At the close of every day Dirksen would return from the Senate floor and ask, "Well boys, what have you done today?" After he was briefed, he would open up the bar, and when one or two conservative Republicans stopped by for a drink, the lawyers from Justice had a chance to lobby for the bill.[63]

In contrast to the previous year, this time Dirksen faced no organized effort from within his ranks to dismantle the administration bill. From his home in Scottsdale, Arizona, Barry Goldwater fired off a letter to Dirksen ridiculing Johnson's "We Shall Overcome" address to a joint session of Congress as "one of the corniest and [most] unusual speeches ever made from such a high rostrum in this country." To Goldwater, the White House legislation was the "end of the democratic processes and the republican form of government we have so long enjoyed." Goldwater's disgust, however, was inconsequential. He was no longer a player, and

Dirksen virtually ignored his histrionics. Bourke Hickenlooper was another matter. Though the Iowan was opposed to the scope of the bill, his legislative assistant wrote his boss and praised Dirksen for trying to "head off more radical infringement of states rights . . . and to get some credit for Republicans on civil rights. . . . He probably is right in assuming that in the present mood of the country and Congress, some voting rights legislation is going to pass."[64]

Dirksen's agreement to introduce the administration's voting rights legislation with Mansfield was a major achievement for Johnson. He wrote Eisenhower that Dirksen's "contribution" on voting rights "was immeasurably helpful to the national interest and unity." To express gratitude for Dirksen's support, Johnson told him to contact White House aide Harry McPherson "when he wanted to pass on recommendations and other matters of interest." Dirksen quickly contacted McPherson about three nominations. McPherson wrote his boss, emphasizing that when "he actively urges a nomination, I will send it to you at once." Dirksen's interaction with Johnson at this time was so close that he took the "presumptuous" step of recommending an Illinois Democrat for the Interstate Commerce Commission. In this case, the White House had already filled its opening.[65]

Dirksen, Mansfield, and the White House cooperated to keep the voting rights legislation intact when what was known as the "Dirksenbach" bill began its tortuous path through Congress. Both sides compromised. Though Dirksen favored legislation enforced by local federal district courts, Katzenbach's lobbying and the crisis atmosphere convinced him to support the combined power of the Justice Department and the executive branch to administer the program. Liberal Democrats made a concerted effort to include a provision that would ban all poll taxes. Dirksen argued that not every poll tax discriminated solely on the basis of race and held that such a move represented an unwarranted imposition of federal power on states' rights. Katzenbach and the administration agreed that the poll tax ban might be ruled unconstitutional. Moreover, they needed to keep the minority leader on board. As the attorney general explained to Johnson, "I have proceeded on the assumption that the continued support of Senator Dirksen is necessary to assure the votes for cloture." When the liberals tried to add the poll tax ban to the Mansfield-Dirksen bill on the floor, only vigorous White House lobbying kept the legislation intact. Dirksen ignored Strom Thurmond's (R-SC) efforts to gut the bill in order to "avoid the obvious intent of penaliz[ing] the southern states" and killing off the Republican party there. On May 25, with little of the drama that had so captured the nation the year before, Dirksen delivered twenty-three of his thirty-two Republicans for a successful cloture vote of 70 to 30. Adding the poll tax ban, the House voted for their version in early July.[66]

Before the House-Senate conference committee could resolve the differences between the two bills, ongoing deterioration in Vietnam turned the Washington establishment's attention to Southeast Asia and called into question the legitimacy of global containment. Through the summer Dirksen supported the administration's escalating efforts to halt the spread of communism into South Vietnam. A sequence of meetings on July 15 demonstrated his unflinching commitment to the White House. Before he and Ford met the press for what was now termed the "Ev and Jerry Show," Dirksen caucused with the House and Senate leadership to hammer out a statement. The leaders discussed the responsibility of the opposition in the field of foreign policy. Their language was at odds with the actions Dirksen had taken since the situation in Vietnam had deteriorated in the early months of the Johnson presidency. In their statement the GOP leaders emphasized that "debate . . . should be encouraged. Only in the crucible of full and candid debate can the nation force a foreign policy which will lead to the ends which all Americans seek to attain—peace, freedom, and security." But departing from his text and the obligations he had to his colleagues, Dirksen again narrowed the margin for legitimate debate when he took questions from the press. He asked rhetorically, "Is there any other alternative except to fight through to a victorious conclusion? And besides, don't forget for a moment that the prestige and the face of this country is involved in all of Southeast Asia."[67]

By mid-July Johnson faced the most difficult decisions yet with regard to Vietnam. Despite the increased sorties scheduled under Rolling Thunder, a flurry of coups and countercoups in South Vietnam made it impossible for the United States to achieve even a measure of political stability there. With the exceptions of George Ball and Clark Clifford, every one of the president's formal and informal advisers urged the introduction of U.S. ground forces to bolster the south and to stem the military advances of the North Vietnamese and the Viet Cong. By the time Johnson summoned a friendly group of bipartisan leaders to the White House for a foreign policy discussion, he had made up his mind to send American ground troops to Vietnam.[68]

The only issue for debate was how to pay for the buildup. Though it would have been possible to declare a national emergency and call up the reserves, Johnson told the leaders that he preferred to "give the commanders the men they say they need" and ask Congress for the necessary appropriation in January 1966. When Ford questioned Johnson's tactics, the president stammered that the "reserves really won't be ready." McGeorge Bundy recalled that Johnson's "unspoken object" was to downplay the crisis atmosphere in order to "protect his legislative program." Johnson was angered that the leaders did not immediately agree with his predetermined course of action. He resorted to the suprapartisan language of the Washington establishment to force through his decision: "I've asked you to come here not as Democrats and Republicans but as Americans. . . . Let me appeal to you as Americans to show your patriotism by not talking to the press."

Dirksen had been sitting quietly, directly across the table from Johnson. He assured the president that "I quite agree with your premise." But, he counseled, the administration should "tell the country that we are engaged in very serious business." He gauged the American people as "apathetic" and insisted that "we don't need to withhold information." Johnson agreed. Dirksen then argued that "five months is a long time. I don't think you can wait. If you need the money, you ought to ask for it." While Johnson wanted to protect the Great Society, Dirksen and his Republican colleagues hoped that the bipartisan agreement to escalate the Vietnam War would adversely affect the White House's ambitious domestic agenda.

Johnson, however, would not let Dirksen's cosmetic criticism derail his twin goals: upholding the nation's commitment to the worldwide containment of communism and updating the New and Fair Deals in his Great Society. "When you come back in January," Johnson assured Dirksen, "you'll have a bill of several billion dollars." He then tried to wrap up the meeting: "Is there any other comment?" Mansfield had a prepared statement that criticized Johnson's policies. As his colleagues looked on in astonishment, the majority leader insisted, "We owe this [present] government nothing—no pledge of any kind. . . . Escalation begets escalation." Courageous as Mansfield was, he assured Johnson and the others that in public he would "support the president's position." One day later

Johnson told the American people that a total of 125,000 men had been sent to serve in Vietnam. On July 31 White House aide Jack Valenti wrote the minority leader to assure him that the "Dirksen interests are well cared for at this end of Pennsylvania Avenue."[69]

The escalation of the Vietnam War dulled the shine on the final debate on the voting rights bill. The major stumbling block in the conference remained the issue of the ban on poll taxes for local elections, the provision Dirksen continued to resist. Only when Katzenbach made public a letter in which Martin Luther King supported the Senate version of the bill was the stalemate broken. John Lewis of SNCC described the bill as a "milestone every bit as momentous and significant . . . as the Emancipation Proclamation or the 1954 Supreme Court decision." Though his support for the voting rights bill was not nearly as crucial as was his endorsement of the 1964 civil rights bill, Dirksen's unwavering commitment to the administration's suprapartisan approach was an instrumental part of the "most significant liberal accomplishment of the 1965 congressional session."[70]

Two days before Johnson signed the voting rights bill, Mike Mansfield called the president from Dirksen's office to report that they were finishing their work on the measure. Alone in the White House, Johnson asked if he could stop by the Twilight Lodge for a visit. When he got to Dirksen's office, Johnson asked for a root beer. "A root beer?" scoffed Dirksen. "We don't have root beer up here." Johnson settled for a scotch and soda. Dirksen delighted in telling the press of Johnson's "courtesy call." He had an attentive audience. "Well, all I can say is: the dog came in first and then came. . . . [drowned out by laughter]. Now whether the dog came in just as a security measure, I don't know [more laughter]." Dirksen reported that Johnson stayed about one hour and that "it was a little like old times—when we used to sit either in his office or in my office and discuss the affairs of the day."[71] In style as well as substance, the suprapartisan Washington establishment dominated the national politics of the day.

Membership in the inner circle, however, was by invitation only. Johnson's visit to the Twilight Lodge came on the heels of a public feud with Ford, whom Johnson accused of leaking confidential information from a White House briefing on Vietnam for cheap partisan gain. Because he "breached the rules of the political game," one reporter noted that "the House leader is being laid low as a teller of tales out of school, a young and inexperienced man, and a bitter partisan. And his name is never mentioned." By contrast, Dirksen remained Johnson's most trusted Republican confidant.[72]

Notwithstanding the success of his politics, Dirksen had clear obligations to his Republican colleagues. Shortly after the voting rights bill was signed into law, he continued a developing pattern by searching for an issue that he hoped would unify his troops and distinguish the GOP from the White House. Most Republicans chose not to criticize the president for his handling of the Vietnam War. Dirksen and Ford did write Eisenhower and reported "dissatisfaction . . . with the president's peacemeal [sic] handling of the increased military appropriations for Vietnam," but they made clear that their letter was to be kept strictly confidential. Moreover, Dirksen chose not to question the thrust of the Great Society. While he often rebuked the president for his idealism, he joined heavy congressional majorities by voting for federal aid to local schools, federal college scholarships, governmental medical insurance, the federal government's manpower retraining program, regional development in Appalachia, and highway beautification.[73]

A "great amender," Dirksen rarely engaged in principled opposition against a heavy majority. Even so, his demoralized troops needed a partisan victory to boost their flagging spirits. Johnson accommodated the minority leader by promoting the repeal of Section 14(b) of the 1947 Taft-Hartley labor law, which gave states the right to ban the union shop. Organized labor had long considered Taft-Hartley a noxious threat to their interests, and they retained a special hatred for Section 14(b), which supporters described as a state right-to-work law. Having given widespread support to Johnson in the 1964 election and seen the Democratic majority in the Congress swell dramatically, labor lobbied for the repeal of 14(b). Dirksen argued that such a move was "an unwarranted intrusion of the federal government into the sovereign rights of states," and in early June he made clear to his colleagues that he opposed the administration.[74]

In late July the House passed the repeal by a vote of 221 to 203. Conservative Republicans agreed with Dirksen that the GOP should fight the White House on the issue. John Tower told his colleagues that if 14(b) were eliminated, "there would be approximately 350,000 more people [in Texas] forced to join the unions and to pay dues, giving the unions more money to use in campaigns against Republican candidates." As the repeal made its way out of committee, Dirksen organized a filibuster to prevent its enactment. He visited the White House to assess Johnson's commitment to the bill. Neither side gave. When George Meany of the AFL–CIO came to visit, Dirksen opened by saying, "George, I'm glad to see you. How's Mrs. Meany?" Meany was in no mood for pleasantries: "Everett, you know why I'm here. All we want is a straight up-and-down vote." Dirksen rejoined, "George, you're not going to get a straight up-and-down vote. I am no spring chicken, but so long as there is any breath and energy in this carcass, we will go ahead. We mean business." Though Mansfield supported the repeal, he chose not to schedule around-the-clock sessions. On October 11 he failed by a vote of 47 to 45 to invoke cloture and bring the bill to the Senate floor. Johnson promised to try again in the upcoming session, but meanwhile, Dirksen had won a notable victory that strengthened his reputation as a partisan leader. Karl Mundt wrote that Dirksen's "inspirational leadership made it easier for me and the team." More important, the administration's failure on the repeal of 14(b) was a harbinger of setbacks to follow.[75]

Though Dirksen's commitment to the Washington establishment accounted for his national importance, his efforts to deny the repeal of 14(b) reflected a developing ideology that crystallized in the early part of 1966 and characterized his final years in public life. Working in his notebooks before the beginning of the second session of the Eighty-ninth Congress, he articulated his concerns for the growing imbalance between state and federal power. He dismissed the perception that with machine-like consistency he represented the interests of big business and private capital. Instead, he contended that the real issue with 14(b) was organized labor's effort to deny the several states and individual Americans the "right to work, to earn a living, to survive." He feared the domination of labor in state legislatures and promised to "fight" the administration when it brought up the repeal in the coming session.[76] In part because of Dirksen's efforts, the administration never succeeded in winning the two-thirds support necessary to bring the repeal of 14(b) up for consideration.

Dirksen's defense of states' rights in the case of 14(b) dovetailed neatly with his proposed constitutional amendments to permit state legislatures to apportion one house on a basis other than population and to permit voluntary prayer in public schools. Both amendments failed in the Senate; nevertheless, Dirksen's efforts demonstrated a growing disdain in the GOP for unchecked majority rule in state legislatures and the further secularization of American society. Dirksen lashed out at the Supreme Court for creating "chaos and distress" through its threats to the "integrity and continuance of our FEDERAL-STATE SYSTEM."[77] The combined exigencies of the cold war abroad and civil rights at home encouraged him to embrace the modern presidency, but he never abandoned his intuitive and conservative belief in a small government. By early 1966, he turned his indignation to the Supreme Court's decisions to apportion state legislatures by the one-man, one-vote ratio and to prohibit prayer in public schools.

Essentially, he opposed what he believed to be the recent trend of the Court to act as a third legislative chamber. After the failure of his proposal in the previous session, Dirksen offered another constitutional amendment to protect the rights of states to organize their own legislatures. He railed at "judicial decree" and at the "seeds of destruction" that would ultimately "destroy our traditional concept of assuring the small and weak and the minority a forum from which to be heard." To Dirksen, the Court's decision left organized labor unchecked, for they "know they can control both branches of many state legislatures with one-man, one-vote." Like 14(b), one-man, one-vote was to Dirksen a conspiratorial scheme to concentrate power in the hands of a "selfish few who can control the greatest blocs of voters within the few greatest cities."[78]

Dirksen also objected to the Court's efforts to eliminate prayer in the public schools. In *Engel v. Vitale* (1962) the Court held by a 6-to-1 majority that a prayer composed by New York state officials for daily narration was a clear violation of the religion clause in the First Amendment. In 1963 the Court ruled against Bible reading and the recitation of the Lord's Prayer, again citing the religion clause. In December 1965 the Supreme Court chose not to review *Stein v. Oshinsky,* in which the Second Circuit Court of Appeals in New York ruled that the state was not obligated to permit prayer (even voluntary) in public schoolrooms. Dirksen lambasted the *Oshinsky* decision. He scorned the Court's disregard for individual rights and its intrusion into state affairs. For one audience, he created a melodramatic scene: "Here were these children, unspoiled, unsullied, with nothing but glow in their hearts. In the morning they would sing 'God is great, God is good, and we thank Him for our food.'

So the august justices, bearded and unbearded, say there is something wrong with that. . . . What in God's name do you make of it?" He argued that "prayer is the road map to God" and that healthy habits demanded the "building of spiritual muscle." He criticized the "quaint legalism and the jargon of church and state" and asserted that it was important to "give Caesar what he requires, but give God a little also." He promised action before the year was out.[79]

To whip up support for these issues, Dirksen cast himself as a populist who was fighting to defend the majority against the unconstitutional concentration of power. For one who had for so many years left local Illinois politics to his trusted associates, Dirksen's identification with a small-town, traditional, and conservative constituency outside Washington represented an ironic twist in his evolving political style. In his notes he wrote that Johnson's "commitment" was to George Meany, "mine to the people." Writing for the Committee for Government of the People on the issue of reapportionment, he put himself on the side of the "voiceless voters" against the "party functionaries, labor leaders, and other self-servers." In an article for the *Farm Journal* on the same issue, he concluded that "six judges . . . left you no choice. They left you no opportunity even to discuss or debate the question! . . . What is really at issue here is not whether 'equal population' districts are, or are not, better. The issue is simply whether the people can continue to make the choice."[80]

Dirksen's efforts to reclaim a simpler, more traditional America were in part a response to the social unrest and turmoil he saw swirling around him in urban areas and on college campuses. He mocked student demonstrators who opposed the Vietnam War, calling them "craven souls, wailing, quailing, protesting young men" ignorant of America's sacrifice to the "cause of freedom." In a January speech to the Sigma Delta Chi fraternity he described his ideal American as "the guy who is square in everything, in doing his duty for his country and paying his taxes; and praying to his God and doing all those things that mankind expects of him." Dirksen's self-defined goal as a political leader was to shelter the liberties of the people from what he deemed to be the insatiable appetite of the federal government. He struggled to define "freedom," though he conceded that it did not equal food that could be eaten or money that could be spent. But in a speech to the Republican Women's Conference, he created a colorful (if hokey) analogy that made clear his commitment to the nebulous notion of freedom: "There is something about that mysterious relationship between a little baby and a parent when that baby puts its chubby arms around your neck and slobbers down your collar—you can't eat that either—but you can't replace that."[81]

Returning to the realm of Washington politics, Dirksen began 1966 by encouraging Johnson to escalate the Vietnam War. In December the administration ordered a bombing halt to induce negotiations with North Vietnam. Without criticizing Johnson's leadership directly, Dirksen urged the United States to increase its pressure on North Vietnam by imposing a naval blockade of Haiphong Harbor. He argued that the White House should pursue a complete military victory before entering into peace talks. When the media highlighted Dirksen's belligerence and suggested that he was edging away from the administration's more moderate position, Johnson telephoned the minority leader. Dirksen explained that his comments had been taken out of context, and though he had "some political things this year," nothing would "take precedence over his country." After Johnson's call, Dirksen tempered his remarks by warning that the bombing of urban centers like Hanoi and Haiphong might induce terrorist attacks in the south and quash all prospects for an honorable settlement.[82]

In general, however, Dirksen kept the pressure on. He told Arthur Goldberg, the U.S. ambassador to the United Nations, that he was "on the whole sympathetic to the president's position" but asked for "sympathy if to keep his own forces in line he was compelled from time to time to make 'Republican' noises." The effect of his aggressiveness, however, was to narrow Johnson's options for waging war in Southeast Asia. In his GOP State of the Union address that focused on foreign affairs, Dirksen ridiculed the possibility of de-escalation and withdrawal: "To retreat and get out would be deemed a confession that we are a paper tiger. . . . To forsake our pledges would shatter confidence in us and further diminish our prestige." For the first time, Dirksen's saber-rattling resulted in muted criticism from his GOP colleagues. One New England senator reported, "There I was waiting for the chance to applaud, and I'll be damned if I could hear one thing that was worth applauding."[83]

Dirksen seemed not to care. He continued to undermine the Great Society by promoting his patriotic support for Vietnam. Hoping that the penny-conscious Johnson would have to scale back his domestic agenda to keep the budget balanced, Dirksen feigned sympathy for his friend's position. He maintained that "we must fight the war first," and he felt

Johnson's pain: "This is the biggest headache the president has. To keep expenditures in balance, he is going to have to cut somewhere, and he certainly can't cut on the war." Dirksen also chafed at increasing congressional interest in Vietnam. Innately distrustful of specialists, he bristled when some of his colleagues veered out of the loop by going to Southeast Asia before the start of the second congressional session: "There must have been 100 members of Congress out there. We'll have experts running out our ears."[84]

Independently of Dirksen, Johnson had concluded by the end of January that the monthlong bombing halt was increasing the communist incursion from the north. Knowing that a resumption of Rolling Thunder would generate some political criticism, he singled out Dirksen as a key ally who would support the decision he had already made. He told his foreign policy advisers, "We ought to—quietly—visit with Dirksen and see how he feels" before meeting with the full leadership and informing them of his decision to resume the bombing. Secretary of State Dean Rusk urged Johnson to consult Fulbright and Hickenlooper as well. Nothing in the record indicates that Johnson sought to widen the scope of his talks with Capitol Hill. Later in the year Dirksen admitted in his correspondence that Johnson had shunned "the old-style conference" because he would have to battle a growing number of Democratic critics.[85]

At the leadership meeting on January 25 Johnson reported his decision to resume Rolling Thunder. Of the nineteen members from the Senate and the House who attended the meeting, only Mansfield and Fulbright disagreed with the President's policy. Dirksen prefaced his remarks by insisting, "I am sensitive to young blood as any man." But he then derided the possibility of withdrawal and advised against fighting a status quo war of attrition. Instead, he counseled the president to "go in to win. If we are not winning now, let's do what is necessary to win. I don't believe you have any other choice. I believe the country will support you in anything you do to win this war."[86] Having lost the support of key Democrats, and with the emergence of Republican grumbling, Johnson increasingly looked to Dirksen as the White House's indispensable agent for maintaining the prowar consensus.

Despite an embryonic dissatisfaction with the president's leadership within the Republican ranks, Dirksen pointed to the disloyal Democrats who were turning on the White House. When a number of Democratic critics discussed a rescission of the Gulf of Tonkin resolution and a cut in the military appropriations for the war, Dirksen insisted that the fault-finders "do NOT come from our side because when the chips are down . . . I think you'll find that on the minority side [we] will be almost solid." He exaggerated. John Sherman Cooper was one of several Republicans who had begun to challenge the president's leadership. He held that "this war should be settled by negotiation and not by total war" and under-lined the "fear that there are no limits being placed by our own country on expansion of this war." Dirksen countered by endorsing the presi-dent's constitutional power to make and execute the most important for-eign policy decisions.[87]

On Capitol Hill, Dirksen enjoyed almost unparalleled prestige. A strong supporter of Johnson's leadership and the power of the presidency, he was invaluable to the administration's foreign policy designs. As criti-cism of his policies increased in the Congress, Johnson turned more and more to Dirksen. In early March Federal Bureau of Investigation (FBI) assistant director Cartha "Deke" DeLoach visited Dirksen in an off-the-record meeting. Expressly ordered to do so by Johnson, DeLoach passed Dirksen confidential information that pointed to Morse's and Fulbright's "entanglements" with communist interests. Dirksen agreed that Fulbright's recent decision to open Foreign Relations Committee hearings on Red China was the result of instructions from "certain contacts." William C. Sullivan, who served as the FBI's assistant director for the Intelligence Division, remembered that DeLoach's meeting with Dirksen was part of a larger pattern established by Johnson. According to Sullivan, the presi-dent's "paranoia" drove him to order the FBI to investigate the activities of all his congressional critics. While Johnson took responsibility for leaking FBI material on Republicans to the press, his "reluct[ance] to at-tack members of his own party" motivated him to supply Dirksen with the dirt on Democrats.[88]

In the legislative arena, Dirksen contributed mightily to the failure to repeal 14(b), and though the minority leader did little to oppose the tor-rent of Great Society legislation that passed in the Eighty-ninth Con-gress, Attorney General Katzenbach continued to view him as "probably the key" to enacting more civil rights legislation. Bryce Harlow wrote Eisenhower that in the Senate, "the entire apparatus can be summed up in one word—Dirksen." Though the "press curtain is still largely drawn against the Republican party," Dirksen's "influence in the Senate and with his Republican associates has grown to an unbelievable degree."

Harlow wrote that Dirksen was a "favorite" of the press and that the minority leader "constitutes his own research staff, and his power of publicity is such that . . . he easily outdistances Gerry Ford and the rest of the Republican congressmen in gaining national attention."[89]

Dirksen used his political influence to secure gains for the Republicans in preparation for the 1966 midterm elections. Though conservative weeklies like the *National Review* denounced the GOP's "gloating over the dissension on Vietnam in the Democratic party" without supporting the anticommunist movement with more clarity and vision, Dirksen continued to snipe at the disloyal Democrats who had abandoned the White House. "Who should come over to our side?" he asked one audience. "Not the Morses, McGoverns, Fulbrights, Hartkes, [or] Kennedys, but the GOP which has stood by the commander in chief." On another occasion he cited inflationary pressures resulting from a combination of the war and the Great Society programs as one more threat to his notion of freedom: "Every housewife who shops in a grocery store knows this. They are the living, breathing, signs of this destructive burglarizing force." When rampant inflation resulted in government controls over prices and wages, "that is when freedom is done. It's not down the road, it's not remote, it's here."[90]

Johnson dismissed Dirksen's jousting as little more than political posturing. He kept the minority leader well within his administration's loop. Johnson was at his ranch in Texas when one Saturday night in May Dirksen fell out of his bed at Walter Reed Hospital in Washington and broke his hip. Contacted by the White House, Johnson called Walter Reed at 6:22 A.M. on Sunday. Mrs. Johnson joined him in the kitchen at 6:45, and at 7:30 they called Louella, who was visiting Joy and Howard Baker in Knoxville, Tennessee. Johnson sent a telegram to Dirksen from Air Force One on the way back to Washington: "We know your love of life and your friends love for you will give you strength while you recuperate and rebuild for all of us." He then dispatched one of his JetStars to Knoxville to take Mrs. Dirksen back to Washington, and she was there to meet the Johnsons at Andrews Air Force base at 12:30.[91]

Dirksen's broken hip forced him to cut back his schedule, but he continued to provide the administration with significant support. Long worried over increased inflation, Johnson convened a bipartisan leadership meeting at the White House to discuss the importance of "fiscal responsibility." Johnson was convinced that he had cut expenditures in the

executive branch at every opportunity. Knowing that the war was heat-
ing up the economy and driving up inflation, the president told the leaders, "I am concerned . . . that Congress could add $5 to 6 billion to the
budget this year." When Ford urged Johnson to veto a bill to "put all of
us on the spot," Dirksen disagreed: "You can't win on a veto in an election year. There are too many sacred cows." Instead, Dirksen counseled
Johnson to "defer some of these expenditures" to cool the economy.[92]

Later, at a meeting with his GOP colleagues, Dirksen emphasized that
he "wanted to help the president carry the torch . . . to keep the budget
to a minimum." His disgust for an unbalanced budget outweighed any
lingering concerns about a powerful presidency. Dirksen discussed a proposal that would "grant the president authority to impound funds from
any programs and use the appropriated moneys for other emergency programs as he sees fit." While he hoped that the thrust of his plan would
have the effect of "put[ting] the monkey on the president's back," some
of his colleagues chafed at the power that Dirksen was surrendering
to the White House. Several weeks later Karl Mundt argued against
Dirksen's proposal. He held that such a move "would transfer the constitutional powers of Congress over to the president"; and by the end of the
session, the minority leader's plans for giving the White House even more
control over the national economy lay dead in the water.[93]

Though he had given the White House crucial support in 1964 and
1965, Dirksen in 1966 abandoned the administration's civil rights agenda.
In his State of the Union message on January 12, Johnson announced
that he would call for legislation that would ban racial discrimination in
the sale and rental of all housing. Though Attorney General Katzenbach
eventually agreed to amendments that would exempt single owners and
small landlords, Dirksen deemed the housing title "completely unconstitutional." Unlike the civil rights bills of 1964 and 1965 that singled out
basic constitutional rights and targeted the segregated South, the 1966
measure would have outlawed a more subtle, less obvious discrimination
that persisted throughout the nation. Though the vast majority of non-
southerners had favored the earlier bills, the administration in 1966 acknowledged that "there is no great push for civil rights legislation this
year." To make matters worse for the White House, the radicalization of
the civil rights movement through black power raised fears of a white
backlash and threw supporters of the legislation on the defensive. For the
third summer running, riots erupted in the nation's urban areas. In 1966

the violence spread to Chicago, Cleveland, Jacksonville, Atlanta, and New York City.[94]

Dirksen objected to the bill before the violence hit Chicago. Uncharacteristically, he spoke out early and often against the administration's proposal. Before the bill passed the House, he told his colleagues that he could not accept the "ugly compulsion and illegality" of the housing provision. Holding that the bill was "offensive," he stated that "in his opinion there could be no compromise." Dirksen saw no reason to change his mind after the bill made its way through the House by a narrow margin. His willingness to negotiate the other provisions of the bill did not assuage the administration. Though Katzenbach met with Dirksen several times in early September, the minority leader maintained his firm opposition and refused to help the White House muster the votes necessary for cloture. Katzenbach wrote Johnson, "I don't believe there is any advantage to seeking a civil rights bill without the housing provision. Civil rights groups are adamantly opposed and I think it better to let Dirksen take total responsibility." After a fruitless meeting at the White House on September 13, Dirksen told the press, "I know nobody under the canopy of the bright blue heavens that can say anything to change my mind."[95]

Securing only fifty-two votes, Mansfield failed to invoke cloture on September 19. Ignoring the fact that the movement had lost the momentum necessary to pass increasingly controversial legislation, Roy Wilkins attacked Dirksen, arguing that he "led the axmen who killed" the 1966 civil rights bill. Clarence Mitchell was equally critical, charging that the minority leader's "intransigence and subtle appeals to race prejudice" undercut the efforts of civil rights leaders. Dirksen, of course, was more sanguine. His opposition promoted the "nation's best interest," and he defended the "right of every American to preserve the integrity of his own judgment and determine the future of his own home." He applauded the role of the minority, and in a departure from his conception of the minority's responsibility to the party in power in the realm of foreign affairs, insisted that "only as a majority is repeatedly questioned and checked by a strong minority can the foundations of this republic be preserved."[96]

Fond as he was of a principled and patriotic minority, Dirksen would have preferred a heavier majority when he brought his amendment for voluntary prayer in public schools to the Senate floor for debate.

Throughout the summer he had been working to amass the public support essential in gaining the necessary two-thirds vote. He argued that the separation of church and state was not intended to "strip" the state of the opportunity to engage in organized prayer. He suggested that "organized atheists in our society today are striving for supremacy and as a minority are forcing their opinions on the majority." Writing for the conservative journal *Human Events,* he resorted to cold war rhetoric and worked to distinguish the United States from the communist heathen: "I would hate to have it said that our attitude toward prayer begins to approximate the lack of respect for prayer and its spiritual refreshment which appears to be the attitude of the Soviet Union." On the Senate floor he pointed to the growing social unrest in the nation and his efforts to provide an antidote to turn the country back to its traditional moorings: "There is a godless mass. You cannot contemplate the gangs in our large cities, and the mass of atheistic communism, and all of these other forces that are trying to destroy the religious traditions of this country, without coming to the conclusion that they have made a lot of progress."[97]

His efforts were insufficient. Though he attracted strong grassroots support for his amendment, Jewish, Protestant, and Catholic leaders warned against the modification of the First Amendment and underlined the inevitable disputes that would fracture local communities as they tried to determine the appropriate prayer for their public schools. In the Senate Sam J. Ervin (D-NC) argued that Dirksen's amendment was nothing less than an "annihilation of the principle of the First Amendment." The measure, he contended, would empower school boards across the country to "make a law respecting the establishment of religion." Mike Mansfield rejected the amendment because prayer was "too personal, too sacred, too private to be influenced by the pressures for change each time a new school board is elected to office." After three days of debate, Dirksen's proposal fell nine votes short of the two-thirds majority needed to propose a constitutional amendment.[98]

Though he failed to move the voluntary prayer amendment to the states, Dirksen's campaign restored his reputation as a conservative traditionalist fighting to recommit his nation to its righteous foundations. Often critical of his penchant for compromise, the *National Review* praised Dirksen's efforts to beat back "a small minority of zealots . . . to impose its dislike of prayer or of God upon the great majority." However willing he was to distance himself from mainstream liberalism in 1966, Dirksen never edged too far away from the White House loop. He continued to maintain that "politics is the art of the possible" and that "you can't let a problem sit . . . when it cries out for action."[99]

Dirksen was most compliant on the Vietnam issue. When Ford and Nixon questioned the president's attendance at a peace conference in Manila one month before the 1966 midterms, Dirksen sprang to Johnson's defense. When Nixon accused Johnson of courting votes for Democratic candidates, Dirksen pointed to the cynicism of the charge: "I like to take everybody at face value. You project yourself into the other fellow's position. Suppose I were going out there on something of a similar mission? I don't think I would like to have my motives demeaned." Even while he backed Johnson's leadership, however, he continued to take a hard line on Vietnam. In a mid-October interview he insisted, "We cannot retreat. If we retreated from there, we would lose face not only in the Oriental world, but in the Moslem world as well. And all of the prestige that's still left would go into a hand-basket before we got through with it. . . . God perish the thought that we would ever surrender."[100]

On the Friday after Thanksgiving congressional leaders from both parties flew to Johnson's ranch on the Pedernales River in central Texas. After rattling around the bottoms of the ranch and showing the leaders a ten-prong buck named Clarence who ate unfiltered cigarettes, Johnson briefed his guests on Vietnam and the administration's plans to dampen increasing inflation by reducing nonessential expenditures. At a press conference that evening, Mansfield noted that the bipartisan leadership meeting was the fifty-seventh of Johnson's three-year presidency. Despite the heavy Democratic majorities Johnson commanded in Congress, the partisan peculiarities of the civil rights crisis, the perceived need to maintain a nonpartisan consensus for waging the cold war, and the president's own predilection for the politics of the Washington establishment combined to render Dirksen a critical member of the White House team.

Obsequiously, Dirksen told reporters of a "most enjoyable outdoor occasion. I have enjoyed it to the full, and I am deeply grateful for the opportunity to come here and see this section of Texas—but, very particularly, to see the LBJ Ranch; and more especially, to see the distinguished president and his very gracious and very lovable spouse, Lady Bird." Though the other leaders took their leave at the end of the day,

Dirksen and the Mansfields spent the night with the Johnsons.[101] In the politics of both style and substance, Dirksen remained committed to the inner circle. As urban riots and antiwar demonstrations spread, however, it remained unclear how much longer the suprapartisan Washington establishment could dominate the politics of the day.

6. "Ev Dirksen Will Leave Us"

As Everett Dirksen approached the last complete Congress of his political career, his power and prestige appeared at an all-time high. Early in 1967 William S. White called the minority leader "the second most powerful and responsible man in the United States." Later that year he described the "statesmanlike" Dirksen as the "balance wheel of the Senate itself." Lyndon Johnson continued his cultivation of Dirksen. Before a White House dinner for Chief Justice Earl Warren and Vice President Hubert Humphrey, Johnson invited Dirksen and Mike Mansfield to his private quarters to discuss "the most important thing I have talked to you about since I became president." After swearing the two leaders to secrecy, he read the latest cables detailing the administration's diplomatic efforts to win a negotiated peace in Southeast Asia. Johnson insisted that both the critics who wanted him to escalate the war and the faultfinders who urged him to stop the bombing undercut the administration's bargaining position with Ho Chi Minh. While Johnson's principal goal was for Mansfield and Dirksen to get Fulbright and Hickenlooper to postpone divisive Senate hearings on the Vietnam War, his tactics indicated Dirksen's importance to the administration and buttressed his place in the Washington establishment.[1]

Appearances, however, were deceiving. Dirksen's hold on his GOP colleagues was slipping. His failing health and repeated stints at Walter Reed resulted in long absences from Congress and diminished his ability to engage in the "eyeball to eyeball confrontations" that effective leadership requires.[2] His efforts to overturn the Supreme Court's rulings on one-man, one-vote and on prayer in public schools distracted his attention, preventing him from hearing the cacophony of party voices urging varied solutions to a wide array of foreign and domestic crises. More and more Republicans chafed at his close cooperation with Johnson and his penchant for supporting the White House at crucial times. Fundamen-

229

tally, however, changes in the Senate Republican membership were most responsible for the gradual decline of Dirksen's importance.

The 1966 elections were an unalloyed success for the GOP. Falling well short of gaining a congressional majority, Republicans nevertheless captured forty seven House seats, three Senate seats, eight governorships, and over five hundred seats in state legislatures. With the Goldwater debacle of 1964 fresh in their minds, Republican Senate candidates worked to extricate themselves from the strictures of conservative dogma. One victor, Tennessee's Howard Baker, was Dirksen's son-in-law. Another was Michigan's Robert Griffin, who won a full term for himself after filling in for Pat McNamara in early 1966. A former member of the House, Griffin was a shrewd and ambitious operator who relished the role of the underdog and made a name for himself by challenging the party hierarchy. "Don't underestimate this young man," Charlie Halleck warned Dirksen. Three other winners in 1966 were liberal Republicans who also bucked the established patterns of Dirksen's leadership. Edward Brooke of Massachusetts promised to address the decay of the nation's urban areas. An African American, Brooke supported the open housing law that Dirksen had helped to kill in the previous congressional session. Mark Hatfield, the forty-three-year-old former governor of Oregon, won a Senate seat in part by calling for a reappraisal of the containment doctrine and criticizing the administration's escalation of the Vietnam war.[3]

In Dirksen's home state of Illinois, Charles Percy won Paul Douglas's Senate seat. A forty-seven-year-old millionaire industrialist, Percy was quick to distance himself from Dirksen's leadership in his campaign. Like Hatfield, Percy criticized Johnson for what he considered to be the administration's thoughtless prosecution of the war. And like Brooke, Percy was a strong supporter of open housing. When asked how to reconcile his own views with Dirksen's, Percy reported that he and the senator had signed a preelection "declaration of independence," enabling the two to go their own ways when they differed on issues. One insider remembered that Dirksen "detested" Percy, in part because he had considered a run against Dirksen in the 1962 GOP primary. Whether Dirksen realized it or not, the Republican Senate was embroiled in a generational change that threatened his leadership style and eventually shaped Washington's political culture. Hatfield and his fellow freshmen resented the hierarchical structures and the emphasis on deference that dominated Washington politics. John Tower, by contrast, later looked back at the 1966 elections and scolded the "new boys" for their determination to "cut a wide swath." According to Tower, the youngsters chose not to bow to their elders, and the Senate folkways of times past began to crumble.[4]

Though a growing number of Republicans were finding fault with the White House, Dirksen continued to back the administration, endorse the sanctity of the presidency as an institution, and drive the war out of the political arena. He and Ford divided the 1967 Republican State of the Union into two sections, the senator responding to international issues and Ford highlighting domestic policy concerns. Though Ford emphasized the administration's "credibility gap," Dirksen praised Johnson's presentation of his policies in Southeast Asia as "realistic and candid." He pledged his support for the president's determination to keep the region noncommunist: "We must do all that is necessary until the freedom and independence of Vietnam is assured."[5]

The rest of Dirksen's speech was equally indifferent to conflicting views in the party. Though Percy had just supported trade with the communist bloc "as a bargaining weapon to get a quieting down of the cold war in Europe," Dirksen ridiculed East-West trade as a "structure for the conveying of our bounty and treasure to unfriendly and uncooperative nations." The most important difference between Dirksen and a growing number of his colleagues, however, revolved around Vietnam. *Time* asserted that Dirksen's rock-ribbed support for the war did not reflect the views of younger, more independent-minded GOP senators who questioned U.S. involvement in Southeast Asia. When pressed to explain his reluctance to confer with party colleagues, Dirksen snapped, "I've tried that consultation business and I find it takes a year to get consensus. The devil with that. If they want to try me for party deviation, they can."[6]

Dirksen's efforts to hold the party together while supporting the administration created restless rumblings among veteran Republicans as well. When Clifford Case pointed to the unease dividing Republican centrists and declared that there was "a very definite possibility" that some GOP senators would rebel against Dirksen's "hard line" support for Johnson, the minority leader took exception. He told reporters, "When anybody spoils for a fight, they are going to get one," and he maintained that Case's views fell outside the scope of the GOP's foreign policy position. Remembering that war critic and Democrat Wayne Morse had once been a nominal Republican, Dirksen compared the faultfinding Case to the Oregonian: "[Case] belongs on the other side of the aisle more than Morse. He never votes with the party anyway." Self-aware enough to realize that he had violated his commitment to Republican inclusiveness, Dirksen called Case to apologize for his intemperate remarks. Though he blamed the press for needling him, he explained later that "when there is a little friction, I feel I should be the first one to move in with the oil can." Later in the day, Dirksen apologized to Case in front of the entire GOP caucus, making clear his commitment to a unified party even when he took a position that frustrated his Republican colleagues.[7]

Though Dirksen questioned the extent to which the president could keep South Vietnam noncommunist through diplomatic means, he at least conceded the possibility of negotiations. Such a position separated the senator from the right wing of the GOP, another group of Republicans that threatened Dirksen's party leadership in 1967. On March 1 the Senate approved a resolution endorsing the efforts of Johnson and "other men of goodwill" to contain the conflict and to achieve a negotiated settlement to the war. Supporters added the resolution to an amendment appropriating $4.5 billion for the war effort. Though the administration endorsed the innocuous and nonbinding resolution, Sen. Norris Cotton (R-NH) voted against the substitute, calling the result "an indication to the world that we are furnishing the money but our heart isn't in the war." Although noting that he had "never been mistaken for a dove," Dirksen endorsed the substitute, nonetheless.[8] Dirksen's zigzagging tactics for ending the war placed him squarely in the middle of the GOP spectrum. If his position was murky and contradictory, the minority leader appeared to approve of Johnson's emphasis on negotiation from a position of strength. From the left, Case supported increased diplomatic efforts through de-escalation, and Cotton, on the right, promoted a military solution to the conflict. Though relatively inconsequential at this stage, both Case's criticism and the row over the meaning of the March resolution indicated the degree to which Dirksen's middle-of-the-road leadership was falling out of favor.

The battle over the ratification of the U.S.–Soviet Consular Treaty revealed growing divisions within the Republican Senate and increasing frustration with Dirksen's off-the-record interaction with President Johnson. The agreement contained two basic provisions. First, consular officials and employees were to be given complete criminal and diplomatic immunity. Second, each country agreed to notify the other when they arrested a visiting citizen and to provide access to the accused at regular intervals. Though largely a symbolic gesture, the treaty appealed to those Republicans and Democrats who favored improving relations between the superpowers and a thawing of the cold war in Europe. Though the pact had been signed in 1964, Johnson, preoccupied with what he deemed to be more important political issues, chose not to make the treaty a priority until Kentucky's Thruston Morton urged ratification in late January 1967.[9]

Dirksen had long opposed the treaty. Although he did not refer directly to the agreement in his GOP State of the Union address, he denounced increased interaction with communist countries "while these nations are supplying most of the guns and missiles that are killing American soldiers" in Vietnam. He advised his colleagues "to keep an open mind" on the pact but reported to the media that he had been contacted by a Soviet diplomat pushing for the treaty. Dirksen told the press that he had brusquely dismissed the emissary: "You're always talking about cooperation, but what you want is to hit someone on the head with a baseball bat and then say, 'Let's cooperate.'"[10]

Johnson assigned his top Dirksen troubleshooter, Nicholas Katzenbach, to win the minority leader's support. Katzenbach worked up a memo for a White House meeting with Johnson that addressed Dirksen's reluctance to "enter into an agreement with the Russians during the Vietnamese conflict." The key, Katzenbach argued, was that the treaty gave the United States immediate and regular access to Americans arrested in the Soviet Union. He promised that the White House would not open up any new Soviet consular offices in the near future and made clear that FBI Director J. Edgar Hoover could handle the strain of ten to fifteen more Soviet officials who might serve on the side as espionage agents. Secretary of State Dean Rusk wrote Dirksen a similar letter of assurance.[11]

Lobbied by the White House and pressed by a growing number of Republican moderates dissatisfied with a status quo foreign policy, Dirksen reversed field and supported the treaty. He explained his change of heart to his colleagues during a heated party conference. In a "lengthy and detailed" presentation, Dirksen insisted that Katzenbach, Rusk, and Hoover had satisfied his concerns. He offended the rank and file by declaring that his decision was based on confidential information that he had received from the White House. In short, he was asking his colleagues to trust his judgment and to honor his privileged place in the

Washington establishment. An angry Gordon Allott (CO) insisted that he "and others are entitled to have all of the information necessary, the same as any other senator, before they are asked to vote upon this treaty."[12]

In mid March, just as the debate on the treaty was winding down, an ailing Dirksen checked himself into Walter Reed. Yet again, Johnson kept up with his prognosis. Dr. G. G. Burkley wrote that "Dirksen does not have a malignancy. He tends to overextend himself and has a limited reserve of his cardiovascular system and also has marked emphysema. When he is supposed to be on restricted activity, he tends to overwork. This results in some degree of heart failure." He was well enough to leave the hospital and vote for the Consular Treaty, which passed with just three votes to spare, 66 to 28. Johnson fired off a quick note of appreciation, telling Dirksen, "You did a great job for your country and your president."[13] While the two resorted to the politics of the Washington establishment to pass the treaty, the early part of the Ninetieth Congress made clear Dirksen's declining influence within the caucus. GOP moderates like Morton and the freshmen made the Consular Treaty an important issue and flexed enough muscle to win Dirksen's grudging support. Most important, Dirksen's intimate place in the behind-the-scenes workings of the Johnson administration was irritating Republicans who expected more partisan direction from their leader.

Though the struggle to ratify the treaty revealed an embryonic erosion of Dirksen's prestige on Capitol Hill, proposals to end the war provided a larger test to his leadership. On March 3 Sen. Robert Kennedy (D-NY) argued that the United States should suspend the bombing of North Vietnam in order to encourage the communists to begin peace talks. Maintaining that the administration had attempted unsuccessful cease-fires in the past, Dirksen sided with the president's refusal to stop the bombing without an "equivalent action" by the North Vietnamese. Percy endorsed the creativity of the Kennedy speech, calling Johnson's policies "simply too vague to be practical." After the speech, Dirksen met with journalists outside the Senate chamber. In response to a reporter's statement that he seemed "pretty much on the side of LBJ," Dirksen thundered, "Pretty much? I'm entirely with LBJ!"[14]

On May 1, 1967, the Senate Republican Policy Committee released a staff paper, "The War in Vietnam." Jacob Javits pushed for the paper at a party caucus in mid-March, when Dirksen was convalescing at Walter

Reed. The New Yorker acknowledged the "different and varied" views among his colleagues but hoped that the committee's paper might generate some "consensus or party view" on the war. Bourke Hickenlooper endorsed the Javits proposal but warned that the contents of the report had to be kept "confidential" until the full conference had the opportunity to discuss its implications. Hospitalized in early May, this time with a case of pneumonia, Dirksen wrote Hickenlooper that the completed study "is by all odds one of the finest, if not the finest, all-inclusive reports on the whole subject that I have encountered at any time."[15]

Despite Hickenlooper's instructions, bits and pieces of the report were leaked to the press. Thrown on the defensive, Hickenlooper and Margaret Chase Smith released the study in its entirety without consulting Dirksen. Describing the conflict in Southeast Asia as a "weary nightmare," the GOP white paper argued that Johnson had assumed "enormous discretionary powers" at the expense of Congress, distinguished the administration's policies from Eisenhower's "limited commitment," and questioned the usefulness of bipartisanship. The ninety-one-page document concluded by encouraging Republicans to define the precise national interest in Southeast Asia and to establish clearly the "lengths we are prepared to go in support of this interest."[16]

Though only a staff document, the paper created a rift among Republicans concerned about party policy heading into the 1968 election. Nothing in Dirksen's eight-year tenure as minority leader had generated as much divisiveness on a major national issue. One week before the report was released, Morton had distinguished between the "flagburners" and those on Capitol Hill "exercising their responsible rights of dissent" during a "period of bloody conflict." George Aiken (R-VT) backed the paper and doubted Johnson's ability to achieve an acceptable peace. Aiken, the second-ranking representative on the Senate Foreign Relations Committee, argued that the administration was limited by "its own predilections" and "emotional commitments" and was unable to "see the interest of the nation except in terms of its own survival as the government in power."[17]

Aiken appreciated the extent to which the war was dividing the GOP, noting that "there is almost as much divergence of view among prominent Republicans as among prominent Democrats." As early as spring 1967 he was looking forward to the next presidential election. Maintaining that a Republican president could negotiate America out of the conflict, Aiken was one of the first Republicans to link the war to party politics. His views, expressed at an impromptu news conference on May 2, coincided with Walter Lippmann's column in the *Washington Post* on the same day. A consistent critic of Johnson's war policies, Lippmann pointed to Eisenhower's election and compared the stalemate in Vietnam to the Korean War: "There was no solution then except through the election of a Republican president. And that may well turn out to be the only solution now."[18]

Not all newspaper accounts agreed. The *Washington Evening Star* argued that making the war into a partisan issue would result in the GOP's "self-destruction" and warned against the "harmful consequences for a country which has or soon will have half a million of its young men fighting in Vietnam." A cadre of the younger, more moderate Republicans, however, fell in behind senior party figures like Aiken and Morton and challenged Dirksen's commitment to the suprapartisan Washington establishment and the basic assumptions of global containment. Mark Hatfield echoed Aiken's assessment, suggesting that the Republicans form "alternatives to administration policies which have been unable to bring either victory or solution" to the conflict. Though supporting South Vietnamese independence, Senators Javits, Hugh Scott, and Percy issued a policy statement urging "greater efforts" to achieve a negotiated peace. In anticipation of the coming election, all seemed to agree on the importance of arriving at some sort of Republican position on the war.[19]

Dirksen never admitted that, in the opinion of one perceptive reporter, he had "hailed the report while it was a family secret." Determined to cuff his critics and to redouble his support for the administration, he attacked the journalists who had (in his mind) blown the staff paper out of proportion and widened divisions among Republicans. In order to set the record straight with reporters and his fellow senators, Dirksen left his hospital bed to appear at a weekly GOP conference. There he delivered a response to the committee paper (which he had composed between 2:30 and 4:00 A.M. on May 3). The minority leader wanted to "reiterate our whole-hearted support of the commander in chief." Though Dirksen acknowledged the "right of full and fair inquiry and criticism," he dismissed the war as a legitimate partisan issue and emphasized "our position standing four-square behind the president." The fallout from the report reflected the first stages of the crystallization of GOP foreign policy factions. Dirksen positioned himself in the middle of the fray and on the side of the administration, a stance that miffed his party colleagues. One Republican groaned, "Old Ev keeps saying, 'We stand for this' and 'we stand for that,' but the 'we' is more apt to be Ev and Lyndon than Ev and us Republicans."[20]

Johnson's May 3 press conference highlighted his dependence on Dirksen's support. When asked his views of the staff paper, Johnson chose not to mention Aiken, Hatfield, Percy, Javits, or Scott but did refer vaguely to the leader of the loyal opposition: "I haven't read the details of the Senate Republican leader's statement. What I have observed of his statements I am in general agreement with. I do not know what senators . . . are tied to this document. It looks kind of like—well, I don't know." Associating the faithful Dirksen with the GOP position, the president failed to acknowledge the fluidity of Republican support for his policies. The two were so close that reporter Neil MacNeil, without any proof to substantiate his view, wrote that Dirksen most likely assisted in the choice of North Vietnamese bombing targets. At the very least, Dirksen's central place in the establishment deadened his partisan instincts and discouraged him from attacking the president's leadership. Even as a growing number of Republicans questioned the information driving White House policymaking, Dirksen backed the administration: "I go on the theory that in his corner he has the Chiefs of Staff, he has the best military talent we have, he has these reports from Vietnam. Obviously . . . he is in a better position to know about what the situation is than a layman back here 12,000 miles from the scene."[21]

Though intraparty conflict over foreign policy in general and Vietnam in particular dominated GOP Senate politics through the first half of 1967, events at home soon captured the nation's attention. In July urban riots in Newark and Detroit lasted for almost a week, leaving sixty-six dead and hundreds injured. Though scholars have shown that the rioting was primarily a class-based attack on the nation's economic structures, Dirksen, like many of his Capitol Hill colleagues, viewed the violence as an illegitimate, radically organized attack on established institutions of authority. The GOP's response to the riots revealed fissures within the party. Gov. Ronald Reagan (CA), for instance, characterized the looters as "riffraff." Brooke's reaction was more subtle and sophisticated. He urged the creation of a congressional committee charged with investigating the social conditions that contributed to "one of the most urgent domestic problems we have ever faced." Arguing that the United States was committing a disproportionate amount of its resources to a failed foreign policy, Percy held that the national government was obligated to address the socioeconomic problems of urban America: "If we continue to spend $66 million a day trying to save the 16 million of South Vietnam, while leaving the 20 million urban poor in our own country unresolved, then I think we have our priorities terribly confused."[22]

Unable or unwilling to appreciate the demographic and economic issues behind the riots, Dirksen charged that radical agitators with communist ties were directing the urban tumult. He told the press that he had secret information showing that radicals were making Molotov cocktails in New York City factories. When pressed to explain his assertions, he uncharacteristically clammed up, retorted that he was under no obligation to answer, and stormed off the platform. Dirksen's hold on his colleagues was slipping. In response to the growing unrest in urban America that he was unequipped to understand, Dirksen resorted to the politics of the early 1950s. He was dissatisfied with Brooke's perception of what drove the riots, and he suggested that the special congressional committee assess the extent to which there was a "touch of Red" behind the violence. Johnson relayed Dirksen's view when he told his advisers that "Senator Dirksen thinks we are soft on communists. But I have no evidence of communist participation." One week later, however, Johnson was more sympathetic. When Attorney General Ramsey Clark reported that the Justice Department had no "hard evidence of a conspiracy or of overall organization," the president replied, "There may be more to this than we see at the moment." The wide array of responses to the July riots exposed a generational divide that threatened not only Dirksen's hold over the GOP but also the legitimacy of the Washington political establishment.[23]

Thrown on the defensive, Dirksen used a drawn-out legislative battle over the Subversive Activities Control Board (SACB) to reassert his importance as a conservative traditionalist while at the same time providing the country with a "shotgun behind the door" in its ongoing campaign against communist agitators. Not surprisingly, he cooperated closely with Johnson to achieve his most important political goals. Driven by the anticommunist hysteria that had overwhelmed the nation's political culture, Congress established the SACB in 1950 as part of the Internal Security Act. Passed over President Truman's veto, the board investigated radical individuals and organizations in order to determine if they were communist-controlled or -motivated. If so, the 1950 act demanded that such groups register with the attorney general. A series of Supreme Court decisions in the 1960s ruled such requirements unconstitutional, and the board had since been foundering without a mission.[24]

The first eruption over the SACB occurred during the July riots, when the Senate confirmed Simon F. McHugh to fill a vacant seat on the board. After the vote, critics charged that the twenty-nine-year-old McHugh's only qualification for the position was his recent marriage to the former Victoria McCammon, who had once served as one of the president's secretaries. Though remaining employed by the government, the very attractive Mrs. McHugh resigned her position in the White House when she married in August 1966. On July 20, three days after the Senate confirmed McHugh's nomination, the *Wall Street Journal* disclosed his personal association with Johnson and questioned his fitness for service. Surprised by the revelations and the resulting controversy, the White House struggled to explain McHugh's appointment. (Press Secretary George Christian has recently recalled, "How well I remember the pounding I took over Si McHugh.") Sen. John J. Williams (R-DE) entered two motions into the *Congressional Record,* one urging the upper chamber to reconsider its confirmation and the other requesting Johnson to return his nomination to the Senate. Though both motions failed, liberal Democrats and penny-conscious Republicans used the McHugh episode to argue for the board's abolition.[25]

After a private White House conference with Johnson and McHugh, Dirksen took the Senate floor to defend the nominee. His meager grasp of McHugh's dubious professional qualifications did not prevent him from delivering a flowery monologue about courtship and the potential evils of senatorial oversight. As members from both sides of the aisle laughed good-naturedly, Dirksen wove a little magic and used his sense of humor to argue against an intrusive Washington press corps and a hypercritical Senate: "I believe in quiet weddings. I do not believe in probing into them. Love is one of those great, all-consuming powers that knows no rules, no evidence, nothing." *Newsweek* concluded that Dirksen backed McHugh and the SACB "primarily as a means of saving Mr.

Johnson from embarrassment." Though he would have gone to some lengths to protect the president from overly partisan attacks, Dirksen's genuine interest in subversive activities was part of an intuitive belief system that was rooted in his fervid support of the Vietnam War, his disgust with the fallout that conflict created at home, and his dislike of a growing welfare state that in his mind sapped individual will and initiative.[26]

Despite the pleas of Democratic senators such as Edward Kennedy (MA), William Proxmire (WI), and Joseph D. Tydings (MD) and the objections of influential newspapers such as the *Washington Post*, Dirksen confirmed his commitment to the board in a Senate speech: "I want to say now that I will be the last man on the floor of the Senate to stand by quietly and see the board shoved into limbo." He framed his arguments around the notion that the growing Communist Party presented a dangerous menace to American society. Noting that some of his fellow Americans no longer perceived communism as a threat, Dirksen countered that "communism today is a greater danger than it ever was before." Though his speech never explicitly referred to the riots, Newark and Detroit uprisings had occurred twelve days and two days before his remarks. When the *New York Times* criticized his reference to the construction of Molotov cocktails in New York factories, Dirksen retorted, "That must have aggravated the pink-shirted editorial writers who sit in Times Square."[27]

Despite pointed disagreement within his administration, Johnson cooperated with Dirksen to resuscitate the SACB. The fallout from the McHugh nomination prevented the president from taking a more public stand, but he fought for the board in part to keep Dirksen within the White House loop. After the Judiciary Committee approved a continuation of the board's existence, Dirksen planned to bring the bill to the Senate floor in late August. When aide Sherwin Markman informed Marvin Watson that Edward Kennedy and Tydings were planning to stage a filibuster, Johnson ordered Watson to "have Joe Califano get [Larry] Levinson to write some tomorrow and get [Ramsey] Clark to talk to Tydings and Ted Kennedy and keep them from being ugly." Though he and Mansfield decided to delay a Senate vote, Dirksen maintained his anticommunist, antiradical slant through the summer. Moreover, he appeared to appreciate Johnson's efforts to salvage the board. When most of Capitol Hill returned to their districts for the Labor Day recess, Dirksen called Watson and reported, "I will be available if he needs me."[28]

Circumstances soon gave Dirksen another opportunity to play the anti-communist card. On September 17 editor and writer Harry S. Ashmore of Arkansas charged that President Johnson had "effectively and brutally canceled" a covert peace initiative sponsored by the State Department between Ashmore and Ho Chi Minh. Ashmore had visited Hanoi and met with Ho at the behest of the State Department in early January, re-porting back to Washington that the North Vietnamese leader seemed "deliberately conciliatory" regarding the possibility of negotiations. Ac-cording to Ashmore, the State Department encouraged him to write Ho a letter describing the Americans as "prepared for secret discussions at any time without conditions." Ashmore argued that Ho never responded to his February 5 letter because Johnson had cut off the peace feeler by delivering a bellicose message to the North Vietnamese leadership on February 2. Limiting Ho to a four-day deadline, the president's letter re-quired the communists to halt infiltration of the south before he sus-pended the bombing of North Vietnam. Deriding the demands as the "most stringent" terms yet imposed, Ashmore indicted the administration for "crude duplicity" and "double-dealing." On September 18 Ashmore sharpened his attacks and pointed to intrabureau infighting between two State Departments, "one sympathetic to conciliatory efforts and the other taking a hard line toward Hanoi."[29]

The Johnson administration and Senator Dirksen responded quickly to Ashmore's charges. Assistant Secretary of State William P. Bundy ac-knowledged State's cooperation with Ashmore but minimized the mis-sion's importance: "Ashmore yields to an understandable feeling that his own channel was the center of the stage. It was not. It was a very, very small part of a total picture." NSC adviser Walt Rostow, one of John-son's most important foreign policy lieutenants and a strong supporter of the war, wrote a speech for Dirksen criticizing the Arkansan's exagger-ated sense of self: "Mr. Ashmore should remember that private citizens who get involved in diplomacy have a duty to all parties to keep their mouths shut and leave their memoirs for their grandchildren." Though Johnson authorized Rostow to send the speech to the senator, Dirksen chose not to deliver it on the Senate floor, preferring instead to support the president at an impromptu news conference. He followed his de-fense of Johnson with an attack on Ashmore's patriotism. Dirksen in-sisted that Ashmore was "tainted" by his association with the Center for the Study of Democratic Institutions, an organization that in his mind was connected to the "creative disorder" of the New Left. Rostow wrote to thank Dirksen for his "wise and helpful words." But Dirksen was primarily pursuing his own agenda. He had Ashmore pegged for attack before the Arkansan's trip to Southeast Asia. At a GOP fundraiser at the Carlton Hotel in June, Dirksen maintained that the Center for the Study of Democratic Institutions represented a "dangerous philosophic trend." Noting that the group had held a worldwide meeting in Geneva, the minority leader concluded, "They mean business."[30]

Dirksen not only supported the president but also, and for his own political purposes, resorted to his long-held belief that there was something sinister and traitorous about the people protesting against the war. In his mind, the liberal left disturbed the equilibrium of American society and threatened to overturn the traditional values that had made the country great. From a political standpoint, identifying and rebuking the most prominent antiwar critics was a way to promote his image in the GOP as a hardened cold warrior protecting the nation's interest. The Ashmore controversy enabled Dirksen to weave together foreign and domestic threats to his notion of freedom and played into his unfailing commitment to preserve the SACB.

On September 26 Senator Case sharply criticized the president's handling of the war. Known for his even-handed demeanor and his "patrician courtesy," the New Jersey Republican shocked his colleagues when he charged that Johnson had created a "crisis of confidence" through the "misuse" and "perversion" of the 1964 Gulf of Tonkin resolution. Case "paced back and forth across the center of the aisle pounding on desks" during his speech and the ensuing debate. He described Johnson's escalation of the war as "highly irresponsible" and argued that the president had "squandered his credibility" by using the resolution to justify the expansion of an unpopular war. Case's speech was the most vocal assault on the president by a Republican in 1967.[31]

Senators from both sides of the aisle rose to defend the president. Mansfield maintained that "it is too late now to point the finger of blame," and John Stennis (D-MS) warned that the Case speech gave "hope and comfort" to the North Vietnamese. Dirksen disagreed with Case's attack on Johnson's interpretation of the Gulf of Tonkin resolution, arguing that Congress had been neither duped nor deceived by the administration's use of it to justify a wider war: "It was our business to examine it. There are enough lawyers in this body . . . to know that it is the language that governs; and they ought not complain afterwards if the language rises up and hits them in the face." He then belittled Case's intelligence by observing that congressmen in general knew the implications of the resolution's language, "and if they did not, it is a pretty tragic confession, and might well cause the American people to go back and reexamine their conscience about the fitness of people to sit in this body." Even though Dirksen diffused the crisis by yet again springing to Johnson's defense, Case's speech showed the growing vigor of Republicans who were fed up with the president's handling of the war.[32]

In mid-October Rostow, at Johnson's request, compiled the foreign policy views of the most likely Republicans to run for the presidency. Rostow's report revealed the wide array of GOP strategies to terminate the conflict. Some promoted a negotiated settlement. Maintaining that the North Vietnamese had matched each American escalation, Percy concluded that it was "incumbent on the U.S. to accelerate its diplomatic initiatives to bring the war to the conference table." The junior senator from Illinois lambasted Johnson's failure to pursue negotiations more actively and introduced a resolution stipulating that "the armed forces of the U.S. should not continue to bear an ever-increasing proportion of the fighting." Dirksen expressed his frustration with the proliferation of congressional resolutions, responding to Percy's effort, "If we will just let the people alone who are running the war, particularly the military, we will get somewhere."[33]

Though a number of public officials pointed to the popularity of de-escalation, John Tower noted that his Texas constituents preferred "decisive military steps . . . to shorten the war." Former vice president Richard Nixon also favored a more aggressive policy. Arguing that it was "time to fish or cut bait," Nixon charged that the president, "by gradual escalation, has frittered away the advantage that massive pressure should have given us." Reagan endorsed escalation "to win the war as quickly as possible." Viewing the U.S. arsenal of nuclear weapons as a valuable deterrent, he maintained that "the last person in the world that should know we wouldn't use them is the enemy." The governor then suggested that Johnson might consider using atomic weapons, as he "would like to see the end in twenty-four hours if it could be done."[34]

Thruston Morton was the most established Republican senator who questioned the president's policies. On September 27 the former GOP national chairman and assistant secretary of state in the Eisenhower administration reversed his earlier support of Johnson's leadership. Indicative of the loss of the White House's "middle ground" of public support, Morton reevaluated his position not for moral or political reasons but because the war demanded unacceptable costs to achieve ambiguous goals. He maintained that Johnson's policy of strategic bombing "is not paying off." Calling for staged de-escalation, including the unilateral cessation of American bombing in North Vietnam, Morton pointed to the malignant atmosphere of the times. He asserted that "extremists of both the left and the right are poised to destroy our basic social fabric." He ridiculed the administration's policies and attacked Johnson's leadership: "He has been mistakenly committed to a military situation in Vietnam for the past five years, with only a brief pause during the election campaign to brainwash the American people with 'the war in Vietnam ought to be fought by Asian boys.'"

As an additional affront to Dirksen's stance, Morton identified the war as an electoral issue. He charged that if Johnson ignored a diplomatic solution to the conflict, "All hell's going to break loose in November of 1968. The American people will speak out through the ballot box." Beginning early in the year when he lobbied for the Consular Treaty and urged the administration to pursue trade opportunities with the communist East, Morton had nipped at Dirksen's heels and provided the GOP freshmen with the leadership necessary to buck Dirksen's agenda. Reporters began to write about Morton's interest in the minority leadership. He denied the accounts and insisted that "I not only wouldn't think of opposing Ev Dirksen for minority leader, but would fight any one else opposing him as long as he wants the job." Dirksen clipped this report from the *Chicago Tribune* and pasted it into his notebooks, showing that he was conscious of those prestigious Republicans like Morton who denounced his efforts to protect Johnson from congressional critics. He could, however, hardly fathom Morton's use of the war for partisan advantage: "My God, you're confronted with an enemy."[35]

In the face of the most sustained Republican attack on its policies, the administration worked with Dirksen to salvage congressional backing for the president's prosecution of the war. In a memorandum to Johnson, Acting Secretary of State Katzenbach showed that the administration recognized the increasing criticism and took steps to strengthen support for the president's leadership: "Senator Gruening praised Senator Morton's change of position on Vietnam. We have supplied material to Senator Dirksen to counteract Morton's speech." Downplaying the importance of Morton's defection, Johnson asked Rostow during his Tuesday luncheon session, "Walt, did you get the information to Senator Dirksen and Senator Mansfield? They are battling with Senator Case today."[36]

Armed with the administration's resources, Dirksen took the Senate floor on October 3 to admonish GOP faultfinders. What began as an attempt to solidify Republican party ranks resulted in a fierce dispute over the obligations of citizenry during wartime as well as U.S. war aims in Vietnam. "Pounding his desk until his curly hair shook in all directions," Dirksen first recognized the existence of "dissident views" before explaining his responsibility to the head of state in a time of crisis: "I cannot in my position, and I cannot under any circumstances, denigrate him or demean him in the eyes of the world." Without naming his target, Dirksen had Morton in mind when he referred to those critics characterizing Johnson as "brainwashed by the military-industrial complex." If America were to maintain its prestige in troubled times, Congress would have to fall in line and support the president: "Have you heard the British demean their King and Queen? No, you do not demean the ruler." Having just compared Johnson to royalty, Dirksen wisely backtracked and acknowledged that "the president is not our ruler, but you do not demean him in the eyes of the world." Earlier in his career Dirksen had been a jealous protector of congressional power and an avid critic of all things British. Yet, even as his influence began to wane, he continued to celebrate the power of the presidency, and he paraphrased Winston Churchill from the Senate floor: "Let me say that I was not made senator to preside over the liquidation of the holy fabric of freedom."[37]

Dirksen's speech touched off an extemporaneous debate lasting nearly two hours. Case defended the GOP critics by arguing that it was the responsibility of those who differed "to state that disagreement as clearly and distinctly as possible, whether in peace or in time of war." Fulbright challenged Dirksen's belief in the enormity of the communist threat, maintaining that Soviet and Chinese support for North Vietnam did not "mean the Soviets are intending to use South Vietnam as a stepping stone to attack us." Dirksen countered by stressing the importance of a "holding line" between Southeast Asia and Singapore and asserting that defeat in Vietnam would jeopardize American security in the Pacific and freedom around the world: "I still believe in the general field of global strategy that is our defense line, and if we lose it by having the flank turned, the Pacific will no longer be a real defense to our country. When [freedom] is impaired in one place, that impairment continues."[38]

One week later Fulbright made a formal reply to Dirksen's speech. He informed Dirksen about his remarks, but the minority leader chose not to attend. In fact, most senators were watching the Boston Red Sox defeat the St. Louis Cardinals in game six of the 1967 World Series. Nevertheless, the Arkansan cut to the heart of Dirksen's support for Johnson's leadership and his ceding of congressional power to the White House. Noting that Dirksen was entrusted with the leadership of the opposition, he pointed to the irony of his concession to Johnson of "the right to conduct the war virtually without criticism." The trouble, Fulbright contended, was that Dirksen was "being generous with something that is not his—or any other senator's—to give away, namely the responsibility for foreign military commitments entrusted to Congress by the Constitution." Unruffled, Dirksen carried on with his established policy. In an off-the-record speech to Republican staff members he "pounded the rostrum and castigated those who would demean the president."[39]

Dirksen used his relationship with Johnson to wage an intense campaign for the preservation of the SACB. In his eyes, freedom at home was under siege. Before delivering a speech defending the board, Dirksen issued into the record an article from the *Washington Daily News,* "Communist Party Gaining." He linked criticism of the board with the betrayal of the soldiers in Vietnam, asking rhetorically, "Who do senators think have killed 15,000 American troops, if it has not been the Reds? Are we going to play ducks with our own freedom, and let them run loose here in this country, or are we going to come to grips with them?" Believing that the growth of radicalism in the United States was part of a worldwide conspiracy attacking democracy, Dirksen concluded, "We are at a time when we have to call a spade a spade in this country. The time for fooling is past."[40]

Dirksen undermined Democratic arguments by revealing Johnson's promotion of his own efforts to revitalize the board. When Joseph Tydings asked Dirksen why he had voted against hearings on the board to determine the administration's position, the minority leader referred to one of his off-the-record meetings with Johnson: "Why do we have to find out from the administration how they feel, when the president, your president, calls me to the White House and says he wants the bill?" To emphasize the administration's support for his position (as well as his own access to Johnson), Dirksen asked, "Did he call the senator from Maryland down there and say he did not want the bill?" Tydings was forced to admit that he had not visited with the White House about the board. Majority Leader Mansfield added, "I haven't heard from the president on this."[41]

The final push for the SACB coincided with Dirksen's early October defense of the administration's prosecution of the war. Congressional critics at first stymied his efforts to revitalize the board when it became clear that Attorney General Ramsey Clark had no intention to refer any new cases to the SACB. Just forty years old, Clark had an unpretentious, scholarly manner that masked his fierce commitment to civil rights and liberties. Frustrated by the attorney general's intransigence, Dirksen called Marvin Watson at the White House and asked Johnson to direct Clark to send a letter to Congress outlining his intention to comply with the provisions of his legislation. Johnson told Watson that "[we] cannot let Dirksen down." He directed Watson to order Clark to write the letter and threatened, "If [he] can't work for [the] boss, changes are needed." A few days later a chastened Clark sent a letter to Dirksen promising that the law "will be enforced." With the administration's goodwill in his pocket, Dirksen backed a compromise that agreed to abolish the SACB at the end of fiscal year 1969 if the board had not initiated hearings by December 31, 1968. After weeks of wrangling, Congress passed the measure on December 14, and Johnson signed the bill into law in early 1968.[42] Though a limited victory for Dirksen, the temporary preservation of the SACB enabled him to make productive use of his ties to the White House while preserving his ties to the right wing of the GOP.

The Republican right proved far more concerned with Vietnam than with the SACB. A headline for *Human Events* read "Republican Doves Sully Party's Image." Unmoved, increasing numbers of moderate Republicans continued to question Johnson's leadership. Holding that dissent "should be welcomed," Brooke argued that "because of the war, the needs of our cities have been left untended. Conservation projects and educational programs have been postponed. The resources to effectively wage war on poverty have been decreased." He urged Johnson to initiate a unilateral cessation of hostilities to lure the North Vietnamese to the negotiating table. Other Republicans stepped up their criticism of Dirksen's tactics and began to question his party leadership. One GOP senator lashed out at his reluctance to distinguish himself from the administration, saying, "If and when the Republican party dies, its epitaph will read, 'Ev Dirksen killed it.'" His efforts to avoid a party split widened the divide among Republicans, according to one congressman who argued that "Dirksen is polarizing the party on the war issue, leaving a gap so wide that Johnson can drive a truck down the middle by election time." A Republican moderate joined the chorus: "We are fed up to the teeth with Dirksen's constant efforts to save Johnson."[43]

Party discontent threatened to spread beyond his control, yet Dirksen continued to support the president. Though he would never cut himself off from the administration, fall 1967 represented the apex of Dirksen's personal and political relationship with President Johnson. Still in the White House's corner, he addressed his Illinois constituents and rehashed the theme of a growing communist threat to freedom. Relating Vietnam to Nazi aggression, Dirksen insisted that "the grab is on again." He maintained that Red China, with its "hulking population," was destined to pour into resource-rich Southeast Asia: "You see, those leaders on the other side are looking down the long road." Describing communism as a "relentless force that continues to move all over the world," Dirksen insisted that the Soviets would gobble up the Panama Canal "if we weren't guarded and cautious about it."[44]

Dirksen's continued emphasis on freedom under attack derived from his belief that the nation was underestimating the communist menace. Increasingly isolated by a mounting barrage of critics, yet having gone past the point of no return in Vietnam, Johnson welcomed Dirksen's loyalty and supported him politically and personally. In an October cabinet meeting an embittered Johnson pointed specifically to those Republicans and Democrats who had betrayed the White House before he reported that "Dirksen is the only one standing up for us now." In the same meeting Attorney General Clark backtracked and acknowledged that "extreme left-wing groups with long lines of Communist affiliations" were sponsoring the March on the Pentagon. One month later Dirksen called on the White House to present the president with a Thanksgiving turkey. In a move that rightly infuriated Democratic party regulars, Johnson virtually endorsed Dirksen's efforts to win reelection in 1968: "I just hope that whatever time I'm allowed in Washington, I'll always have a turkey brought in, and more than that, I hope that Senator Dirksen will always bring it."[45]

Dirksen lapped up Johnson's efforts to support his leadership. Relishing the praise he won when presenting Johnson with the turkey, Dirksen orchestrated a surprise visit from the president at the annual dinner of the Veterans for Strategic Services. That group honored Dirksen with the William J. Donovan Award, bestowed annually upon that public official who had most effectively promoted the cause of freedom throughout the world. Dirksen was rhapsodizing about the "indivisible fabric of freedom" at home and abroad when Johnson arrived unannounced at the Mayflower Hotel. Dirksen surrendered the stage to Johnson, who chose the obligations and limitations of partisanship as his theme: "If Senator Dirksen has established his reputation for fulfilling the duties of partisanship, he has also quite avoided the temptations of irresponsibility." Knowing in advance that he was speaking to a group of servicemen who had dropped behind enemy lines during World War II, Johnson dotted his address with clever references to the art of espionage. He identified the loyal Dirksen as "one of my dearest friends" and his fifth column on Capitol Hill, as the "only column I haven't complained about all year long." Acknowledging that some of his detractors deemed Dirksen to be a double agent, the president noted the senator's support for issues in the national interest. Carrying on with his portrayal of Dirksen the double agent, Johnson mused, "I am comforted to know that Gerry Ford sometimes thinks so, too."[46]

Yet Dirksen's loyalty to Johnson was neither absolute nor unconditional. Within weeks he inched away from the president's position. Despite his best efforts, the festering situation in Southeast Asia had become an undisputed electoral issue. He could no longer deny the importance of the war and its rightful place in partisan politics. On December 9 Dirksen addressed the GOP Governors' Conference in Palm Beach, Florida. He focused on the election as never before. "All eyes," he told his audience, "are on 1968." He recited a litany of Democratic party failures, including efforts to control inflation and achieve an acceptable breakthrough in Vietnam. He claimed that the Great Society had eroded the notion of "common purpose, of sacrifice, of individuality." Dirksen concluded by targeting the upcoming election: "A Republican victory is imperative, and it is for us to lead the forces through to victory."[47]

On December 15 Dirksen issued his report on the first session of the Ninetieth Congress into the *Congressional Record*. Often used by party leaders to frame the debate for the upcoming election, Dirksen's report was a halfway break with Johnson that enabled him to snipe at the White House without the fanfare of a public address. He intensified his attack on the president's inability to extricate the nation from the war: "For there is no prospect of peace, no promise of stability, no hope for the better in the policies of this administration." Dirksen also modified his understanding of the passive role to be played by Capitol Hill during wartime, maintaining that Congress and the American people should continue "thoughtful discussion [to] guide and strengthen the hand of the commander in chief."[48]

Most surprising was not that Dirksen edged away from Johnson but that he maintained his self-defined role of chief advocate for as long as he did. Wooed and coddled by the White House, Dirksen possessed worldviews similar to Johnson's that drove the senator into the administration's camp as America fought the expansion of communism in Southeast Asia and struggled to come to grips with the fraying of the social fabric at home. Preoccupied with foreign and domestic threats to freedom, the two seasoned cold warriors cooperated for most of 1967 to protect what they deemed to be the nation's interest. Yet national interest and the ideals of a bipartisan foreign policy camouflaged the political dynamics of the times. Dirksen never devoted himself blindly to the president. He supported the revitalization of the SACB for his own political purposes and outpaced the White House in his determination to stamp out communism at home. His support for Johnson's handling of the war was at once instinctive and intentional, impulsive and calculated. Because Republicans were so badly divided by the war, Dirksen enjoyed little room for maneuver if he wanted to protect himself and maintain a façade of party unity. To bind his troops together, Dirksen resorted to the politics of suprapartisanship and lashed out at those who urged the White House to negotiate a peace and at those who advised Johnson to do whatever it took to win the war.

In the end, such a strategy proved unworkable, primarily because the fabric of the party was beginning to rip despite Dirksen's efforts to control the extremes from his more moderate position. After receiving from the White House an electoral endorsement and accolades from a grateful commander in chief, Dirksen backed away. If he failed to offer an alternative policy to bring the conflict to an end, he at last acknowledged that the war rightfully belonged in the political arena. Johnson's former ally even opened fire on the administration's foreign policy leadership, hinting that only a Republican president could achieve peace with honor in Southeast Asia. For Johnson, the minority leader's criticism was potentially disastrous: no longer could the increasingly isolated president conduct the war with the unquestioned support of Capitol Hill's most influential Republican. Moreover, Dirksen showed that when pushed to the limit, his commitment to his own interests and to the GOP far outstripped his devotion to the president's ill-fated efforts to wage an unpopular war thousands of miles away from American shores. For the first time since Dwight Eisenhower occupied the White House in the early 1950s, Dirksen hinted at the limitations to presidential power in the foreign policy arena.

Though Dirksen's reevaluation of his support of Johnson's war leadership was in part political posturing in anticipation of 1968, his deepening despair about the state of the nation was heartfelt and genuine. Dirksen's dissatisfaction mirrored the GOP's increasing willingness to soft-pedal bread-and-butter economic issues while focusing on the fundamental need for social control. In an October speech he denounced the protesters as pampered sycophants thumbing their collective noses at established authority. Like Lyndon Johnson and millions of other Americans of his generation, he never grasped any significant meaning behind the unrest. Befuddled and thrown on the defensive, his only answer was to urge a crackdown on the agitation. Whether the dissidents were engaged in lie-ins, teach-ins, draft card burnings, or protracted efforts to delay the embarkation of troops for Vietnam, Dirksen insisted that "when the law is violated, it must be enforced. . . . No disorderly country ever survived." In a private letter to Mansfield before Christmas, he admitted that he wondered "whether we haven't seen the best of this country." The style of politics he had come to dominate was under attack, but he had in mind the social unrest swirling around him when he told Mansfield that there was "all the more need for us to stand steadfast and be forthright in our devotion to the Republic."[49]

At the start of the second session of the Ninetieth Congress, Dirksen reverted to his practice of supporting the White House on the most important issues. The *National Review* feared that his December criticism of

Johnson's war leadership would entangle him in the "net" of the "dove program." Dirksen insisted that he had not changed his position. Though he reserved "the right to criticize the methods" employed by the White House, he assured the press corps that he supported the administration's objectives in Southeast Asia. But he sensed the futility of the present policy: "We can't retreat, we can't pull out, and we can't get the other side to negotiate."[50] Dirksen's diving and ducking masked one important change in his approach to the most explosive of political issues. Although he never came out and rebuked Johnson in a public speech, he had abandoned the practice of defending the White House on the Senate floor and protecting the administration from its more vocal critics.

Dirksen accepted the fact that Vietnam had become an undisputed political issue, but he chose not to soften his instinctive anticommunism, which he laced with harsh cold war invective. When North Korea captured an American spy ship, the *Pueblo,* and held its crew hostage for eleven months, Dirksen suggested that the White House reconsider its efforts to solve the dispute through diplomatic means. He held that a "clammy spirit of fear seems to be upon us," and he linked the dispute to morale in the field: "What would our troops fighting in Vietnam think if we let these fourth-, fifth-, and sixth-rate Communist countries kick us around?" Though he appeared to be breaking with the White House, he and Johnson were in close contact throughout the crisis. Dirksen read the president his speech over the telephone before delivering it on the Senate floor and acknowledged that Johnson "modified" his remarks "a little" to make it clear that Dirksen supported the administration's diplomatic efforts to resolve the crisis. In late January Johnson invited Dirksen and Ford to the White House for a two-hour private briefing on the *Pueblo* crisis and on the Tet offensive.[51]

Dirksen continued to affirm Johnson's efforts to manage his most vexing problems with the support and cooperation of the leaders of the Washington political establishment. Given the spreading social unrest of the late 1960s, Dirksen maintained that the White House sessions between party leaders were models of conflict resolution. He wrote a newspaper column, "Here, They Reason Together." Dirksen argued that the "veterans of legislative wars" expressed sharp differences on policy issues at White House meetings. Even so, "these old legislative friends . . . sit down around the same big table with the president and, in the spirit of friendships that were formed in honorable political conflict, seek sensible solutions for problems where the national interest is involved." In a national interview Dirksen, piqued by a question that suggested he would prefer Johnson to win reelection in 1968, responded, "The fact that he is a Democrat, I am a Republican, does that mean I have got to take a knife and suddenly cut that friendship . . . in two? I think I should feel honored, I think my party should be honored, that the president seeks my advice."[52]

Convinced that he was an indispensable part of the establishment and determined to hold the GOP together through the upcoming campaign, the seventy-two-year-old Dirksen announced his candidacy for reelection. His fragile health was increasingly troublesome, but he would not allow himself to think of retirement. He sensed that the nation and the world were confronted with an unresolved crisis that demanded commitment and sacrifice. "The easy course," he admitted, "would be to walk away and let the fire burn. But to retreat from an unfinished war or from the unsolved challenges and baffling problems would be alien to every conviction I cherish." He took steps to address the age issue directly, but most Capitol Hill observers sensed that Dirksen's hold over his party colleagues had slipped and that more than ever he was reacting to the changing dynamics within the GOP caucus.[53]

Nowhere was this more clear than on the volatile issue of civil rights. For the third time in as many years, Johnson called for a fair housing bill in 1968. Though few in the administration or in Congress expected the measure to pass, Walter Mondale (D-MN) introduced an amendment to the House bill that offered exemptions to religious organizations and to rentals in owner-occupied buildings of up to four units. By instinct, the national media pointed to Dirksen's "pivotal position" in the legislative process. Mansfield held out little hope for winning Dirksen's support and told the White House that he planned to dispose of "civil rights one way or another . . . and proceed with other Senate business." Even though Johnson argued that the legislation was "essential if we are to relieve the crisis in our cities," Dirksen balked at the cloture vote scheduled for February 20. As expected, the motion failed, but the 55-to-37 margin encouraged proponents of the bill. More interestingly, the GOP caucus divided 18 to 18, which represented a marked shift from the 12-to-21 and 10-to-20 votes of 1966. The freshman Republicans made the difference.[54]

Mansfield filed another cloture motion for February 26. In the meantime, Senators Javits, Brooke, Percy, Mondale, and Philip Hart (D-MI) met with Ramsey Clark and Warren Christopher of Justice. They agreed that without Dirksen on board, "there can be no cloture." The group was hopeful, however, that he would support a bill exempting single-family dwellings sold by the owner without the use of a brokerage agency. Christopher asked the president to call the minority leader and encourage the compromise, but Clark was adamant that the package appear as if it came from Javits, a veteran Republican legislator who had served with Dirksen since the 1950s. On February 26 the Senate failed to invoke cloture by a vote of 56 to 36. This time the GOP caucus divided 19 to 17 in favor of the motion, with Norris Cotton's vote representing the difference.[55]

Seeing his charges peeling away, Dirksen backtracked and told the press that he was committed to a compromise measure. He requested a meeting with Mansfield to discuss the essentials. On February 27 he announced his support for a bill that closely resembled what he believed to be the Javits initiative. Chain-smoking and gulping cups of cold coffee, he explained his reversal to the Washington press corps: "Time and reality makes you older and wiser." When one reporter asked if his influence within the GOP conference had waned, he would not answer but did admit to feeling the pressure: "Maybe I can find comfort in the fact that you have to be a pretty strong bastard to take the slings and arrows." Even though he knew that he was being pushed and pulled more than ever before, he took full credit for "pulling [the bill] out of the fire. I don't know who has if I haven't."[56]

If Dirksen expected that his theatrics alone would win over the necessary number of Republicans, he was to be greatly disappointed. Louis Martin of the Democratic National Committee wrote the White House that Dirksen "has not been able to swing his cronies [Roman] Hruska and [Carl] Curtis of Nebraska." Dirksen admitted to Mansfield that he was struggling to find the votes: "It's easier to line up votes on your side of the aisle. I have to deal with some real sons of bitches." Trying to win conservative support, Dirksen rocked the liberal and moderate consensus when he introduced amendments to weaken the bill without consulting his colleagues. Backed by Baker, Dirksen proposed that all single-family homes with federally financed mortgages be exempted from the bill.[57]

His efforts were to no avail. Supporters of the bill rejected his amendment out of hand and instead introduced a third cloture motion that failed by a margin of 59 to 35. Visibly weary from the negotiating, the weakened Dirksen won the votes of only two other Republicans. Sensing that the minority leader had lost his edge, Percy asked presidential candidate Richard Nixon to prevail upon Karl Mundt for his vote. After securing some minor modifications, Mundt supported the bill. In last-minute negotiations before the fourth and final cloture vote, Dirksen, with Brooke's cooperation, convinced Jack Miller to back the motion. Ultimately, the Senate voted for cloture by a margin of 65 to 32, exactly the two-thirds majority it needed to pass. Dirksen explained that the 1967 riots forced him to revisit his opposition to open housing: "I do not want to worsen the . . . restive condition in the United States. I do not want to have this condition erupt and have a situation develop for which we do not have a cure and probably have more violence and damage done."[58] His apparent concern for the conditions driving social unrest in the nation's urban areas was a sham. His notion that the riots had been organized and directed by domestic communists and that the unrest was nothing more than an unmasked contempt for authority revealed his indifference to the structural and demographic problems plaguing urban America. What moved Dirksen to support fair housing in 1968 was an accurate sense that he had lost control of his caucus.

The liberal and moderate Republicans made the difference. The bill outlawed racial segregation in the sale and rental of 80 percent of the nation's housing. Exemptions were granted to religious organizations, private clubs, owner-occupied dwellings of up to four living units in which the owner lived, and individuals who sold up to three of their own homes a year and did not discriminate in their advertising. Like the civil rights acts of 1964 and 1965, complainants were empowered to file suit in federal courts only after local and state remedies had been exhausted. Johnson passed along the obligatory congratulations. Noting that the package was stymied just one month before, Johnson thanked Dirksen for his efforts and wrote that the bill "is a step toward racial justice in America."[59] Though the 1968 Fair Housing Act would not have passed without his support, it was clear that Dirksen had been pushed to endorse the bill by the growing number of Republicans who bucked his leadership.

Though Dirksen did not endorse Johnson's leadership as he had in the past, he remained close to the administration. When the president shocked the country by announcing his decision not to run for reelection, Dirksen issued a statement that empathized with Johnson because of the vitriolic criticism he had endured. Sympathetic though he was, Dirksen could not resist the opportunity to fire a partisan arrow at the Democrats for driving Johnson into submission. His argument that the president was "pilloried for alleged mistakes in judgment and mainly by members of his party" was a fallacy, simply because the growing number of Republican critics narrowed the margin of essential support on Capitol Hill the president needed to prosecute the war.[60]

Johnson's abandonment of his political future temporarily increased Dirksen's stature on Capitol Hill. Just two days after the president's announcement, the Senate capitalized on the goodwill and passed a $6 billion spending cut and a 10 percent tax surcharge to dampen the inflation generated by the war. Dirksen had supported the plan since fall 1967, arguing then that such a proposal "was based on faith by both sides." Though the pace of Dirksen's public support of Johnson's leadership had slowed, the White House continued to honor his faithfulness. Johnson included Dirksen and Mansfield in discussions with his negotiating team traveling to Paris to seek a settlement of the war. Secretary of Defense Clark Clifford warned against a "certain euphoria" and promised that the "discussions will be lengthy and difficult." The key, he told the Senate leaders, was to "present an appearance of unity during these talks." Dirksen gave his support, telling the group, "I haven't let you down yet."[61]

Despite the flurry of activities that temporarily restored his prominence in the nation's political scene, Dirksen could not overcome the dejection he felt at the social unrest plaguing the country. He was angry at the Justice Department for refusing to refer cases to the SACB. He called Mike Manatos and reported that he had caught "hell and damnation" from his colleagues for supporting the board and told him to ask Johnson to "direct [Clark] to live up to the agreement [Dirksen] believes he has." The true depth of Dirksen's melancholy, however, came through in his speeches and writings. In the article "Let's Not Make Patriotism a Dirty Word," he argued that love of country had ensured America's greatness in the past by inspiring a selfless sacrifice for the common good. He defined patriotism as "that pulsing, throbbing sense of devotion which rises in a citizen when a flag goes by or when the band strikes up the national anthem," and he maintained that when that "ennobling spirit" faltered, a "spiritual sickness is indeed upon us." To Dirksen, the withering of patriotism was at the core of the rot that was eating at the nation's sense of self. He worried that patriotism would be replaced by "some sordid, material consideration," and he feared that the national malaise would "weaken our respect for one another, for law and order, and for the free institutions of this land." In language that echoed his commitment to voluntary prayer in public schools, Dirksen insisted, "Patriotism *is* love of God *and* devotion to our country, one and inseparable."[62]

In his remarks to the Illinois State Republican Convention, Dirksen continued to underscore his traditionalist concern for the nation's social and moral fabric. Pointing to the assassinations of Martin Luther King and John and Robert Kennedy, Dirksen contended that "the sanctity of human life has been scorned and disdained." To him, the protest language that marked the late 1960s was "uncouth, coarse, and un-American." He told his audience that "burn, baby, burn" was an "evil cry" and nothing more than a "call to violence." Like Richard Nixon, Dirksen in 1968 spoke for the silent American who loved his God, paid his taxes, and hoped to protect his private property but was overcome by a "brooding fear of insecurity which hangs like a miasma over our country." He loathed the desecration of the American flag at home and abroad and wondered aloud "whether there is a ring of conviction in what we recite when we say, 'One nation, under God, indivisible with liberty and justice for all.'"[63]

Meanwhile, in the arena of the Washington establishment, Lyndon Johnson turned to Dirksen one last time. The occasion was Earl Warren's announced intention to retire as chief justice of the Supreme Court. Warren's decision, made after Johnson opted not to run for reelection, presented the president with the opportunity to nominate a successor. Johnson's goal was to mold the Court's direction for years to come, thus preserving the social achievements of his administration. Before settling on a choice, Johnson invited Dirksen to the White House for a private conference. At this late date in his presidency Johnson knew that Dirksen's support would be crucial if his nominee were to be confirmed.

The two met in Johnson's study off the Oval Office for nearly an hour, Johnson presenting Dirksen with the situation and asking if he had any suggestions. Dirksen, confident that the president had his own design, yet eager to secure a favorable trade in exchange for his ultimate endorsement, ducked and dived: "Well, why don't you trot out some of yours?"

Still unwilling to play his hand, Johnson rattled off names he had considered but ultimately rejected. Dirksen took the bait and proposed Secretary of the Treasury Henry Fowler, a man who commanded unquestioned respect on both sides of the aisle. Johnson demurred, stating that Fowler was too important to the administration: "We've got this gold imbalance and these problems abroad; Fowler knows the European bankers. If I got somebody who didn't know them, to start fresh and uninformed, that'd be quite a handicap."[64]

The negotiations were at a standstill, but the president buttered Dirksen up by asking if he would like the nomination. As Johnson must have expected, an emboldened Dirksen refused but then threw Johnson off balance by suggesting William Campbell, a federal district judge in Chicago. Campbell's nomination would have restored a modicum of Dirksen's influence in Washington, and Johnson was momentarily caught off guard. "Great idea," he responded as he searched for a reasonable out. He remembered that William Brennan held the so-called Catholic seat on the Court and was thus able to parry, "of course, Bill's Catholic. I don't think I'd like to disturb the religious balance on the Court, and I'm afraid perhaps I couldn't take him."

Working quickly, the two men exchanged more names, and then Johnson played his hand: "What do you think of Abe Fortas?" Fortas possessed a first-rate legal mind and was at the time an associate justice and the Court's only Jewish member. One of the president's most trusted confidants before and after he entered the Court, Fortas was an intimate friend of the Johnsons who could be trusted to protect the liberal legacy of the Great Society. Dirksen knew Fortas well and gave an early boost to Johnson's plan: "He's a bright, brilliant lawyer, in fact, now he's been on the Court for three years. I know of nothing that has come to my attention to impeach his record in any way." Fortas was Johnson's choice, and the president had already anticipated that the nominations (he proposed U.S. Circuit Court judge Homer Thornberry of Texas to fill Fortas's vacancy and secure the support of Richard Russell) would be contentious. At issue, then, was the extent to which Dirksen would fight for Johnson's nominees.[65]

The two combatants were wise and experienced enough to know that Dirksen's commitment would come at a cost. Dirksen was still miffed over Clark's unwillingness to refer new cases to the SACB. Johnson called Larry Temple, who served as the White House's liaison with the

Justice Department, into the conversation. Wanting a smiling Dirksen to see the deal in action, Johnson ordered Temple, "Get in touch with Ramsey Clark and tell him to refer some cases to the SACB." When Clark hesitated, Johnson called him and told him that the nominations depended on his use of the board. On July 1 Clark held his nose and referred seven cases to the SACB. As Temple remembered, "Ramsey did it knowingly, intentionally, reluctantly, and unwillingly."[66]

Dirksen blundered badly by pledging his support to Johnson without first taking the temperature of his caucus. He dined with Howard Baker the evening of his discussion with the president. Baker listened to Dirksen discuss his promise to back the nominees and then gave his own reaction: "Mr. D., I can't go along with you. I'll fight confirmation until we convene a new Congress and install a new administration." Alarmed by Baker's immediate resistance, Dirksen sounded out more of his colleagues before a 12:30 meeting of the entire Republican conference. He called the White House and warned that the nominations were likely to create a firestorm on Capitol Hill. He told Mike Manatos that he thought highly of Thornberry but feared that the nomination "could open the president to charges of cronyism." He again advised Johnson to name Fowler as Warren's successor.[67]

Dirksen was not the only senator to sound off. James Eastland (D-MS), still chairman of the Judiciary Committee, told Manatos that "Dirksen is opposed to Fortas, contrary to the impression he may be giving." Fortas's loyalty to the liberal majority of the Warren court piqued conservative Republicans and Democrats, who sought to use the nomination to test the vitality of liberalism and the strength of the Washington political establishment. John McClellan (D-AR) hoped that Eastland would get "that SOB formally submitted to the Senate" so he could fight the nomination on the floor. Eastland warned Manatos that a long, hard-fought debate on Warren's successor would "tear this country apart." A non-Southern Democrat added his opposition and commented on the shifting mood of the country: "Liberalism is dead."[68]

But when the administration confirmed its plan to proceed with the Fortas and Thornberry nominations, Dirksen pledged his support and began his search for the necessary votes to confirm the nominees. The GOP conference on June 25 was a disaster. He told his colleagues, "There's nothing about lame ducks in the Constitution," but because the White House had not yet formally announced the nominees, he postponed a full discussion of the issue until the next week's conference. George Murphy (CA) turned to Robert Griffin and declared, "To hell with waiting a week for the next policy luncheon to decide on a position. Let's get up a statement declaring our opposition and get some of our colleagues to sign it." Nineteen GOP senators wrote the Murphy-Griffin manifesto, which concluded that the signers would vote against any Supreme Court nominee chosen by Johnson and would filibuster until he withdrew his current nominees. Less than twenty-four hours after Dirksen had reported to his colleagues that he would back the White House, more than half the GOP caucus had deserted him.[69]

His troops had backed him against the wall, and Dirksen saw there was nothing to do but fight. Despite the heavy odds, he remained supremely confident that he would prevail. Even though he preferred another chief justice and had anticipated the charges of cronyism that were plaguing the nominations, Dirksen defied his GOP critics in the caucus and defended the nominees. Johnson calculated that Fortas's Judaism would ensure his speedy confirmation, sensing that no Republican would want to open the party up to charges of anti-Semitism in an election year. Many Republicans, however, were not so easily discouraged. They objected to Fortas's liberalism, Johnson's intimate friendships with both his nominees, and the White House's bald-faced assumption that the administration could retool the Court even when the president had made himself a lame duck. Though Dirksen acknowledged the rationale behind the cronyism charge, his commitment to the modern presidency and to the Washington establishment conditioned him to regard the lame-duck argument as "offensive." He told Manatos that he was chipping away at the GOP opposition and urged the administration to "let it simmer a while. We'll take care of it."[70]

Attorney General Clark must have been privately pleased when the press badgered Dirksen in an attempt to determine if the White House had traded the SACB for the minority leader's support for Fortas and Thornberry. Dirksen denied that there was any link between Clark's decision to resuscitate the board and his decision to support the administration in an election year against a majority of Senate Republicans. According to him, "The Fortas and Thornberry nominations had as much to do with all this as the nuclear proliferation treaty would have to do with Bob Hope." The administration's decision to revive the board, Dirksen believed, was nothing more than a function of his perseverance:

"This is just a case where I mowed Clark down. . . . When you play for keeps, you play for keeps." Capitol Hill reporters were not satisfied with his halfhearted explanation. When one journalist asked again if he had struck a deal with Johnson, Dirksen lost his temper: "That's, that's crass. This is a goddamned outrage to suggest I would do this on the basis of a handout! Why, my life would have been impoverished if I lived that way, only doing something in return for something. What makes me sore is a guy who can't take me straight. That is an insult."[71] Insult or not, the charge was true. He used Johnson's need for his support to lock up a concession that he deemed to be an important political goal.

Dirksen's mounting petulance was one more sign that his influence among his colleagues was waning. On the surface, he continued to exude an almost arrogant certainty that he would prevail. He promised the White House, "We will win this one," and he took great pleasure in reporting to Manatos when he was able to secure a GOP convert. But when a reporter asked if Griffin's dogged stubbornness represented a threat to his leadership, he exploded in outrage: "Don't throw that kind of tripe at me. When you write that kind of tripe, the people back home say, 'Sonny Boy's leadership is being challenged'—now that's just billingsgate and you know it. . . . I'm their leader, not their dictator. No one challenges my leadership. Nothing happens around here without me."[72]

To this point, the White House was pleased with Dirksen's commitment to the nominations. Temple wrote the president after a Judiciary Committee meeting on Fortas and Thornberry and reported that Dirksen "was never in more eloquent form."[73] Though he addressed Eastland, Dirksen made no secret that his real target was Griffin. He continued to extol the power of the presidency. Calling the lame duck charge "entirely improper and . . . very offensive," Dirksen maintained that it was Johnson's privilege to make appointments until the end of his term. He held that the lame duck argument, taken to its logical extreme, would have excused every senator retiring from public life or defeated in the 1968 primaries from voting on the matter. Detailing the history of Supreme Court appointments, he scoffed at the assertion that Johnson had acted inappropriately by promoting his closest friends to the bench. After all, Dirksen opined, "You do not go out looking for an enemy to put on the Court."

He ridiculed Griffin's efforts and employed his wide-ranging vocabulary to assert his superiority over the rebellious upstart. The cronyism charge, he maintained, was a "frivolous, diaphanous—you know what that means, don't you—gossamer—you know what that means, don't you—argument that just does not hold water. And I have not seen an argument yet that will stand up, durably stand up, against the nomination and confirmation of the two men." When George Smathers (D-FL) asked if Charles Fairman, the Supreme Court authority Dirksen had contacted about the nominations, was a "crony" of his, Dirksen chided, "Yes, a crony; that is right. He was a second lieutenant in artillery in World War I. So was I. That makes us closer cronies." Above the laughter and snickering, Smathers was heard to say, "Terrible."[74]

The *New York Times* wrote that confirmation was "inevitable" and urged the Senate "irresponsibles" to give in gracefully. But Griffin and his supporters did not let go. Their tenacity delayed proceedings long enough for more damaging information to come to light. Until then, Griffin had hammered away at what he considered to be Johnson's blatant usurpation of congressional power. To Griffin, the issues "involved in this struggle reach far beyond party lines to the very core of our system of government." He resented Johnson's assumption that a retiring president and a few anointed leaders on Capitol Hill could ram contentious nominations through the Senate. Immediately after his minority leader tried to show him up, Griffin pounded the witness table and lashed out at what he considered to be Johnson's extraconstitutional effort to have his way: "He has only half the power and it is about time the Senate realized that, especially with regard to the Supreme Court."[75] Griffin's sustained efforts to thwart Johnson's designs were a frontal assault on the politics of suprapartisanship and on the modern presidency that Dirksen embraced.

Confident that he had struck Griffin with an effective counterblow, Dirksen put the nominations aside to focus on the GOP's national convention in Miami Beach. Charged with the chairmanship of the party platform, Dirksen arrived with a guard, armed with a shotgun, who sat in a jumpseat behind the cockpit of Dirksen's plane in order to prevent a possible hijacking. After months of maneuvering, Dirksen had won the chairmanship of the platform committee despite a barrage of protests from Republican governors who wanted to modernize the party image and downplay the importance of the congressional leadership anchored in Washington. Dirksen appeared unruffled by their rancor and threatened to write the platform himself on a portable typewriter on the trip down to Miami.

As it turned out, the 1968 GOP platform made clear Dirksen's diminished prestige. Remembering the divisive effects of the Goldwater effort four years earlier, he reported that he would push for a platform that "any candidate can stand on." But he failed to appreciate the extent to which the writing of the document would result in an intraparty feud that magnified how much his hold on the GOP had slipped. Not surprisingly, Dirksen hoped to avoid making a partisan issue of the Vietnam war. Jack Miller disagreed, insisting that the committee make clear Johnson's "deception" and "misperception."[76] Dirksen's draft did little more than criticize the administration for its "piecemeal" escalation of the conflict. Though he had supported the negotiations in public and cooperated with the White House in off-the-record meetings, he proposed language that would reject any diplomatic settlement "unless it assures the Vietnamese people full opportunity for self-determination."

Pushed hard by Rockefeller and several other Republican moderates, probable nominee Richard Nixon cabled the platform committee and endorsed a "phasing out" of American troops. Nixon emphasized that the war "must be ended honorably, consistent with America's limited aims and with the long-term requirements of peace in Asia." The final version of the platform included phrases taken from Rockefeller's earlier speeches that pledged a "coherent program for peace" and promised "to develop a clear and purposeful negotiating position." Backed against the ropes, Dirksen could do little more than accept the amendments to his handiwork, revealing that the torch of the GOP leadership had been passed to a new generation of leaders.[77]

Disappointing as writing the platform must have been for Dirksen, the convention was not a total loss. In addition to giving a rousing "stump speech in the grand style" and performing his duties as head of the platform committee, Dirksen participated with other GOP leaders in Nixon's selection of a vice presidential candidate. At some point in the meeting Hatfield's name came into the conversation. Though other established Republicans resented Hatfield for substantive reasons, Dirksen spoke against his candidacy because he had not matched the social expectations that the senator deemed crucial for any leader in the establishment. "Mark's a nice boy," Dirksen told Nixon. "However, one is not even served a soupçon of wine when invited to his house for dinner." According to Tower, Thruston Morton asked Dirksen more pointedly, "You mean he's a square?" Dirksen replied, "Yes, he's a square," and that ended all talk of Hatfield serving on the ticket with Nixon. The Republican congressional leaders, however, had a limited effect on Nixon's ultimate decision. According to Dirksen, no one in the group mentioned the possibility that Maryland governor Spiro Agnew might be Nixon's vice president.[78]

In Washington again, Dirksen confirmed reports that more than his political life was under attack. In March 1968 he began to receive anonymous death threats. The sheriff from Loudon County in Virginia knocked on his door one night in March 1968, informing Dirksen that "there's a man who wants to blow your head off." Thereafter, Dirksen received protection from the Secret Service, the FBI, and local policemen, and the potential for violence accounted for the guard with a shotgun who had traveled with the minority leader to Miami Beach. In September Dirksen seemed unmoved by the situation, telling reporters, "I didn't want anybody to blow my head off because the flowers were in bloom and they need me. I told [the sheriff] whoever this creature is, I hope he waits till the frost comes and the barn swallows are gone."[79]

Dirksen had less cover in the ongoing struggle to protect his political power. On the surface he remained closely connected to the key provisions of the administration's agenda; as always, he couched his support in personal terms. On September 5 he sent a photograph of himself to Johnson inscribed, "To my longtime colleague, my steadfast friend, with esteem and warm personal wishes." Desperate to retain Dirksen's support for the Fortas and Thornberry nominations, Johnson wrote back, "As much as I like your picture, I like the inscription even more. It was good and kind of you to let me have such a magnificent reminder of our service together, and the richness of friendship those years will always assure. The photograph will always be near me. I hope you will too." For the moment, Dirksen was on board, still confident that the Senate would confirm Fortas and Thornberry. Johnson, however, began to sense that "Dirksen will cut and run." Larry Temple reassured his boss, pointing to the fact that Dirksen had given the White House his commitment to the nominations. Johnson was not assuaged, telling Temple, "I know him. I know the Senate. If they get this thing drug out very long, we're going to get beat. Ev Dirksen will leave us if we get this thing strung out very long."[80]

Johnson was right to be concerned. The White House was struggling to get the nominations out of the Judiciary Committee. Johnson's opponents had centered their original objections on the idea that a lame-duck president should not have the power to nominate Supreme Court justices. They then argued that Johnson erred by promoting his intimate friends to the High Court. Conservative Republicans upped the ante. By charging that Fortas's liberal and activist interpretation of the First Amendment made it easier for pornographers to sully the nation's collective conscience, Strom Thurmond ensured that the nominations would be stalled in the Judiciary Committee. Johnson was exasperated. He told his staffers, "We're a bunch of dupes down here. They've got all the wisdom. All the sagacity is reposed up there. They're just smarter than we are. We're a bunch of ignorant, immature kids who don't know anything about this." After the pornography charges were leveled against Fortas, Harold "Barefoot" Sanders wrote Johnson that neither Mansfield nor Dirksen "is approaching this fight with any enthusiasm, confidence, or sense of outrage."[81]

Thurmond and Griffin had Johnson on the ropes, and Dirksen began to edge away. Previously he had predicted smooth sailing for the nominations, but on September 14 he reported that there were not enough votes for the Senate to act before adjournment. Two days later, in an effort to take some of the heat off Fortas, he offered an amendment to relieve federal courts of all authority to review the obscenity convictions handed down by state courts. Fortas scholar Bruce Allen Murphy points to the "hollow ring" of the Dirksen amendment: "It was a little like defending the virtue of your daughter to others by announcing that you are locking her in a closet."[82] Dirksen had served notice that he was on the brink of turning tail on the White House.

Just before 7:00 P.M. on September 16 Dirksen was ushered into the little lounge just off the Oval Office. He had told Manatos that he planned "to lay it on the line" with Johnson. Dirksen told the president that he expected the Judiciary Committee to report out the nominations by a two-to-one margin. In a conversation with Manatos earlier in the day, Mansfield and Dirksen agreed "that the 'dirty movies' issue has taken its toll on Fortas, and that the $15,000 fee [the amount of an honorarium for teaching a seminar at American University], while a secondary issue, has been hurtful." Dirksen counted twenty-six Republicans opposed to cloture. The two predicted that the floor debate on pornography would be long and "dirty." Though no one questioned Fortas's qualifications, Thurmond "tastes blood," and "the movies were what the opposition needed to make their positions jell." Dirksen bemoaned what he deemed to be the "danger" to the separation of powers if Congress thwarted a presidential appointment and chose to deny "any nominee for the Court not on his qualifications, but on decisions he has rendered." According to Manatos, both Senate leaders agreed that "win or lose, the stain of this terrible ordeal will remain with Fortas on or off the Bench."[83]

With a heavy majority of his troops committed to defeating the nominations, Dirksen needed a reasonable pretext to separate himself from the White House. Even at this late date he moved slowly, and John Sherman Cooper predicted that Dirksen was "throwing a lot of sand in everybody's eyes. No doubt he would like to come out as the savior of the nomination after a while." Cooper's impression, however, was that the appointments could be salvaged. Dirksen knew that the game was up. On September 24 he proposed that the Senate vote to recommit the nominations to the Judiciary Committee or, because Warren had agreed to retire only when a successor was "qualified," pass a sense of the Senate resolution that no vacancy existed.[84]

The White House chose not to pursue the offer, and on September 27, Dirksen announced that he would not support cloture on the Fortas nomination. When asked to explain his change of heart, Dirksen was far too canny to admit that his party colleagues had whipped him. Armed with a memo from one of his assistants, Dirksen referred to a 1968 Supreme Court case, *Witherspoon v. Illinois,* in which Fortas and the Court ruled unconstitutional the Illinois law excluding all prospective jurors who expressed conscientious objections to the death penalty in capital punishment cases. The case had become a hot political issue in Illinois when the attorney for Richard Speck, convicted for the murders of eight nursing students, claimed that he would use the Court's ruling to challenge the constitutionality of the verdicts. Though Fortas's opponents had grilled the nominee about the case in his mid-July hearings before the Judiciary Committee, Dirksen claimed that he had delayed his reversal because the whole issue deserved "far better scrutiny than I have been able to devote to it." The *Witherspoon* case was simply a veneer. Fortas's mounting troubles and the headstrong efforts of an unbreakable cadre of GOP renegades forced a diminished Dirksen to betray the White House and to clarify his ultimate commitment to his own party leadership.[85] Just as important, the Senate's rejection of Fortas's nomination was a successful attack on the powers of the modern presidency. Moreover, the Senate rejected the palace politics that Johnson had mastered with the help of confidants like Abe Fortas and Everett Dirksen.

Meanwhile, Dirksen had paid little attention to his own campaign for reelection. In early June he drubbed Roy C. Johnson in the GOP primary. A truck driver by trade, Johnson compromised any chances he might have had for the nomination when he argued for the immediate invasion of Cuba and China.[86] His opposition in the general election appeared only slightly more formidable. In early 1968 Adlai Stevenson III and Sargent Shriver tested the waters and hinted at a run for Dirksen's seat. But Chicago mayor Richard Daley, the unchallenged boss of the Illinois Democratic party, passed over these two prominent figures and settled on William G. Clark, the state's unknown attorney general. Daley snubbed Stevenson because the son of the former Illinois governor and Democratic nominee for the presidency was unwilling to pledge unconditional support for Johnson's position on the Vietnam War.

Daley's announcement of Clark as the party's nominee coincided with Dirksen's February decision to reverse field and support the administration's open housing legislation. The timing was so eerie that one suspicious member of the Democratic party's Central Committee reported that he was convinced that "Lyndon told them not to rock the boat on Ev." Dirksen was surprised when reporters informed him that a political lightweight he hardly knew would be his opponent. When he was asked if Johnson actually wanted him to triumph because the president was more comfortable with the minority leader than with any of his potential successors, Dirksen replied, "God, I'm glad somebody's comfortable with me."[87]

Once nominated, Clark shucked off Daley's mantle and sharply criticized Johnson's handling of the war. Though Clark's tactics won him the backing of Senate doves like Edward Kennedy and Eugene McCarthy, Daley repudiated his nominee and hung him out to dry. Cut off from the financial and logistical support of the Democratic machine, Clark was forced to open a Washington office in order to raise the necessary money to continue his campaign. Organized labor in Illinois, for years the greatest coordinated threat to Dirksen's political life, provided only $10,000 for Clark's coffers. Dirksen gave his opponent little heed. Two weeks before the election, the *Chicago Sun-Times* released a poll giving Dirksen a 62-to-38 percent lead.[88]

Starved for funds and deprived of all support from party functionaries, Clark savagely attacked the style of politics that Dirksen and Johnson had come to dominate and that appeared to be quickly falling out of favor. He lashed out at Johnson's leadership in the Fortas fiasco. Without attacking Fortas's qualifications, Clark assailed the "arrogant intrigue" and "political overkill" that Johnson employed to gain Dirksen's support in an effort to "ram through" the Fortas nomination. Clark was not privy to the quid pro quo arrangements that had for so many years characterized the suprapartisan Washington establishment, but he sensed that palace politics was eating away at the nation's democratic impulse: "It is the concept of the stacked deck in which aces tumble from the highest places in the mistaken belief that democracy belongs to those in power. But it is this very concept of wheel and deal that has created a mass cynicism in this land, particularly among young people. . . . Public office is a public trust, but the public shouldn't have to do all the trusting."[89]

More interested in the political effects of Johnson's last-minute bombing halt than in his own affairs, Dirksen saw little reason to answer his opponent's charges. But just as he had done six years before, Dirksen rushed away from his obligations in Washington to patch up his concerns in Illinois. On one particular day he invited author Fred Bauer along for a downstate tour. As Bauer climbed on the plane, the pilot warned that flying as low as 3,500 feet might get a little rough. When Bauer asked why they were flying so low, the copilot explained, "It's his lungs," and the pilot added, "Emphysema." Bauer remembered that the exhausted Dirksen was suffering from a miserable cold and that as he slept "his breathing, rattly and labored, was the only sound competing with the engines." When the plane touched down in Peoria, however, Dirksen seemingly recovered and put on a show: "Like gangbusters, he came on strong, shaking hands, smiling, making small talk, signing autographs." Later in the evening, as Dirksen prepared for a radio interview near a cocktail lounge, he asked Bauer to fetch him a Jack Daniels with water. When Bauer returned and handed over the drink, he saw the senator grimace. He knew right away that the bar had run out of Jack Daniels and had dirtied up his drink with another bourbon.[90]

Bauer was especially impressed that Dirksen spoke without a manuscript, that he held forth without even a single note to prompt his memory. Despite the Dirksen magic, it was clear that even the people of Illinois were turning against him late in his career. In his final campaign he won reelection by a 53-to-47 percent margin that was closer than anyone had anticipated.[91] How the election might have gone had Clark had Daley's money and manpower is pure speculation. Though his alienation from the Democratic machine threatened the very existence of his campaign, Clark was able to cast himself as a free agent battling the entrenched powers for the public interest. From Dirksen's perspective, the narrowness of the result may not have phased him. He knew that 1968 was his last campaign, and in the final analysis, he was safely reelected. His hold on the Senate Republican leadership had already slipped; his future in that capacity would be dictated not by Illinois politics but by the way he handled the GOP conference.

Though his prestige had ebbed and he had endured an election scare, Dirksen remained at the center of the national establishment through the end of the Johnson administration. Just five days after the election, on Saturday, November 9 at 9:00 A.M. Dirksen arrived unannounced at the residence of South Vietnam's ambassador to the United States, Bui Diem. Diem opened the door to find Dirksen, standing alone and bracing himself against the November chill. Worried that South Vietnam's steadfast resistance to peace talks would "create difficulties" for Nixon's administration, Dirksen underscored the importance of South Vietnamese participation in the talks: "I am here," he explained, "on behalf of two presidents, President Johnson and President-elect Nixon. South Vietnam has got to send a delegation to Paris before it's too late."[92]

In addition to the role he played as an intermediary between Johnson and Nixon, Dirksen served as chairman of the Inaugural Committee. In that ceremonial capacity he went out of his way to invite the Johnsons and their daughters to the Senate luncheon following the swearing-in. Eager to leave Washington and already committed to a luncheon at the Clark Cliffords, Johnson sent his regrets. More important, at White House bidding, Dirksen went to bat one last time for Johnson and lobbied for a bill to increase the presidential salary to $200,000 and to boost the pay of former presidents, beginning with Johnson. Three days before the inauguration Johnson wrote Dirksen one last time: "I am indeed proud to call you 'my friend'—a good friend, a steadfast friend, a loyal friend. You have helped lighten the load that I have carried as president and you have enriched my heart." Johnson captured the spirit of the suprapartisan Washington establishment, but he sidestepped the essential expedience of their interaction and the recent erosion of a relationship that marked the ebb of the political culture so crucial to their power and prestige. At 11:05 A.M., January 20, 1969, Johnson, Dirksen, and the president-elect motored together to Capitol Hill for the ceremony. In style and substance, the drive from the White House signaled the end of an era and the start of a new chapter in America's political life.[93]

Epilogue

Richard Nixon's ascendancy to the White House was the finishing blow to Dirksen's importance in Washington politics. At seventy-three, he and the fifty-six-year-old Nixon were of different generations and had a professional relationship based on "mutual respect" rather than a personal relationship of genuine friendship. Even more important, Nixon departed from recent custom and established a leadership style that isolated his administration from the crucial players on Capitol Hill. No longer Washington's most important Republican, Dirksen tried to preserve his independence by stalling a handful of presidential nominations. His tactics appeared to be a back-handed slap at Nixon's leadership. One national weekly wondered "whether Richard Nixon really needs enemies when he has friends like Ev Dirksen." On the defensive, Dirksen countered that he was protecting Nixon "from people I feel do him no good and could do him harm."[1]

Dirksen's GOP colleagues refused to accept his explanation that he was merely doing the administration's dirty work in order to save Nixon from political embarrassment. One frustrated Republican complained, "There's a growing resentment over Ev's announcements that he's going to stop this nomination or block that one. If he continues to be the man on horseback, there'll be a blowup. We're no children." Even his friends in the Washington press corps began to turn on him. *Newsweek* ran a feature article exposing his connection with special interests and pointing to the perks he received for his constant support of their agendas. Through it all, Dirksen retained his equanimity and appeared to accept the more aggressive inquisitiveness of the new investigative journalism. He told a story from World War I about a frightened recruit on his first aerial mission behind enemy lines. The private panicked when his balloon came under fire, shrieking, "Sergeant, the Germans are shooting at us!" "That's right, my boy," the sergeant answered. "They're allowed to."[2]

271

It was as if he knew that his greatest challenges lay behind him and that the end was near. His staff sensed that his health was more fragile than ever. In August 1969 their worst fears were confirmed. The doctors at Walter Reed found what they suspected was a malignant tumor on his right lung, no doubt the result of his three-pack-a-day addiction to his beloved cigarettes. He spent the few weeks before his surgery getting his affairs in order and writing an autobiography of his political career through 1950. Because his body was wracked by emphysema, a stomach ulcer, and a fluttering heart, it was doubtful that he could survive the surgery. The doctors gave him a 10 percent chance. Having prepared for the worst, his family and friends were shocked that he survived the three-hour ordeal in decent shape. Perhaps eager for more political cover, Nixon wrote to praise the "famed Dirksen spirit and zest for life."[3]

But his recovery was short-lived. Just four days after his surgery, on September 7, 1969, Dirksen, with Louella, Joy, and Howard Baker at his side, was overwhelmed by sudden cardiac and respiratory arrest and died an hour later. Reaction from his Capitol Hill colleagues was swift and heartfelt. Liberal Democrat George McGovern (SD) was speaking at a rally in Libertyville, Illinois, when he heard of Dirksen's death and informed the audience. "I shall never forget," McGovern recalled, "the hush which fell over that partisan Democratic audience as they thought about our common mortality and those fundamental concerns that cut across political lines." Mike Mansfield, known for his understated and laconic manner, nonetheless saluted Dirksen's "capacity for change in a changing world." He remembered his friend's "tolerance, understanding, and unfailing kindness. I remember, too, the laughter, now stilled, which a short time ago he engendered in the Senate. I remember the tears which, on occasion, he provoked among us with the passionate vividness of his words. I remember the fierce divisions and triumphant reconciliations in the Senate—both of which he was often the prime mover."[4]

After Nixon's eulogy and the memorial on Capitol Hill, the cortege traveled to Washington's National Presbyterian Church for the funeral, and finally, on September 12, 1969, back to Pekin for a graveside service. Leaving behind the Washington establishment that had redoubled the importance of his political career, Dirksen came home for the final time to the small midwestern town where it had all begun. Though he no doubt would have preferred more time, he was blessed with a mental sharpness and a love of life until the very end. He escaped the purposeless malaise that plagues so many public servants who have been shunned by the voters or superseded by a younger generation. Until the day he died, Dirksen was in the arena, mixing it up, ducking and diving, savoring every moment of his existence as minority leader of the Republican Senate.

Assessing the whole of Dirksen's career is no easy task. On one level, he never escaped the caricature of a purposeless ham, well-meaning and good-natured but nevertheless a puppetlike buffoon who used the nation's political stage more to entertain and amuse than to lead and inspire. David Halberstam offers such a perspective, in the late 1970s writing that "Dirksen was marvelously over-blown, like a huge and rich vegetable that has become slightly overripe; watching him, one had the sense that he was always winking at the audience, winking at the role that he had chosen to play, the stereotype of a slightly corrupt old-fashioned senator."[5]

Dirksen's unpredictability as a legislator and as minority leader gives some weight to the notion that he was a chameleon, ever ready to adapt to changing circumstances. Abrupt reversals on important policy issues marked his career from beginning to end. Ideological elasticity is currently out of fashion in today's politics, but Dirksen never apologized for his bobbing and weaving. He once explained "I am a man of principle, and one of my principles is flexibility." Although some interested parties remain critical of Dirksen's inconsistencies, his son-in-law Howard Baker, himself a former Senate Republican leader, has a different take. "Virtually every idea he held," Baker has recently written, "he held tentatively. The world would be better off if more people did that these days."[6] Dirksen's discomfort with a rigid set of ideas was a function of his awareness that changing times and dangerous conditions require pragmatic cooperation with the other side of the aisle. As minority leader he sensed intuitively that his first obligation was to ensure that the Senate functioned smoothly as a governing institution, not that it screech to a halt for mere ideological posturing.

Dirksen's theatrical inclinations also masked the fact that he was a master legislator. Through hard work and sheer determination he shaped countless laws in the course of his career. Baker recently described Dirksen as a "semi-insomniac" and recalled that "he used to get up at 4:30

in the morning. On those occasions when I was with him, at that hour I'd wake up and see the light on at his desk." Robert Novak suggested that Dirksen's emphysema contributed to his insomnia. "He'd go back out on his screen porch in Leesburg with an old portable typewriter and he'd take every bill that came out of committee, read the bill, read the report, and write a one-page precis on it." Thomas Kuchel's legislative assistant Stephen Horn remembered that Dirksen's work continued after the close of the legislative day. "When his chauffeur-driven car took him out to his home in Virginia," Horn recalled, "you could see the light on in the back seat and Dirksen reading his bills under that light."[7]

Horn argued that "there was no senator more serious about the study of legislation than Everett Dirksen." Novak agreed, insisting that Dirksen "knew the legislation better than anybody in the Senate." Dirksen's herculean work habits were just part of what made him a throwback to an earlier era. In addition to writing his own legislation and the vast majority of his speeches, he campaigned without advance teams or personal aides to control his contact with the public. In 1962 Novak saw Dirksen arrive in a small downstate Illinois town, walk into a popular cafe, and approach the nearest waitress. "Tell everyone I'm here," he said.[8]

Dirksen's work ethic and his hands-on political style overturn the notion that he was little more than a charlatan spoofing his way through public service, but the wisdom of his actions and the meaning of his leadership remain open for debate. In his early Senate years he was driven by an unquenchable ambition and an exaggerated sense of self. As a Republican he was more of a divider than a unifier. In one of the ugliest periods of his tenure, Dirksen gave unbroken support to Joe McCarthy and showed a blatant disregard for civil liberties and an unseemly indifference to the national interest. Age, experience, and reality tempered Dirksen's ambition. Once it became clear that he would never be president, he channeled his every energy into public service. He wisely used his relationship with Dwight Eisenhower to edge his way into a position of national leadership and a revered place in the suprapartisan establishment.

Once there he exceeded expectations and developed into a Senate giant. Always leading the minority, Dirksen nevertheless controlled the pace and the outcomes of several of the most important debates in his Senate career. Eisenhower, Kennedy, and Johnson worked feverishly to keep him in the White House camp. Each president knew that Dirksen's loyalty was rarely unconditional and that his cooperation was never completely assured. Dirksen profited from his importance and his unpredictability, winning favors for himself and his outnumbered Republican colleagues. At critical times he went to the wall for Democratic presidents who would have been left reeling without his support for unpopular but essential foreign policy programs. As the civil rights crisis peaked and threatened to tear the country apart, he rallied his troops and ensured that the Senate he so dearly loved responded to the call.

There were, to be sure, missed opportunities, glaring miscalculations, and important failures. Perhaps too comfortable in the minority, Dirksen spent very little time shaping a wideranging partisan agenda to compete for a congressional majority. Unlike many of his GOP colleagues, he ignored the emergence of the South as a Republican stronghold. At the height of the 1964 civil rights debate he wrote that the "future of the Republican party does not lie in Georgia or the Deep South."[9] At the very least, Dirksen would today regret the one-party tendency that courses through southern culture and the way that race continues to polarize the nation at the turn of the twenty-first century.

Dirksen's most glaring shortcomings surfaced at the end of his career. As time wore on he focused more on establishment politics, presumed subversive activities, and amendment crusades than on urban decay and a realistic assessment of the nation's arrogant and open-ended commitment to global containment. For too long he impulsively backed Johnson's Vietnam policy, and in the end he failed the Republican party and the American people. Although some observers might excuse Dirksen's actions as necessary and appropriate when troops are engaged in the field, the cost of the war at home required more statesmanlike leadership than he or Johnson was able to muster. As a revered Republican, Dirksen had the prestige and courage necessary to urge Johnson privately to promote a national discussion on the war that might have expedited an end to the conflict. Instead, he couched himself as the ultimate American patriot supporting the nation's war effort against mounting odds.

Dirksen's greatest fault, in the final analysis, was not his membership in the establishment but his unbroken reverence for it. At his peak, he realized that ever-changing conditions create opportunities and alter responsibilities for national leaders; at the end of his career, however, he wrongly assumed that the suprapartisan establishment was the most effective means for addressing every national crisis. In the case of Vietnam, angry Americans were lashing out at "the system," and Dirksen and his establishment colleagues chose to ignore their calls and deny them a partisan outlet to vent their frustration. By loyally supporting the commander in chief, the fiercely patriotic Dirksen snubbed the nation's democratic impulse and ironically exacerbated the social unrest he had hoped to limit. In the process, he contributed to the public's mounting disgust with the establishment and the nation's turn toward the politics of resentment.[10]

It was somehow fitting that in just eight short months Lyndon Johnson retired and Dwight Eisenhower and Everett Dirksen died. Their demise signaled the end of suprapartisanship and the emergence of a more acrimonious and contentious political culture that welcomed differences, capitalized on discord, and deemed national consensus an unrealized and foolhardy dream of the broken past. Assessing the two political cultures is inherently problematic and extraordinarily difficult, but several observations are in order. Suprapartisan politics served the nation well from Eisenhower's inauguration through the mid-1960s. Though there were cracks in the mold and important issues were left unaddressed, a strong consensus in the body politic held that it was appropriate for the establishment and the White House to provide for the social welfare, contain the spread of communism, and ensure the basic civil rights of all Americans. Suprapartisan leaders from both sides of the aisle gathered behind closed doors, and, in sessions relatively insulated from public view, debated the most effective means for achieving common goals. Pollsters and political consultants were far less prolific, giving the leadership appropriate time and space to deliberate a given course of action. For better or worse, emphasis was on a common good and a corporate endeavor rather than on a selfish interest or an individual triumph. Members were loyal to each other and to the establishment. They enjoyed their times together, and they found comfort and community in the whole.

If suprapartisanship proved capable of serving democratic ends, however, the politics of the time were by today's standards hardly democratic. Membership in the club was by invitation only, and important voices and points of view never made it to the table where the dealing was done. As antiwar protests and urban riots intensified, the suprapartisan leadership hunkered down and walled itself in, choosing to resort to the palace politics that previously had served the nation well. The profoundly undemocratic abuses in presidential power were even more problematic. The emergence of suprapartisanship had always been inextrica-

bly linked to the consolidation of the modern presidency, but by the end
of Dirksen's career the national disgust with a bloated and deceitful
White House that routinely handled the nation's business from behind
closed doors was building in intensity. In some ways, the Watergate
cover-up was merely the most arrogant and farcical exercise of power in
a pattern of executive aggrandizement that began most conspicuously in
the presidency of Franklin Roosevelt.

Watergate finished off suprapartisanship for good and ushered in a
flurry of democratic reforms meant to make the system more open and
responsive to a wider array of Americans. Interest groups flourished, and
a jaundiced media launched exposé after exposé detailing the sordid and
corrupt behavior of our public servants. Loyalty to the system, the establishment, and the administration became a relic of the past. Those who
work at the highest level are expected to sell their stories to the highest
bidder long before the president has concluded his time in office. Lobby-
ists and political consultants are more influential than ever, and most
would prefer that the politician/client defend his or her selfish interest
and frame the hot-button issues in incendiary press conferences and with
negative television ads than pursue the common good. Political scientist
Hugh Heclo bemoans today's "hyperdemocracy," and though he does
not yearn for the suprapartisan palace politics of Dirksen's era, he certainly calls into question the utility of the finger-pointing and backbiting
that dominate the airwaves today.[11]

Hyperdemocracy has bled into Senate culture as well. In 1986 C-SPAN
began gavel-to-gavel television coverage of Senate floor proceedings in
order to satisfy the national urge to know what our leaders are doing
and how they are serving our interests. Though the Senate remains a
change-resistant institution whose subtle but unbroken mores and rhythms
escape the eye of the untrained observer, the upper house nevertheless
has endured great pressures from technological advances and a more aggressive and adversarial media. Most experts interviewed for this book
point to a decline in the human relationships that have made the Senate
the world's most deliberative legislative body; a few senators privately
admit that their lives are lonelier than they could have ever expected.
Dirksen's successors have not replaced the famed Twilight Lodge, and
opportunities for fellowship and camaraderie on Capitol Hill are more
scant today than ever. Except for party caucus luncheons, the weekly
Senate Prayer Breakfast, and roll-call votes on the Senate floor, there are

precious few chances for members to engage each other in off-the-record conversations. Howard Baker admits that the Senate is less "clubby" now than in Dirksen's day, and he identifies the television media as a contributing cause. Robert Dole, who served in the Senate from 1969 to 1992, agrees, and he suggests that media obtrusiveness narrows the space necessary for compromise and conciliation on the most important issues. Most senators crave public attention, and the media magnify conflict and celebrate personal differences. By contrast, Dole remembers fondly the end of the Dirksen era: "We had more debates in those days. Now it's more back and forth in the press. There's now more focus on the media and less on what takes place in the Senate."[12]

Not surprisingly, today's journalists are less than sympathetic. Those whose careers span the course of the two political cultures agree that much has changed, but they rightly place most of the blame on the never-ending need to raise more money for the next campaign. Washington is more than ever a transient town. When Congress is in session, money-hungry senators expect to leave for their states on Thursday evening and not return until Monday afternoon. By contrast, Dirksen and his colleagues spent most of their time in Washington and entertained each other on the weekend. Relationships today are thinner and more transparent, largely because senators do not know each other. "Now," Robert Novak asserts, "there's a mad rush to get to the airports to go home." Senators from both sides of the aisle sadly but not surprisingly reported a "bonding experience" during President Bill Clinton's impeachment trial. Until then, they had not sat and listened to one another as a complete legislative body in a media-free environment.[13]

The relentless need to raise more money calls into question the vitality of democracy in today's America. At the very least, the constant coming and going and the endless posturing have created a poor working environment for thoughtful and deliberative legislation. Dirksen hammered out most of his legislative deals during face-to-face confrontations with his colleagues. Today, as Rowland Evans Jr. argues, too many senators too often fail to master the critical details in pending legislation. "Well," Evans imagines one senator telling another, "I'll have Harry look at it and why don't you tell your guy to call Harry."[14]

Dirksen would have deemed such behavior a dereliction of his duty. But even more than the changed atmosphere for carrying on Senate politics, the alienation that hovers over today's political culture would have especially saddened him. Young people who distrust their government and feel disconnected from their leaders would have weighed heavily on his conscience. In a very real way, even his hamlike theatrics were a lasting contribution to our culture. Dole marveled that "you could watch in the gallery and see people peering over the edge trying to find Senator Dirksen." In his obituary for Dirksen in the *New York Times,* E. W. Kenworthy remembered the "voice—modulated to the words, now a whimper, now a deep growl, now rolling thunder—that for years had sent the cry through the press galleries, 'Ev's up.' "[15] Every American who deems politics a worthwhile endeavor and public service a noble undertaking and who yearns for a time in this country when voters might reconnect with their leaders and be moved by their public personalities would be wise to recall the life and career of Everett Dirksen. He was a giant of a man.

Notes

Introduction

1. *Pekin (Illinois) Daily Times,* September 9, 1969, Biographical File, Senate Historical Office (SHO), Washington, D.C.; *Public Papers of the Presidents, 1950–1968,* selected vols. (Washington, D.C.: GPO, 1950–1968) (hereafter *PPP*), Richard M. Nixon, September 9, 1969, pp. 715–717; *National Review,* September 23, 1969, pp. 950–951.

2. *New Republic,* December 2, 1967, p. 4; in addition to my own efforts, Frank Mackaman, executive director of the Dirksen Center in Pekin, Illinois, has scoured the senator's papers and failed to find a quote that matches "sooner or later you're talking about real money."

3. Everett Dirksen, oral history, May 8, 1968, interview by William S. White, p. 4, Lyndon B. Johnson Library (LBJL).

1. "He Should Be in Politics"

1. Frank J. Fonsino, "Everett McKinley Dirksen: The Roots of an American Statesman," *Journal of Illinois State Historical Society* (spring 1983): 17–34; Everett Dirksen, *The Education of a Senator* (Urbana: University of Illinois Press, 1998), p. 4.

2. Dirksen, *Education of a Senator,* pp. 4–6; "Everett Dirksen's Washington," Remarks and Releases (RR), January 22, 1968, Everett McKinley Dirksen Congressional Leadership Center (EMDC); Louella Dirksen, *The Honorable Mr. Marigold: My Life with Everett Dirksen* (Garden City, N.Y.: Doubleday, 1972), p. 35; Fonsino, "Dirksen," pp. 18–19.

3. Dirksen, *Education of a Senator,* pp. 10–11.

4. Fonsino, "Dirksen," pp. 19–20; *Saturday Evening Post,* August 26, 1950, p. 20.

5. Frank H. Mackaman's introduction to Dirksen's *Education of a Senator,* p. xiii; Personal File (PF), folder 41, EMDC.

6. Dirksen, *Education of a Senator,* pp. 14–15; Fonsino, "Dirksen," p. 20; "Everett Dirksen's Washington," RR, January 22, 1968, EMDC.

7. Dirksen, *Education of a Senator,* pp. 14–16; PF, folder 44, EMDC.

8. Fonsino, "Dirksen," p. 23; Louella Dirksen, *Mr. Marigold,* pp. 39–40; Dirksen, *Education of a Senator,* pp. 22.

9. Fonsino, "Dirksen," p. 23.

10. Dirksen, *Education of a Senator,* p. 49; Mackaman, introduction, p. xiv; *Pekin Daily Times,* December 7, 1923, p. 7.

11. Louella Dirksen, *Mr. Marigold,* p. 23; Everett Dirksen to Louella Carver, September 30, 1924, PF, folder 11, EMDC.

12. Dirksen to Louella Carver, July 1924 letters, PF, folder 11, EMDC.

13. *Pekin Daily Times,* December 8, 1923, p. 5, and December 6, 1923, p. 5.

14. Fonsino, "Dirksen," p. 23; Louella Dirksen, *Mr. Marigold,* pp. 23–46.

15. Neil MacNeil, *Dirksen: Portrait of a Public Man* (New York: World Publishing Company, 1970), p. 25.

16. Fonsino, "Dirksen," pp. 24–26; Dirksen, *Education of a Senator,* p. 68; "Voters Must Clean House," April 1927, Clippings File (CF), folder 1, EMDC.

17. Fonsino, "Dirksen," pp. 24–30.

18. "Congressman Hull," *Peoria Star,* March 31, 1930, CF, folder 1, EMDC; "Dirksen Fails to Declare He Is Wet or Dry," *Peoria Star,* March 28, 1930, CF, folder 1, EMDC; Dirksen, *Education of a Senator,* p. 88; *Pekin Daily Times,* April 9, 1930, CF, folder 1, EMDC.

19. CF, folder 1, EMDC. For background, see Fonsino, "Dirksen," pp. 28–32.

20. Everett Dirksen, "Mr. Dirksen (R.) Goes to Congress," *New Outlook,* March 1933, p. 25.

21. Ibid., p. 26.

22. Dirksen, *Education of a Senator,"* p. 107; MacNeil, *Dirksen: Portrait of a Public Man,* pp. 41, 51–52.

23. MacNeil, *Dirksen: Portrait of a Public Man,* p. 59; Tony Buttitta, *Uncle Sam Presents: A Memoir of the Federal Theatre, 1935–1939* (Philadelphia: University of Pennsylvania Press, 1962), p. 218. See also Clyde P. Weed, *The Nemesis of Reform: The Republican Party During the New Deal* (New York: Columbia University Press, 1994), p. 121.

24. Louella Dirksen, *Mr. Marigold,* pp. 85–89.

25. Ibid., p. 93; *Congressional Record* (CR), 77th Cong., 1st sess., September 18, 1941, pp. 7478–7479.

26. For the *Fortune* article, see April 1943, p. 764; *CR,* October 1, 1942, pp. 7696–7700; Elliot A. Rosen, "The Midwest Opposition to the New Deal" in *The New Deal Viewed from Fifty Years: Papers Commemorating the Fiftieth Anniversary of the Launching of President Franklin D. Roosevelt's New Deal in 1933,* ed. Lawrence E. Gelfand and Robert J. Neymeyer (Iowa City: Center for the Study of the Recent History of the United States, 1983), pp. 76–77.

27. Republican National Committee Papers, News Clippings and Publications, 1932–1965, box 26, Dwight D. Eisenhower Library (DDEL); Edward L. Schapsmeier and Frederick H. Schapsmeier, *Dirksen of Illinois: Senatorial Statesman* (Urbana: University of Illinois Press, 1985), p. 38; Dirksen, *Education of a Senator,* p. 176.

28. Louella Dirksen, *Mr. Marigold,* p. 111.

29. Harold Rainville, oral history, March 22, 1974, interviewed by Josh Lee, p. 26, EMDC; Louella Dirksen, *Mr. Marigold,* pp. 124–125.

30. Louella Dirksen, *Mr. Marigold,* p. 128; MacNeil, *Dirksen: Portrait of a Public Man,* p. 82.

31. Mackaman, introduction, p. xxi; Schapsmeier and Schapsmeier, *Dirksen of Illinois,* p. 7; Dirksen, *Education of a Senator,* p. 232.

32. Louella Dirksen, *Mr. Marigold,* pp. 128–130.

33. Ibid., p. 135.

34. Arthur Summerfield, speech to the Republican National Strategy Committee at the Hotel Stevens in Chicago, December 13, 1949, Papers of the Republican Party, Part 1: Meetings of the Republican National Committee, 1911–1980 (Series A: 1911–1960), reel 9, p. 0589.

35. David McCullough, *Truman* (New York: Simon and Schuster, 1992), p. 813; David R. Kepley, *The Collapse of the Middle Way: Senate Republicans and the Bipartisan Foreign Policy, 1948–1952* (New York: Greenwood Press, 1988), chapters 5 and 6.

36. Record Group 4, box 915, folder 4, 1949–1955, Karl Mundt Papers, Karl E. Mundt Archival Library, Madison, South Dakota; *Chicago Daily News,* September 27, 1949, Republican National Committee (RNC) Papers, News Clippings–Publications, 1932–1965, box 26, Dirksen, Everett M., DDEL.

37. Papers of the Republican Party, Werner W. Schroeder, address to the Executive Session of the Midwest Regional Conference of the RNC, September 15, 1950, reel 10, p. 0306; Dirksen to David Annan, May 17, 1950, Chicago Office File (COF), folder 1, EMDC; *Chicago Daily News,* September 27, 1949, News Clippings–Publications, 1932–1965, box 26, Dirksen, Everett M., *Elgin Daily Courier-News,* December 2, 1949, *Chicago Daily News,* September 27, 1949, and January 21, 1950, all in RNC Papers, DDEL; "The Undefeated Lock Horns in Illinois," June 10, 1950, CF, folder 20, EMDC.

38. *PPP,* Harry S. Truman, January 19, 1950, p. 118.

39. *Illinois State Journal,* January 20, 1950, RNC Papers, News Clippings–Publications, 1932–1965, box 26, Dirksen, Everett M., DDEL; Paul Powell to William Boyle, Chairman of the Democratic National Committee (DNC), May 18, 1950, President's Secretary's Files, Political File, box 56, Illinois, Harry S. Truman Library (HSTL).

40. Harold Rainville to Ruth McCormick Miller, editor of the *Times Herald,* February 13, 1950, COF, folder 3899, EMDC; Edward L. Schapsmeier and Frederick H. Schapsmeier, "Scott W. Lucas of Havana: His Rise and Fall as Majority Leader in the United States Senate," *Journal of the Illinois State Historical Review* (November 1977): 302–320.

41. Schapsmeier and Schapsmeier, "Lucas," p. 312.

42. CF, folder 22, and Notebook 33, folder 117, EMDC.

43. Louella Dirksen, *Mr. Marigold,* p. 111; Louella Dirksen to Harold Rainville, September 26, 1949, COF, and CF, folder 24, EMDC; for 1,200 speeches and three cars, see *New York Times (NYT),* October 15, 1950, sect. 4, p. 6.

44. Dirksen's postprimary letter to his fellow Republicans, News Clippings

and Publications, 1932–1965, box 26, Dirksen, Everett M., *Chicago Daily News,* May 12, 1950, and *Chicago Tribune (CT),* January 31, 1950, all in RNC Papers, DDEL.

45. Ibid., *Christian Science Monitor,* January 6, 1950, and *CT,* October 11, 1949.

46. Record Group 3, Legislation, box 690, folder 1, 1950, Mundt Papers; Richard M. Fried, *Nightmare in Red: The McCarthy Era in Perspective* (New York: Oxford University Press, 1990).

47. Records of the Democratic National Committee, Meetings of the DNC and Subordinate and Related Committees, box 4, May 13, 1950, meeting in Chicago, executive session, HSTL; *PPP,* Truman, May 15, 1950, p. 409; *NYT,* May 16, 1950, p. 1; *Louisville Times,* May 17, 1950, p. 6; Truman to Lucas, May 20, 1950, President's Personal File, box 532, folder 1774, HSTL.

48. McCarthy, speech in Chicago to the Steuben Society German-American Club, October 21, 1950, RR, October 1950, EMDC.

49. *NYT,* October 27, 1950, p. 21; *Chicago Daily News,* December 30, 1949, RNC Papers, News Clippings–Publications, 1932–1965, box 26, Dirksen, Everett M., DDEL; Notebooks, folder 97, "The Man from Havana," and for "faster," see Notebooks, folder 116, EMDC.

50. *Saturday Evening Post,* August 26, 1950, p. 20.

51. Lucas to J. D. McDonald, September 21, 1950, box 168, Dirksen–General Information; Lucas to Andrew Biemiller, September 26, 1950, box 169, Dirksen–McCarthy Income Tax Information; Lucas, speech, September 2, 1950, Ana, Illinois, box 168, Dirksen–Description of House Votes, all in Scott W. Lucas Papers, Illinois State Historical Society, Springfield.

52. "Dirksen Must Rely on Inspiration," and also *Wall Street Journal,* October 26, 1950, CF, folder 22, EMDC.

53. *Saturday Evening Post,* August 26, 1950, p. 20; *Kankakee Daily Journal,* October 26, 1950, p. 12, CF, folder 22, EMDC; Edward L. Schapsmeier and Frederick H. Schapsmeier, *Dirksen of Illinois,* p. 62; *NYT,* November 6, 1950, p. 22.

54. *NYT,* August 11, 1950, p. 38; Campaign Literature, 1950 (3 of 3 folders), Lucas Papers; *NYT,* August 18, 1950, p. 12; *CT,* November 6, 1950, p. 1.

55. *NYT,* November 5, 1950, p. 1; *PPP* (Truman), 1950, p. 697.

56. For the 1950 Illinois Senate election, see *America Votes* (Washington, D.C.: Elections Research Center, Congressional Quarterly, 1950), pp. 78–87.

57. *CT,* November 8, 1950, p. 4.

58. *U.S. News and World Report,* November 17, 1950, p. 32; RR, November 1950, EMDC; William Howard Moore, *The Kefauver Committee and the Politics of Crime, 1950–1952* (Columbia: University of Missouri Press, 1974), p. 157.

59. Joe Alsop to Bernard Baruch, December 28, 1950, General Correspondence, box 6, Joe Alsop Papers, Library of Congress (LC); David M. Oshinsky, *A Conspiracy So Immense: The World of Joe McCarthy* (New York: Free Press, 1983), p. 176; *CT,* November 9, 1950, p. 16; Alonzo L. Hamby, *Man of the*

People: A Life of Harry S. Truman (New York: Oxford University Press, 1995), pp. 550–551.

60. Hoover's and Dirksen's November 1950 correspondence, Post-presidential File, box 48, Everett Dirksen, Herbert C. Hoover Library (HCHL); Lucas to Dirksen, November 12, 1950, Glee Gomien Papers (Private Collection); Dirksen to Lucas, November 17, 1950, box 169, Dirksen–Acknowledgment of Congratulations by Senator Lucas, Lucas Papers; *Beacon News,* December 5, 1950, CF, folder 24, EMDC.

61. Louella Dirksen, *Mr. Marigold,* pp. 140–141; *CT,* August 5, 1951, CF, folder 25, EMDC.

62. Notebooks, folders 102 and 107, EMDC.

63. Dirksen to John Morley, September 18, 1951, Morley Papers, box 1, Dirksen folder, HCHL.

64. Robert E. Wood Papers, box 3, Dirksen, HCHL; *CR,* 82d Congress, 1st sess., March 15, 1951, p. 2480; *CR,* March 15, 1951, p. 2477.

65. Taft to Vandenberg, November 11, 1950, Subject File, Correspondence with Senators, box 1064, Robert A. Taft Papers, LC.

66. Notebooks, folder 103, EMDC.

67. Ronald J. Caridi, *The Korean War and American Politics: The Republican Party as a Case Study* (Philadelphia: University of Pennsylvania Press, 1968), chapter 6; *CT,* April 12, 1951, pp. 1–2.

68. Caridi, *The Korean War.*

69. Norman A. Graebner, *The New Isolationism: A Study in Politics and Foreign Policy Since 1950* (New York: Ronald Press Company, 1956).

70. *CR,* June 26, 1951, p. 7126, August 24, 1951, p. 10626, and August 31, 1951, p. 10876; remarks to the Chicago Defender Conference, June, 1951, RR, EMDC; *CR,* August 30, 1951, p. 10812.

71. *CR,* June 28, 1951, p. 7306; Dirksen's September 11, 1951, interview on NBC's *Meet the Press,* RR, EMDC.

72. *CR,* March 6, 1951, p. 1980, and August 31, 1951, p. 10876; *NYT,* August 31, 1951, p. 14.

73. Dirksen's September 11, 1951, interview on *Meet the Press,* RR, EMDC.

74. Dwight Eisenhower, *At Ease: Stories I Tell My Friends* (Garden City, New York: Doubleday, 1967), pp. 371–372; Stephen E. Ambrose, *Eisenhower: Soldier, General of the Army, President-Elect, 1890–1952* (New York: Simon and Schuster, 1983), p. 498. See also James T. Patterson's *Mr. Republican: A Biography of Robert A. Taft* (Boston: Houghton Mifflin Co., 1972), p. 484.

75. *NYT,* October 2, 1951, p. 1.

76. Ibid., November 19, 1951, p. 17; Taft to Dirksen, November 21, 1951, Subject File, Correspondence with senators, 1951, box 1064, Taft Papers.

77. Louella Dirksen, *Mr. Marigold,* pp. 140–141; MacNeil, *Dirksen: Portrait of a Public Man,* p. 98.

78. Dirksen to Beling, January 24, 1952, Working Papers, folder 2645, EMDC; *NYT,* January 17, 1952, p. 17; see also Robert Griffith, *The Politics of Fear:*

Joseph R. McCarthy and the Senate (Lexington: University of Kentucky Press, 1970), pp. 167–168.

79. RR, February 12, 1952 EMDC; *NYT,* February 13, 1952, p. 49.

80. Notes for WGN, week of April 20, 1952, Notebooks, folder 109, EMDC.

81. Kepley, *Collapse of the Middle Way,* p. 134.

82. *NYT,* March 20, 1952, p. 3; *CR,* March 19, 1952, pp. 2500–2506, and March 20, 1952, p. 2575; *CT,* March 20, 1952, p. 16.

83. Patterson, *Mr. Republican,* pp. 492–496; Kepley, *Collapse of the Middle Way,* p. 140.

84. May 24, 1952, newspaper article, CF, folder 48, EMDC; *CT,* June 24, 1952, p. 1.

85. Patterson, *Mr. Republican,* pp. 547–552.

86. Author's interview with Baker, August 9, 1999; *NYT,* July 10, 1952, p. 18; *CT,* July 10, 1952, p. 1.

87. Richard H. Rovere, *Affairs of State: The Eisenhower Years* (New York: Farrar, Straus, and Cudahy, 1956), p. 32.

88. "McCarthy Probe Delayed," undated column from *Peoria Journal,* 1952, CF, folder 43; "A Republican Victory Is Indispensable," Notebooks, folder 107; "Keep U.S. Solvent," CF, folder 48, all in EMDC.

89. COF, folder 4014, EMDC; *Washington Post (WP),* July 11, 1952, p. 1.

90. *WP,* July 11, 1952; *NYT,* July 11, 1952, p. 16; Sherman Adams, oral history, April 1967, interview by Ed Edwin, OH 162, DDEL; Herbert S. Parmet, *Eisenhower and the American Crusades* (New York: MacMillan, 1972), p. 100; Stephen E. Ambrose, *Eisenhower: Soldier, General of the Army, President-Elect,* p. 542; Ed McCabe, oral history, September 5, 1967, interview by Paul L. Hopper, OH 41, DDEL.

91. Butler's undated letter to Dirksen, Republican Congressional Leadership File (RCLF), folder 108, EMDC; Hoover to Dirksen, July 23, 1952, Hoover Papers, Post-presidential File, box 48, Dirksen correspondence, HCHL.

92. MacNeil, *Dirksen: Portrait of a Public Man,* p. 107; minutes of the January 17, 1953, meeting in executive session, RNC Papers (Series A), reel 13, p. 0782.

93. *CT,* August 2, 1952, p. 3; *NYT,* August 2, 1952, p. 1.

94. *NYT,* August 3, 1952, p. 50; *CT,* August 5, 1952, p. 1; Butler to Taft, July 31, 1952, Subject File, Correspondence with senators, 1952, box 1184, Taft Papers.

95. Taft to Dirksen, August 6, 1952, Subject File, Correspondence with senators, 1952, box 1184, Taft Papers; Dirksen to Carlson, August 7, 1952, RCLF, folder 118, EMDC.

96. *NYT,* August 5, 1952, p. 13; Dirksen's August 21, 1953, appearance in Gardiner, Maine, Scrapbooks, volume 115, pp. 21–23, Margaret Chase Smith Papers, Skowhegan, Maine.

97. Butler to Carlson, August 23, 1952, RCLF, folder 109, EMDC; Dirksen's reply to Butler comes from the same folder; Patterson, *Mr. Republican,* pp. 576–578.

98. James T. Patterson, *Grand Expectations: The United States, 1945–1974*

(New York: Oxford, 1995), pp. 249–260; J. Ronald Oakley, *God's Country: America in the Fifties* (New York: Dembner Books, 1990), p. 135.

99. *NYT,* September 19, 1952, p. 16.

100. Ibid., August 19, 1952, p. 18; MacNeil, *Dirksen: Portrait of a Public Man,* p. 109; Lewis Summaries, Everett Dirksen, Margaret Chase Smith Papers.

101. Butler to Dirksen, September 16, 1952, RCLF, folder 109; Purtell to Dirksen, November 12, 1952, RCLF, folder 178; Goldwater to Dirksen, July 15, 1964, Alpha File, all in EMDC.

102. Dirksen to Sen. Ralph Flanders, September 26, 1952, RCLF, folder 131, EMDC; Taft to Sen. Herman Welker, August 18, 1952, Subject File, Correspondence with senators, 1952, box 1184, Taft Papers; Dirksen to Hoover, August 7, 1952, RCLF, folder 109, EMDC.

2. "A Foot . . . in Every . . . Camp"

1. Stephen E. Ambrose, *Eisenhower: Soldier, General of the Army, President-Elect, 1890–1952* (New York: Simon and Schuster, 1983), p. 572.

2. Dirksen's February 7, 1965, interview on ABC's *Close-Up,* RR, EMDC; NYT, December 3, 1952, p. 18; James Patterson, *Mr. Republican: A Biography of Robert A. Taft* (Boston: Houghton Mifflin, 1972) pp. 584–585; CT, December 3, 1952, p. 18, and December 2, 1952, p. 14.

3. *American Economic Security* 10, 4 (May–July, 1953): 9–17 (Chamber of Commerce, Washington, D.C.); Chester J. Pach and Elmo Richardson, *The Presidency of Dwight D. Eisenhower* (Lawrence: University Press of Kansas, 1991), p. 18.

4. *CT,* March 22, 1953, p. 11; Taft, report to the president, March 9, 1953, microfilmed copies of Eisenhower's Meetings with Legislative Leaders, reel 1, p. 0205; David Oshinsky, *A Conspiracy So Immense: The World of Joe McCarthy* (New York: Free Press, 1983), pp. 287–288; Stephen E. Ambrose, *Eisenhower: The President* (New York: Simon and Schuster, 1984), 2: 59–61; Charles E. Bohlen, *Witness to History, 1929–1969* (New York: W. W. Norton, 1973), p. 320; Athan G. Theoharis, *The Yalta Myths: An Issue in U.S. Politics, 1945–1955* (Columbia: University of Missouri Press, 1970), p. 6.

5. Ambrose, *Eisenhower,* 2: 59; PPP, Dwight D. Eisenhower, March 26, 1953, p. 130.

6. *CR,* 83d Cong., 1st sess., March 27, 1953, p. 2385; NYT, March 22, 1953, p. 1; Bohlen, *Witness to History,* p. 323; CT, March 26, 1953, p. 1; Robert H. Ferrell, ed., *The Eisenhower Diaries* (New York: W. W. Norton, 1981), pp. 226, 234.

7. *The Scribner Encyclopedia of American Lives: Notable Americans Who Died Between 1986 and 1990* (New York: Charles Scribner's Sons, 1999), 2: 128–130.

8. Duane Tananbaum, *The Bricker Amendment Controversy: A Test of Eisen-*

hower's Political Leadership (Ithaca, New York: Cornell University Press, 1988), p. 72; U.S. Congress, Senate, Committee on the Judiciary, *Treaties and Executive Agreements, Hearings Before a Subcommittee of the Committee on the Judiciary,* 83d Cong., 1st sess., 1953, pp. 225–227.

9. *WP,* April 7, 1953, p. 1; *NYT,* April 8, 1953, p. 1. For transcripts of Dirksen's questioning of Dulles and Brownell, see U.S. Senate, *Treaties and Executive Agreements,* pp. 867–873 and 936–941.

10. Dwight D. Eisenhower Diaries (DDED), reel 2, p. 0932; Meetings with Leaders, June 4, 1953, reel 1, p. 0313.

11. Dirksen, speech to the RNC, April 10, 1953, Papers of the Republican Party, reel 14, p. 0029; *NYT,* May 14, 1953, p. 25; *CR,* May 14, 1953, pp. 4913–4914; *CT,* May 15, 1953, p. 1.

12. DDED, May 4, 1953, reel 2, p. 0051.

13. Meetings with Leaders, reel 1, p. 0315; *NYT,* June 3, 1953, p. 1.

14. *CR,* May 20, 1953, p. 5198; *NYT,* May 17, 1953, p. 1; *CR,* July 1, 1953, p. 7794, and June 30, 1953, pp. 7605–7606; *CT,* July 3, 1953, p. 8.

15. *NYT,* July 5, 1953, p. 33; Milton Eisenhower, oral history 345, November 6, 1975, interview by Robert F. Ivanov, p. 5, DDEL; White House Office: Office of the Staff Secretary, L. Arthur Minnich Series, box 1, Misc., "M," April 1953–July 1955, DDEL.

16. *WP,* July 12, 1953, p. 2; Notebook 36, folder 136, EMDC; *DDED,* reel 1, p. 0939.

17. *CR,* July 29, p. 10331; *NYT,* July 30, 1953, p. 1.

18. Eisenhower to Dirksen, July 27, 1953, White House Central File (WHCF), Official File (OF), box 665, 133-L, and Office of the Staff Secretary, Notes of July 31, 1953, Cabinet Meeting, box 1, C-6 (4), p. 71, both in DDEL; *CT,* July 30, 1953, p. 1; Gary W. Reichard, *The Reaffirmation of Republicanism: Eisenhower and the Eighty-Third Congress* (Knoxville: University of Tennessee Press, 1975), p. 70.

19. George Reedy Memos, box 413, 1953 (2 of 3), Lyndon B. Johnson Senate Papers, Lyndon B. Johnson Library (LBJL); *NYT,* September 8, 1953, p. 20, and September 20, 1953, p. 62.

20. *NYT,* September 20, 1953, sect. 4, p. 2, and November 1, 1953, p. 67.

21. Dirksen, speech to the RNC, January 17, 1953, Meetings of the RNC, reel 13, p. 0873; Sherman Adams, *Firsthand Report: The Story of the Eisenhower Administration* (New York: Harper and Brothers, 1961), p. 57; Minnich Series, Box 1, Misc., "R," January 1953–June 1958, DDEL; Sidney M. Milkis, *The President and the Parties: The Transformation of the American Party System Since the New Deal* (New York: Oxford University Press, 1993), pp. 161–163.

22. George Reedy Memos, box 413, 1954, LBJ Senate Papers, LBJL; "Ike's First Year," Notebooks, folder 161, EMDC; *DDED,* February 7, 1954, reel 3, p. 0099.

23. *CR,* January 11, 1954, pp. 113–120; *NYT,* January 13, 1954, p. 1.

24. Ambrose, *Eisenhower,* 2: 152; Meetings with Leaders, January 11, 1954,

reel 1, p. 0113; DDED, January 9, 1954, reel 3, p. 0436; Ambrose, *Eisenhower,* 2: 154–155; Tananbaum, *Bricker Amendment Controversy,* p. 184.

25. CR, February 1, 1954, pp. 1060–1068, and February 26, 1954, p. 2357.

26. Ibid., February 26, 1954, pp. 2374–2375; Tananbaum, *Bricker Amendment Controversy,* pp. 179–180; Minnich Series, Box 1, Misc., "A," (3), March 1954–April 1956, DDEL.

27. DDED, March 12, 1954, reel 3, p. 0849.

28. Fred I. Greenstein, *The Hidden Hand Presidency: Eisenhower as Leader* (New York: Basic Books, 1982), chapter 5, and p. 169.

29. DDED, March 9, 1954, reel 3, p. 0890.

30. James Patterson, *Grand Expectations: The United States, 1945–1972* (New York: Oxford University Press, 1995), p. 197.

31. Ambrose, *Eisenhower,* 2: 57; for a more critical account, see Jeff Broadwater, *Eisenhower and the Anti-Communist Crusade* (Chapel Hill: University of North Carolina Press, 1992), chapter 6.

32. Oshinsky, *A Conspiracy So Immense,* pp. 359–377.

33. Ibid., pp. 385–386; *Time,* March 8, 1954, p. 24; Fulton Lewis Jr., undated article, CF, folder 66 and 67, EMDC.

34. DDED, February 25, 1954, reel 3, p. 0383; Greenstein, *Hidden Hand Presidency,* p. 186.

35. Greenstein, *Hidden Hand Presidency,* p. 186.

36. DDED, March 2, 1954, reel 3, p. 0379, and March 5, 1954, reel 3, p. 0079.

37. Office of the Staff Secretary, Notes of March 5, 1954, cabinet meeting, box 1, C-12 (2), p. 22, DDEL.

38. Greenstein, *Hidden Hand Presidency,* p. 188; DDED, March 5, 1954, reel 3, p. 0376, March 9, 1954, reel 3, p. 0890, and March 12, 1954, reel 3, p. 0894.

39. Robert H. Ferrell, ed., *The Diary of James C. Hagerty: Eisenhower in Mid-Course, 1954–1955* (Bloomington: Indiana University Press, 1983), p. 28; Greenstein, *Hidden Hand Presidency,* p. 198; Oshinsky, *A Conspiracy So Immense,* p. 416.

40. Rainville to Mrs. Miner Austin, March 23, 1954, Alpha File (AF), "McCarthy, Joseph," EMDC; Oshinsky, *A Conspiracy So Immense,* p. 406.

41. DDED, reel 3, p. 0722.

42. Ibid., reel 3, p. 0753; Notebooks, folder 146, EMDC.

43. NYT, April 8, 1954, p. 1; Mundt to the committee, April 2, 1954, Government Operations, box 558, folder 3, 1954, Mundt Papers; Oshinsky, *A Conspiracy So Immense,* chapters 28–31.

44. DDED, reel 3, p. 0362, and reel 4, p. 0158; Oshinsky, *A Conspiracy So Immense,* p. 417.

45. Papers as President, Ann C. Whitman Diary Series, April 27–28, 1954 (1), DDEL.

46. Dirksen oral history, July 19, 1966, interview by Richard D. Challener, John Foster Dulles Oral History Project, Princeton University; Patterson, *Grand*

Expectations, pp. 282–284; Ambrose, *Eisenhower,* 2: 20–22; Office of the Staff Secretary, Notes of May 21, 1954, cabinet meeting, box 1, C-14 (3), p. 48, DDEL.

47. Oshinsky, *A Conspiracy So Immense,* p. 435; McCarthy to the committee, March 31, 1954, Working Papers, folder 1789, EMDC; U.S. Senate, Committee on Government Operations, Special Subcommittee on Investigations, *Hearings, Charges and Counter Charges Involving Secretary of the Army Robert T. Stevens, John G. Adams, H. Struve Hensel, and Senator Joe McCarthy, Roy M. Cohn, and Francis P. Carr* (hereafter Army-McCarthy Hearings), 83d Cong., 2d sess., 1954, p. 998; Oshinsky, *A Conspiracy So Immense,* pp. 436–437; WP, CF, folder 67, EMDC.

48. Oshinsky, *A Conspiracy So Immense,* pp. 441–442.

49. Army-McCarthy Hearings, 1954, p. 1184 (for "kill those subpoenas," see p. 1178); Roy Cohn, *McCarthy* (New York: Lancer Books, 1968), pp. 158–161.

50. DDED, March 2, 1954, reel 3, p. 0379; Oshinsky, *A Conspiracy So Immense,* pp. 442–443; Minnich Series, box 1, Misc., "Mc.," May 1953–June 1955, DDEL.

51. Army-McCarthy Hearings, 1954, pp. 1269–1274; Notebooks, folder 182, EMDC; Army-McCarthy Hearings, 1954, pp. 2977–2981.

52. Oshinsky, *A Conspiracy So Immense,* pp. 395–396 and 474–475; CR, July 30, 1954, pp. 12729–12736.

53. NYT, July 31, 1954, pp. 1, 4, and August 3, 1954, p. 11; WP, July 31, 1954, p. 1; CR, July 30, 1954, pp. 12736–12742. The Dirksen Center houses the gold clock that McCarthy gave to his friend and supporter.

54. Papers of the Republican Party, reel 14, p. 0486; Ann C. Whitman Diary, July 20, 1954 (3), DDEL; DDED, reel 4, p. 0878.

55. Papers of the Republican Party, reel 14, p. 0473; Saltonstall to Dirksen, October 15, 1954, RCLF, folder 180, EMDC; John Sherman Cooper, oral history, April 1980, interview by William Cooper, 80 OH 64, Coop 24, John Sherman Cooper Oral History Project, Lexington, Kentucky.

56. James P. Selvage to Dirksen, August 8, 1954, RCLF, folder 119, EMDC; *Papers of the Republican Party,* reel 14, pp. 504–505; Dirksen to Mrs. Horace A. Woodward, August 12, 1954, RCLF, folder 120, EMDC.

57. Dirksen, speech to the RNC, August 30, 1954, Papers of the Republican Party, reel 14, p. 0473; RR, September 22, 1954, EMDC.

58. NYT, September 22, 1954, p. 21; Ambrose, *Eisenhower,* 2: 221; *DDED,* reel 3, p. 0037.

59. NYT, November 8, 1954, p. 1; Oshinsky, *A Conspiracy So Immense,* pp. 470–482.

60. M. F. Walter to Bricker, November 8, 1954, box 11, "McCarthy," John Bricker Papers, Ohio Historical Society, Columbus; CR, November 8, 1954, pp. 15951–15954.

61. NYT, November 15, 1954, p. 17; Dirksen, interview on NBC, November 7, 1954, RR, EMDC.

62. CR, November 18, 1954, p. 16136; Neil MacNeil, *Dirksen: Portrait of*

a Public Man (New York: World Publishing Company, 1970), pp. 125–126; Oshinsky, *A Conspiracy So Immense*, pp. 487–488. For the letter Dirksen wrote for McCarthy, see Working Papers, folder 1790, EMDC.

63. Eisenhower to Cliff Roberts, December 7, 1954, DDED, reel 5, p. 0337; Eisenhower to Swede Hazlett, December 8, 1954, DDED, reel 5, p. 0330; Dirksen to McCarthy, December 6, 1954, AF, EMDC.

64. Reichard, *The Reaffirmation of Republicanism*, p. 204.

65. *CR*, 84th Cong., 1st sess., January 10, 1955, p. 180; *NYT,* January 19, 1955, p. 1; Oshinsky, *A Conspiracy So Immense*, p. 496.

66. Dirksen, interview on *Face the Nation*, January 9, 1955, RR, EMDC; *NYT,* February 13, 1955, pp. 1, 54; "Patterns for America's Tomorrow," RR, February 12, 1955, EMDC.

67. MacNeil, *Dirksen: Portrait of a Public Man*, p. 130; Dirksen, interview on the Mutual Broadcasting System, March 21, 1955, RR, EMDC.

68. MacNeil, *Dirksen: Portrait of a Public Man*, p. 132.

69. *NYT,* March 21, 1955, p. 8; Meetings with Leaders, March 29, 1955, reel 1, p. 0628; Dirksen to Eisenhower, June 1, 1955, WHCF, OF, box 707, 138-B, and Jack Martin's notes of Dirksen's June 3, 1955, meeting with Eisenhower, Subject Series, White House Subseries, box 1, Conferences–Staff coverage (6), both in DDEL.

70. *CR*, July 22, 1955, pp. 11256–11261.

71. *Reporter,* August 11, 1955, pp. 3–4; *CR*, July 22, 1955, pp. 11263–11264.

72. *NYT,* July 23, 1955, p. 1, and July 24, 1955, p. 7.

73. *NYT,* August 27, 1955, p. 13; MacNeil, *Dirksen: Portrait of a Public Man,* p. 139; Lyn Ragsdale, *Vital Statistics on the Presidency: Washington to Clinton* (Washington, D.C.: Congressional Quarterly Press, 1996), p. 195.

74. *NYT,* October 7, 1955, p. 12; *CT,* October 7, 1955, p. 5; *NYT,* November 12, 1955, p. 1.

75. Edward L. Schapsmeier and Frederick H. Schapsmeier, *Dirksen of Illinois: Senatorial Statesman* (Urbana: University of Illinois Press, 1985), p. 97.

76. DDED, Reel 4, p. 0004; Ferrell, ed., *The Diary of James C. Hagerty,* p. 14; Tananbaum, *Bricker Amendment Controversy,* pp. 203–206.

77. Dirksen to A. T. Burch, March 19, 1956, Working Papers, folder 427, EMDC; *Chicago Sun Times,* March 9, 1956, COF, folder 4150, and *Olney Daily Mail,* March 20, 1956, COF, folder 4151, EMDC.

78. Office of the Staff Secretary, Notes of the March 13, 1956, legislative leaders' meeting, box 3, L-28 (3), p. 75, DDEL; Dulles to Eisenhower, April 30, 1956, DDED, reel 3, p. 0954.

79. Meetings with Leaders, reel 1, p. 0920; *NYT,* May 3, 1956, p. 30; Dulles, memorandum of his conversation with Eisenhower, May 9, 1956, John Foster Dulles and Christian Herter Series, microfilm, reel 3, p. 0086; Tananbaum, *Bricker Amendment Controversy,* p. 206.

80. Tananbaum, *Bricker Amendment Controversy,* p. 63; *Rock Island (Illinois) Argus,* April 7, 1956, COF, folder 4152, EMDC.

81. Notebooks, folder 130, EMDC; Meetings with Leaders, reel 1, p. 0887.

82. MacNeil, *Dirksen: Portrait of a Public Man,* pp. 142–144; *CR,* July 24, 1956, p. 14177.

83. Rainville to Andrew Schoeppel, April 9, 1956, COF, folder 4249, EMDC; COF, handwritten notes, folder 4209, EMDC; *Reporter,* November 1, 1956, p. 13.

84. *Centralia (Illinois) Sentinel,* August 1, 1956, CF, folder 91, EMDC; Eisenhower to Dirksen, August 9, 1956, WHCF, OF, box 368, 99-V (2), DDEL; *PPP* (Eisenhower), September 25, 1956, p. 976.

85. *WP,* July 22, 1956, CF, folder 90, EMDC; *NYT,* January 7, 1953, p. 14.

86. *Chicago Sun-Times,* COF, folder 4152, EMDC; *NYT,* August 17, 1956, p. 10.

87. Ambrose, *Eisenhower,* 2: 327–328; *NYT,* August 21, 1956, p. 15.

88. *CT,* October 4, 1956, CF, folder 100, EMDC; *Reporter,* November 1, 1957, p. 13.

89. Henry E. Seyfarth to Robert E. Merriam, October 22, 1956, box 187, Illinois, 1956–1957, Len Hall Papers, DDEL; Alice V. McGillivray and Richard M. Scammon, *America at the Polls, 1920–1956: A Handbook of American Presidential Election Statistics* (Washington, D.C.: Congressional Quarterly Press, 1994), p. 196; Howard W. Allen and Vincent A. Lacey, *Illinois Elections: Candidates and County Returns for President, Governor, Senate, and House of Representatives* (Carbondale: Southern Illinois University Press, 1992), pp. 458–459.

90. Eisenhower to Dirksen, November 9, 1956, AF, box 848, "Dirksen," 1956, DDEL; Herbert Brownell, *Advising Ike: The Memoirs of Herbert Brownell* (Lawrence: University Press of Kansas, 1993), chapter 14; DDED, reel 10, p. 1028.

3. *"We Can Always Count on Ev"*

1. *PPP* (Eisenhower), November 7, 1956, p. 1090.

2. DDED, November 19, 1956, reel 10, p. 0565. Dirksen promoted Brennan's confirmation, despite Joseph McCarthy's criticism of the judge's "guerrilla warfare" against congressional investigations of communism in America when Brennan served on the New Jersey Superior Court. Brennan was confirmed by a voice vote, with McCarthy bellowing a no. See *WP,* March 20, 1957, p. A2.

3. Neil MacNeil, *Dirksen: Portrait of a Public Man* (New York: World Publishing Company, 1970), pp. 147–148; *NYT,* January 8, 1957, p. 9.

4. *PPP* (Eisenhower), January 16, 1957, pp. 38–59; Stephen E. Ambrose, *Eisenhower: The President* (New York: Simon and Schuster, 1984), 2: 389–390.

5. Chester J. Pach and Elmo Richardson, *The Presidency of Dwight D. Eisenhower* (Lawrence: University Press of Kansas, 1991), p. 160; *PPP* (Eisenhower), January 5, 1957, pp. 6–16.

6. Office of the Staff Secretary, Notes of January 23, 1957, Legislative Meeting Series, box 4, L-34 (2), DDEL; Robert Alan Goldberg, *Barry Goldwater* (New Haven: Yale University Press, 1995), p. 119.

7. *CR*, 85th Cong., 1st sess., February 25, 1957, pp. 2528–2533 and 2535.

8. Burton I. Kaufman, *Trade and Aid: Eisenhower's Foreign Economic Policy, 1953–1961* (Baltimore: Johns Hopkins University Press, 1982), chapter 6; Ambrose, *Eisenhower,* 2: 379; Eisenhower to Robert W. Woodruff, August 6, 1957, DDED, reel 12, p. 1044.

9. Meetings with Leaders, May 9, 1957, reel 2, p. 0187; *PPP* (Eisenhower), May 21, 1957, pp. 372–385.

10. Emmet John Hughes, *The Ordeal of Power: A Political Memoir of the Eisenhower Years* (New York: Atheneum, 1963), p. 234; *WP,* May 21, 1957, p. A1; DDED, May 21, 1957, reel 12, p. 0779; *CR*, May 22, 1957, p. 7341.

11. Meetings of Leaders, May 1, 1957, reel 2, p. 0213; *PPP* (Eisenhower), January 23, 1957, pp. 72 88; David W. Reinhard, *The Republican Right Since 1945* (Lexington: University Press of Kentucky, 1983), pp. 138–139; Welton to Dirksen, April 26, 1957, COF, folder 453, EMDC.

12. Meetings with Leaders, March 5, 1957, reel 2, p. 0213; Office of the Staff Secretary, Notes of March 5, 1957, Legislative Meeting Series, box 4, L-36 (1), p. 4, DDEL; Meetings with Leaders, March 5, 1957, reel 2, p. 0153.

13. *CR,* April 8, 1957, pp. 5258–5261.

14. *CT,* April 9, 1957, p. 1, and April 10, 1957, p. 16; Dirksen, interview on "Meet the Press," May 19, 1957, RR, EMDC.

15. Stephen F. Lawson, *Running for Freedom: Civil Rights and Black Politics in America Since 1941* (New York: McGraw-Hill, 1991), chapters 2 and 3; Robert F. Burk, *The Eisenhower Administration and Black Civil Rights* (Knoxville: University of Tennessee Press, 1984). For analysis of the 1957 bill, see chapter 10.

16. *NYT,* February 21, 1957, p. 28; U.S. Congress, Senate, Committee on the Judiciary, *Hearings Before the Subcommittee on Constitutional Rights,* 85th Cong., 1st sess., 1957, pp. 392–395.

17. *CR,* July 2, 1957, pp. 10771–10777, and July 2, 1957, p. 10772; Gilbert E. Fite, *Richard B. Russell Jr.: Senator from Georgia* (Chapel Hill: University of North Carolina Press, 1991).

18. Robert Dallek, *Lone Star Rising: Lyndon Johnson and His Times, 1908–1960* (New York: Oxford University Press, 1991), p. 522; Ambrose, *Eisenhower,* 2: 407.

19. Warren Olney to Gerald Morgan, July 9, 1957, WHCF, OF, box 430, 102-B-3, DDEL; Ambrose, *Eisenhower,* 2: 408; *CR,* July 10, 1957, pp. 11212–11221; Ann C. Whitman Diary, July 25, 1957 (1), DDEL; Eisenhower to Robert W. Woodruff, August 6, 1957, DDED, reel 13, p. 1044.

20. Dallek, *Lone Star Rising,* pp. 524–526; Meetings of Leaders, July 23, 1957, reel 2, p. 0246.

21. Dirksen to Roy Wilkins, July 30, 1957, Group 3, A69, Congressmen and Senators, General, 1956–1965, NAACP Papers, LC; Taylor Branch, *Parting the Waters: America in the King Years, 1954–1963* (New York: Simon and Schuster, 1988), p. 221; Ambrose, *Eisenhower,* 2: 411–412; Office of the Staff Secretary, Notes, August 13, 1957, Legislative Meeting Series L-42 (2), p. 32, DDEL.

22. Burk, *Eisenhower Administration and Black Civil Rights*, pp. 225–226; Ambrose, *Eisenhower*, 2: 413 (for Ambrose's overall assessment of Eisenhower's place in history, see pp. 618–627).

23. *CR*, July 10, 1957, pp. 11212–11221.

24. Ambrose, *Eisenhower*, 2: 390–391; Kaufman, *Trade and Aid*, pp. 108–110.

25. Eisenhower to Dirksen, June 28, 1957, AF, "Dirksen, Everett M.," 1957, box 848, and for "deserve congratulations even more," see Eisenhower to Dirksen, September 13, 1957, both in DDEL.

26. David Oshinsky, *A Conspiracy So Immense: The World of Joe McCarthy* (New York: Free Press, 1983), p. 505; Dirksen to Jean McCarthy, May 27, 1957, AF, 1957, EMDC; *CR*, August 14, 1957, pp. 14681–14683.

27. For this August 1957 correspondence, see AF, "McCarthy," EMDC.

28. Burk, *Eisenhower Administration and Black Civil Rights*, chapter 9; J. Ronald Oakley, *God's Country: America in the Fifties* (New York: Dembner Books, 1990), p. 341; RR, September 16, 1957, EMDC.

29. Robert A. Divine, *The Sputnik Challenge: Eisenhower's Response to the Soviet Satellite* (New York: Oxford University Press, 1993); George E. Reedy, memorandum to Johnson, October 17, 1957, LBJ Senate Papers, Office of George Reedy, box 420, Reedy: Memos, October 1957, LBJL; Ambrose, *Eisenhower*, 2: 436–438.

30. Reedy, memo to Johnson, October 17, 1957, LBJ Senate Papers, Office of George Reedy, box 420, October 1957, LBJL.

31. *NYT*, January 24, 1958, p. 1; *CR*, 2d Cong., 85th sess., January 23, 1958, pp. 884–885, and January 23, 1958, p. 860.

32. RR, February 13, 1958, EMDC.

33. Pach and Richardson, *Presidency of Eisenhower*, p. 177; Meetings of Leaders, February 25, 1958, reel 2, p. 0311.

34. Meetings of Leaders, May 15, 1958, reel 2, p. 0334; Office of the Staff Secretary, Notes, April 29, 1958, Legislative Meeting Series, L-47 (3), p. 60, DDEL; Meetings of Leaders, May 19, 1958, reel 2, p. 0438; Office of the Staff Secretary, Notes, July 1, 1958, Legislative Meeting Series, L-50 (1), p. 21, DDEL; Dirksen, speech on foreign aid, July 21, 1958, RR, EMDC.

35. Stephen E. Ambrose, *Eisenhower: Soldier and President* (New York: Simon and Schuster, 1990), pp. 463–464.

36. Office of the Staff Secretary, Notes, June 17, 1958, Legislative Meeting Series, L-49 (4), pp. 79–80, DDEL.

37. *Human Events*, December 22, 1958, p. 1; internal memorandum, September 5, 1959, General Correspondence, Series 320, box 217, "Dirksen, Everett," Richard M. Nixon Pre-presidential Papers, National Archives, Pacific Southwest Region; Dwight D. Eisenhower, *The White House Years: Waging Peace, 1956–1961* (Garden City, New York: Doubleday, 1965), p. 315.

38. Meade Alcorn to Eisenhower, September 29, 1958, DDED, reel 18, p. 0741; Eisenhower to Dirksen, October 3, 1958, COF, folder 521, EMDC; *Los Angeles Times*, November 5, 1958, p. 1; Goldberg, *Barry Goldwater*, p. 132; *NYT*, November 6, 1958, p. 1.

39. Eisenhower to Paul Helms, April 30, 1955, DDED, reel 4, 0436; Dallek, *Lone Star Rising*, p. 438; Eisenhower's diary entry for January 10, 1955, reel 5, p. 0759, DDED.

40. *CT*, November 6, 1958, p. 1; Ann C. Whitman Diary, December 15, 1958, DDEL.

41. Theodore White, *The Making of the President: 1960* (New York: Atheneum, 1961), pp. 82–94.

42. Case's interview on *Face the Nation*, December 21, 1958, CBS News, Holt Information Systems, c. 1972, p. 394; Drew Pearson, "The Washington Merry-Go-Round," *WP*, December 21, 1958, CF, folder 142, EMDC.

43. Ann C. Whitman Diary, December 15, 1958, DDEL; *NYT*, December 20, 1958, and *Washington Evening Star*, December 20, 1958, both in CF, folder 142, EMDC; *New Republic*, December 29, 1958, p. 2; *Face the Nation*, January 4, 1959, p. 1.

44. Eisenhower's December 18, 1958, meeting with Johnson, reel 19, p. 0363, DDED.

45. Internal memo to Styles Bridges, December 30, 1958, Speech Materials, Confidential File, File 82, folder 79, Leadership Fight, Styles Bridges Papers, New Hampshire State Archives, Concord; Aiken biographical file, SHO; George Aiken, oral history, May 24, 1976, interview by Bill Cooper, Coop 01, pp. 16–17, John Sherman Cooper Oral History Project; Richard C. Smoot, "John Sherman Cooper: The Early Years, 1901–1927," in *Register of the Kentucky Historical Society* (spring 1995): 1–26; Cooper, telegram to Bourke Hickenlooper, December 31, 1958, Political File, National Politics, box 51, Republican Conference, General, 1957–1959, Bourke Hickenlooper Papers, HCHL.

46. Interoffice memorandum, December 17, 1958, General Correspondence, Series 320, Dirksen, Everett, box 217, Nixon's Pre-presidential Papers; *Washington Evening Star*, December 31, 1958, CF, folder 143, EMDC.

47. Senator Carl T. Curtis, oral history, January 26, 1981, interview by Terry Birdwhistell, 81OH09, pp. 8–10, Cooper Oral History Project; Prescott Bush, oral history 31, July 1966, interview by John Mason, p. 195, DDEL; MacNeil, *Dirksen: Portrait of a Public Man*, p. 163.

48. *NYT*, December 20, 1958, CF, folder 142, EMDC; internal memo to Bridges, January 3, 1959, Speech Materials, Confidential File, File 82, folder 79, Leadership Fight; Bridges Papers; Milton Young's wire to Dirksen, January 3, 1959, ibid.; Bill Cooper, "John Sherman Cooper: A Senator and His Constituents," *Register of the Kentucky Historical Society* (spring 1986): 199–200.

49. *Harper's*, December 1959, p. 47; Clifford Case, oral history, June 10, 1980, interview by Bill Cooper, 80 OH 122, Coop 24, p. 23, Cooper Oral History Project; Smith, speech to the Sanford Lion's Club, September 20, 1958, Statements and Speeches, volume 17, pp. 169–174, Margaret Chase Smith Papers.

50. Senator George Smathers, oral history, October 24, 1989, interview no. 3, SHO.

51. *Face the Nation*, December 21, 1958, p. 393; *Washington Evening Star*, December 31, 1958, CF, folder 143, EMDC.

52. *CT,* January 8, 1959, pt. 1, p. 3; Nicol C. Rae, *The Decline and Fall of the Liberal Republicans from 1952 to the Present* (New York: Oxford University Press, 1989); Dirksen to Bridges, January 12, 1959, AF, EMDC.

53. Robert H. Ferrell, ed., *The Eisenhower Diaries* (New York: W. W. Norton, 1981), p. 348; Dallek, *Lone Star Rising,* p. 438.

54. Office of Staff Secretary, Notes, January 13, 1959, Legislative Meeting Series, L-53 (1), p. 27, DDEL; notes on January 13, 1959, legislative meeting, reel 19, p. 0985, DDED; MacNeil, *Dirksen: Portrait of a Public Man,* chapter 6.

55. Office of Staff Secretary, Notes, January 26, 1959, Legislative Meeting Series, L-54 (1), p. 28, and for "Bryce is right," notes of February 17, 1959, L-54 (3), p. 59, both in DDEL.

56. Undated article, *Chicago American,* CF, folder 144, EMDC; Jack Anderson's notes of July 3, 1959, meeting with Thruston Morton, Republican Candidates and Party, F168 (2 of 3), Drew Pearson Papers, LBJL; Office of Staff Secretary, Notes, January 13, 1959, Legislative Meeting Series, L53 (1), p. 31, DDEL.

57. Eisenhower to Dirksen, January 17, 1959, WHCF, OF, 99-B, box 339, 1959–1960 (1); the president to Dirksen, March 7, 1960, AF, 1960, box 848; and Eisenhower to Dirksen, April 7, 1960, all in DDEL.

58. R. Alton Lee, *Eisenhower and Landrum-Griffin: A Study in Labor-Management Politics* (Lexington: University Press of Kentucky, 1990).

59. *NYT,* January 28, 1959, p. 1; *CR,* March 11, 1959, p. 3806.

60. Stewart E. McClure, chief clerk, Senate Committee on Labor, Education, and Public Welfare, oral history, interview no. 3, SHO; Lee, *Eisenhower and Landrum-Griffin,* p. 171; Eisenhower, *Waging Peace,* p. 329.

61. Ann C. Whitman Diary, June 19, 1959, and Eisenhower, oral history 106, July 13, 1967, interview by Raymond Henle, both in DDEL; Name and Subject Series, Commerce Department Hearing, box 243, Dirksen, Everett, Lewis L. Strauss Papers, HCHL; *NYT,* June 22, 1959, p. 14.

62. Malcolm E. Jewell, *Senatorial Politics and Foreign Policy* (Lexington: University of Kentucky Press, 1962), p. 67; George Aiken to Dirksen, September 15, 1959, AF, EMDC.

63. Author's interview with Reedy, July 30, 1998.

64. DDED, reel 19, p. 0744; *CR,* April 8, 1959, pp. 5506–5510; *NYT,* April 9, 1959, p. 9.

65. Post-presidential Files, Secretary's Office Files, box 14, folder D, Harry S. Truman Papers, HSTL; Dirksen letter, October 26, 1959, Johnson Senate Papers, Papers of the Democratic Leader, box 369, 1959 Congressional File "D," LBJL, and also Dirksen to the majority leader, September 12, 1959; for Johnson's September 14 reply, see AF, EMDC.

66. *NYT,* July 10, 1959, p. 24; *Harper's,* December, 1959, pp. 44–49.

67. A. M. Kennedy to Walter Trohan, January 23, 1959, Name and Subject Series, box 16, Everett Dirksen, Walter Trohan Papers, HCHL; *NYT,* February 1, 1960, p. 21; *Reporter,* March 31, 1960, pp. 5–6; author's interview with Evans, August 5, 1999.

68. Dirksen to Aiken, November 5, 1959, AF, EMDC; *NYT,* January 6, 1960, p. 28; *Washington Evening Star,* January 6, 1960, p. C1.

69. Iwan W. Morgan, *Eisenhower Versus the Spenders: The Eisenhower Administration, the Democrats, and the Budget, 1953-1960* (New York: St. Martin's Press, 1990); *NYT,* January 14, 1959, p. 16, and May 21, 1959, p. 7.

70. Notebook 44, January 27, 1960, EMDC; Burk, *Eisenhower Administration and Black Civil Rights,* pp. 241-248; Dallek, *Lone Star Rising,* p. 562.

71. *CR,* February 15, 1960, p. 2445; *NYT,* February 27, 1960, p. 20.

72. *NYT,* March 2, 1960, p. 28.

73. *Ibid.,* February 9, 1960, p. 1, and March 2, 1960, p. 1.

74. Legislative Meeting Series, March 8, 1960, reel 25, p. 0170, DDED; *NYT,* March 2, 1960, p. 1; Dirksen to Wilkins, March 8, 1960, Group 3, A69, Congressmen and Senators, General, 1956-1965, NAACP Papers.

75. *NYT,* March 9, 1960, p. 1; Meetings of Leaders, April 5, 1960, reel 2, p. 0774.

76. Meetings of Leaders, April 26, 1960, reel 2, p. 0756; for reaction to the vote, see *NYT,* March 23, 1960, p. 1; *CR,* April 8, 1960, p. 7808, and April 8, 1960, p. 7807.

77. Eisenhower's July 1, 1960, breakfast meeting with GOP Senate leaders, Subject Series, White House Subseries, box 1, Conferences, Staff Coverage (4), and Ann Whitman Diary, July 1, 1960, both in DDEL.

78. Pearson Papers, G294 (3 of 3), Republican Convention, 1960, LBJL.

79. Reinhard, *The Republican Right Since 1945,* pp. 153-154; *NYT,* July 24, 1960, p. 1; *Washington Evening Star,* July 24, 1960, p. A12; *CR,* September 1, 1960, p. 19108.

80. *U.S. News and World Report,* August 10, 1959, p. 84; Cooper to Dirksen, September 5, 1960, Senatorial Series 2, Office Copy File, box 696, John Sherman Cooper Papers, University of Kentucky, Lexington; Saltonstall's note to Dirksen, August 31, 1960, Mundt to Dirksen, August 31, 1960, and Bennett to Dirksen, September 1, 1960, all in RCLF, folder 0003, EMDC.

81. Meetings with Leaders, April 28, 1959, reel 2, p. 0586; Clarence Mitchell's notes of August 6, 1959, meeting with Dirksen, Group 3, A69, Congressmen and Senators, General, 1956-1965, NAACP Papers.

82. Eric F. Goldman, *The Crucial Decade and After: America, 1945-1960* (New York: Knopf, 1966); Arthur Schlesinger, *The Vital Center: The Politics of Freedom* (Cambridge, Massachusetts: Riverside Press, 1962); Godfrey Hodgson, *America in Our Time* (Garden City, New York: Doubleday, 1976); Patterson, *Grand Expectations,* chapter 14.

4. *"He Is My President"*

1. *NYT,* May 7, 1961, sect. 6, p. 22.

2. George Smathers, oral history, July 10, 1964, recorded interview by Don Nelson, part 3, p. 18, John F. Kennedy Oral History Project, John F. Kennedy Library (JFKL); Neil MacNeil, *Dirksen: Portrait of a Public Man* (New York: World Publishing Company, 1970), pp. 182-183; William "Fishbait" Miller, *Fishbait: The Memoirs of a Congressional Doorkeeper* (Englewood Cliffs, New

Jersey: Prentice-Hall, 1977), p. 277; Drew Pearson and Jack Anderson *The Case Against Congress* (New York: Simon and Schuster, 1968), p. 110.

3. Robert F. Kennedy and Burke Marshall, oral history, December 22, 1964, interview by Anthony Lewis, part 7, pp. 563–564, JFKL; Stuart Symington, oral history, June 9, 1980, interview by William Cooper, 80OH124, Coop 25, Cooper Oral History Project; author's interview with David Broder, March 16, 1999; "Everett Dirksen's Washington," January 22, 1968, RR, EMDC; Louella Dirksen, *The Honorable Mr. Marigold: My Life with Everett Dirksen* (Garden City, N.Y.: Doubleday, 1972), pp. 162–163.

4. Donald A. Ritchie, "The Senate of Mike Mansfield," *Montana: The Magazine of Western History* (winter 1998): 50–62; author's interview with Mansfield, June 6, 1996.

5. *WP,* January 28, 1961, p. C15.

6. DDED, reel 28, p. 0326, and reel 28, p. 0337; *NYT,* January 25, 1961, p. 20; Henry Z. Scheele, "Response to the Kennedy Administration: The Joint Senate-House Republican Leadership Press Conferences," *Presidential Studies Quarterly* (fall 1989): 825–846; *CT,* October 8, 1961, pt. 1, p. 12.

7. *NYT,* March 12, 1961, p. 11; *WP,* May 21, 1961, p. E4; Bryce Harlow's February 1961 correspondence with Eisenhower, Dwight D. Eisenhower Papers, Post-presidential File (PPF), 1961–1969, Special Names Series, Harlow, Bryce, box 6 (4), DDEL; Javits to Dirksen, February 10, 1961, AF, EMDC; *National Review,* May 8, 1962, pp. 314–315.

8. *NYT,* March 12, 1961, sect. 4, p. 11; Halleck, oral history, April 26, 1977, interview by Thomas Soapes, OH 489, DDEL; author's interview with David Broder, March 16, 1999; *Chicago American,* April 6, 1961, CF, folder 213, EMDC.

9. *NYT,* May 1, 1961, p. 21; "Washington Conversation," March 5, 1961, RR, EMDC.

10. *A History of the United States Senate Republican Policy Committee: 1947–1997,* prepared by Donald A. Ritchie, associate historian, U.S. Senate Historical Office, 105th Cong., 1st sess., Senate Document 105–5 (Washington, D.C.: GPO, 1997).

11. Senator Smith's speech to the Business and Professional Women's Club, October 23, 1961, Statements and Speeches, vol. 23, pp. 274–279, Smith Papers; Wallace Bennett, oral history, June 17, 1970, interview by Jean Torcom, p. 3, Carl Curtis, oral history, June 23, 1970, interview by Jean Torcom, p. 2, Dirksen's 1961 correspondence with Tower, AF, all three in EMDC; Ross K. Baker, *Friend and Foe in the U.S. Senate* (New York: Free Press, 1980), p. 198.

12. Robert Dallek, *Lone Star Rising: Lyndon Johnson and His Times* (New York: Oxford University Press, 1991), p. 540. Associate Historian of the Senate Don Ritchie and Robert Wilkie in the Office of the majority leader kindly gave me a guided tour of the private Senate offices on Capitol Hill.

13. *New York Herald Tribune,* August 7, 1963, *New York Herald Tribune* Morgue, Dirksen, Everett M., Center for American History (CAH), Austin, Texas; Dirksen to Javits, December 18, 1963, AF, EMDC; MacNeil, *Dirksen: Portrait of a Public Man,* p. 168.

14. Author's interview with Robert Novak, August 4, 1999; John G. Tower, *Consequences: A Personal and Political Memoir* (Boston: Little, Brown, 1991), pp. 56-58; John Tower, oral history, July 8, 1970, interview by Jean Torcom, p. 5, EMDC; Francis R. Valeo, oral history, interview no. 17, December 11, 1985, pp. 776-777, SHO; Baker, *Friend and Foe*, p. 26.

15. *NYT,* January 5, 1961, p. 24; "The GOP Conference," Notebooks, folder 157, EMDC.

16. *NYT,* April 8, 1962, sect. 6, p. 30; RCLF, folder 0005, and Notebooks, folders 102 and 107, both in EMDC.

17. Notebooks, folder 150, and RR, January 23, 1961, both in EMDC; *NYT,* January 14, 1961, p. 1.

18. Manatos to Larry O'Brien, February 23, 1961, WHCF, Name File (NF), Everett M. Dirksen (EMD), JFKL; Dirksen's March 6, 1961, radio-television broadcast, RR, and *Chicago Sunday-Times,* April 9, 1961, p. 26, CF, folder 212, both in EMDC.

19. *NYT,* January 23, 1961, p. 6.

20. "Washington Conversation," March 5, 1961, RR, EMDC; Dirksen's speech to the RNC, January 6, 1961, National Republican Committee Series, Political File, 1958-1968, Box 12, transcript of RNC proceedings, Thruston Morton Papers, University of Kentucky, Lexington.

21. Joint Republican Congressional Leaders Meeting, March 16, 1961, RCLF, folder 0012, EMDC.

22. *WP,* April 11, 1961, CF, folder 212, and Joint Republican Congressional Leaders, April 13, 1961, RCLF, folder 0014, both in EMDC.

23. Dirksen and Halleck press conference, April 20, 1961, RCLF, folder 0014, EMDC; Richard Reeves, *President Kennedy: Profile of Power* (New York: Simon and Schuster, 1993), p. 100.

24. Herbert S. Parmet, *JFK: The Presidency of John F. Kennedy* (New York: Penguin Books, 1983), pp. 176-177; *NYT,* May 2, 1961, p. 1; May 1, 1961, RNC press conference, RCLF, folder 0015, EMDC; *NYT,* May 4, 1961, p. 11.

25. RR, May 1, 1961, EMDC.

26. *NYT,* May 3, 1961, p. 25.

27. Ibid., May 11, 1961, p. 26.

28. Michael R. Beschloss, *The Crisis Years: Kennedy and Khrushchev, 1960-1963* (New York: Harper Collins, 1991), chapters 10 and 11.

29. Montague Kern, Patricia W. Levering, and Ralph B. Levering, *The Kennedy Crises: The Press, the Presidency, and Foreign Policy* (Chapel Hill: University of North Carolina Press, 1983), pp. 65-76; Dirksen's press release, July 27, 1961, RCLF, folder 0019, EMDC.

30. Press release following August 15, 1961, GOP leadership meeting, RR, EMDC.

31. James Fetzer, "Clinging to Containment: China Policy," in *Kennedy's Quest for Victory: American Foreign Policy, 1961-1963,* ed. Thomas G. Paterson (New York: Oxford University Press, 1989), chapter 7; Dirksen's statement to the press, June 28, 1961, RCLF, folder 0018, and for Dirksen-Halleck press release, August 24, 1961, see RCLF, folder 0021, both in EMDC.

32. Fetzer, "Clinging to Containment," p. 179; *Washington Daily News*, September 7, 1961, CF, folder 225, EMDC.

33. Dirksen to John Sherman Cooper, July 16, 1961, AF, EMDC; Louella Dirksen, *The Honorable Mr. Marigold*, p. 167.

34. Dirksen to Thruston B. Morton, March 22, 1961, AF, and Eisenhower's speech, September 16, 1961, on behalf of Dirksen, RR, both in EMDC; *NYT*, September 17, 1961, p. 1; Notebooks, folder 147, EMDC; *NYT*, September 23, 1961, p. 9.

35. *NYT*, January 11, 1961, p. 1; *Washington Daily News*, January 11, 1962, p. 3, CF, folder 231, EMDC.

36. Dirksen's statement to the press, January 18, 1962, RCLF, folder 0023, EMDC; *NYT*, January 19, 1962, p. 13; Robert Humphrey Papers, Box 12, 1961–1965, Senate and House Leadership (2), DDEL.

37. *Foreign Relations of the United States: 1961–1963*, vol. 24, *Laos Crisis* (Washington, D.C.: GPO, 1994), p. 632; *NYT*, February 11, 1962, p. 52.

38. Arthur M. Schlesinger Jr., *Robert Kennedy and His Times* (Boston: Houghton Mifflin, 1978), pp. 385–387; Bobby Baker, *Wheeling and Dealing: Confessions of a Capitol Hill Operator* (New York: W. W. Norton, 1978), pp. 97–98.

39. Beschloss, *The Crisis Years*, p. 635; Dirksen's January 1962 correspondence with Eisenhower, Eisenhower Papers, Post-presidential File (PPF), 1961–1969, Signature File, box 32, Gig, DDEL.

40. *NYT*, February 18, 1962, p. 52.

41. Paul H. Douglas, *In the Fullness of Time: The Memoirs of Paul H. Douglas* (New York: Harcourt Brace Jovanovich, 1972), p. 573; Claude DeSautels to Larry O'Brien, February 20, 1962, White House Staff Files, O'Brien Papers, box 17, Dirksen, Everett, JFKL.

42. *Wall Street Journal*, March 9, 1962, RG 7, Political, box 1142, folder 10, 1962, Mundt Papers; *NYT*, June 11, 1962, p. 16.

43. Robert Alan Goldberg, *Barry Goldwater* (New Haven: Yale University Press, 1995), p. 158.

44. Dirksen on "Youth Wants to Know," March 1962, RR, EMDC; *NYT*, March 26, 1962, p. 18.

45. *Human Events*, April 7, 1962, p. 236.

46. *CT*, April 2, 1962, CF, folder 248, EMDC; Morse's biographical file in SHO.

47. *CT*, April 4, 1962, p. 3.

48. *NYT*, April 4, 1962, p. 42; *CR*, April 5, 1962, pp. 6090–6092; *Washington Evening Star*, April 6, 1962, CF, folder 249, EMDC.

49. *CR*, April 4, 1962, p. 6092; Benjamin C. Bradlee, *Conversations with Kennedy* (New York: W. W. Norton, 1975), p. 73; *Chicago Sun-Times*, April 7, 1962, CF, folder 249, and *Chicago Daily News*, April 7, 1962, CF, folder 249, both in EMDC; *Time*, April 20, 1962, p. 29; *CT*, April 7, 1962, p. 8; MacNeil, *Dirksen: Portrait of a Public Man*, p. 196.

50. *St. Louis Globe-Democrat*, April 10, 1962, CF, folder 251, EMDC; *Time*, April 20, 1962, p. 29.

51. Daniel Ruge to Ralph H. Kunstadter, July 5, 1962, COF, folder 4394,

EMDC; *National Review,* May 8, 1962, p. 315; Bryce Harlow to Eisenhower, April 24, 1962, Eisenhower Papers, PPF, Special Names Series, box 7, Harlow, Bryce, DDEL; Eisenhower's statement, May 10, 1962, Humphrey Papers, box 12, 1961–1965, Senate and House Leadership (2), DDEL.

52. *CR,* June 18, 1962, p. 10758; John Lewis Gaddis, *Strategies of Containment: A Critical Appraisal of Postwar American National Security Policy* (New York: Oxford University Press, 1982), p. 200; David Halberstam, *The Best and the Brightest* (New York: Random House, 1969), pp. 156–162; *Foreign Relations of the United States: 1961–1963,* vol. 8, *National Security Policy* (Washington, D.C.: GPO, 1996), p. 331.

53. Executive Sessions of the Senate Foreign Relations Committee, vol. 14, 87th Cong., 2d sess., June 26, 1962, p 551; *Human Events,* July 7, 1962, p. 496.

54. *CR,* August 22, 1962, p. 17265; Douglas to Larry O'Brien, August 29, 1962, WHCF, NF, EMD, JFKL.

55. *Time,* September 14, 1962, p. 28; MacNeil, *Dirksen: Portrait of a Public Man,* pp. 204–205; *NYT,* October 11, 1962, p. 35.

56. *NYT,* September 8, 1962, p. 2; Hickenlooper Papers, Political File, National Politics, Minutes of October 2, 1962, Republican Policy Committee meeting, box 70, folder 0032, HCHL; Dirksen to Charles Percy, August 7, 1962, AF, EMDC.

57. *Washington Sunday Star,* October 14, 1962, p. A1; author's interview with Broder, March 16, 1999; CT, October 8, 1962, President's Office File, Subject File, box 101, Illinois-Part 1, JFKL.

58. *New York Herald Tribune (NYHT),* October 18, 1962, *NYHT* Morgue, Elections-Congress-Republicans, CAH.

59. Ibid., *NYHT,* October 19, 1962.

60. *NYT,* October 20, 1962, p. 10; *PPP,* John F. Kennedy, October 19, 1962, pp. 802–804; Robert Kennedy, oral history, April 30, 1964, interview by John Bartlow Martin, part 3, p. 216, JFKL; Beschloss, *Crisis Years,* p. 461.

61. Louella Dirksen, *The Honorable Mr. Marigold,* p. 168; Reeves, *Profile of Power,* p. 392; Beschloss, *Crisis Years,* p. 480.

62. Reeves, *Profile of Power,* p. 393; for Russell's notes of the meeting, see General Series, Red Line, Special Presidential, October 23, 1962, Richard B. Russell Papers, University of Georgia, Athens.

63. Dirksen's statement about the crisis, October 22, 1962, RR, EMDC; Presidential Recording Log, Tape 37: Cuba, Item 37.1, tape recording of congressional leadership meeting at the White House, October 24, 1962, JFKL.

64. *NYT,* November 4, 1962, p. 60; Louella Dirksen, *The Honorable Mr. Marigold,* p. 172.

65. *NYT,* November 4, 1962, p. 60, and November 7, 1962, p. 16; Howard W. Allen and Vincent A. Lacey, *Illinois Elections: Candidates and County Returns for President, Governor, Senate, and House of Representatives* (Carbondale: Southern Illinois University Press, 1992), pp. 471–473.

66. Dirksen's January 1963 remarks to the GOP leadership conference, Notebooks, folder 169, EMDC; notes of the January 30, 1963, Republican Policy

Committee meeting, Hickenlooper Papers, Political File, National Politics, box 70, folder 1962, HCHL; Dirksen's February 3, 1963, appearance on *Meet the Press*, RR, EMDC.

67. Dirksen's February 1963 letter to his GOP colleagues, RCLF, folder 0006, EMDC; *WP,* February 13, 1963, p. A8; Mike Manatos to Larry O'Brien, February 15, 1963, White House Staff Files, Mike Manatos Papers, Congressional Liaison Office, box 1, Memoranda, JFKL.

68. *New York Times Magazine,* October 28, 1962, sect. 6, p. 26; *NYHT,* June 2, 1963, *NYHT* Morgue, Dirksen, Everett, CAH; author's interview with Elspeth Rostow, August 9, 1999.

69. Dirksen's statement to the press, February 28, 1963, RCLF, folder 0034, EMDC; Taylor Branch, *Parting the Waters: America in the King Years, 1954–1963* (New York: Simon and Schuster, 1988), chapters 18–20.

70. James Patterson, *Grand Expectations: The United States, 1945–1972* (New York: Oxford University Press, 1995), pp. 479–480.

71. June 3, 1963, Johnson-Sorensen telephone conversation, Theodore Sorensen Papers, Subject File, box 30, Civil Rights Legislation, 1963, JFKL.

72. *PPP* (Kennedy), June 11, 1963, pp. 468–471; *NYT,* June 12, 1963, p. 21.

73. Mansfield's June memorandum to the White House, President's Office Files, box 53, Civil Rights, JFKL.

74. Eisenhower to Dirksen, June 14, 1963, Eisenhower Papers, PPF, Secretary's Series, box 9, "Da," DDEL; *NYT,* June 18, 1963, p. 1, and June 20, 1963, p. 32.

75. Mansfield to Kennedy, June 18, 1963, Sorensen Papers, Subject Files, 1961–1964, box 30, Civil Rights, JFKL.

76. *NYT,* June 22, 1963, p. 8; *NYHT,* June 19, 1963, *NYHT* Morgue, Republicans-General, CAH.

77. *PPP* (Kennedy), June 10, 1963, pp. 459–464; Glenn T. Seaborg, *Kennedy, Khrushchev, and the Test Ban* (Berkeley: University of California Press, 1981), pp. 213–216.

78. *NYT,* June 11, 1963, p. 17; Dirksen-Halleck press conference, July 11, 1963, RCLF, folder 0039, EMDC; Kennedy's conversation with Rusk, July 24, 1963, President's Office Files, Recordings and Transcripts, Winning Support for the Nuclear Test Ban Treaty, 1963, JFKL.

79. Dirksen's Radio and Television address, July 29, 1963, RR, and Dirksen's January 1963 remarks to the GOP leadership conference, Notebooks, folder 169, both in EMDC.

80. *NYT,* July 30, 1963, p. 1; U.S. Senate, Committee on Foreign Relations, *Hearings Before the Committee on Foreign Relations: Nuclear Test Ban Treaty,* 88th Cong., 1st sess., August 19, 1963, p. 353.

81. Manion Forum and attached correspondence with Dirksen, September 1, 1963, AF, EMDC; *NYHT,* August 1, 1963, *NYHT* Morgue, Republicans-General, CAH.

82. Beschloss, *Crisis Years,* pp. 628–635.

83. Fulbright's telephone conversation with Kennedy, August 23, 1963, President's Office Files, Presidential Recordings and Transcripts, Winning Senate Sup-

port for the Nuclear Test Ban Treaty, 1963, JFKL; Baker, *Wheeling and Dealing,* pp. 98–99; Eisenhower to Fulbright, August 23, 1963, Series 48.5, box 20.3, J. William Fulbright Papers, University of Arkansas, Fayetteville.

84. George H. Gallup, *The Gallup Poll: Public Opinion, 1935–1971, 1959–1971* (New York: Random House, 1972), 3: 1837; Dirksen's September 3, 1963, Radio and Television address, RR, EMDC; Reeves, *Profile of Power,* p. 594.

85. Notes of Republican Policy Committee meeting, September 11, 1963, Hickenlooper Papers, Political File, National Politics, Box 70, HCHL; *NYT,* September 12, 1963, p. 20.

86. *CR,* September 11, 1963, pp. 16788–16791; Kuchel to Rainville, January 19, 1970, COF, folder 5431, EMDC; Theodore Sorensen, *Kennedy* (New York: Harper and Row, 1965), p. 740.

87. *National Review,* August 13, 1963, p. 107; Goldberg, *Barry Goldwater,* p. 174; *PPP* (Kennedy), September 12, 1963, p. 672; *Christian Science Monitor,* September 14, 1963, CF, folder 329, EMDC; *NYT,* September 12, 1963, p. 36.

88. *NYT,* August 29, 1963, p. 17.

89. Nicholas deB. Katzenbach, oral history, November 16, 1964, pp. 168–169, JFKL Oral History Program; Dirksen to Kennedy, November 3, 1963, WHCF, NF, EMD, JFKL.

90. *CR,* November 22, 1963, p. 22665 22693; William Manchester, *The Death of a President: November 1963* (New York: Harper and Row, 1967), pp. 197–198; notes of the Republican Policy Committee Meeting, November 22, 1963, Hickenlooper Papers, Political File, National Politics, Box 70, folder 1963, HCHL.

5. *"You're My Kind of Republican"*

1. Paul Conkin writes that "Johnson handled the difficult, post-assassination period almost to perfection." See Conkin, *Big Daddy from the Pedernales: Lyndon Baines Johnson* (Boston: Twayne Publishers, 1986), p. 174; Dirksen's interview on *Face the Nation,* CBS News, Holt Information Systems, c. 1972, September 19, 1965, p. 229; Lyndon B. Johnson, *The Vantage Point: Perspectives of the Presidency, 1963–1969* (New York: Holt, Rinehart and Winston, 1971), p. 158.

2. Johnson's telephone conversation with Dirksen, November 23, 1963, Telephone, Tapes, and Transcripts (TTT), K6311.01/9, LBJL.

3. Louella Dirksen, *The Honorable Mr. Marigold: My Life with Everett Dirksen* (Garden City, N.Y.: Doubleday, 1972), pp. 8–9; author's interview with Baker, August 9, 1999.

4. Jack Bell, *The Johnson Treatment: How Lyndon B. Johnson Took Over the Presidency and Made It His Own* (New York: Harper and Row, 1965), p. 40.

5. Johnson's telephone conversation with Dirksen, November 29, 1963, TTT, K6311.04/8, LBJL; Dillon's telephone conversation with Johnson, December 3, 1963, TTT, K6312.03/5, LBJL; Johnson to Dirksen, December 19, 1963, WHCF, NF, EMD, LBJL.

6. Jacob Javits, oral history, June 24, 1970, interview by Jean Torcom, p. 2, EMDC; author's interview with Larry Temple, July 16, 1998; Jack Valenti, oral history no. 5, July 12, 1972, interview by Joe B. Frantz, p. 11, LBJL.

7. For Johnson's conversation with Dirksen, December 20, 1963, see TTT, K6312.10/25, LBJL; WHCF, NF, William Macomber, LBJL.

8. Johnson's conversation with Roy Wilkins, January 6, 1964, TTT, WH6401.06/8, LBJL.

9. Johnson's conversation with Eugene McCarthy, January 6, 1964, TTT, WH6401.06/12, LBJL.

10. Johnson's conversation with Dirksen, February 3, 1964, TTT, WH6402.03/11, LBJL.

11. Charles Whalen and Barbara Whalen, *The Longest Debate: A Legislative History of the 1964 Civil Rights Act* (New York: Mentor, 1985), chapter 4.

12. "The Civil Rights Bill," February 26, 1964, Working Papers, folder 256, EMDC.

13. Johnson's conversation with Kennedy, February 10, 1964, TTT, WH6402.13/14, LBJL; Stephen Horn's Notes of the Capitol Hill Meetings Concerning the Passage of the 1964 Civil Rights Act (Horn Log), Carl Albert Center Archives, Norman, Oklahoma, p. 17. Horn was Republican whip Thomas Kuchel's legislative assistant. For Dirksen's February 20, 1964, press conference with Halleck, see RCLF, folder 0046, EMDC.

14. Hubert H. Humphrey, oral history no. 1, August 17, 1971, interview by Joe B. Frantz, LBJL. See also Timothy Nels Thurber, "The Politics of Equality: Hubert H. Humphrey and the African-American Freedom Struggle, 1945–1978" (Ph.D. diss., University of North Carolina, 1996); Carl Solberg, *Hubert Humphrey: A Biography* (New York: W. W. Norton, 1984), p. 224; Carl T. Rowan, *Breaking Barriers: A Memoir* (Boston: Little, Brown, 1991), p. 248.

15. Hubert Humphrey's memo on the Civil Rights bill, Autobiography Files, Interview Transcripts, Civil Rights bill, 1964, pp. 13–14, Hubert H. Humphrey Papers, Minnesota Historical Society, St. Paul; Dirksen's notes, February 26, 1964, Working Papers, folder 256, EMDC.

16. *Chicago Daily News,* April 10, 1964, CF, folder 338, EMDC; Whalen and Whalen, *The Longest Debate,* p. 166.

17. Horn Log, April 6, 1964, pp. 79–80; Mitchell's letter to Roy Wilkins, April 10, 1964, NAACP Papers, Group 3, A72, Mitchell, Clarence, 1956–1965, LC; Horn Log, April 13, 1964, p. 87; Whalen and Whalen, *The Longest Debate,* p. 167; Horn Log, April 17, 1964, p. 102.

18. *Delta-Democrat Times* (Greenville, Mississippi), April 22 and 23, 1964, LBJL.

19. John Stewart's Notes on the Civil Rights Bill (Stewart Log), April 21, 1964, Humphrey Autobiography Files, Interview Transcripts, Norman Sherman Background and Correspondence Files, 148 B 9 11 (B), box 2, Hubert Humphrey Papers.

20. Horn Log, April 22, 1964, p. 111; Stewart Log, April 24, 1964, p. 2.

21. Horn Log, April 27, 1964, p. 123, and April 29, 1964, pp. 129–130.

22. For Johnson's telephone conversation with O'Brien, April 28, 1964, see TTT, WH6404.14/1, LBJL.

23. For Johnson's telephone conversation with Mansfield, April 29, 1964, see TTT, WH6404.15/4, LBJL; Stewart Log, April 29, 1964, p. 6.

24. Dirksen to Robert E. Wood, April 30, 1964, Wood Papers, box 3, Everett M. Dirksen, HCHL; Horn Log, April 30, 1964, p. 145.

25. Mansfield's memo to the White House, May 4, 1964, 6XLE/HU2, box 65, LBJL; Thurber, "The Politics of Equality," pp. 232–234.

26. Stewart Log, May 6, 1964, pp. 1–2; Drew Pearson's column, *Clinton Herald,* May 16, 1964, Hickenlooper Papers, Legislative Files, Civil Rights, 1964, Newspaper Clippings, HCHL; Hickenlooper to Don Berry, May 4, 1964, Hickenlooper Papers, Legislative File, box 9A, Civil Rights, 1964, Constituent Correspondence, Against, A–M, and Hickenlooper to Robert W. Turner, May 11, 1964, Hickenlooper Papers, Legislative File, box 9A, Civil Rights, 1964, Constituent Correspondence, Against, N–Z, both in HCHL; Horn Log, May 8, 1964, p. 168.

27. Johnson's telephone conversation with O'Brien, May 8, 1964, TTT, WH6405.03/12, LBJL.

28. Horn Log, May 11, 1964, p. 172. For "it's a goddam sellout," see Whalen and Whalen, *The Longest Debate,* p. 183; Stewart Log, May 13, 1964, pp. 5–6.

29. Hugh Davis Graham, *The Civil Rights Era: Origins and Development of National Policy, 1960–1972* (New York: Oxford University Press, 1990), pp. 145–148; Whalen and Whalen, *The Longest Debate,* p. 185; Johnson's conversation with Humphrey, May 13, 1964, TTT, WH6405.06/18, LBJL.

30. Johnson's conversation with Dirksen, May 13, 1964, TTT, WH6405.06/5, LBJL.

31. Humphrey's conversation with Johnson, May 13, 1964, TTT, WH6405.06/18, LBJL; Whalen and Whalen, *The Longest Debate,* pp. 187–188.

32. Pavlik's memo to Hickenlooper, May 19, 1964, Hickenlooper Papers, Legislative File, box 8, Civil Rights, BBH Working File, May, 1964, HCHL; Whalen and Whalen, *The Longest Debate,* p. 194; Humphrey memo on the Civil Rights bill, Autobiography Files, Interview Transcripts, Civil Rights Bill, 1964, Hubert Humphrey Papers; *Des Moines Register,* May 21, 1964, Hickenlooper Papers, Legislative File, Civil Rights, 1964, Newspaper Clippings, HCHL.

33. *CR,* 88th Cong., 2d sess., May 26, 1964, p. 11935–11943.

34. George C. Herring, *America's Longest War: The United States and the Vietnam War, 1950–1975,* 2d ed. (New York: Alfred A. Knopf, 1986); Brian VanDeMark, *Into the Quagmire: Lyndon Johnson and the Escalation of the Vietnam War* (New York: Oxford University Press, 1991).

35. Dirksen-Halleck press conference, February 27, 1964, RCLF, folder 0046; Dirksen on *Meet the Press,* February 2, 1964, RR, p. 10; Dirksen's statement to the press, May 26, 1964, RCLF, folder 0049, all in EMDC; William Conrad Gibbons, *The U.S. Government and the Vietnam War, Part II: 1961–1964* (Princeton: Princeton University Press, 1986), p. 264; Dirksen-Halleck press conference, May 26, 1964, RCLF, folder 0049, EMDC.

36. Johnson's conversation with Russell, May 27, 1964, TTT, WH6405.10/3–5, and for his conversation with Bundy later that day, see TTT, WH6405.10/6, both in LBJL.

37. Dirksen to Robert E. Wood, June 1, 1964, Wood Papers, box 3, Everett M. Dirksen, HCHL; Whalen and Whalen, *The Longest Debate*, p. 193.

38. Hickenlooper to Don Berry, June 2, 1964, Hickenlooper Papers, Legislative File, box 9A, Civil Rights, 1964, Constituent Correspondence, Against, A–M, HCHL; Stewart Log, Final Thoughts, p. 2; Whalen and Whalen, *The Longest Debate*, pp. 193–195.

39. Robert D. Loevy, *To End All Segregation: The Politics of the Passage of the Civil Rights Act of 1964* (Lanham, Maryland: University Press of America, 1990), p. 321.

40. Whalen and Whalen, *The Longest Debate*, pp. 197–203; *CR*, June 10, 1964, p. 13308; for Dirksen's remarks, see *CR*, June 10, 1964, pp. 13319–13320.

41. Loevy, *To End All Segregation*, p. 319.

42. Cooper to Rockefeller, June 13, 1964, Office Copy File, box 763, Cooper Papers; King to Dirksen, June 24, 1964, AF, EMDC; NAACP Papers, Administrative Files, 1956–1965, General Office File, box A67, Civil Rights, Cloture Vote, 1964; for Johnson's conversation with Dirksen, June 23, 1964, see TTT, WH6406.15/2, LBJL.

43. J. D. Stetson to Hickenlooper, May 28, 1964, Hickenlooper Papers, Personal Files, box 10, Everett M. Dirksen, HCHL; Von Dreele's June 16, 1966, poem for the *National Review*, CF, folder 342, EMDC; Loevy, *To End All Segregation*, p. 301.

44. GOP Policy Committee meeting, June 20, 1964, Hickenlooper Papers, Political File, National Politics, HCHL.

45. "Barry Captures Dirksen," *WP*, July 1, 1964, *NYT*, July 2, 1964, and *WP*, July 6, 1964, all in CF, folder 346, EMDC; Neil MacNeil, *Dirksen: Portrait of a Public Man* (New York: World Publishing Company, 1970), p. 241; David W. Reinhard, *The Republican Right Since 1945* (Lexington: University Press of Kentucky, 1983), p. 191.

46. Goldwater to Dirksen, July 15, 1964, AF, and RR, July 15, 1964, both in EMDC.

47. MacNeil, *Dirksen: Portrait of a Public Man*, p. 243; author's interview with MacNeil, September 26, 1996; author's interview with Stolley, August 9, 1999.

48. Herring, *America's Longest War*, pp. 119–122.

49. White House notes, meeting of congressional leaders, August 4, 1964, Meeting Notes File, box 1, LBJL.

50. Gibbons, *U.S. Government and the Vietnam War*, 2:302–303.

51. *CR*, August 7, 1964, p. 18462.

52. Ibid.

53. Dirksen to Johnson, November 10, 1964, AF, EMDC; Hickenlooper to Dirksen, December 3, 1964, and Dirksen's response, Hickenlooper Papers, Personal Files, box 10, Everett M. Dirksen, HCHL.

54. For Joe Alsop, "The Baffled Republicans," January 8, 1965, and for Roscoe

Drummond's January 25, 1965, article, see *NYHT* Morgue, Republicans: Party Conflict, CAH.

55. Joseph A. Califano, *The Triumph and Tragedy of Lyndon Johnson: The White House Years* (New York: Simon and Schuster, 1991), p. 63; Jack Valenti, oral history no. 5, July 12, 1972, interview by Joe B. Frantz, pp. 10–13, LBJL; author's interview with Temple, July 16, 1998.

56. Louella Dirksen, *The Honorable Mr. Marigold,* p. 180; C. V. Clifton, memo to the president, February 23, 1965, WHCF, NF, EMD, LBJL.

57. *WP,* July 6, 1964, CF, folder 346, EMDC; author's interview with Broder, March 16, 1999.

58. *WP,* July 6, 1964, CF, folder 361, EMDC.

59. National Security Council (NSC) Meetings File, box 1, Bi-partisan Congressional Leadership Meeting with NSC, February 8, 1965, LBJL.

60. Gibbons, *U.S. Government and the Vietnam War, Part III,* p. 129; Drummond, "Johnson's GOP Support: Pillar of No-Yield Policy," March 5, 1965, *NYHT* Morgue, Republicans, CAH.

61. Morton to Mrs. Nancy Dancinger, January 6, 1965, Senatorial Series, Legislative File, box 19, Foreign Relations, 1965, Morton Papers; Johnson's meeting with Eisenhower, February 17, 1965, Meeting Notes File, Box 1, LBJL; Dirksen's radio and television speech, "The Vietnam Crisis," February 22, 1965, RR, EMDC.

62. David J. Garrow, *Protest at Selma: Martin Luther King, Jr., and the Voting Rights Act of 1965* (New Haven: Yale University Press, 1978); Garrow, *Bearing the Cross: Martin Luther King, Jr., and the Southern Christian Leadership Conference* (New York: William Morrow, 1986), chapter 7.

63. Rowland Evans and Robert Novak, "Dirksen and Katzenbach, Inc.," March 14, 1965, *NYHT* Morgue, Republicans, CAH; Humphrey to Johnson, March 10, 1965, White House Files, Memos to LBJ from HHH, Civil Rights, 1965, 144.A.6.8F, Humphrey Papers; Stephen F. Lawson, *Black Ballots: Voting Rights in the South, 1944–1969* (New York: Columbia University Press, 1976), p. 309; minutes of GOP Policy Committee Meeting, March 9, 1965, Hickenlooper Papers, Political File, National Politics, Box 70, Republican Policy Committee, HCHL; Stephen Horn, "Roundtable of Participants in the Passage of the Civil Rights Act of 1964," *This Constitution* 19 (fall 1991): 36.

64. Goldwater to Dirksen, March 16, 1965, and Dirksen's tepid reply, AF, EMDC; Pavlik to Hickenlooper, March 1965, Hickenlooper Papers, box 10, Civil Rights, 1965, BBH Working File, HCHL.

65. Johnson to Eisenhower, March 16, 1965, WHCF, NF, EMD; McPherson memo to Johnson, March 24, 1965, Office Files of Harry McPherson, box 7, Dirksen; Dirksen to Jack Valenti, April 6, 1965, WHCF, NF, EMD, all in LBJL.

66. For "Dirksenbach," see article by Arthur Krock, May 11, 1965, *NYHT* Morgue, Congress: Senate, CAH; Garrow, *Protest at Selma,* pp. 98–132; Lawson, *Black Ballots,* p. 315; minutes of GOP Policy Committee Meeting, May 3, 1965, Hickenlooper Papers, Political File, National Politics, box 70, Republican Policy Committee, HCHL.

67. Dirksen's statement following the Joint Senate–House Republican Leadership Meeting, July 15, 1965, RCLF, folder 0059 and also folder 0060, EMDC.

68. VanDeMark, *Into the Quagmire*, pp. 173–207.

69. Meeting Notes File, July 27, 1965, Box 1; McGeorge Bundy's Notes of the Congressional Leadership Meeting, July 27, 1965, Meeting Notes File, box 1; Jack Valenti to Dirksen, July 31, 1965, WHCF, NF, EMD, all in LBJL.

70. Lawson, *Black Ballots*, p. 321; James T. Patterson, *Grand Expectations: The United States, 1945–1972* (New York: Oxford University Press, 1995), p. 579.

71. Evans and Novak, "Inside Report," August 15, 1965, *NYHT* Morgue, Congress: Senate, CAH; Dirksen-Ford press conference, August 5, 1965, RCLF, folder 0060, EMDC.

72. Andrew Glass, "Playing No-Name Politics," August 7, 1965, *NYHT* Morgue, Republicans, CAH.

73. Dirksen's and Ford's letter to Eisenhower, August 26, 1965, RCLF, folder 0060, and *Chicago Sun-Times*, October 25, 1965, CF, folder 368, both in EMDC.

74. Loevy, *To End All Segregation*, chapter 11; Irving Bernstein, *Guns or Butter: The Presidency of Lyndon Johnson* (New York: Oxford University Press, 1996), chapter 11; Notes of Republican Policy Committee Meeting, June 2, 1965, Hickenlooper Papers, Political File, National Politics, Minutes, HCHL.

75. Notes of Republican Policy Committee Meeting, August 10, 1965, Hickenlooper Papers, Political File, National Politics, Minutes, HCHL; Bernstein, *Guns or Butter*, pp. 307–312.

76. Notebooks, folder 199, EMDC.

77. Ibid., folder 165.

78. Dirksen's publication in *Committee for Government of the People*, January 1966, RG 3, box 600, folder 4, Mundt Papers; Dirksen's interview with *U.S. News and World Report*, December 27, 1965, RR, EMDC.

79. Dirksen, speech to the Sigma Delta Chi Fraternity in Washington, D.C., January 19, 1966, Working Papers, folder 2071, and "Constitutional Amendment to Permit Voluntary Prayer in Public Schools," March 22, 1966, RR, both in EMDC.

80. Notebooks, folder 199, EMDC; Dirksen's publication in *Committee for Government of the People*; Dirksen, "Let the People Choose! How You Can Help Me Win the Reapportionment Battle," *Committee for Government of the People*, February 1966.

81. Gibbons, *U.S. Government and the Vietnam War*, 4:89; Dirksen, speech to the Sigma Delta Chi Fraternity, January 19, 1966, Working Papers, folder 2071, and Dirksen, speech to the Fourteenth Annual Republican Women's Conference, May 6, 1966, RR, both in EMDC.

82. Gibbons, *U.S. Government and the Vietnam War*, 4:141; "Presidential Telecons," January 12, 1966, Papers of George Ball, box 6, LBJL.

83. Goldberg to Johnson, January 16, 1966, Confidential File, ND19/CO 230, box 71, ND19/CO 312, Vietnam, LBJL; Gibbons, *U.S. Government and the Vietnam War*, 4:141; *Newsweek*, January 31, 1966, p. 22.

84. *NYHT*, January 2, 1966, and January 5, 1966.

85. Jack Valenti's Notes of Meeting with Foreign Policy Advisers on Resumption of Bombing, January 24, 1966, Meeting Notes File, box 1, LBJL; Dirksen to Charles Percy, May 26, 1966, AF, EMDC.

86. Notes of Bi-partisan Leadership Meeting, January 25, 1966, Diary Back-up, box 28, LBJL; Meeting with Congressional Leadership on Resumption of Bombing, Meeting Notes File, box 1, LBJL.

87. Ford-Dirksen press conference, February 24, 1966, RCLF, folder 0063, EMDC; Cooper to Kirby B. Crowe, March 4, 1966, Vietnam, 1966, box 481, Cooper Papers; Dirksen's radio-television speech, "The Commander-in-Chief," February 21, 1966, RR, EMDC.

88. Athan Theoharis, ed., *From the Secret Files of J. Edgar Hoover* (Chicago: Elephant Paperbacks, 1993), pp. 237–238; William C. Sullivan, *The Bureau: My Thirty Years in Hoover's FBI* (New York: W. W. Norton, 1979), p. 65; Gibbons, *U.S. Government and the Vietnam War*, 4:229.

89. Katzenbach to Joe Califano, March 11, 1966, Personal Papers of Nicholas deB. Katzenbach, Civil Rights Legislation, 1966 (2 of 2), JFKL; Harlow to Eisenhower, March 3, 1966, Eisenhower Post-presidential Papers, 1961–1969, Special Names Series, box 7, Harlow, Bryce, DDEL.

90. Frank S. Meyer, "Vietnam—The Republican Performance," *National Review*, April 5, 1966, p. 326; Dirksen's notes for his speech at a Chicago dinner, April 26, 1966, Notebooks, folder 214, and Dirksen, speech to the Fourteenth Annual Republican Women's Conference, May 6, 1966, RR, both in EMDC.

91. Daily Diary, May 10, 1966, box 6, LBJL; Johnson's telegram to Dirksen, May 10, 1966, WHCF, NF, EMD, LBJL.

92. Tom Johnson's Notes of Bipartisan Leadership Meeting, July 18, 1966, Appointment File, Diary Back-up, box 39, LBJL.

93. Minutes of GOP Policy Committee Meeting, July 19, 1966, and minutes of September 13, 1966, Hickenlooper Papers, Political File, National Politics, box 70, Republican Policy Committee, HCHL.

94. PPP, Lyndon B. Johnson, January 12, 1966, pp. 3–12; Dirksen to Frank Kinne, May 20, 1966, Working Papers, folder 319, EMDC; Katzenbach to Califano, March 11, 1966, Katzenbach Papers, Civil Rights Legislation, 1966 (2 of 2), JFKL; *Congressional Quarterly Almanac (CQA)* (Washington, D.C.: Congressional Quarterly, 1966), p. 451.

95. Minutes of GOP Policy Committee Meeting, June 21, 1966, Hickenlooper Papers, Political File, National Politics, box 70, Republican Policy Committee, HCHL; Katzenbach to Johnson, September 9, 1966, LE/HU2, Box 65, and Daily Diary, September 13, 1966, box 8, both in LBJL; CQA, 1966, p. 470.

96. CQA, 1966, p. 472; Denton L. Watson, *Lion in the Lobby: Clarence Mitchell's Struggles for the Passage of Civil Rights Laws* (New York: William Morrow, 1990), p. 680; Ford-Dirksen press conference, September 22, 1966, RCLF, folder 0071, EMDC.

97. Dirksen's statement to the Long Island Federation of Women's Clubs, August 2, 1966, Working Papers, folder 2079, EMDC; Dirksen's article in *Human Events,* September 3, 1966, p. 5; CR, September 21, 1966, p. 23533.

98. *CR,* pp. 23547–23549. For a general summary of the prayer issue in and out of the Congress, see *CQA,* 1966, pp. 512–516.

99. *National Review,* August 23, 1966, p. 834; Dirksen's interview on *Meet the Press,* August 7, 1966, RR, EMDC.

100. Dirksen's interview on *Face the Nation,* October 2, 1966, RR, and Dirksen's interview on "Opinion in the Capital," October 16, 1966, RR, both in EMDC.

101. Daily Diary, November 25, 1966, box 9, LBJL; *PPP* (Johnson), November 25, 1966, pp. 1398–1405.

6. *"Ev Dirksen Will Leave Us"*

1. Working Papers, folder 449, EMDC; *WP,* August 21, 1967, p. A15; Diary Back-up, January 17, 1967, box 52, LBJL.

2. Neil MacNeil, *Dirksen: Portrait of a Public Man* (New York: World Publishing Company, 1970), p. 306; Mac Mathias, oral history, July 9, 1970, interview by Jean Torcom, p. 3, EMDC.

3. *CQA,* pp. 1387–1396; Bruce Allen Murphy, *Fortas: The Rise and Ruin of a Supreme Court Justice* (New York: William Morrow, 1988), pp. 274–275.

4. *Congressional Quarterly Weekly,* week ending October 21, 1966 (Washington, D.C.: Congressional Quarterly, 1966), p. 2537; author's interview with Neil MacNeil, September 26, 1996; John Tower, oral history, July 8, 1970, interview by Jean Torcom, p. 2, EMDC.

5. *Vital Speeches of the Day* (New York: City News Publishing Company, 1967), 33:258–260.

6. *Meet the Press,* January 15, 1967, box 497, Subject File, Vietnam, EWB Position and Statements, 1967–1970, Edward Brooke Papers, LC; *Time,* January 27, 1967, p. 18.

7. *NYT,* February 3, 1967, p. 15; *WP,* February 4, 1967, p. A2; *NYT,* February 8, 1967, p. 35; Minutes of Republican Policy Committee Meeting, February 7, 1967, Hickenlooper Papers, Political File, National Politics, box 70, HCHL.

8. *CR,* 90th Cong., 1st sess., February 28, 1967, p. 4766, and March 1, 1967, pp. 4940–4948; *NYT,* March 2, 1967, p. 1.

9. *CQA,* 1967, pp. 188–195.

10. Minutes of Republican Policy Committee Meeting, January 31, 1967, Hickenlooper Papers, Political File, National Politics, box 70, HCHL; *NYT,* January 27, 1967, p. 16.

11. Katzenbach to Johnson, January 27, 1967, Diary Back-up, box 53, LBJL; Rusk to Dirksen, February 23, 1967, Working Papers, folder 452, EMDC.

12. Minutes of Republican Policy Committee Meeting, February 28, 1967, Hickenlooper Papers, Political File, National Politics, box 70, HCHL.

13. G. G. Burkley to Johnson, March 13, 1967, Confidential File, FG430, box 34, and Johnson to Dirksen, March 18, 1967, WHCF, NF, MD, both in LBJL.

14. *CR,* March 3, 1967, pp. 5279–5284; *NYT,* March 4, 1967, p. 1; *CT,* March 4, 1967, p. 4.

15. Minutes of Republican Policy Committee Meeting, March 14, 1967, and Minutes of April 18, 1967, Hickenlooper Papers, Political File, National Politics, box 70; Dirksen to Hickenlooper, May 1, 1967, Hickenlooper Papers, Political File, National Politics, box 79, Republican Policy Committee, Vietnam Report, General 1967–1968, all in HCHL.

16. *CQA*, 1967, p. 940.

17. *WP*, May 3, 1967, p. 1; *CR*, April 27, 1967, p. 11002–11003; George Aiken's statement, May 2, 1967, box 481, Vietnam, 1967, Cooper Papers.

18. *WP*, May 2, 1967, p. A17.

19. *Washington Evening Star*, May 3, 1967, p. A22; *CQA*, 1967, p. 939.

20. *Cedar Rapids (Iowa) Gazette*, May 9, 1967, Hickenlooper Papers, Political File, National Politics, box 79, Republican Policy Committee, Vietnam Report, Clippings, 1967, HCHL; *WP*, May 3, 1967, p. A1; *NYT*, May 3, 1967, p. 1; undated issue of *Des Moines Tribune*, Hickenlooper Papers, Political File, National Politics, box 79, Republican Policy Committee, Vietnam Report, Clippings, 1967, HCHL.

21. For Johnson's press conference, May 3, 1967, see *PPP* (Johnson), p. 500; author's interview with MacNeil, September 26, 1996; MacNeil, Dirksen: Portrait of a Public Man, p. 274; *Face the Nation*, August 6, 1967, CBS News, Holt Information Systems, c. 1972, pp. 228–229.

22. Charles Morris, *A Time of Passion: America, 1960–1980* (New York: Harper and Row, 1984), pp. 117–128; Brooke to Dirksen, July 20, 1967, Correspondence, Master File, Di, 1967, Brooke Papers; *NYT*, July 26, 1967, p. 1.

23. *NYT*, July 25, 1967, p. 20, and July 26, 1967, p. 1; Tom Johnson's Notes of Meetings, July 25, 1967, box 3, and Diary Back-up, August 2, 1967, both in LBJL.

24. Notebooks, folder 226, EMDC; *CQA*, 1967, p. 742.

25. *CT*, July 21, 1967; *Wall Street Journal*, July 20, 1967, p. 1; author's interview with George Christian, July 16, 1998; *CR*, July 21, 1967, p. 19625.

26. *CR*, July 24, 1967, p. 19814; *CT*, July 25, 1967, sect. 1, p. 16; *Newsweek*, October 30, 1967, p. 27.

27. *WP*, August 19, 1967, p. A12; *CR*, July 24, 1967, p. 19813.

28. Harry McPherson to Califano, July 19, 1967, McPherson Papers, Memos to Califano, box 50; Johnson to Watson, August 27, 1967, and Watson to Johnson, August 31, 1967, WHCF, NF, EMD, all in LBJL.

29. *NYT*, September 18, 1967, pp. 1, 3, and September 19, 1967, p. 20.

30. *NYT*, September 19, 1967, pp. 1, 20; National Security File, Country File, Vietnam, Congressional Attitudes and Statements, file 4, and Rostow to Dirksen, September 18, 1967, WHCF, NF, EMD, both in LBJL; Notebooks, June 19, 1967, folder 215, EMDC.

31. *CR*, September 26, 1967, pp. 26704–26705; Working Papers, March 9, 1982, biographical file, SHO; *NYT*, September 27, 1967, pp. 1, 14.

32. *CR*, September 26, 1967, pp. 26706–26707.

33. Files of Marvin Watson, box 27, "Richard Nixon," LBJL; *CT*, October 6, 1967, p. 5.

34. *NYT*, October 8, 1967, pp. 1, 42; for Nixon's interview with Godfrey

Sperling of the *Christian Science Monitor,* August 21, 1967, see Files of Marvin Watson, box 27, "Richard Nixon," LBJL.

35. Don Oberdorfer, *Tet!* (New York: Doubleday, 1971), pp. 84–86; Morton to Robert Hubbard, August 24, 1967, Senatorial Series, Legislative File, box 19, Foreign Relations, 1967, Morton Papers; *CR,* September 28, 1967, p. 27131; *CT,* August 17, 1967, Notebooks, folder 215, EMDC; *CT,* September 28, 1967, sect. 1, p. 1.

36. Katzenbach to Johnson, September 29, 1967, Files of Marvin Watson, Vietnam (1 of 2), box 32, and Tom Johnson's notes of the president's Tuesday luncheon, October 2, 1967, box 1, both in LBJL.

37. *CR,* October 3, 1967, pp. 27577–27579; *NYT,* October 4, 1967, p. 1.

38. *CR,* October 3, 1967, pp. 27580–27584.

39. Fulbright's speech, October 11, 1967, Series 71, Box 33.12, Fulbright Papers; Randall Bennett Woods, *Fulbright: A Biography* (New York: Cambridge University Press, 1995), pp. 464–465; *NYT,* October 12, 1967, p. 5, and October 16, 1967, p. 20.

40. *CR,* October 10, 1967, pp. 28376–28377.

41. Ibid., p. 28377; *Newsweek,* October 30, 1967, p. 27.

42. Watson's notes of his meeting with Johnson, October 12, 1967, and Clark to Dirksen, October 16, 1967, Ex., WHCF, LE/ND7-2, box 140, LBJL; *CQA,* 1967, p. 742.

43. *Human Events,* October 14, 1967; Brooke's speech at Springfield Technical High School, October 11, 1967, box 497, Subject File, Vietnam, EWB Position and Statements, 1967–1970, Brooke Papers; *Newsweek,* October 30, 1967, p. 27; *US News and World Report,* December 11, 1967, p. 74; *Oklahoma City Times,* September 29, 1967, Files of Marvin Watson, box 5, Illinois-A, Senate-Illinois, LBJL.

44. Radio–TV Weekly Report, November 6–12, 1967, RR, EMDC.

45. Minutes of October 4, 1967, cabinet meeting, Cabinet Papers, box 10, LBJL; *NYT,* November 17, 1967, p. 7.

46. Watson to Johnson, September 27, 1967, Diary Back-up, box 83, LBJL; Notebooks, folder 227, EMDC; *PPP* (Johnson), November 20, 1967, pp. 1065–1067.

47. RR, December 9, 1967, EMDC.

48. *CR,* December 15, 1967, pp. 37425–37427.

49. RR, October 9, 1967, EMDC; Dirksen to Mansfield, December 18, 1967, AF, EMDC.

50. *National Review,* January 16, 1968, p. 16; *NYT,* January 15, 1968, p. 15.

51. *CR,* January 29, 1968, p. 1233; *NYT,* January 29, 1968, p. 1, and January 30, p. 1; Daily Diary, January 30, 1968, box 14, LBJL.

52. RR, January 30, 1968, EMDC; Dirksen's interview on *Issues and Answers,* February 4, 1968, WHCF, PR18-1, box 368, LBJL.

53. RR, February 17, 1968, and Radio–TV Weekly Report, January 29, 1968, RR, both in EMDC.

54. *PPP* (Johnson), January 24, 1968, pp. 55–62; *CR,* 90th Cong., 2d sess.,

February 6, 1968, pp. 2270-2274; *NYT,* February 8, 1968, p. 42; Manatos to Johnson, February 13, 1968, WHCF, NF, EMD, and Johnson to Philip Hart, February 19, 1968, Ex, WHCF, LE/HU2, 4/12/67-3/11/68, box 66, both in LBJL; *CR,* February 20, 1968, p. 3427; Hugh Davis Graham, *The Civil Rights Era: Origins and Development of National Policy, 1960-1972* (New York: Oxford University Press, 1990), p. 271.

55. Temple to Johnson, February 23, 1968, WHCF, NF, EMD, LBJL; *CR,* February 26, 1968, pp. 4064-4065.

56. Mary Rather to Johnson, February 26, 1968, WHCF, NF, EMD, LBJL; *NYT,* February 28, 1968, p. 1.

57. Martin to Johnson, March 1, 1968, WHCF, NF, EMD, LBJL; Edward L. Schapsmeier and Frederick H. Schapsmeier, *Dirksen of Illinois: Senatorial Statesman* (Urbana: University of Illinois Press, 1985), p. 188; *CR,* February 29, 1968, p. 4690.

58. *CR,* March 1, 1968, p. 4845; Manatos to Johnson, March 5, 1968, Ex, WHCF, LE/HU2, 4/12/68-3/11/68, box 66, LBJL; *Life,* March 15, 1968, p. 32; *CR,* March 4, 1968, p. 4960; *CQA,* 1968, p. 159.

59. Graham, *Civil Rights Era,* pp. 270-273; Johnson to Dirksen, March 13, 1968, WHCF, NF, EMD, LBJL.

60. RR, March 31, 1968, EMDC.

61. *NYT,* April 3, 1968, p. 1; Tom Johnson's Notes of the President's Meeting with the Democratic Leadership (joined by Republican leaders), October 23, 1967, box 1, and Tom Johnson's Notes of the President's Meeting with Negotiating Team, May 8, 1968, box 3, both in LBJL.

62. Manatos to Johnson, April 30, 1968, WHCF, NF, EMD, LBJL; RR, May 16, 1968, EMDC.

63. RR, June 29, 1968, EMDC.

64. Daily Diary, June 24, 1968, Box 103, LBJL; Dirksen, oral history no. 2, March 21, 1969, interview by William S. White, pp. 12-14, LBJL; Dirksen's undated notes, "The Abe Fortas Story," Notebooks, folder 222, EMDC.

65. Murphy, *Fortas: Rise and Ruin of a Supreme Court Justice,* pp. 280-282.

66. *Ibid.,* pp. 296-297; Neil D. McFeeley, *Appointment of Judges: The Johnson Presidency* (Austin: University of Texas Press, 1987), p. 59.

67. Samuel Shaffer, *On and Off the Floor: Thirty Years a Correspondent on Capitol Hill* (New York: Newsweek Books, 1980), pp. 83-84; Manatos to Johnson, June 25, 1968, WHCF, NF, EMD, LBJL.

68. Manatos to Johnson, June 25, 1968, Fortas-Thornberry Special File, box 1, Chron File: 6/13/68-6/25/68, LBJL.

69. Shaffer, *On and Off the Floor,* pp. 84-85.

70. Manatos to Johnson, June 26, 1968, Fortas-Thornberry Special File, box 1, Chron File: 6/13/68-6/25/68, LBJL.

71. Working Papers, folder 1799L, EMDC; *Washington Star,* July 3, 1968, p. 1; *WP,* July 3, 1968, p. A11.

72. *Newsweek,* July 15, 1968, p. 27; Murphy, *Fortas: Rise and Ruin of a Supreme Court Justice,* p. 325.

73. Temple to Johnson, July 12, 1968, Fortas-Thornberry Special File, box 2, Chron File: 7/7/68–7/13/68, LBJL.

74. U.S. Senate, Committee on the Judiciary, *Hearings, Nominations of Abe Fortas and Homer Thornberry,* 90th Cong., 2d sess., July 11–23, 1968 (Washington, D.C.: GPO, 1968), pp. 51–54 (hereafter Confirmation Hearings); *NYT,* July 13, 1968, pp. 1, 26.

75. Confirmation Hearings, p. 58; Murphy, *Fortas: The Rise and Ruin of a Supreme Court Justice,* p. 376.

76. *NYT,* July 29, 1968, p. 1.

77. Ibid., August 6, 1968, p. 23; Stephen E. Ambrose, *Nixon: The Triumph of a Politician, 1962–1972* (New York: Simon and Schuster, 1989), p. 167.

78. *NYT,* August 7, 1968, p. 1; Manatos to Johnson, August 15, 1968, WHCF, Exec., FG 2, box 39, LBJL; John G. Tower, *Consequences: A Personal and Political Memoir* (Boston: Little, Brown, 1991), p. 58.

79. *NYT,* September 6, 1968, p. 33.

80. WHCF, PR 6, September 5, 1968, Box 75; Johnson to Dirksen, September 5, 1968, WHCF, NF, EMD; Larry Temple, oral history no. 1, August 11, 1970, p. 42, all in LBJL; Murphy, *Fortas: The Rise and Ruin of a Supreme Court Justice,* pp. 367–368.

81. Larry Temple, oral history no. 1, August 11, 1970, p. 42, and Sanders to Johnson, September 12, 1968, Fortas-Thornberry Special File, box 3, Chron File, 9/3/68–9/24/68, both in LBJL.

82. *NYT,* September 15, 1968, p. 76, and September 17, 1968, p. 50; Murphy, *Fortas: The Rise and Ruin of a Supreme Court Justice,* p. 509.

83. Daily Diary, September 16, 1968, box 17, and Manatos to Johnson, September 16, 1968, WHCF, NF, EMD, both in LBJL.

84. Harry McPherson to Manatos, September 20, 1968, Fortas-Thornberry Special File, box 3, Chron File: 9/16/68–9/30/68, LBJL; *NYT,* September 24, 1968, p. 1.

85. *WP,* September 28, 1968, p. 1; Bernard J. Waters to Dirksen, September 26, 1968, Working Papers, folder 968, EMDC; *CR,* October 1, 1968, pp. 11687–11688.

86. *NYT,* June 12, 1968, p. 28.

87. Ibid., February 28, 1968, pp. 1, 35.

88. Ibid., October 23, 1968, p. 21.

89. Ibid., September 24, 1968, p. 34.

90. Fred Bauer, ed., *Ev: The Man and His Words* (Old Tappan, New Jersey: Hewitt House, 1969), pp. 16–17.

91. Howard W. Allen and Vincent A. Lacey, *Illinois Elections: Candidates and County Returns for President, Governor, Senate, and House of Representatives* (Carbondale: Southern Illinois University Press, 1992), pp. 488–489.

92. Lloyd C. Gardner, *Pay Any Price: Lyndon Johnson and the Wars for Vietnam* (Chicago: Ivan R. Dee, 1995), pp. 518–519.

93. Jim Jones to Johnson, December 18, 1968, Manatos to Johnson, January

10, 1969, and Johnson to Dirksen, January 17, 1969, all in WHCF, NF, EMD, LBJL; Daily Diary, January 20, 1969, box 18, LBJL.

Epilogue

1. *U.S. News and World Report*, May 19, 1969, pp. 46–47; *Newsweek*, May 12, 1969, p. 36; *Time*, May 9, 1969, pp. 26–27.

2. *Newsweek*, May 12, 1969, p. 36, June 16, 1969, pp. 26–29, and September 22, 1969, pp. 34–35.

3. Author's interview with Glee Gomien, June 7, 1996; *NYT*, September 13, 1969, p. 25; Nixon to Dirksen, September 3, 1969, AF, EMDC.

4. U.S. Senate, *Memorial Services Held in the Senate and House of Representatives of the United States, Together with Tributes Presented in Eulogy of Everett McKinley Dirksen* (Washington: GPO, 1970), p. 154 and pp. 39–40.

5. David Halberstam, *The Powers That Be* (New York: Knopf, 1979), p. 387.

6. Jean E. Torcom, "Leadership: The Role and Style of Everett Dirksen," in *To Be a Congressman: The Promise and the Power*, ed. Sven Groennings and Jonathan P. Hawley (Washington, D.C.: Acropolis Books, 1973), p. 217; Howard Baker, foreword, in Everett Dirksen, *The Education of a Senator* (Urbana: University of Illinois Press, 1998), p. viii.

7. Author's interview with Baker, August 9, 1999; author's interview with Novak, August 4, 1999; "Roundtable of Participants in the Passage of the Civil Rights Act of 1964," *This Constitution* 19 (fall 1991): 35.

8. "Roundtable of Participants in the Passage of the Civil Rights Act of 1964," *This Constitution* 19 (Fall 1991): 35; author's interview with Novak, August 4, 1999.

9. David Broder, "The Struggle for Power," *Atlantic*, April 1966, pp. 68–69; Dirksen to Robert E. Wood, June 1, 1964, Wood Papers, Box 3, Everett M. Dirksen, HCHL.

10. Garry Wills, *Nixon Agonistes: The Crisis of the Self-Made Man* (Boston: Houghton Mifflin, 1969), chapter 3.

11. Hugh Heclo, "Hyperdemocracy," *Wilson Quarterly* (winter 1999): 62–71.

12. Author's interview with Harry McPherson, August 26, 1999; author's interview with Baker, March 24, 1999; author's interview with Dole, March 11, 1999.

13. Author's interview with Novak, August 4, 1999; author's interview with Broder, March 16, 1999.

14. Author's interview with Evans, August 5, 1999.

15. Robert Dole, oral history, July 9, 1970, interview by Jean Torcom, p. 2, EMDC; *NYT*, September 8, 1969, p. 26.

Bibliography

Other scholars have appreciated Everett Dirksen's importance to post–World War II American politics, and I am indebted to each of them for their early work on his life and career. Neil MacNeil's *Dirksen: Portrait of a Public Man* is an insightful and revealing account from one of Washington's most seasoned journalists. MacNeil drew on his close relationship with Dirksen and provides the reader with in-depth interviews that the minority leader gave the author in the late 1960s. As such, however, the work is slanted to Dirksen's point of view. A journalist by trade, MacNeil paints a vivid portrait of Dirksen's political and personal abilities, but he avoids a historical analysis of the most important issues of the day. Political scientist Jean Torcom completed a 1973 dissertation, "Minority Leadership in the United States Senate: The Role and Style of Everett Dirksen." Torcom conducted twenty-seven interviews with Dirksen's Senate colleagues, an oral history collection now housed at the Dirksen Center in Pekin, Illinois. Useful as it is, Torcom's account is less a study of Dirksen's Senate career and his place in modern American history than a revealing evaluation of his minority leadership within a loosely defined and decentralized two-party system. In 1985 Edward and Frederick Schapsmeier published *Dirksen of Illinois: Senatorial Statesman.* The authors were the first to mine the senator's papers, and their book is the first scholarly biography of Dirksen and his career. Even though they drew on a number of interesting and revealing sources, their book provides only a cursory examination of that career. Too often the authors present Dirksen as having acted in a vacuum, neither pushed nor pulled by forces in and out of the Republican party. Their account, in short, assumes that Dirksen enjoyed more power than he did, and they avoid a re-creation of the political reality and the Washington milieu within which the senator operated.

Scholarship of the Republican party has its own limitations. Political historians have generally focused more on the Democratic party and the successes and failures of liberalism than on a textured understanding of the GOP. Those historians who have written on Republicans have paid too little attention to the changing dynamics in the party. To the extent that scholars acknowledge that Republicans were not cut from the same mold and were more than reproducible parts of a monolithic whole, they overemphasize a linearlike, almost inevitable triumph of the Republican right that culminated in Ronald Reagan's election in 1980. Work on Barry Goldwater, for instance, has flourished since Reagan's inauguration and the GOP's dramatic victory in the 1994 congressional elections. In these accounts, the liberal and moderate Republicans who controlled the national GOP in the Dirksen era are largely overlooked, as scholars and readers impose too much of the present on the past and fashion a historical continuum that never existed.

In *Everett Dirksen and the Modern Presidents,* I devoted much of my energy to a re-creation of the many voices that shaped Washington politics and impacted Dirksen's career. Not surprisingly, I spent many hours in Pekin, Illinois, at the senator's library which houses his papers. Researchers must persevere in the Dirksen papers, simply because the sources tend to be unrevealing. Dirksen preferred to conduct most of his business in private conversations (if notes were kept, they do not survive) or on the telephone. He maintained no private diary, and his tersely written letters rarely expose his point of view. Though Dirksen was not the most reflective of senators, his papers were nonetheless indispensable in my research. His private notebooks reflect his changing impressions and the development of his ideas, but the collection is not organized chronologically and must be pieced together with other sources. The Remarks and Releases File contains the written texts of most of his speeches and public appearances, but these records must be supplemented with the Clippings File and other newspaper accounts because the senator often deviated from his prepared remarks. Although resourceful researchers can find untapped nuggets in the Chicago Office File, Personal File, and Working Papers, anyone hoping to profit from Dirksen's papers should expect a lengthy stay in Pekin.

In addition to the Dirksen Papers, the presidential libraries were critical sources of information. Dwight Eisenhower's legendary diary is a good place for any scholar of the era to begin, but just as important for me was the L. Arthur Minnich Series. Minnich was a White House aide who kept handwritten notes of legislative leaders' and cabinet meetings. Because I went to graduate school at the University of Texas in Austin, I spent most of my research time at the Lyndon B. Johnson Library. Recorded telephone conversations between Johnson and Dirksen and Johnson and others about Dirksen were some of the most fascinating historical sources I have ever encountered. Reviewing the conversations is laborious work, and much of the collection remains closed to researchers, but scholars interested in any part of the Johnson presidency should begin with the tapes.

I supplemented my basic research with trips to archives and libraries that house the papers of Dirksen's Senate colleagues. Politicians often save reams of uninspiring material for fund-starved researchers to plow through at breakneck speed. Even so, I found the Bourke Hickenlooper, Hubert Humphrey, Margaret Chase Smith, John Sherman Cooper, and Thruston Morton collections well organized and informative. Hickenlooper kept copies of the Republican Policy Committee Papers that shed light on party dynamics. Newspaper clippings were rich and revealing sources. When Dirksen strayed from his prepared remarks, reporters were often there to record the results. More important, journalists painted brilliant pictures of Dirksen's manner and demeanor. He thoroughly enjoyed his interaction with the press, and even if the reporters were too sympathetic by today's standards, they nonetheless provided historians with a textured milieu of the world I try to re-create. Used carefully and backed up with manuscript references whenever possible, oral histories provided a critical body of information. The principal characters of the book were often more open about change, continuity, and conflict when they left the arena and had time to reflect. My own personal interviews rarely if ever changed the point of view that I honed from the sources but did add immensely to my understanding of Dirksen and the world in which he lived.

Archives

Carl Albert Center Archives, Norman, Oklahoma: Stephen Horn's Notes Concerning the 1964 Civil Rights Act
Center for American History, Austin, Texas: *New York Herald Tribune* Morgue
Everett McKinley Dirksen Congressional Leadership Center, Pekin, Illinois:
    Everett McKinley Dirksen Papers
        Alpha File
        Chicago Office File
        Clippings File
        Notebooks
        Personal File
        Remarks and Releases
        Republican Congressional Leadership File
        Working Papers
Dwight D. Eisenhower Library, Abilene, Kansas
        Dwight D. Eisenhower Papers
            Alpha File
            Papers as President: Ann Whitman Diary Series
            Post-presidential File
            President's Official Files
            White House Central File
        Len Hall Papers
        Robert Humphrey Papers
        Republican National Committee Papers
        Subject Series, White House Subseries: Conferences–Staff Coverage
        White House Office, Office of the Staff Secretary
            Cabinet Meeting Series
            Legislative Meeting Series
            L. Arthur Minnich Series
Herbert C. Hoover Library, West Branch, Iowa
        Bourke B. Hickenlooper Papers: Republican Policy Committee Papers
        Herbert Hoover Papers: Post-presidential File
        Felix Morley Papers

Lewis L. Strauss Papers
Walter Trohan Papers
Robert E. Wood Papers
Illinois State Historical Library, Springfield, Illinois: Scott W. Lucas Papers
Lyndon B. Johnson Library, Austin, Texas
George Ball Papers
Lyndon B. Johnson Papers
Aides Files: Harry McPherson; Marvin Watson
Appointment File, Diary Backup
Cabinet Papers
Confidential File
Daily Diary
Fortas-Thornberry Special File
Meeting Notes File
National Security File
Senate Papers: Papers of the Democratic Leader; George Reedy Memos
Telephone Tapes and Transcripts
White House Central Files
Tom Johnson Papers: Notes of Meetings
Drew Pearson Papers
John F. Kennedy Library, Boston, Massachusetts
Nicholas deB. Katzenbach Papers
John F. Kennedy Papers
White House Central Files
President's Office Files: Presidential Recordings and Transcripts
Theodore Sorensen Papers
White House Staff Files
Mike Manatos Papers
Larry O'Brien Papers
Library of Congress, Washington, D.C.
Joe Alsop Papers
Edward Brooke Papers
Papers of the National Association for the Advancement of Colored People
Robert A. Taft Papers
Manuscripts on Microfilm
John Foster Dulles and Christian Herter Series
Dwight D. Eisenhower Diaries
Dwight D. Eisenhower's Meetings with Legislative Leaders
Papers of the Republican Party. Part 1: Meetings of the Republican National Committee, 1911–1980 (Series A: 1911–1960)
Minnesota Historical Society, St. Paul: Hubert H. Humphrey Papers, John Stewart's Notes on the Civil Rights Bill
Karl E. Mundt Archival Library, Madison, South Dakota: Karl Mundt Papers
National Archives, Pacific Southwest Division: Richard M. Nixon Pre-presidential Papers

New Hampshire State Archives, Concord: Styles Bridges Papers
Ohio Historical Society, Columbus: John W. Bricker Papers
Private Collections: Glee Gomien Papers
Senate Historical Office, Washington, D.C.: Biographical Files
Margaret Chase Smith Library, Skowhegan, Maine: Margaret Chase Smith Papers
Harry S. Truman Library, Independence, Missouri
    Records of the Democratic National Committee
    Harry S. Truman Papers
      General File
      Official File
      Post-presidential Office Files
      President's Personal Files
      President's Secretary's Files
University of Arkansas, Fayetteville: J. William Fulbright Papers
University of Georgia, Athens: Richard B. Russell Papers
University of Kentucky, Lexington
    John Sherman Cooper Papers
    Thruston B. Morton Papers
University of Virginia, Charlottesville: Hugh Scott Papers

Oral Histories

John Sherman Cooper Oral History Project, Lexington, Kentucky
    George Aiken, May 24, 1976
    Clifford Case, June 10, 1980
    Carl T. Curtis, January 26, 1981
    John Sherman Cooper, 80 OH 64, April 1980
    Hugh Scott, January 27, 1981
    Stuart Symington, June 9, 1980
Everett McKinley Dirksen Congressional Leadership Center
    Harold Rainville, March 22, 1974
    Jean E. Torcom Oral History Project
      Wallace Bennett, June 17, 1970
      Carl Curtis, June 23, 1970
      Robert Dole, July 9, 1970
      Jacob Javits, June 24, 1970
      Mac Mathias, July 9, 1970
      John G. Tower, July 8, 1970
John Foster Dulles Oral History Project, Princeton, New Jersey: Everett M.
    Dirksen, June 19, 1966
Dwight D. Eisenhower Library
    Sherman Adams, April 1967
    Prescott Bush, July 1966
    Dwight D. Eisenhower, July 13, 1967

Milton Eisenhower, November 6, 1975
Charles Halleck, April 26, 1977
Ed McCabe, September 5, 1967
Lyndon B. Johnson Library
Everett Dirksen, May 8, 1968, March 21, 1969
Lawrence F. O'Brien, February 12, 1986
Larry Temple, August 11, 1970
John G. Tower, November 1, 1971
Jack Valenti, July 12, 1972
John F. Kennedy Library
Nicholas deB. Katzenbach, November 16, 1964
Robert F. Kennedy, April 30, 1964
Robert F. Kennedy and Burke Marshall, December 22, 1964
George Smathers, July 10, 1964
Senate Historical Office, Washington, D.C.
Leonard H. Ballard, September 1, 1983
Stewart E. McClure, 1982–1983
George Smathers, October 24, 1989
Francis R. Valeo, December 11, 1985

Interviews

Howard Baker, March 24, 1999, and August 9, 1999
David Broder, March 16, 1999
George Christian, July 16, 1998
Robert Dole, March 11, 1999
Rowland Evans Jr., August 5, 1999
Glee Gomien, June 7, 1996
Neil MacNeil, September 26, 1996
Mike Mansfield, June 6, 1996
Harry McPherson, August 26, 1999
Robert Novak, August 4, 1999
George E. Reedy, July 30, 1998
Elspeth Rostow, August 9, 1999
Richard Stolley, August 9, 1999
Larry Temple, July 16, 1998

Dissertations

Jean Torcom Cronin, "Minority Leadership in the United States Senate," Ph.D.
diss., Johns Hopkins University, 1973.
Timothy Nels Thurber, "The Politics of Equality: Hubert H. Humphrey and the
African-American Freedom Struggle, 1945–1978," Ph.D. diss., University of
North Carolina, 1996.

Books

Adams, Sherman. *Firsthand Report: The Story of the Eisenhower Administration.* New York, 1961.

Allen, Howard W., and Vincent A. Lacey. *Illinois Elections: Candidates and County Returns for President, Governor, Senate, and House of Representatives.* Carbondale, Illinois, 1992.

Ambrose, Stephen E. *Eisenhower: Soldier, General of the Army, President-Elect, 1890–1952.* New York, 1983.

———. *Eisenhower: The President.* Volume 2. New York, 1984.

———. *Eisenhower: Soldier and President.* New York, 1990.

———. *Nixon: The Triumph of a Politician, 1962–1972.* New York, 1989.

Andrew, John A., III. *The Other Side of the Sixties: Young Americans for Freedom and the Rise of Conservative Politics.* New Brunswick, New Jersey, 1997.

Baker, Bobby. *Wheeling and Dealing: Confessions of a Capitol Hill Operator.* New York, 1978.

Baker, Ross K. *Friend and Foe in the U.S. Senate.* New York, 1980.

Bauer, Fred, ed. *Ev: The Man and His Words.* Old Tappan, New Jersey, 1969.

Bell, Jack. *The Johnson Treatment: How Lyndon B. Johnson Took Over the Presidency and Made It His Own.* New York, 1965.

Berman, William C. *William Fulbright and the Vietnam War: The Dissent of a Political Realist.* Kent, Ohio, 1988.

Bernstein, Irving. *Guns or Butter: The Presidency of Lyndon Johnson.* New York, 1996.

———. *Promises Kept: John F. Kennedy's New Frontier.* New York, 1991.

Beschloss, Michael R. *The Crisis Years: Kennedy and Khrushchev, 1960–1963.* New York, 1991.

Bohlen, Charles E. *Witness to History, 1929–1969.* New York, 1973.

Bradlee, Benjamin C. *Conversations with Kennedy.* New York, 1975.

Branch, Taylor. *Parting the Waters: America in the King Years, 1954–1963.* New York, 1988.

Brennan, Mary C. *Turning Right in the Sixties: The Conservative Capture of the GOP.* Chapel Hill, North Carolina, 1995.

Broadwater, Jeff. *Eisenhower and the Anti-Communist Crusade.* Chapel Hill, North Carolina, 1992.

Brownell, Herbert. *Advising Ike: The Memoirs of Herbert Brownell.* Lawrence, Kansas, 1993.

Burk, Robert F. *The Eisenhower Administration and Black Civil Rights.* Knoxville, Tennessee, 1984.

Buttitta, Tony. *Uncle Sam Presents: A Memoir of the Federal Theatre, 1935–1939.* Philadelphia, 1962.

Califano, Joseph A. *The Triumph and Tragedy of Lyndon Johnson: The White House Years.* New York, 1991.

Caridi, Ronald J. *The Korean War and American Politics: The Republican Party as a Case Study.* Philadelphia, 1968.

Cohn, Roy M. *McCarthy.* New York, 1968.

Congressional Quarterly Almanac. Selected volumes. Washington, D.C., 1966–1968.

Congressional Quarterly Weekly. Selected issues. Washington, D.C., 1966–1968.

Congressional Record, 1941–1968. Selected Volumes. Washington, D.C., 1941–1968.

Conkin, Paul K. *Big Daddy from the Pedernales: Lyndon Baines Johnson.* Boston, 1986.

DeBenedetti, Charles. *An American Ordeal: The Anti-War Movement of the Vietnam War.* Syracuse, New York, 1990.

Dallek, Robert. *Lone Star Rising: Lyndon Johnson and His Times, 1908–1960.* New York, 1991.

Dirksen, Everett. *The Education of a Senator.* Urbana, Illinois, 1998.

Dirksen, Louella. *The Honorable Mr. Marigold: My Life with Everett Dirksen.* Garden City, New York, 1972.

Divine, Robert A. *Eisenhower and the Cold War.* New York, 1981.

———. *Politics and Diplomacy in Recent American History.* 2d ed. New York, 1979.

———. *The Sputnik Challenge: Eisenhower's Response to the Soviet Satellite.* New York, 1993.

Douglas, Paul H. *In the Fullness of Time: The Memoirs of Paul H. Douglas.* New York, 1972.

Eisenhower, Dwight D. *At Ease: Stories I Tell My Friends.* Garden City, New York, 1967.

———. *The White House Years: Waging Peace, 1956–1961.* Garden City, New York, 1965.

Face the Nation. CBS Television Network, New York, 1972.

Ferrell, Robert H., ed. *The Diary of James C. Hagerty: Eisenhower in Mid-Course, 1954–1955.* Bloomington, Indiana, 1983.

———, ed. *The Eisenhower Diaries.* New York, 1981.

Fite, Gilbert E. *Richard B. Russell Jr.: Senator from Georgia.* Chapel Hill, North Carolina, 1991.

Foreign Relations of the United States: 1961–1963. Vol. 24. *Laos Crisis.* Washington, D.C., 1994.

Foreign Relations of the United States: 1961–1963. Vol. 8. *National Security Policy.* Washington, D.C., 1996.

Fried, Richard M. *Nightmare in Red: The McCarthy Era in Perspective.* New York, 1990.

Gaddis, John Lewis. *Strategies of Containment: A Critical Appraisal of Postwar American National Security Policy.* New York, 1982.

Gallup, George H. *The Gallup Poll: Public Opinion, 1935–1971.* Vol. 3. *1959–1971.* New York, 1972.

Gardner, Lloyd C. *Pay Any Price: Lyndon Johnson and the Wars for Vietnam.* Chicago, 1995.

Garrow, David J. *Bearing the Cross: Martin Luther King Jr. and the Southern Christian Leadership Conference.* New York, 1986.

——. *Protest at Selma: Martin Luther King Jr. and the Voting Rights Act of 1965*. New Haven, Connecticut, 1978.

Gelfand, Lawrence E., and Robert J. Neymeyer, eds. *The New Deal Viewed from Fifty Years: Papers Commemorating the Fiftieth Anniversary of the Launching of President Franklin D. Roosevelt's New Deal in 1933*. Iowa City, 1983.

Gibbons, William Conrad. *The U.S. Government and the Vietnam War: Executive and Legislative Roles and Relationships*. Princeton, New Jersey, 1986.

——. *The U.S. Government and the Vietnam War, Part II: 1961–1964*. Princeton, New Jersey, 1986.

——. *The U.S. Government and the Vietnam War, Part III: January–July 1965*. Princeton, New Jersey, 1989.

——. *The U.S. Government and the Vietnam War, Part IV: July 1965–January 1968*. Princeton, New Jersey, 1995.

Goldberg, Robert Alan. *Barry Goldwater*. New Haven, Connecticut, 1995.

Goldman, Eric F. *The Crucial Decade and After: America, 1945–1960*. New York, 1966.

Graebner, Norman A. *The New Isolationism: A Study in Politics and Foreign Policy Since 1950*. New York, 1956.

Graham, Hugh Davis. *The Civil Rights Era: Origins and Development of National Policy, 1960–1972*. New York, 1990.

Greenstein, Fred I. *The Hidden Hand Presidency: Eisenhower as Leader*. New York, 1982.

Griffith, Robert. *The Politics of Fear: Joseph R. McCarthy and the Senate*. Lexington, Kentucky, 1970.

Groennings, Sven, and Jonathan Hawley, eds. *To Be a Congressman: The Promise and the Power*. Washington D.C., 1973.

Halberstam, David. *The Best and the Brightest*. New York, 1969.

——. *The Powers That Be*. New York, 1979.

Hamby, Alonzo L. *Man of the People: A Life of Harry S. Truman*. New York, 1995.

Herring, George C. *America's Longest War: The United States and the Vietnam War, 1950–1975*. 2d ed. New York, 1986.

Hodgson, Godfrey. *America in Our Time*. Garden City, New York, 1976.

Hughes, Emmet John. *The Ordeal of Power: A Political Memoir of the Eisenhower Years*. New York, 1963.

James, D. Clayton. *The Years of MacArthur: Triumph and Disaster, 1945–1964*. Boston, 1985.

Jewell, Malcolm E. *Senatorial Politics and Foreign Policy*. Lexington, Kentucky, 1962.

Johnson, Lyndon Baines. *The Vantage Point: Perspectives of the Presidency, 1963–1969*. New York, 1971.

Kalman, Laura. *Abe Fortas: A Biography*. New Haven, Connecticut, 1990.

Kaufman, Burton I. *Trade and Aid: Eisenhower's Foreign Economic Policy, 1953–1961*. Baltimore, 1982.

Kepley, David R. *The Collapse of the Middle Way: Senate Republicans and the Bipartisan Foreign Policy, 1948–1952*. New York, 1988.

Kern, Montague, Patricia W. Levering, and Ralph B. Levering. *The Kennedy Crises: The Press, the Presidency, and Foreign Policy.* Chapel Hill, North Carolina, 1983.

LaFeber, Walter. *Inevitable Revolutions: The United States and Central America.* New York, 1984.

Lawson, Stephen F. *Black Ballots: Voting Rights in the South, 1944–1969.* New York, 1976.

———. *Running for Freedom: Civil Rights and Black Politics in America Since 1941.* New York, 1991.

Lee, R. Alton. *Eisenhower and Landrum-Griffin: A Study in Labor-Management Politics.* Lexington, Kentucky, 1990.

Levy, David W. *The Debate over Vietnam.* Baltimore, 1991.

Loevy, Robert D. *To End All Segregation: The Politics of the Passage of the Civil Rights Act of 1964.* Lanham, Maryland, 1990.

Lurie, Leonard. *The King Makers.* New York, 1971.

MacNeil, Neil. *Dirksen: Portrait of a Public Man.* New York, 1970.

Manchester, William. *The Death of a President: November 1963.* New York, 1967.

McCullough, David. *Truman.* New York, 1992.

McFeeley, Neil D. *Appointment of Judges: The Johnson Presidency.* Austin, Texas, 1987.

McGillivray, Alice V., and Richard M. Scammon. *America at the Polls, 1920–1956: A Handbook of American Presidential Election Statistics.* Washington, D.C., 1994.

Miles, Michael W. *The Odyssey of the American Right.* New York, 1980.

Milkis, Sidney M. *The President and the Parties: The Transformation of the American Party System Since the New Deal.* New York, 1993.

Miller, William. *Fishbait: The Memoirs of a Congressional Doorkeeper.* Englewood Cliffs, New Jersey, 1977.

Moore, William Howard. *The Kefauver Committee and the Politics of Crime, 1950–1952.* Columbia, Missouri, 1974.

Morgan, Iwan W. *Eisenhower Versus the Spenders: The Eisenhower Administration, the Democrats, and the Budget, 1953–1960.* New York, 1990.

Morris, Charles. *A Time of Passion: America, 1960–1980.* New York, 1984.

Murphy, Bruce Allen. *Fortas: The Rise and Ruin of a Supreme Court Justice.* New York, 1988.

Oakley, J. Ronald. *God's Country: America in the Fifties.* New York, 1990.

Oberdorfer, Don. *Tet!* New York, 1971.

Oshinsky, David M. *A Conspiracy So Immense: The World of Joe McCarthy.* New York, 1983.

Pach, Chester J., and Elmo Richardson. *The Presidency of Dwight D. Eisenhower.* Lawrence, Kansas, 1991.

Parmet, Herbert S. *Eisenhower and the American Crusades.* New York, 1972.

———. *JFK: The Presidency of John F. Kennedy.* New York, 1983.

Paterson, Thomas G., ed. *Kennedy's Quest for Victory: American Foreign Policy, 1961–1963*. New York, 1989.

Patterson, James T. *Grand Expectations: The United States, 1945–1972*. New York, 1995.

———. *Mr. Republican: A Biography of Robert A. Taft*. Boston, 1972.

Pearson, Drew, and Jack Anderson. *The Case Against Congress*. New York, 1968.

Phillips, Kevin B. *The Emerging Republican Majority*. Garden City, New York, 1969.

Public Papers of the Presidents, 1950–1968. Selected volumes. Washington, D.C., 1950–1968.

Rae, Nicol C. *The Decline and Fall of the Liberal Republicans from 1952 to the Present*. New York, 1989.

Ragsdale, Lyn. *Vital Statistics on the Presidency: Washington to Clinton*. Washington, D.C., 1996.

Reeves, Richard. *President Kennedy: Profile of Power*. New York, 1993.

Reichard, Gary W. *The Reaffirmation of Republicanism: Eisenhower and the Eighty-third Congress*. Knoxville, Tennessee, 1975.

Reinhard, David W. *The Republican Right Since 1945*. Lexington, Kentucky, 1983.

Ripley, Randall B. *Power in the Senate*. New York, 1969.

Rovere, Richard H. *Affairs of State: The Eisenhower Years*. New York, 1956.

Rowan, Carl T. *Breaking Barriers: A Memoir*. Boston, 1991.

Scammon, Richard M., and Ben J. Wattenberg. *The Real Majority*. New York, 1970.

Schapsmeier, Edward L., and Frederick H. Schapsmeier. *Dirksen of Illinois: Senatorial Statesman*. Urbana, Illinois, 1985.

Schlesinger, Arthur M., Jr. *Robert Kennedy and His Times*. Boston, 1978.

———. *The Vital Center: The Politics of Freedom*. Cambridge, Massachusetts, 1962.

Seaborg, Glenn T. *Kennedy, Khrushchev, and the Test Ban*. Berkeley, California, 1981.

Shaffer, Samuel. *On and off the Floor: Thirty Years a Correspondent on Capitol Hill*. New York, 1980.

Smith, Richard Norton. *The Colonel: The Life and Legend of Robert R. McCormick, 1880–1955*. Boston, 1997.

Solberg, Carl. *Hubert Humphrey: A Biography*. New York, 1984.

Sorensen, Theodore. *Kennedy*. New York, 1965.

Sullivan, William C. *The Bureau: My Thirty Years in Hoover's FBI*. New York, 1979.

Tananbaum, Duane. *The Bricker Amendment Controversy: A Test of Eisenhower's Political Leadership*. Ithaca, New York, 1988.

Theoharis, Athan G. *The Yalta Myths: An Issue in U.S. Politics, 1945–1955*. Columbia, Missouri, 1970.

———, ed. *From the Secret Files of J. Edgar Hoover.* Chicago, 1993.

Tower, John G. *Consequences: A Personal and Political Memoir.* Boston, 1991.

U.S. Senate. Committee on Foreign Relations. *Executive Sessions of the Senate Foreign Relations Committee,* 1962.

———. *Hearings Before the Committee on Foreign Relations: Nuclear Test Ban Treaty,* 1963.

———. Committee on Government Operations, Special Subcommittee on Investigations. *Charges and Countercharges Involving Secretary of the Army Robert T. Stevens, John G. Adams, H. Struve Hensel, and Senator Joe McCarthy, Roy M. Cohn, and Francis P. Carr,* 1954.

———. Committee on the Judiciary. *Hearings Before the Subcommittee on Constitutional Rights,* 1957.

———. *Hearings, Nominations of Abe Fortas and Homer Thornberry,* 1968.

———. *Treaties and Executive Agreements,* 1953.

———. *Memorial Services Held in the Senate and House of Representatives of the United States, Together with Tributes Presented in Eulogy of Everett McKinley Dirksen,* 1970.

———. Senate Historical Office. *A History of the United States Senate Republican Policy Committee: 1947–1997,* 1997.

VanDeMark, Brian. *Into the Quagmire: Lyndon Johnson and the Escalation of the Vietnam War.* New York, 1991.

Vital Speeches of the Day. New York, 1967.

Watson, Denton L. *Lion in the Lobby: Clarence Mitchell's Struggles for the Passage of Civil Rights Laws.* New York, 1990.

Weed, Clyde P. *The Nemesis of Reform: The Republican Party During the New Deal.* New York, 1994.

Whalen, Charles, and Barbara Whalen. *The Longest Debate: A Legislative History of the 1964 Civil Rights Act.* New York, 1985.

White, Theodore H. *The Making of the President: 1960.* New York, 1961.

Wills, Garry. *Nixon Agonistes: The Crisis of the Self-Made Man.* Boston, 1969.

Woods, Randall Bennett. *Fulbright: A Biography.* New York, 1995.

Articles

Cooper, Bill. "John Sherman Cooper: A Senator and His Constituents." *Register of the Kentucky Historical Society* (spring 1986).

Heclo, Hugh. "Hyperdemocracy." *Wilson Quarterly* (winter 1999).

Horn, Stephen. "Roundtable of Participants in the Passage of the Civil Rights Act of 1964." *This Constitution* (fall 1991).

Fonsino, Frank J. "Everett McKinley Dirksen: The Roots of an American Statesman." *Journal of the Illinois State Historical Society* (spring 1983).

Ritchie, Donald A. "The Senate of Mike Mansfield." *Montana: The Magazine of Western History* (winter 1998).

Schapsmeier, Edward L., and Frederick H. Schapsmeier. "Scott W. Lucas of Havana: His Rise and Fall as Majority Leader in the United States Senate." *Journal of the Illinois State Historical Review* (November 1977).

Scheele, Henry Z. "Response to the Kennedy Administration: The Joint Senate-House Republican Leadership Press Conferences." *Presidential Studies Quarterly* (fall 1989).

Smoot, Richard C. "John Sherman Cooper: The Early Years, 1901–1927." *Register of the Kentucky Historical Society* (spring 1995).

Index